"*Healing Haunted Histories* shows how it is possible—even necessary—to braid together the truth of family stories of immigration, including their traumatic silences; a thoughtful inhabitation of places and watersheds; a radical Christianity, not the religion of power and whiteness; and a deep commitment to confronting the settler mythologies of entitlement in North America. Practical and personal, this book will be a trustworthy guide for many in the decolonizing work that lies ahead."

—Roger Epp
Professor of Political Science, University of Alberta

"I didn't know how Enns and Myers would hold it all together, but they did! I was especially impressed (coming from a historian's perspective) with their ability to traverse the Canada/US divide. The histories are different, but the book showed us both the common ground and the differences seamlessly, and didn't let either side of the border off the hook! The insistent and yet compassionate interrogation of the authors' own family narrative is a rare gift—and a model. The personal threads woven throughout the work help keep it indeed 'intelligible and accessible,' but without sparing us the important critical theory or the necessary details."

—Sandra Beardsall
Professor of Church History and Ecumenics, St. Andrew's College, Saskatoon, Saskatchewan

"Beautifully written, I can feel the heart, courage, and passion that went into this text. I learned a ton about Mennonite history, trauma, and the importance of 'bloodlines work.' I was inspired by the compassionate and bold call to imagine and dance a reparative future. More importantly, *Healing Haunted Histories*, through its careful weaving of personal narrative, decolonizing theory, and biblical imagination, fills a real gap. I know nothing like it! Routinely, I paused while reading and said to myself, this is going to be used in church circles, and it's going to make a difference."

—Steve Heinrichs
Director of Indigenous-Settler Relations for Mennonite Church Canada

"I was inspired and challenged and re-oriented. I'm so grateful to have been part of this conversation over the years, and reading this now (in a time when my mind/heart/body is caught up with many complex institutional responsibilities in a very unstable time) has been life-giving. The authors' re-membering and discipleship have lifted my eyes to broader horizons and deeper longings. Their explorations of archaeology and cartography were deeply engaging for me."

—**Eileen Klassen Hamm**

Executive Director, Mennonite Central Committee Saskatchewan

"This is an excellent book. The rubric of 'haunted histories' is a compelling one with real heuristic value. It is well-written, well-organized, remarkably well-researched, and combines very powerful storytelling with outstanding analysis. I think it sparked about five hundred sermon ideas! *Haunted Histories* has put into words so many of the 'deep knowings' that I have as a settler/aspiring ally. I'm very grateful for that, knowing that I'll be much more articulate on these matters as I continue in the work and continue as a preacher."

—**Russell Daye**

Lead Minster, St. Andrew's Church, Halifax, Nova Scotia, and author of *Political Forgiveness*

"I will use this book in materials I continue to develop for the United Church of Canada. I really feel like it is a piece that we can use to take responsibility for our ongoing complicity in colonization. Thanks to the authors for doing the work, which I know is hard."

—**Sara Stratton**

Reconciliation and Indigenous Justice Animator, Toronto, The United Church of Canada

"The themes resonate deeply with me, as they are parallel to what I also continue to examine. I am very grateful for Enns' and Myers' careful and insightful work. They have wrestled hard with many difficult storylines—and at the same time opened up avenues for the reader to explore their own storylines."

—Luke Gascho

Executive Director Emeritus of Merry Lea Environmental Learning Center of Goshen College, Indiana

"Intimate, rigorous, accountable, and transformative—Enns and Myers offer both challenge and accompaniment to white settler Christians striving to bring their whole selves to the necessary work of deep, authentic, and radical solidarity with Indigenous peoples. The centering of women's voices and experiences makes this book an even more essential read for those prepared to risk being truly 'unsettled' in the pursuit of justice."

—Jennifer Henry

Executive Director, KAIROS: Canadian Ecumenical Justice Initiatives, Toronto

"In *Healing Haunted Histories* Elaine Enns and Ched Myers excavate the traumatic impact of settler colonialism and reckon the resulting settler amnesia with a Christian model of restorative justice that foregrounds Indigenous perspectives, experiences, and histories."

—Jonathan Cordero

(Ohlone and Chumash), Assistant Professor of Sociology, California Lutheran University

"*Healing Haunted Histories* is a powerful testimony, a prophetic witness, and a humble gesture toward 'saving the soul of America' through deep engagement with our own family stories. The 'bloodlines, landlines, and songlines' motif echoes the ancient Hebrew folk wisdom 'a cord of three strands is not quickly broken' (Eccl 4:12). The interbraiding of all three strands is what will make these transformational conversions hold strong. As people of faith, we trust that it is possible to heal the past. The authors' healing work here is skilled and true. Each one of us must learn and practice telling our own stories in a restorative justice mode. That is how we enter the joyful ceremony of mature humanity. If you were to map all the place names mentioned here in North America, it almost creates a circle: Saskatchewan, British Columbia, Pacific Coast, Laguna Pueblo, New Orleans, across the South, up to DC, New York, Toronto, and back to Saskatchewan. A great Turtle Island round dance for the healing of the nations!"

—Rose Marie Berger

Author of *Bending the Arch: Poems*, and senior editor at *Sojourners* magazine

"Rarely is a book so timely, urgent, and compelling. I believe that people will feel their hearts woven into the stories, the healing, and the challenge. Will we be made whole? This book of discipleship, filled with knowledge, insight, and information that you will find both practical and revolutionary at the same time, has quite a few artifacts from the world to come. I hope that many will be read by it."

—Mark MacDonald

National Indigenous Anglican Archbishop for that part of Turtle Island that is often called Canada

Healing Haunted Histories

CENTER AND LIBRARY FOR THE BIBLE AND SOCIAL JUSTICE SERIES

Laurel Dykstra and Ched Myers, editors
Liberating Biblical Study
Scholarship, Art, and Action in Honor of the Center and Library for
the Bible and Social Justice

Norman K. Gottwald
Social Justice and the Hebrew Bible
3 volumes

Elaine Enns and Ched Myers
Healing Haunted Histories
A Settler Discipleship of Decolonization

Healing Haunted Histories

A Settler Discipleship of Decolonization

By ELAINE ENNS
and CHED MYERS

Foreword by JUNE L. LORENZO
Afterword by HARRY LAFOND

CASCADE *Books* • Eugene, Oregon

HEALING HAUNTED HISTORIES
A Settler Discipleship of Decolonization

Cascade Books
An Imprint of Wipf and Stock Publishers
199 W. 8th Ave., Suite 3
Eugene, OR 97401

www.wipfandstock.com

PAPERBACK ISBN: 978-1-7252-5535-7
HARDCOVER ISBN: 978-1-7252-5536-4
EBOOK ISBN: 978-1-7252-5537-1

Cataloguing-in-Publication data:

Names: Enns, Elaine, author. | Myers, Ched, author. | Lorenzo, June L., foreword. | Lafond, Harry, afterword. | Nozik, Sherri, annotated bibliography.

Title: Healing haunted histories : a settler discipleship of decolonization / Elaine Enns and Ched Myers ; foreword by June L. Lorenzo; afterword by Harry Lafond; and annotated bibliography by Sherri Nozik.

Description: Eugene, OR: Cascade Books, 2021. | Includes bibliographical references and index.

Identifiers: ISBN 978-1-7252-5535-7 (paperback). | ISBN 978-1-7252-5536-4 (hardcover). | ISBN 978-1-7252-5537-1 (ebook).

Subjects: LCSH: Decolonization. | Reconciliation—Religious aspects—Christianity. | Whites—Relations with Indians. | Bible—Postolonial criticism. | Mennonite history—North America.

Classification: BS521.2 .H45 2021 (print). | BS521.2 (ebook).

JANUARY 19, 2021

To my ancestors, who despite their suffering
passed on neither resentment nor antipathy,
but a commitment to faith, compassion, gratitude, and determination,
and the belief that we as church have a responsibility
to peacemaking in the world.

So Joshua made a covenant with the people that day ... at Shechem ... He took a large stone, and set it up there under the oak in the sanctuary of the LORD. Joshua said to all the people, "See, this stone shall be a witness against us; for it has heard all the words of the LORD that God spoke to us; therefore it shall be a witness against you, if you deal falsely ..."

—JOSHUA 24:25–27 (NRSV)

History, despite its wrenching pain,
Cannot be unlived, but if faced
With courage, need not be lived again.

—MAYA ANGELOU[1]

1. Angelou, "On the Pulse of Morning," 265.

Contents

Images

Figure 01: Left to right: Ched, Elaine, June Lorenzo, Harry, and Germaine Lafond at Bartimaeus Kinsler Institute, February 2020, Oak View, CA. Photo: Tim Nafziger (used with permission)

Foreword

by June L. Lorenzo

I LEARNED ABOUT THE *Healing Haunted Histories* project in October 2019, after a weekend at the Kayla McClurg Memorial Writing Residency. Elaine, Ched, Rose Berger, and Demetria Martinez had led this unique gathering for a small group of activists of faith. Elaine and Ched drove me from the Wellspring Retreat Center in Maryland to downtown Washington, DC, and we discussed their book project, and the related work of their upcoming 2020 Bartimaeus Kinsler Institute (BKI)-themed "Unsettling Histories | Decolonizing Discipleship | hukišunuškuy." Their focus on settler colonialism, and the work of settler descendants to unpack that history through family stories, sounded ambitious but promising. Yet I found it difficult to imagine, as I knew of few people who had done such work in great depth.

Four months later at the BKI, I was delighted to see Elaine and Ched weaving draft sections of this book into plenary sessions. It was my second BKI, and I was honored to have been asked to participate as an "Indigenous interlocutor," along with Harry Lafond, Germaine Lafond, Matthew Vestuto, Jonathan Cordero, Brooke Prentis, and Bob Two Bulls. We moderated "Councils" to reflect on the day's plenary discussions and small-group processing work. It was a privilege to get a glimpse of participants' journeys as they examined their settler ancestry and what it means for them today.

It was important that Elaine and Ched modeled this work, shared their own wrestling with complex family histories and complicity in settler colonialism. The focus of the 2020 BKI was to offer some structure and support for participants to do their own work, and I witnessed firsthand the difficulty of engaging it authentically. I have done anti-racism training for years in the context of the Presbyterian Church (USA), and have also advocated against racist laws and policies as an attorney and human rights advocate, both domestically and internationally. I have experienced resistance to anti-racist work from descendants of white settlers, who have told me they are "not responsible for the sins of their ancestors," or that I should "just admit that Indigenous peoples lost the war, and became American like everyone else." So to be among settlers who were willing to devote their resources, time and energy to begin, or continue, their own work was a gift.

Healing Haunted Histories encapsulates this decolonization journey in a very readable and "breatheable" way. The organization of the book into Landlines, Bloodlines, and Songlines can help those willing to probe their settler ancestry with mind, body, and spirit. Since we are all these things, why wouldn't we want to embrace this journey with our whole selves? After decades of doing this work as an Indigenous woman, a person of faith, a human rights advocate, and a descendant of two peoples who experienced genocide, it warms my heart to see this book come to fruition. Elaine and Ched invite readers deeper into their own journeys of discovery, reflection, and commitment to live differently. I am grateful.[1]

August 2020
Laguna Pueblo, New Mexico

---

1. June L. Lorenzo (Laguna Pueblo and Diné) is an attorney and judge in New Mexico. She has worked in Congress, for the U.S. Department of Justice, for Indigenous nongovernmental organizations, and both the Laguna Pueblo and Navajo Nations. She advocates for implementation of the UN Declaration of Rights for Indigenous Peoples. An elder at Laguna United Presbyterian Church, she coauthored a report on the Doctrine of Discovery for the Presbyterian Church (USA). For more on the BKI 2020, see below 8B; for June's cited publications see chapter 7, note 65 and chapter 8, note 37.

Acknowledgments

Neither of us could (or would) have taken on this project without the other, and love and honor that which the other brought to the task. A decade in the making, it required many helping hands and hearts along the way:

Family: I felt commissioned by my parents to write this book (see preface). Though different from the family histories their generation curated—thank you, Mom and Dad; Aunt Irma and Uncle Frank; Aunt Irene and Uncle Ernie; Great-uncle George and many others—it shares their commitment to preserving a precious legacy. My siblings have been very supportive of this project, especially my sister Janet, who has accompanied and encouraged me at each stage. I am grateful to my extended family (aunts, uncles, and cousins) for their hospitality and vulnerable conversations (see 3A). After being with my family over the course of our wedding in 1999, Ched's mentor Ladon Sheats summed it up: "There is so much human goodness here!" We hope you all feel honored and loved.

Indigenous Partners: Our deep appreciation to Harry Lafond and June L. Lorenzo for their contributions to this volume and gracious friendship. Thanks to our local collaborators Julie Tumamait-Stenslie, Jonathan Cordero, Matthew Vestuto, and Carol Pulido. And gratitude to the above six, and to those below (across three countries and many nations), who have helped lead one or more of our Bartimaeus Institutes pertaining to the work of this book (below 8B):

- Germaine Lafond, Bob Two Bulls, Brooke Prentis, and Cheryl Bear (Oak View, 2020);

- Jim Bear Jacobs, Randy and Edith Woodley, Lenore Three Stars, and Safina Stewart (Oak View, 2019);

- Mark MacDonald, Sylvia McAdam, Leah Gazan, Lorna Standingready, A.J. Felix, Adrian Jacobs, Vivian Ketchum, Lorraine Vandall, Deb Anderson-Pratt, Gary LaPlante, and Erica Littlewolf (Saskatoon, 2016);

- Sharon Day and Bob Klanderud (Minneapolis, 2015).

Thanks to Harley Eagle for serving on my DMin committee; and to Brander Raven McDonald for teaching us about hauntings at St. Mary's Indian Residential School (see preface).

Faith Communities: Among Canadian Mennonites, thanks to: Nutana Park Mennonite Church for being an incubator of discipleship over many years (especially Pastors Vern Ratzlaff and Anita Retzlaff); to each of the more than fifty people (mostly women) who participated in my DMin research focus groups and interviews; to colleagues at Mennonite Central Committee Saskatchewan, especially Executive Director Eileen Klassen Hamm, Leonard Doell (both for his work and archival resources) and Heather Peters; and to veteran Mennonite peace and justice pioneer Hedy Sawadsky (happy ninetieth!). Among U.S. Mennonites we appreciate the work of Sue and Hyun Hur, Iris de León-Hartshorn, Tim Nafziger, the Dismantling the Doctrine of Discovery Coalition, and Ted and Co. Many other mentors, friends, and colleagues from other traditions have also inspired and aided us; though too numerous to list here, many are named at various places in this book. We thank Jin Kim and Church of All Nations for hosting the Minneapolis Institute, and Lynn Caldwell, Lindsay Mohn, and St. Andrew's College for hosting the Saskatoon Institute. And we are grateful to Janet Wolf for inviting us into the Proctor Institute fold; to Jennifer Henry of KAIROS: Canadian Ecumenical Justice Initiatives for her solidarity; and to Joyce and Nelson Johnson of the Beloved Community Center in Greensboro, North Carolina for their exemplary work and witness.

Readers: Ten stalwart friends agreed to read part or all of the first draft of this project; their feedback, corrections, contributions, and encouragement greatly improved this text. We are indebted to their keen eyes: Sandra Beardsall (my DMin advisor at St. Andrew's College); Eileen Klassen Hamm (MCCS); Steve Heinrichs (director of Indigenous-Settler Relations for Mennonite Church Canada); Russ Daye (pastor of St. Andrew's United Church Halifax); Sara Stratton (Reconciliation and Indigenous Justice Animator for the United Church of Canada); Janet and Rob Regier (my sister and brother-in-law); June L. Lorenzo (Chief Judge at Pueblo of Zia); Luke Gascho (retired professor, Goshen College, Indiana); and Ed Nakawatase (retired National Representative for Native American Affairs for the American Friends Service Committee). Thank you each and all for investing that considerable time and energy.

Writing and Production: Thanks to the team that helped create this text:

- Chris Wight, our communications staff at Bartimaeus Cooperative Ministries, designed many of the illustrations, wrangled images and photos (his own and others), problem-solved, and held down the office for the many months we were preoccupied with this manuscript;

- Rose Marie Berger of *Sojourners* line-edited the entire manuscript twice, significantly strengthening it; Heidi Thompson was our wonderful promotional consultant;

- Sherri Nozik authored the annotated bibliography on trauma studies (Appendix I);

- Adella Barrett copyedited the bibliography;

- Dimitri Kadiev's mural at our home is featured throughout the book; and

- Robert Valiente-Neighbours' print graces the cover (http://artbyrvn.com/about).

At Cascade, Ted Lewis provided advice and Rodney Clapp was our encouraging and patient editor. We are pleased to be part of the CLBSJ series.

Financial Supporters: Early stages of research and writing were enabled through a Pastoral Study Project grant from the Louisville Institute (https://louisville-institute.org/); thanks to Don Richter for his support. Final editing and promotion was helped by a posthumous grant from the late Kayla McClurg of Church of the Saviour in Washington, DC (may you be dancing with the angels). Both of us authors are employed by Bartimaeus Cooperative Ministries, and were freed to do this project because of the faithful partnership of our donors and blessing of our board members (Shady Hakim, Carter Echols, John Parker, and Susan Taylor).

This book is an integral part of our mission at BCM, as is the annual Bartimaeus Kinsler Institute. Our love to elders Gloria and Ross Kinsler, who for the first time this year could not attend the gathering named in honor of them. Gratitude to the following BKI collaborators (program planners, artists, chaplains, co-organizers, and donors) over these last two years: Bob Two Bulls, June L. Lorenzo, Matthew Vestuto, Elizabeth Gibbs Zehnder, Sue Park and Hyun Hur, Grecia and Josh Lopez Reyes, Nathan and Sarah Holst, Art Cribbs, Tim Nafziger, Amardon Team leaders Chris Wight, Lisa Bachman, Tevyn East, Solveig Nilsen-Goodin, Kristina Mata, Jay Beck, Shelby Smith, Tom and Lindsay Airey, Claire Hitchens, and C. John Hildebrand, Marcia and Clancy Dunigan, and the one and only Joshua Grace.

Figure 02: Elaine's great-great-grandfather (paternal) Johann Johann Wiebe, undated. Enns family photo.

Preface

THE LAST TIME I was with my father was October 2003, in Saskatoon, Saskatchewan. My mother had already started down the Alzheimer's journey, so Ched and I had been videotaping interviews with them about family history. The evening before I returned to California I sat with my parents in the family room of the home in which I grew up. Dad was lying on the couch, Mom next to him. He was weak from a damaged heart, and awaiting a transplant that wouldn't come in time.

Ched whispered to me, "Say what you need to say, just in case." I thanked Dad for being such a kind and gentle parent, and for instilling in me a love for music, justice, and family history. He had prepared for this moment too, and pulled out an old, undated photograph. "I want you to have this," he said softly. "This is my mother's grandfather, Johann Johann Wiebe."

I took it from him reverently, like a sacrament. The photo was mounted on cardboard, embossed with gold lettering from a long-forgotten studio in Karassan, Crimea. Written on the back in my grandmother's hand was "*mein grosspapa Wiebe*"; in my Dad's script was a note that Johann "had a vineyard." I later learned from one of our family history books that he was a minister in the church, and an only child, rare in those days. Johann died in 1917—the year that signaled the beginning of the end of the Mennonite Commonwealth in Ukraine.

I became emotional, and soon all three of us were weeping, feeling a shared weight we could not name. I now realize that this sacred moment was not only a farewell. It was a commissioning from my parents to embrace the work of being a "remem-bearer" (below 3A). This book arises from living into that vocation.

∿

Healing Haunted Histories tackles the oldest and deepest injustices on this continent. These violations inhabit every intersection of settler and Indigenous worlds, past and present, and have generated wounds that are inextricably woven into the fabric of our personal and political lives. The purpose of this project is to build capacity for the work of decolonization as a commitment to heal those wounds, as we outline in the introduction.

We explore the places, peoples, and spirits that have shaped us, and invite the reader to do the same. This book is therefore part memoir; part social, historical, and theological analysis; and part practical workbook.[1] Because the genre of this project is neither fish nor fowl, let us explain some idiosyncrasies that shape (and delimit) our approach.

Voice. This is a thoroughly joint venture: every word herein was composed and/or edited by each of us. Because decolonization work cuts across so many vectors, this project required the full expertise, experience, and elocution of both of us. That said, we are two settler authors with very distinct Landlines and Bloodlines, though many shared Songlines (and we are partners in love and life as well as work). At the outset we made a decision to center our narrative on my family story; Ched's surfaces only occasionally to help illustrate themes.[2] Had we attempted to trace and critically engage both our family lines it would have extended an already lengthy book!

Our respective voices and pronouns, therefore, appear differently in this narrative:

- *Elaine* = "I/my": I am always the first-person narrator;
- *Ched* = "He": His voice (when distinct) is always in the third-person;
- "*We*": Sometimes this refers to our joint authorial voice; sometimes to my collective family or community; and sometimes to settler race/class generalizations that include both of us (we trust context will make clear which).

Though this differentiation of voices is unorthodox, and perhaps a bit awkward, we hope you can adjust without confusion.

Scope. There are two main strands (among many threads) developed in this book. One is my communal narrative, which we've attempted to curate in its full affective range, and which is in part an exercise in autoethnography.

---

1. A similar approach is taken by our friend, Canadian Catholic activist theologian Denise Nadeau, whose *Unsettling Spirit: A Journey into Decolonization* was published as we were finishing this book. Her book wrestles with all the same issues in the Canadian context, and we commend it as a kindred volume.

2. To learn more about Ched's storylines see Myers, *Who Will Roll Away the Stone?*, and Myers and Colwell, *Our God Is Undocumented*, 193–200, 207–12.

The other strand is critical engagement with issues of decolonization, which we've tried to cover in representative depth and breadth. The core of our project is the conversation between these two strands, each portrayed through the lens of the other. We think this dialectic of personal story and social analysis is a fruitful way to address the vast topic of settler-Indigenous relations, which otherwise is daunting in scope.

This narrative is both enriched and complicated by the fact that it covers a lot of ground (literally!), weaving my story, and thus also our analysis, across:

- three bioregions (Ukrainian steppes, Saskatchewan prairies, and California chaparral);[3]
- three centuries (nineteenth to twenty-first);
- three communities (Mennonite settlers, non-Mennonite settlers, and Indigenous peoples); and
- two countries (Canada and the US).

Obviously we cannot do full justice to each of these spatial, temporal, communal, and political contexts, not to mention to all of the issues associated with colonization. We are a restorative justice educator and an activist theologian, respectively. We draw on other disciplines such as history, sociology, and psychology as popular educators and organizers trying to shape a pedagogy of personal and political transformation. We've necessarily had to use broad brush strokes and generalizing frameworks, which we recognize are limiting (though hopefully not overly simplified). These we've tried to illuminate in the finer brushwork involved in my family portrait. We hope our approach offers an intelligible and compelling account of the interrelationships between broad concepts and particular explorations.

Ten trusted colleagues (named in the Acknowledgements) read a rough draft of this text, catching many errors (though probably not all), and nuancing or deepening many of our points. We are profoundly grateful for their help, and take sole responsibility for the shortcomings that remain. As reader Ed Nakawatase put it, when dealing with painful and unsettling issues, "shedding light also adds weight." By any measure, the subject of decolonization could not be heavier, not to mention more multidimensional in its reach, or universal in its relevance, or complex in its implications. But it could also not be more important to both settler and Indigenous health.

---

3. Our 2016 book on bioregional faith and practice focused on building literacy in, and restorative relationship with, one's home watershed (see Myers, *Watershed Discipleship*). *Healing Haunted Histories* makes more explicit that decolonization is constitutive of that reinhabition work.

For some this book will seem too involved or overly polemical, for others not detailed or strident enough. Wherever we settlers are on the journey, we can go deeper; we hope this book will encourage and support that.

Context. We have endeavored to be forthcoming about our own social locations and identities as authors; after all, the examination and transformation of such is the very purpose of this project. It has been challenging to curate a predominately Saskatchewan-centered storyline while writing from a geopolitical location in California (I am somewhat sad I've lived in the latter place longer than the former). Though we aspire to be binational in our work and concerns, we recognize much of our social analysis reflects a U.S. context, since this is the primary arena of our praxis. Canadian readers will feel occasional jolts of asymmetry in our "synoptic" approach, for which we can only apologize, and trust they will fill in the gaps in our depiction of their social and political life. Our *mea culpa* to Indigenous readers as well, who will likely feel even stronger jolts from our blind spots regarding native history and culture. We are a work in progress.

Text is always related to context, and our manuscript was completed during widespread protests across the U.S. (and beyond) after the police murder of George Floyd in Minneapolis on May 25, 2020, the latest in yet another string of racialized killings that have provoked widespread civil unrest. This crisis confirmed our original decision that this book should touch multiple times upon past and present issues of justice for Black lives. Raphael Warnock called the twofold pandemic running through our body politic a double virus of "COVID-19 and 1619."[4] Events in the U.S. through the first half of 2020 have only intensified contradictions that were already widening under the Trump presidency, not to mention the older hauntings that plague our collective unconscious. These necessarily shape our perspective. As adrienne maree brown reminds us: "Things are not getting worse, they are getting uncovered."[5]

Our project is predicated intellectually upon two important recent paradigm shifts that have been emerging over these first two decades of the twenty-first century. One is decolonial theory, the other trauma studies. Both fields have exploded, and have wide influence in therapeutic and social movements for change. The critical literature continues to proliferate, yet both disciplines are still new, such that semantic and analytic frames are still evolving (and often hotly contested). We are not academics, and come

4. See Galloway, "Raphael Warnock and a Sunday sermon." Warnock (pastor of the venerable Ebenezer Baptist Church in Atlanta, Dr. King's historic pulpit) is referring to the disease of racism that landed on the shores of America with the first slave ship in 1619.

5. brown, "Living through the Unveiling," para. 1.

to these studies as practitioners; we trust our shortcomings are made up by the (hopefully representative) literature we cite, and that the reader will delight in (rather than be distracted by) our copious use of footnotes. Our colleague Sherri Nozik graciously provided at-a-glance reviews of some recent literature on trauma in Appendix I. Organizations asterisked in our text are doing work relevant to issues discussed herein, and are listed in Appendix III with contact information.

Vocabulary. Unfortunately, too much academic discourse (including studies we've drawn upon) is overly pedantic, or obfuscates important ideas with jargon. We sought to avoid or minimize technical language and internecine or insular debates, while maintaining a degree of nuance and complexity (each reader will have to judge whether we've been successful). At the outset (introduction A) we offer working definitions of key vocabulary or conceptual frameworks, and follow this pattern throughout.

In that vein, let us clarify the three terms, each with multiple meanings today, which lie at the heart of our own discourse (and the architecture of the book): our triad of Landlines, Bloodlines, and Songlines. Here's what we do and don't mean:

- "Landlines" herein does not refer to telephonic communication, nor to surveying protocols, or national or property borders. In our use, Landlines connotes places of personal, communal, and ancestral inhabitation, past and present. They are geographies and landscapes of memory, struggle and contestation, affection, sustenance, and identity—and hold deep stories of peoples' placement and displacement.

- "Bloodlines" we generally (if with some trepidation) use according to its common definition as "members of a family group over a period of time," but with an important caveat. We are interested in social and kinship identities (including "fictive" ones), *not* technical "blood relations" (which preoccupies so much popular genealogy and ancestry work). And we adamantly divorce our use of this term from its lamentable but persistent association with "blood quantum" and the related racial constructs and racist policies of white supremacy.

- "Songlines" in this book is a poetic rubric referring to traditions of individual and collective conscience and liberation, which inspire practices of justice and compassion, and sustain endurance, resilience, and healing. This term acknowledges a universe of diverse traditions of animating Spirit (we draw here primarily on religious convictions, cultural practices, and social movements). In broader usage, Songlines connotes a lyrical or instrumental phrase of music, such as a refrain or an opening. We rather like this association, given how central singing is to Mennonites (and other renewal movements across time and space).[6]

The introduction will offer a full orientation to our approach and process regarding the "Storylines" that shape (and sometimes misshape) us.

A trigger warning: the story of colonization is a violent one, and should not be narrated otherwise. The same is true of certain (far briefer) chapters of the Anabaptist story from which my people spring. We have not indulged in graphic descriptions of violence in this book, but we cannot truthfully relate Storylines of Indigenous peoples, or of my ancestors, or of current realities, without reference to genocide, dispossession, massacres, executions, home invasions, sexual assault (including rape as a weapon of war), and imprisonment. Readers who might be re-traumatized may choose to skip over our summary accounts of violence; others are encouraged to pause and take the time necessary to metabolize these horrors, so as not to remain aloof from a past and present to which we are accountable.

Commitments. Finally, we are unapologetic about three convictional frameworks (or "biases") that have guided this project:

1. *We believe that past and continuing Indigenous dispossession is the "primal sin" of settler colonialism, haunting us and demanding a reckoning.* This is not to suggest that decolonization and Indigenous solidarity are the only issues on which people of conscience should work, or that Indigenous peoples are first among the oppressed, as if there is a hierarchy of pain. Only that we settlers cannot *not* face this legacy and hope to be a healthy or just people. This book is, then, by, primarily about, and for settlers in North America.

2. *In our use of both primary and secondary sources we tried to address the underrepresentation of women's voices.* This was challenging for two

6. On the other hand, we wish to be clear that our use does *not* allude to Bruce Chatwin's 1988 book *The Songlines.* Chatwin's meaning (which is mostly what comes up in the Googlesphere) tried to interpret and popularize for a Western audience Aboriginal practices of tracing one's way across the landscape through spiritual and geographic literacy. His use has been critiqued as a "fuzzy, ill-defined use of the word-concept" that "has had the effect of generating more heat than light" (Nicholls, "Wild Roguery," 22). On the other hand, Nick Wight of Indigenous Ministries Australia,* who uses Songlines language in solidarity tours for settlers, considers the term "popularist, much like other English expressions (such as 'dreamtime') that try to capture complex Indigenous ideas, which are useful for non-Indigenous folk but certainly not invested with the nuance and depth of the many specific nation or language group words that mean the same thing" (private correspondence with authors, May 23, 2020). Our meaning is unrelated to however Songlines might be understood by Aboriginal or settler Australians.

reasons. On one hand, primary sources for my family story were written by men (my grandmothers, for example, left no journals). On the other, women academics were rare before the last two generations. To restore some balance we took several measures. I prioritized women in my 2014 research interviews (we are delighted to include here many of their comments, though mostly anonymous). We cite here studies by women as much as possible. We critically investigate how women's testimonies (and victimization) were marginalized or silenced in the past (below 3D). And we highlight the prominent role of women in Indigenous activism in the present (7D).

3. *Our perspectives are deeply shaped by Christian faith and practice (reflected in our subtitle).* This orientation means several things. For one, we emphasize repeatedly the interconnection between the personal, communal, and political in decolonization work: all have been deformed, and can be transformed. For another, these pages are leavened with occasional theological and biblical reflections (most intensively in the Interlude). This project is offered *to* and *from* our settler faith communities in the hope that we will struggle harder to rescue the gospel from Christendom, colonization, and white supremacy, even as we are being rescued *by* that gospel. A discipleship of decolonization means facing the ways in which we and our ancestors in the faith have been complicit in colonial violence. We have focused on Mennonites here not because they are the only tradition that has been compromised, but because we are working on our own community. We encourage you to do the same.

You don't have to be a person of faith to engage in decolonization work (or benefit from this book). But persons of faith have to do this work.

We invite you to dance with us around circles of Landlines, Bloodlines, and Songlines, and to straddle the many dialectics in these pages: personal and political, spiritual and material, social and religious, past and present, there and here, settler and Indigenous, us and you. This is a long and involved book, so read it in digestible parts, preferably with a study group. Engage the questions, and make this process your own.

∾

As a little girl I used to crawl into the back of my maternal grandmother's small wardrobe and sit amongst the coats and smell of mothballs, praying the back would open up into Narnia. I sensed it held stories of another world. That armoire didn't become a portal to the fantasy universe I hoped for. But in retrospect, perhaps it was a gateway to the Storylines I explore in this book, though it took me many years.

A much spiritually darker room, in contrast, was also a threshold. In 2011, Ched and I were speaking at an outdoor festival in Mission, British Columbia, in a field beneath the looming, abandoned buildings of St. Mary's Indian Residential School (below 7C). We met Brander Raven, a Cree social worker and musician, who told us he used to have his office at St. Mary's. He asked if we wanted to take a tour of the building, adding: "The people have shared that it's haunted, you know." He took us through a labyrinth of dusky corridors, quietly telling us stories of Stó:lō children who had been abused there. The ghosts were palpable. Then, in the musty, rambling room where he once had a desk, Brander related how at nights when he was alone, he would feel little hands on his shoulders from behind, and hear weeping. He said he would sometimes talk to them without turning around. Being with him in that space was one of the heaviest spiritual experiences we've had.

Reflecting on these two "portals," the rest of adrienne maree brown's exhortation comes to mind: "Hold each other tight and continue to pull back the veil."[7] We pray this book helps you, as it has us, face the ghosts of settler colonialism within and around us, and live into the hope that all this "wrenching pain. . .if faced with courage, need not be lived again."

---

7. brown, "Living through the Unveiling," para. 1.

Figure 03: Graffiti in Nutana Park alley, Saskatoon, SK, May 2020. Photo: Emily Hooge (used with permission).

Prologue

Kihci-asotamâtowin

... as long as the sun shines,
as long as the waters flow downhill,
and as long as the grass grows green ...

—FROM THE TWO ROW WAMPUM[1]

OPWASHEMOE CHAKATINAW RISES GENTLY above the prairies, providing impressive views of the valley between the North and South Saskatchewan Rivers. In Cree, *kisiskâciwani-sîpiy* means "swiftly flowing river." It is a humble hill lying near the northern edge of the Great Plains, that vast stretch of steppe and grassland straddling much of the middle of what is today known as the United States and Canada. This is a sacred site for the Young Chippewayans, a Cree band, the symbolic center of a thirty-square-mile tract selected by their chief for a reserve in 1876 as part of Treaty 6.[2]

A few years ago we discovered the graffiti pictured here (Fig. 03) in my old suburban neighborhood, scrawled across a fence just a block from

---

1. The Two Row Wampum was an agreement made between the Five Nations of the Iroquois (*Haudenosaunee*) and representatives of the Dutch government in what is now upstate New York. In the British colony of Canada the 1764 Treaty of Niagara was confirmed through the sharing of the Two Row Wampum. It affirmed a Royal Proclamation's principles of Indigenous self-determination and jurisdiction, which is recognized in Section 25 of the Canadian Constitution (Borrows, "Wampum at Niagara"). See the Two Row Wampum Renewal Campaign*; more below 5E.

2. See orientation map (Fig. 06) and detailed map (Fig. 26) below. Saskatchewan is also Treaty 2, 4, 5, 8, and 10 territory (see Fig. 24), and traditional homeland of the Métis and seventy First Nations from five main linguistic groups: Cree, Dakota, Dene (Chipewyan), Nakota (Assiniboine), and Saulteaux.

3

where I grew up. This venerable phrase from the Two Row Wampum of 1613 was reiterated in most subsequent agreements between European settlers and Indigenous Peoples in Canada, including Treaty 6, which covers much of southern Saskatchewan. Cree elders use the term *kihci-asotamâtowin* to describe sacred promises made to one another in treaty. Stoney Knoll (the settler name for Opwashemoe Chakatinaw) is one of many places where the settler state broke such promises. It is therefore representative of the past and continuing struggle over history, identity, and justice in Saskatchewan.

My home place.

In the late nineteenth century, Young Chippewayans and other tribes were struggling to survive increasing encroachment by settlers. John Macdonald, Canada's first post-Confederation Prime Minister, was waging an aggressive campaign to "open up" the region. As a Canadian Pacific Railway (CPR) poster put it, the prairies were "The Golden West, a home for all people." Indigenous peoples, however, were not included in that vision, despite treaty agreements. Instead they were targets of a four-pronged assault:

- government policies of starvation, including mass slaughter of bison (the main reason that drove the Young Chippewayans off their assigned land, named Reserve 107, in search of food);
- devastating epidemics from European diseases;
- relentless settler infringement on traditional territories; and
- aggressive assimilationist strategies such as residential schools.

These pressures provoked strong currents of Indigenous dissidence on the prairies.

The Northwest Resistance (March 26–June 3, 1885) was an uprising by the Métis, and an allied insurrection by Cree and Assiniboine bands, against the Canadian colonial government in the Northwest Territories (which included present-day Alberta and Saskatchewan).[3] It was led by Louis Riel, a religiously inspired Métis political leader who sought to preserve the rights, land, culture, and survival of his people. Fort Carlton, just north of Reserve 107, where Treaty 6 had been signed less than a decade earlier, was burned down during the conflict. Various companies of Canadian regular and irregular militia, aided by quick transport from the new railway, rushed into the area and quelled the uprising at the Battle of Batoche.

---

3. Métis is a contested "category," typically defined in Canadian settler culture as "people of mixed Indigenous and Euro-American ancestry." However, many Métis understand their identity in fundamental political terms—not in terms of racial-mixing, but of heritage, language, and culture—as a distinct, post-contact Indigenous nation (see Andersen, *Métis*).

Riel surrendered, was tried a month later by the federal government, and executed for treason on November 16, 1885, at the North-west Mounted Police barracks in Regina. Eleven days later, eight other Indigenous men were publicly hung, the largest mass execution in Canadian history. The *Saskatchewan Indian* newspaper reported: "All the Indian students at the Battleford Industrial School were taken out to witness the event . . . to remind them what would happen if one of them made trouble with the crown, and to provide a lasting reminder of the white man's power and authority."[4]

The government set about punishing other tribes and individuals suspected of participating in the uprising. On May 3, 1897, the Canadian Superintendent General of Indian Affairs recommended that the Department of the Interior regain control of Reserve 107, arguing it "has never been taken possession of nor occupied by [the Young Chippewayans who] . . . also took part in the Rebellion of 1885 and for the most part left the country thereafter or became amalgamated with other Bands."[5] Without consultation or compensation, the federal government reassigned Young Chippewayan land to expand the boundaries of a reserve for Mennonite settlers (and subsequently Lutherans and others), who were being aggressively recruited to help domesticate the prairies.

The first Mennonites had arrived in Saskatchewan from West Prussia, Manitoba, and the U.S., beginning in 1892, just seven years after the Northwest Resistance. They built their first church in 1896, at Eigenheim, fourteen miles from Stoney Knoll. Its founding pastor was Peter Regier, my brother-in-law's great-grandfather. In the years that followed, more churches were built near Reserve 107, including a Lutheran sanctuary on top of Stoney Knoll.[6] Between 1923 and 1929, some 22,000 Mennonite refugees from the Russian Revolution came to Canada, the largest influx of Mennonite immigrants in Canadian history. These *Russländer* immigrants—which included all four of my grandparents—had fled horrific violence in Ukraine and Russia, leaving behind many family members who did not survive the Soviet regime.[7] My grandparents were grateful to have escaped to Saskatchewan,

4. Starblanket, *Suffer the Little Children*, 118. See Ogg, "An Infamous Anniversary."

5. Committee of the Honorable the Privy Council, Canadian Superintendent General of Indian Affairs, Department of the Interior, "Report of the Committee . . . 11th May 1897."

6. This Lutheran church was built in 1910, and moved to nearby Laird in the 1950s. The Lutherans still own the property on the top of the hill, including the old cemetery.

7. "By the time the Soviet government forbade further emigration in 1930, 19,891 Mennonites and 12,310 Lutherans had come to Canada; 7,828 of the Mennonites, joined by a small group of Lutherans, settled in Saskatchewan (close to 3,000 in the Rosthern settlement in 1923 alone)" (Anderson, *Settling Saskatchewan*, 120).

yet, like other *Russländer,* also carried significant trauma. And they were entirely unaware of the violent Indigenous displacement only a generation before that made "available" the lands they now occupied.

My people.

The Saskatchewan River watershed thus became a place where two traumatized peoples lived side by side, though mostly segregated from and ignorant of the other. Mennonites, with their long history of religious dissidence and persecution, fleeing another round of violence in Europe, settled on Cree land and set about building prosperous farms. Cree communities, though resident here for thousands of years, struggled to survive another wave of settlers and continuing subjugation, discrimination, and racist injustices from Canadian colonial society.

Our entangled story.

Today my oldest sister lives just a few miles from Stoney Knoll and adjacent to Beardy's and Okemasis First Nation Reserve, on a farm her husband inherited from his parents. Everyone in my family attended a Mennonite boarding school in nearby Rosthern, where other relatives also reside. Many Mennonites still live in and around Reserve 107. I have walked Opwashemoe Chakatinaw with colleagues who work for justice, and sat with Young Chippewayan leaders who are *still* campaigning for federal recognition and repatriation. We understand this little hill is a wound still unhealed, a haunting microcosm of the wider settler colonial story that has left no corner of Turtle Island untouched.[8]

Our responsibility.

8. "Turtle Island is the name many Algonquian- and Iroquoian-speaking peoples mainly in the northeastern part of North America use to refer to the continent. In various Indigenous origin stories, the turtle is said to support the world, and is an icon of life itself." (Robinson, "Turtle Island," para. 2) We will occasionally use this name in this book.

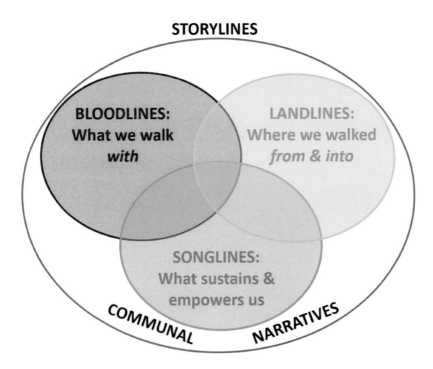

Figure 04: Storylines (LBS model). Design by Elaine Enns.

Introduction

Decolonization as Personal and Political Healing

For too long the depth of racism in American life has been underestimated. The surgery necessary to extract it is necessarily complex and detailed. As a beginning it is necessary to X-ray our history and reveal the full extent of the disease . . .

Our nation was born in genocide, when it embraced the doctrine that the original American, the Indian, was an inferior race. Even before there were large numbers of Negroes on our shore, the scar of racial hatred had already disfigured colonial society . . .

From the sixteenth century forward, blood flowed in battles over racial superiority. We are perhaps the only nation which tried as a matter of national policy to wipe out its indigenous population. Moreover we elevated that tragic experience into a noble crusade. Indeed, even today we have not permitted ourselves to reject or feel remorse for this shameful episode. Our literature, our films, our drama, our folklore all exalt it . . .

It is this tangled web of prejudice from which many Americans now seek to liberate themselves, without realizing how deeply it has been woven into their consciousness.

—Martin Luther King Jr.[1]

---

1. King, *Why We Can't Wait*, 109–10.

A. "TO REVEAL THE FULL EXTENT OF THE DISEASE": GOALS AND KEY TERMS

The extraordinary passage above comes from a book Martin Luther King Jr. published at the end of 1963. It came in the wake of three seminal events that year: the Birmingham Civil Rights campaign, the March on Washington, and the assassination of John F. Kennedy. Dr. King, ever both prophet and pastor, was searching for meaning. The "cascading grief that flooded the country," he suggested, had to do with more than JFK's murder: "We grieved as well for ourselves because we knew we were sick."[2]

Despite posthumous attempts to domesticate King's life and legacy by mainstream hagiographies, his analysis was consistently radical—that is, probing the roots of the "disease" he sought to diagnose and heal. Here King makes the extraordinary claim that U.S. history needs to be "X-rayed" in order to "reveal the full extent of the disease." The civil rights movement, he believed, was doing just that: exposing the roots of "a nation born in genocide" against Indigenous peoples. This remarkable diagnosis, almost six decades old, summarizes the task of this book so precisely that it serves as a focalizer to introduce our theme. Because settlers in the U.S. (and Canada) are *still* struggling to liberate ourselves from "this tangled web of prejudice," and to do so we must "realize how deeply it has been woven" into our consciousness.

The aim of this book is to encourage, challenge, and capacitate *settler* Christians (and other people of faith and conscience) to:

- understand how our histories, landscapes, and communities are *haunted* by the long and continuing history of Indigenous dispossession wrought by *settler colonialism*;

- transform the self-understandings, lifeways, and structures we inhabit; and

- practice restorative solidarity with Indigenous communities as part of a wider movement of *decolonization*.

The italicized terms in this mission statement might be new to some readers, so we offer here a few working definitions, as we will do throughout when strategic vocabulary or conceptual frameworks are introduced. Here are key terms we will use, aware that each has meanings that are evolving in the emerging literature:

---

2. Washington, *Testament of Hope*, 518.

- *Settler*: In this book we use this term to refer primarily to people of European descent whose ancestors immigrated to and established themselves in North America (this includes both of us authors). More prevalent in Canada than the U.S., the rubric of "settler" acknowledges (rather than ignores) the violent and conflicted legacy of settler colonialism in North America since the sixteenth century. Settlers "come to stay," says Patrick Wolfe succinctly, on an "expropriated land base."[3] And settler descendants keep "resettling" as we move around the country (see below 5D). We appreciate Eve Tuck and Wayne Yang's assertion that "Settlers are not immigrants. Immigrants are beholden to the Indigenous laws and epistemologies of the lands they migrate to. Settlers become the law, supplanting Indigenous laws and epistemologies."[4] While we acknowledge the politics of their distinction, we will here use the word *immigrant* for people who came from the "old" country to the "new," and "settler" for their identity once here. Second, while the term *settler* includes non-European immigrants of color, we are aware that these often exploited and marginalized communities face distinct issues. This differentiation is even more acute among those in the African diaspora who are descendants of enslaved peoples (sometimes referred to as "stolen people on stolen land"). We point the reader to the important growing literature arising from these communities.[5]

- *Haunting*: "Hauntology" (a "portmanteau of haunting and ontology") was coined by French philosopher Jacques Derrida to recognize how both identity and history are populated by "ghosts . . . which are neither present nor absent."[6] The concept was picked up and developed by sociologist Avery Gordon to describe ways in which the "spirit" of past violence inhabits both places and people, a framing that has animated a growing body of decolonial-critical literature.[7] We find "haunting" to be an illuminating trope for those of us trying to come to terms

3. Wolfe, "Settler Colonialism and the Elimination of the Native," 388.

4. Tuck and Yang, "Decolonization Is Not a Metaphor," 6–7. As they point out, "the refugee/immigrant/migrant is invited to be a settler in some scenarios, given the appropriate investments in whiteness, or is made an illegal, criminal presence in other scenarios" (17).

5. See for example: Thomas, "Stolen People on Stolen Land"; Thomas, "Who Is a Settler,"; Phung, "Are People of Colour Settlers Too?"; Lee, "Non-White Settler and Indigenous Relations"; Day, "Being or Nothingness"; Tobani, *Exalted Subjects*; King, *Black Shoals*; and Horne, *Apocalypse of Settler Colonialism*.

6. Cited at https://en.wikipedia.org/wiki/Hauntology.

7. Gordon, *Ghostly Matters*.

with the personal (psychosis), communal (possession), and political (occupation) dimensions of colonization (below 1B).

- *Settler colonialism*: This term has "become the 'official' idiolect with substantial influence in the social sciences and the humanities," but has varying and contested definitions.[8] A useful one is: "a distinct type of colonialism that functions through the replacement of indigenous populations with an invasive settler society that, over time, develops a distinctive identity and sovereignty. Settler colonial states include Canada, the United States, Australia, and South Africa."[9] Wolfe adds that settler colonialism's "logic of elimination" toward Indigenous peoples includes "miscegenation, the breaking-down of native title into alienable individual freeholds and citizenship, child abduction, religious conversion, resocialization in total institutions such as missions or boarding schools, and . . . frontier homicide."[10]

- *Restorative solidarity*: This term joins the framework of restorative justice (which we explored in our 2009 *Ambassadors of Reconciliation* volumes) together with the traditional definition of solidarity as "shared interests" across differences and work toward mutual liberation. For those of us who historically have been and continue to be advantaged in and by the settler colonial system, both restorative justice and solidarity are about "making things right." Nikki Sanchez puts it plainly to settlers: "This history is not your fault, but it is absolutely your responsibility."[11] This book is about the latter, not the former. We understand settler restorative solidarity as the practice of "response-ability" in both our "political bodies" and the "body politic" in which we dwell. This entails working to dismantle and heal from settler colonialism, as well as to accompany and collaborate with Indigenous communities, especially those on (or of) lands on which we've settled.[12]

- *Decolonization*: With its popularization over the last decade, this term has become diluted in non-Indigenous discourses. We agree with Tuck and Yang that its core meaning *should* connote the struggle for "the

8. King, "Settler Colonialism and African Americans," para. 1.

9. Barker and Lowman, "Settler Colonialism," para. 1. See also Cox, "Settler Colonialism"; Rindfleisch, "Native American History"; and Cavanagh and Veracini, *Routledge Handbook of the History of Settler Colonialism*.

10. Wolfe, "Settler Colonialism and the Elimination of the Native," 388. See also Henderson, "Imagoed Communities."

11. Sanchez, "Decolonization Is for Everyone," para. 1.

12. See our further discussion below 8C. Also Enns, "Facing History with Courage," and Myers, *Who Will Roll Away the Stone?*, 278–83.

repatriation of Indigenous land and life," and *not* function as "a metaphor for other things we want to do to improve our societies":

> Decolonize (a verb) and decolonization (a noun) cannot eas-
> ily be grafted onto pre-existing discourses/frameworks, even
> if they are critical, even if they are anti-racist, even if they are
> justice frameworks . . . The goal is to break . . . the settler colonial
> triad [which] means repatriating land to sovereign Native tribes
> and nations, abolition of slavery in its contemporary forms, and
> the dismantling of the imperial metropole.[13]

DM Marchand-Lafortune, a Cree-Métis-Jewish colleague, defines this
work as "critically examining the historical, social, economic and political
patterns and systems of power that have been formative in developing one's
own and one's ancestors' worldview, and working to dismantle and transform one's way of being in the world."[14]

We offer this brief summary of theory, like all of the conceptualiza-
tions and semantics we employ in this project, heuristically: their value is
contingent upon their usefulness to actual practices.[15]

Theologian and veteran civil rights activist Ruby Sales is a friend and
esteemed elder. "A movement for racial justice requires White Americans
to save themselves from the strangulation of the spiritual malformation
and social perversity of a culture of Whiteness," says Mother Ruby, and she
agrees with King that it requires us to work "to pull out the root that gets
to the source of the plague."[16] We believe that the personal and political
work of decolonization addresses this "root"—and that it necessitates both
"inward and outward journeys" of transformation.[17]

Swiss psychotherapist Carl Jung wisely warned: "The right way to
wholeness is made up, unfortunately, of fateful detours and wrong turnings.

---

13. Tuck and Yang, "Decolonization Is Not a Metaphor," 1–3, 31, 36. This "manifesto" opened the inaugural issue of *Decolonization: Indigeneity, Education & Society*,
an influential journal for this conversation. See further Smith et al.,*Indigenous and
Decolonizing Studies in Education*.

14. In Marchand-Lafortune's Decolonizing the Heart* workshops, para. 2. See also
Veracini, "Decolonizing Settler Colonialism"; Nadeau, *Unsettling Spirit*.

15. "Any approach to problem solving or self-discovery that employs a practical
method, not guaranteed to be optimal, perfect, logical, or rational, but instead sufficient
for reaching an immediate goal" (https://en.wikipedia.org/wiki/Heuristic).

16. Sales, "Pull Out the Root," para. 1. For more on Ruby's life and work, see Spirit
House Project*, and Sales, "Where Does It Hurt?"

17. This language was popularized by the Church of the Saviour* in Washington,
DC, one of the oldest alternative ecclesial communities in the U.S.; see O'Connor, *Journey Inward, Journey Outward*.

It is the *longissima via*, not straight but snakelike . . . a path whose labyrinthine twists and turns are not lacking in terrors."[18] This is certainly the case when the inward journey focuses, as we do here, on deconstructing settler presumptions of innocence, entitlement, and hegemony. The outward journey, in turn, is the equally challenging work of deepening relationships and practicing restorative solidarity with Indigenous communities. But this is the "way to wholeness" for settler inheritors of a social project "born in genocide."

Our narrative method approaches this journey primarily through the lens of family and communal histories, tracing and analyzing place, people, and spirit ("Storylines" in shorthand). We call these strands:

- "Landlines" of past and present places of inhabitation;
- "Bloodlines" of family and community; and
- "Songlines": liberative traditions that inspire practices of justice and compassion.[19]

In narrative terms these could be considered, respectively, the "setting," "characters," and "plot" of one's Storylines. To illustrate this method, we take a deep dive into my particular communal history, to explore how settler identities are constructed. Our aim is to "re-vise" what has been devised under the colonizing project and "re-member" what has been dismembered, in order to arrive at a more "dis-illusioned" narrative (below 1D). We seek to work with my Storylines empathetically, as befits a personal memoir, but also critically, as befits a political "workbook."

We commend Landlines, Bloodlines and Songlines (hereafter LBS) work to *all* settlers who would deepen and sustain solidarity with Indigenous and other marginalized communities that have been "written out" of colonial history and "written off" in our colonized present. But this work is *necessary* for Christians who would follow a Jesus who was executed by a colonial state; reckon with the long and lamentable history of a colonizing Christendom; and care about a future for the church as "a House for all peoples" (Mark 11:17 and Isa 56:7). This journey into formation (and re-formation) of self and society we call a "discipleship of decolonization."[20]

---

18. Jung, *Psychology and Alchemy*, 6.

19. See more below D; our preface explains why we chose these rubrics, and what we do and don't mean by them.

20. See more below, Interlude. Our friend Chris Budden has outlined a similar project for the Australian context in *Following Jesus in Invaded Space*.

B. WHAT I CARRY IN MY BONES

As the primary subject of the LBS process outlined in this book, I begin by locating myself socially. A cis-gendered heterosexual female, Euro-Canadian white settler, and Christian activist educator, I have worked in the field of restorative justice since 1989 as a practitioner and trainer. I owe the calling into this vocation to my family and faith community: Canadian prairie Mennonites. They nurtured me onto this path in ways I am only now beginning to understand. The following braids of personal narrative offer six snapshots of my journey over the last half century: three vignettes involving young teenage girls, and three wounds from childhood that still haunt me.

Osterwick, Ukraine, 1918. One hundred years ago as I write this, my maternal Grandma, Margreta Schulz, then fourteen, survived a two-week home invasion in her village. This was just one episode in a continuous climate of violence, plundering, rape, and killing endured by Mennonites and other German-speakers during the Russian Revolution and Civil War from 1917–1921. Over Christmas 1918, Margreta's home was commandeered by Ukrainian Anarchist/Nationalist forces under the command of Nestor Makhno.[21] The men had fled into the forest, while my grandma, her older sister, and girl cousins were hidden in the attic. Margreta's mother, Anna, trying to respond to violence with courage and compassion, bandaged the wounds of and fed rough and demanding peasant soldiers. It is difficult to believe that these females escaped sexual violation as assumed by family stories passed down (below 3D). During those days and nights of terror, Margreta experienced severe trauma, yet also witnessed her mother's profound embodiment of her tradition of nonresistance (below 2A). Anna's response to the home invasion may have warded off the worst; some months later her sister and three other relatives were brutally murdered in their home.

Saskatoon, Saskatchewan, 1980. As a child, I knew something horrible had happened to my grandparents, each of whom came to Saskatchewan as refugees of the Russian Revolution. I wanted to understand more, so at age thirteen I interviewed Grandma Margreta, recording her on a cassette tape. I recall that she spoke at length of the beauty and abundance her family had enjoyed during her childhood years in Osterwick. But as her account approached her teenage years, she began to weep, and could not continue. Because she was a joyful person and full of laughter, seeing her cry left an indelible impression, planting in me seeds of both curiosity and trepidation. Long after I had frustratingly lost that tape I would learn how many women of Margreta's generation suffered from PTSD, and how the silence around

21. See Gilley, "Makhno, Nestor Ivanovich"; Peters, *Nestor Makhno*; below, 2A.

their experiences negatively impacted our community. Yet the power of her testimony and her tears inspired me to keep asking questions in the years to come.

Winnipeg, Manitoba, 1988. In my final year of college, I volunteered with the Big Sisters/Little Sisters program in Manitoba. I was paired with a thirteen-year-old Cree girl who had just been released from juvenile detention after three years. She was living in a group home, pregnant for the second time, with twins. Her "crimes" had been sniffing glue, stealing food and clothes, and getting into fights—behaviors I now understand as reactions to a racist colonial system that did not meet her basic human needs. Despite my lack of race or economic analysis at the time, she helped me see that the criminal justice system was unable to address the injustices she faced. She described to me the pain of being forced to give up her first child, and of not knowing where he was. She vowed she would not give up her twins, and wanted them raised "on her reserve by an Indian family."[22] On the cusp of adulthood myself, this encounter raised a new set of questions about how her ancestors had been displaced by mine on the Canadian prairies. It was my first tutorial in the hard truths of colonization, and planted seeds of disillusionment with my comfortable, middle-class, white world.

This book is in part an attempt to understand how the lives of these three barely-teenaged girls—my grandma, my teenaged self, and my Cree "little sister"—are woven together into my history and place. There were other bewildering and frightening experiences that impressed on my young conscience that all was not well in our neighborhood. Again I will name three, each of which added to dissonant chords of alienation in my life, and left me de-formed in ways with which I still wrestle.

Saskatoon, Saskatchewan, 1979. While in grade seven I was walking to school with a white friend when she saw an Indigenous girl with whom she'd been skirmishing. My friend called her a racist name, and the latter pounced and began hitting her. As I tried to pull the native teenager back I ripped her shirt; she let go of my friend and began chasing me. Though she never caught me, I remained so afraid of her that I would run past those blocks on my way to school for the next year. No resources in school or church were available to help me transact such encounters.

Saskatoon, Saskatchewan, 1980. The night of my graduation ceremony from grade eight I was walking home with a white friend through the park.

---

22. While it is hard to forgive myself that as a teenager I lost the tape of my Grandma Margreta's interview, I am grateful I still have a transcript of one of my conversations with my "little sister." It is mysterious how and why we retain (or lose) these important potsherds of our lives—part of the challenge of doing our "archaeological" work (below 1E).

In the bushes I spotted an Indigenous girl who I knew had been adopted into a white settler family. She was on the ground on hands and knees, her adoptive brother behind her, thrusting. I remember the vacant look in her eyes as she stared straight ahead. Without saying a word, my friend and I turned and walked in the opposite direction—and never spoke about what we saw. We did not yet comprehend what we were seeing; but our silence was equally rooted in our ignorance about the racist culture of which we were part.[23] Witnessing this violation added to my sense of haunting.

I know now that this girl was one of an estimated 20,000 Indigenous children who were part of the "Sixties Scoop" in Canada, in which they were placed in foster homes or adopted, primarily by white, middle-class families.[24] This included many Mennonites, not least my own relatives.

Carrot River, Saskatchewan, 1999. I grew up with two Indigenous cousins, Glenn and Larry, who my paternal aunt and uncle adopted separately at ages two and one after having two children of their own. Our family spent many days at their farm in northeast Saskatchewan, where my dad was raised. I have fond memories of playing with Larry; we were the same age and second-youngest of fifty first cousins. My uncle was a gentle man: a beekeeper, farmer, and assistant pastor of the local Mennonite church. My aunt was also kind, with a generous heart and wry sense of humor. They had hoped for more children, and then learned about the Adopt Indian Métis program. But there was a significant dark side to this adoption that impacted our family, even if we did not comprehend it.

Their family was never told what band Larry and Glenn were from, nor given any cultural competence education or training. I remained oblivious to what my cousins were experiencing. As an early teen, Glenn began to battle alcohol abuse, and succumbed to AIDS in early 2001. According to my aunt, Larry has distanced himself; their father's funeral in 1999 was the last time I saw Glenn and Larry. In January 2019, Premier Scott Moe apologized for Saskatchewan's role in the Sixties Scoop, culminating a process of political reconsideration begun in a 1985 report by Justice Edwin Kimelman indicting the actions of the child welfare system during this period as

23. The continuing epidemic of violence against Indigenous girls has given rise to powerful social movements including Murdered and Missing Indigenous Women and Girls (see below 7D).

24. Adoption programs began in the late 1950s and persisted into the 1980s (and also occurred in the U.S. and Europe). From 1967 on, Saskatchewan promoted "Adopt Indian Métis," funded both federally and provincially. As a 2015 Canadian Mennonite article put it: "Some children went to loving homes while others were abused or mistreated by their adoptive or foster families. But nearly all, it seems, were disconnected from their families, language, culture and identities as indigenous people." (Neufeld, "Mennonites Have Yet to Reckon," 20.) See below, chapter 6, nn. 97–98.

"cultural genocide."[25] But such matters were never discussed in our family until very recently (see below 6E).

These are mere glimpses of the wider violence of colonization that intruded on my otherwise insular and privileged suburban existence. As a middle-class white person trying to metabolize these experiences in the absence of any real engagement or explanatory framing, I faced the typical choice: either rationalize the incidents and distance myself from responsibility, or repress the memory. For me it was the latter. So these memories festered below my consciousness, awaiting an awakening.

It has been a long, slow arousal. But I have come to realize I carry in my bones the traumas of my grandparents' generation *and* the haunting of traumas inflicted on Indigenous communities. Both swirled around my childhood as a fog of "dis-ease." These wounds compelled me, if at first unconsciously, into the work of restorative justice. My mentors taught me that this vocation would be a way of life—and indeed it has been. The "turnings" noted in these story braids are important steps on my *longissima via*. Though labyrinthine and "not lacking in terrors," this journey has led me ever deeper into the work outlined in this book.

C. DOING OUR OWN WORK, HERE AND NOW

Two decades ago, friend and mentor Melanie Morrison introduced us to the great writer-activist Audre Lorde's challenge to white folks to "do our own work."[26] There are many ways, and levels at which, to decolonize internalized and externalized patterns of white settler colonialism. We are also cognizant that there are vast differences in circumstances and experiences among descendants of European immigrants. We wish to avoid stereotypes, oversimplified narratives, and above all, essentializing ourselves or others.[27] On the other hand, we emphasize how socialization and historical forces shape us each and all. We offer here a model for decolonization work that aims to "pull on the root" by engaging settler ancestral trauma, historical silences, narratives of superiority, complicity, and moral injury in order to

25. McKenna, "Saskatchewan Premier Scott Moe Apologizes to '60s Scoop Survivors."

26. The phrase is from Lorde's essay "The Transformation of Silence into Language and Action": "I am myself—a Black woman warrior poet doing my work—come to ask you, are you doing yours?" (*Sister Outsider*, 41). Morrison was a key developer of the Doing Our Own Work curriculum with Allies for Change.*

27. That is, characterizing a quality or trait as intrinsic to a particular group; see Chao et al., "Essentializing Race." This is particularly important for those many of us with multiple racial-ethnic identities.

recognize and redress past (and continuing) injustices. It also explores settler legacies of resilience and conscience that can animate restorative solidarity. We hope this book will help others like (and unlike) us to do this work.

In her book, *White Fragility*, Robin DiAngelo points out an inherent paradox in her analysis, which also pertains to ours: "In speaking as a white person to a primarily white audience, I am yet again centering white people and the white voice"—yet for the purpose of *de-centering* whiteness and "building our stamina for the critical examination of white identity."[28] This is obviously tricky, given the inveterate tendency of white settlers to rationalize or absolutize our own perspectives. It requires a determined dance between critically demythologizing our own narratives while genuinely encountering those of Indigenous and other marginalized communities. If we focus *only* on our family stories, in the way hobby genealogists do for example, it becomes another instance of centering whiteness. But if we only focus on *other* people's stories, as some white solidarity activists often do, we can be derailed by dissociation (from our own work) and/or appropriation (of the cultural strength of others).

Our LBS model of inquiry is illustrated through the particularities of my communal and familial Mennonite story over the last 100 years. A second-generation Canadian, I look at how my grandparents' *Russländer* community arrived as victimized but resilient refugees, yet also at how we assimilated into settler privileges. I also examine how their untransacted traumatic experiences may have crippled their ability to "see" the Indigenous inhabitants of the lands to which they came—and how it continues to impact subsequent generations.

We acknowledge this personal approach has certain limitations. We worry, for example, whether my story is representative *enough* to help other white settlers in their LBS work. After all, Mennonites, a historically marginalized and sometimes fiercely persecuted religious minority since the Reformation, are to some degree atypical of European immigrants to the Americas. On the other hand, Mennonite settler negotiation and cooperation with dominant colonial authorities more than once procured advantages, especially regarding access to "frontier" land. Moreover, most European Mennonite settlers in North America have assimilated into white-skin and middle-class privileges. The strange mix of minoritization and mainstreaming, of trauma and opportunism, in my story might resonate across a broad spectrum, perhaps even with some persons of color. But we hope it will encourage white settlers to reckon with the haunting legacies of colonization,

28. DiAngelo, *White Fragility*, xiv.

and to deepen relationships with Indigenous peoples and their ongoing struggles for justice.

There are three main challenges that arise when working with one's own family narrative. One is how we come to terms with the inevitable gaps and silences in the record. These, too, must be interrogated, because what we do *not* know shapes us as much as what we do know (below 3D). This may be particularly acute if you are adopted, if your progenitors were brought to North America under duress, or if your family is highly fragmented. If you have no information about your genealogy, we encourage you to concentrate on your immediate family or personal history.

A second challenge is navigating and negotiating what *has* been recorded or passed on. For example, I have been tempted to omit or reconcile contradictory testimonies; or to downplay ways my people replicated the values of capitalism rather than Anabaptism; or to succumb to paralysis in the face of complexities and incongruities in our communal narratives. I've tried to work against such "harmonizing" tendencies, while remaining committed to handling stories of my living family system with care and respect. Unlike many settlers, I have the problem of "too much" material, chronicled in a formidable corpus of family history books.[29] I have struggled not to get lost in the genealogical maze, and wrestled with how much detail to share (it's *all* fascinating to me!). This project means to be workbook as well as social analysis and memoir; we have thus endeavored to give enough context for my story to be both intelligible and illustrative without being overly self-referential.

A third challenge is to ground our decolonization work in real space and time. So much family history work in popular culture is sentimentalized and acontextualized. It doesn't help that the growing "genealogical industrial complex" offers DNA tests that produce apolitical matrices of kinship that ignore both historical forces and social geographies.

Space. Settler colonialism in North America is all about land—which is why we need to make sure our family stories are *grounded*. This is a twofold task: analyzing our communal narratives in their geographical contexts, and conversely, learning the stories of the places in which our people first settled, as well as where we ourselves now dwell. As we have argued elsewhere, we believe the most appropriate scale for understanding and transforming human inhabitation is that of the bioregion. This is where we most

---

29. It is common for Mennonite families to produce genealogical and clan history books. I have no fewer than seven, and am deeply grateful to elder relatives for their painstaking and careful work in curating them. Our community has also generated a large body of both scholarly and literary accounts of Mennonite history. I recognize that having such voluminous written resources is a privilege.

meaningfully map and measure work for economic, political, and ecological wholeness, and against capitalist illusions of autonomy, rootlessness, and placelessness.[30] More specifically, we each inhabit a particular watershed, every one of which bears deep scars from the environmental and social assault of colonization. Our responsibilities do not end at the watershed level, but they must surely begin there.

The Storylines we trace in this book move between Ukraine and Russia (where my grandparents were born), Saskatchewan (where I was born) and California (where we live). My mobility is not uncommon among twentieth-century North American settler descendants, a middle-class privilege of "re-settling" that often occasions disconnection from place. Our commitment to "Watershed Discipleship" combats these problems, inviting specific covenants to place(s) and engagement in local social and ecological restorative justice. Over the last decade I have become increasingly intentional about bilocationality, seeking to apprentice to the ecological and social Storylines of *both* of my beloved home places: the Ventura River and South Saskatchewan River watersheds (below 5A). Despite their many differences, they share the distinction of having been colonized relatively late in the European occupation of our respective countries, so that their Indigenous peoples struggled to survive colonists who were already well practiced in genocide.

Another reason to focus on one's bioregional inhabitation is because of our tendency as settlers to see issues of injustice "with a clarity and passion inversely proportional to their geographic distance from where we live," a kind of hypermetropia ("defined by Webster as a 'condition of the eye in which distant objects are seen more distinctly than near ones'").[31] For example, my community's peace and justice witness has often seen issues more clearly and responded to needs more quickly in Africa or Latin America than among Indigenous peoples in our own provinces or states. Solidarity with people elsewhere is important, but settlers are fundamentally responsible to help decolonize our *here*.

Time. Our LBS work must also be understood within its social context then and now. In this book, we focus on the last four generations of my kin, covering a span of 150 years, but do so with eyes firmly fixed on our "unsettling" historical moment. On one hand, amidst "signs of the times" such as climate disasters and the COVID-19 pandemic, the U.S. has taken a deeper dive into white supremacist plutocracy. Like many activists in the

30. See Myers, *Watershed Discipleship* (for working definitions of bioregional and watershed paradigms, see 10–15).

31. Myers, *Who Will Roll Away the Stone?*, 228–29. This could be categorized as another "move to innocence" (see below 6C).

fall of 2016, we struggled not to organize reactively to the spectacle politics of the new Trump regime. While continuing resistance to the steady erosion of public ideals of democracy and social equity is crucial, we decided in 2017 to refocus on the roots of the pathology of which Trumpism is only a symptom. This has led us to go deeper into the primal work of decolonization rather than spreading ourselves thin in an attempt to respond to every real and engineered emergency manufactured by this administration and the forces empowered by it.

At the same time, the last half-century has also witnessed long-suppressed voices of native peoples again rising and demanding attention. The occupation of Alcatraz in 1969, the 1992 Columbus Quincentenary, the landmark United Nations Declaration on the Rights of Indigenous Peoples, and recent movements like Idle No More and the resistance to the Dakota Access Pipeline at Standing Rock in North Dakota are all expressions of "Indigenous Resurgence," which represent hopeful Songlines that make settler decolonization work both more imperative and more possible (below 7D). Our project thus revisits issues thought by most settlers to "belong to the past" in order to do our own work in a *now* that is both reactionary and resurgent.

D. LANDLINES, BLOODLINES, AND SONGLINES: AN ORIENTATION TO THIS PROJECT

Our method focuses on examining three interrelated kinds of Storylines:[32]

- *Landlines* (the "where"): our immigrant family histories, whether voluntary or forced, ancestral or personal, from country of origin (chapter 2) to North America (chapter 5).

- *Bloodlines* (the "who"): our embodied story, what we have inherited biologically and psychically from our familial, racial, ethnic, gender, and cultural formation—including the travails or privileges, traumas and impacts, of immigrant leaving (chapter 3) and settling (chapter 6), including the costs of cultural loss and assimilation into settler colonialism.

- *Songlines* (the convictional "why"): traditions of faith and Spirit that animated resilience and redemptive practices in our ancestry (chapter 4) and that help us work for justice and healing today (chapter 7).

32. The semantics of Landlines, Bloodlines, and Songlines has emerged as we have done this work with groups; it is provisional, and not without problems, but we continue to find it illuminating and fruitful.

The circle is only complete as we enact practices of restorative solidarity: re-schooling, reparations, and repatriation (chapter 8) that aspire toward a decolonized future.

As shown on the diagram at the top of this chapter, these circles of story overlap because they do in life. They all inhabit (or contest) the wider circle of our communal narratives. Chapter 1 looks at some of the psychic and social challenges of doing this work, with further suggestions and tools. Chapters 2 through 7 each conclude with "Queries" to help you fill out and wrestle with your own ancestral and communal story. Queries (borrowed from Friends' tradition) seek more than mere information; they are "sacred questions" designed to clarify the meaning of our Storylines and the requirements of our convictions. "They are questions to our life, not accusations, yet they are hard questions, not merely rhetorical ones."[33] Our Queries are offered only as prompts, and we hope you will explore well beyond them.

This is a long book because we are unpacking important and often complex issues, and we hope to have provided enough repetition of key ideas and vocabulary to make the journey intelligible. Two characteristics of our text require explanation. One is our insertion of "road signs" that refer readers backwards or forwards in the text (e.g., "see below 3B"). The fact that we are working with three vectors across multiple contexts made it unavoidable that both our narrative and our process unfold in different places. These "pointers" are meant to help with navigation around a lengthy text: indicating where a concept, theme, person, or place is further elaborated; or assuring the reader that particular ideas will be (or have been) covered elsewhere. They are intended not to promote "hopping around," but to aid in tracking particular threads of argument (should you wish). Secondly, we decided to footnote—rather heavily at times—for several reasons. LBS work involves a wide range of disciplines, and we wish to be transparent about those upon whose expertise we have relied. We believe references and notes empower readers, offering resources and avenues for further exploration. They also allow for some measure of qualification, nuance, or parenthetical correlation. In both cases we hope these "interruptions" to the flow of the narrative will instruct rather than distract; they can be ignored until needed or desired.

Because the backbone of this book's narrative is my family history and its places, it will be helpful for readers to have some orientation to which you can refer along the way:

---

33. For Ched's explication of Quaker "Queries, Testimonies and Advices" as a way of doing practical theology, see *Who Will Roll Away the Stone?*, 34–38.

- Figures 05, 06, and 07 below provide three general maps of the main "settings" of the Storylines we discuss: Ukraine/Russia, the Saskatchewan River Watershed, and the Ventura River Watershed.

- Figures 08 and 09 are another kind of map: an abbreviated family tree outlining four generations of my immediate family, from my great-grandparents' to mine. (You can find individuals by consulting the index.)

- Figures 10 and 11 are timelines marking some events relevant to my Storylines in the three watersheds. The handful of dates plotted are obviously selective, and not in any way representative of the complex histories in each place, which we are still learning!

We appreciate the wisdom of our friend Dee Dee Risher, who wonders: "What to say? How much to share? If we are honest about our pain, will we cause another to falter? And will our vulnerability bring us healing, or will it simply become eviscerated by spectator pity?" But she exhorts: "Tell the truth about everything, especially the things that go wrong."[34]

We conclude this introduction as we began: testifying that our settler "way to wholeness" is one of labyrinthine circles, not straight lines (much less shortcuts). This is true both of an inward journey to "dis-illusionment"—weaning ourselves off of devised and dismembered identities and histories (part I)—and an outward journey of "de-assimilation" and restorative solidarity (part II). A discipleship of decolonization is both demanding and liberating. It is our prayerful hope that this volume equips and inspires white settler Christians (and others) to do *our* work: facing past and present, looking within and around us, struggling for justice here and now. May our journey around many circles of story embrace the promise of the old Shaker Songline:

'Tis the gift to come down, where we ought to be . . .
. . .To bow and to bend we shan't be asham'd,
To turn, turn will be our delight,
Till by turning, turning we come round right.[35]

34. Risher, *Soulmaking Room*, 206.

35. See notes on this venerable song at http://www.americanmusicpreservation.com/SimpleGiftsmultimedia.htm, described there as "written for what the Shakers called a 'Quick Dance' and sung and danced at a lively tempo in their worship service" (para. 4). We return to this image in our Epilogue.

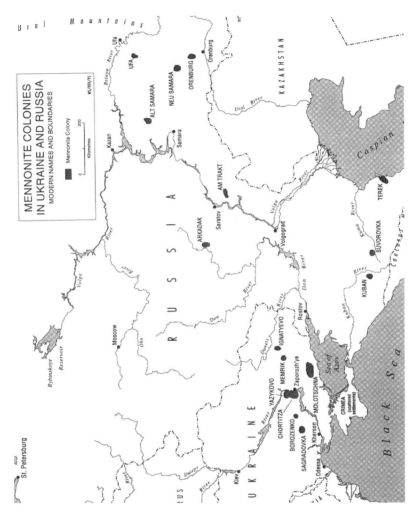

Figure 05: Mennonite Colonies in Ukraine and Russia. Map from *Mennonite Historical Atlas*, 14 (used with permission).

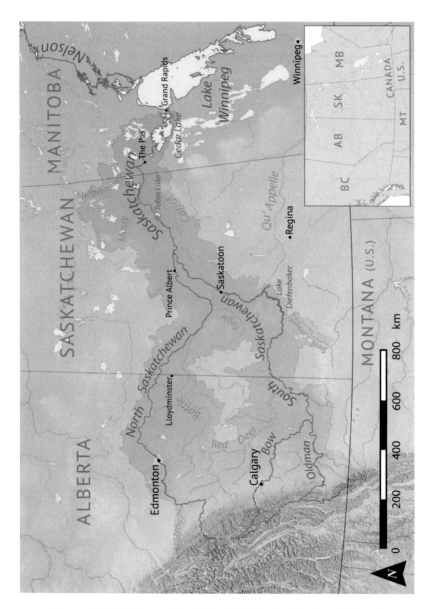

Figure 06: Saskatchewan River Watershed. Map by Alan Ong (at https://en.wikipedia.org/wiki/Saskatchewan_River, used with permission).

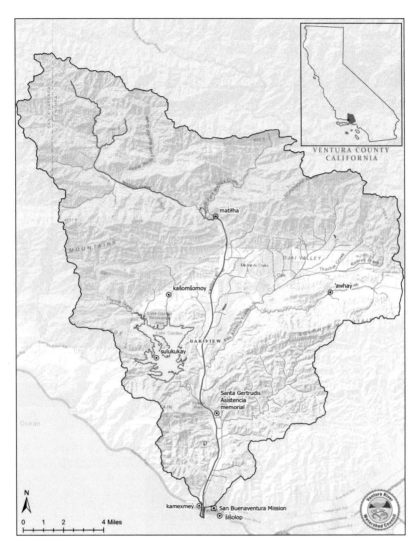

Figure 07: Ventura River Watershed. Custom map provided by Ventura River Watershed Council (venturawatershed.org, used with permission).

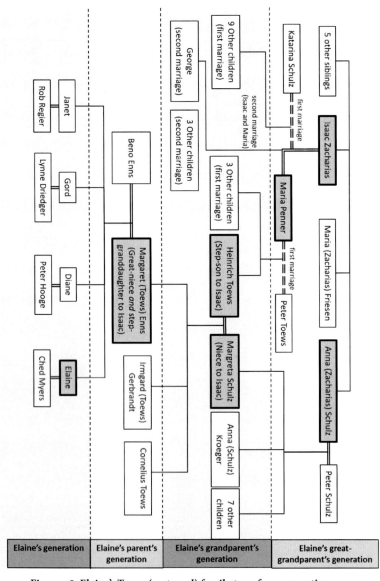

Figure 08: Elaine's Toews (maternal) family tree, four generations.
Design by Chris Wight.

28

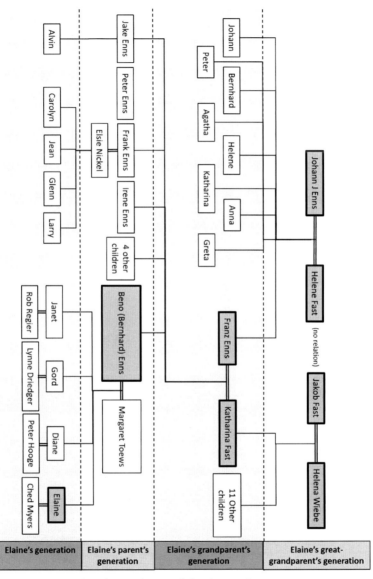

Figure 09: Elaine's Enns (paternal) family tree, four generations.
Design by Chris Wight.

29

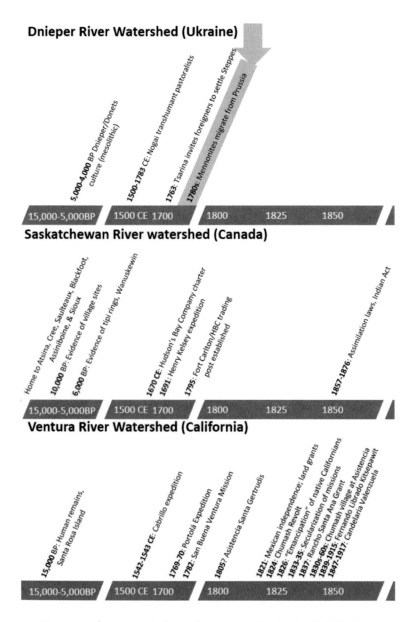

Dnieper River Watershed (Ukraine)

5,000-4,000 BP Dnieper/Donets culture (mesolithic)

1500-1783 CE: Nogai transhumant pastoralists

1763: Tsarina invites foreigners to settle Steppes

1780s: Mennonites migrate from Prussia

| 15,000-5,000BP | 1500 CE 1700 | 1800 | 1825 | 1850 |

Saskatchewan River watershed (Canada)

Home to Atsina, Cree, Saulteaux, Blackfoot, Assiniboine, & Sioux

10,000 BP: Evidence of village sites

6,000 BP: Evidence of tipi rings, Wanuskewin

1670 CE: Hudson's Bay Company charter

1691: Henry Kelsey expedition

1795: Fort Carlton/HBC trading post established

1857-1876: Assimilation laws, Indian Act

| 15,000-5,000BP | 1500 CE 1700 | 1800 | 1825 | 1850 |

Ventura River Watershed (California)

15,000 BP: Human remains, Santa Rosa Island

1542-1543 CE: Cabrillo expedition

1769-70: Portolá Expedition

1782: San Buena Ventura Mission

1805? Asistencia Santa Gertrudis

1821: Mexican independence; land grants

1824: Chumash Revolt

1826: "Emancipation" of native Californians

1833-35: Secularization of missions

1837: Rancho Santa Ana Grant

1830s-60s: Chumash village at Asistencia

1839-1915: Fernando Librado Kitsepawit

1847-1917: Candelaria Valenzuela

| 15,000-5,000BP | 1500 CE 1700 | 1800 | 1825 | 1850 |

Figure 10: Three watersheds timeline, to 1850. Design by Chris Wight.

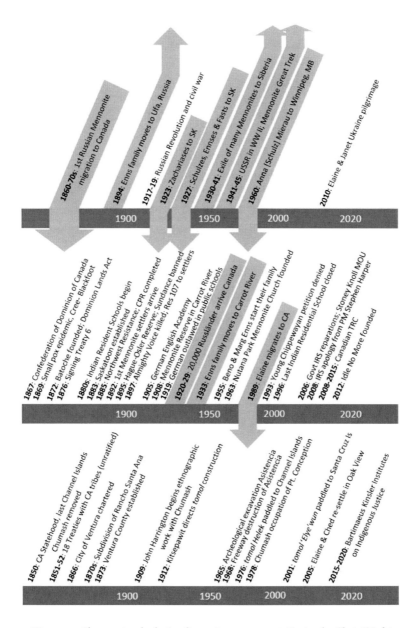

First timeline (top):

1860-70s: 1st Russian Mennonite migration to Canada
1894: Enns family moves to Ufa, Russia
1917-19: Russian Revolution and civil war
1923: Zacharias to SK
1927: Schulzes, Ennses & Fasts to SK
1930-41: Exile of many Mennonites to Siberia
1941-45: USSR in WW II; Mennonite Great Trek
1960: Anna [Schulz] Mierau to Winnipeg, MB
2010: Elaine & Janet Ukraine pilgrimage

1900 | 1950 | 2000 | 2020

Second timeline (middle):

1867: Confederation of Dominion of Canada
1869: Small pox epidemic, Cree- Blackfoot
1872: Batoche founded; Dominion Lands Act
1876: Signing Treaty 6
1880s: Indian Resident Schools begin
1883: Saskatoon established
1885: Northwest Resistance
1892: 1st Mennonite settlers arrive; CPR completed
1895: Hague-Osler Reserve; Sundance banned
1897: Almighty Voice killed; Res 107 to settlers
1905: German English Academy
1908: Mennonite Reserve in Carrot River
1919: German outlawed in public schools
1920-29: 20,000 Russländer arrive Canada
1933: Enns family moves to Carrot River
1955: Beno & Marg Enns start their family
1963: Nutana Park Mennonite Church founded
1989: Elaine migrates to CA
1993: Young Chippewayan petition denied
1996: Last Indian Residential School closed
2006: Gov't IRS reparations; Stoney Knoll MOU
2008: IRS apology from PM Stephen Harper
2008-2015: Canadian TRC
2012: Idle No More founded

1900 | 1950 | 2000 | 2020

Third timeline (bottom):

1850: CA Statehood, last Channel Islands Chumash removed
1851-52: 18 Treaties with CA tribes (unratified)
1866: City of Ventura chartered
1870s: Subdivision of Rancho Santa Ana
1873: Ventura County established
1909: John Harrington begins ethnographic work with Chumash
1912: Kitsepawit directs tomol construction
1965: Archeological excavation Asistencia
1968: Freeway destruction of Asistencia
1976: tomol Helek paddled to Channel Islands
1978: Chumash occupation of Pt. Conception
2001: tomol 'Elye'wun paddled to Santa Cruz Is
2005: Elaine & Ched re-settle in Oak View
2015-2020: Bartimaeus Kinsler Institutes on Indigenous Justice

1900 | 1950 | 2000 | 2020

Figure 11: Three watersheds timeline, 1850 to present. Design by Chris Wight.

Figure 12: Historical Marker for Asistencia Santa Gertrudis (foreground, painting of
Mike Pulido by Robert Valiente-Neighbours), Ventura River Watershed, CA, January
2018. Photo: Chris Wight (used with permission).

CHAPTER 1

Storytelling in a Haunted House

> Haunting . . . is the relentless remembering and reminding that
> will not be appeased by settler society's assurances of innocence
> and reconciliation. Haunting is both acute and general; indi-
> viduals are haunted, but so are societies. The United States is
> permanently haunted by the slavery, genocide, and violence en-
> twined in its first, present and future days . . . Haunting aims to
> wrong the wrongs, a confrontation that settler horror hopes to
> evade.
>
> —Eve Tuck and C. Ree[1]

1A. ASISTENCIA SANTA GERTRUDIS, 2005

In July 2005, we moved up from Los Angeles to the Ventura River Watershed. During our first week, driving along Ventura Avenue, we noticed an
historical marker. Wanting to learn local lore, we pulled over to take a look.
Tucked into some bushes by the side of the road was a stone memorial to
the "Asistencia Santa Gertrudis," marking the approximate location of an
auxiliary chapel to Mission San Buenaventura. Ventura County Historic
Landmark No. 11, erected in 1970, stated murkily: "It served the Indians in
the early days."

Our curiosity piqued, we asked around, but it was years before we
learned the story, and only after some research. Named after Saint Gertrude

---

1. Tuck and Ree, "Glossary of Haunting," 642.

the Great, a thirteenth-century German Benedictine, the Asistencia was constructed sometime between 1792 and 1809. It was located near the Ventura River, five miles from the main mission, by where the El Camino Real—an historical trail linking a system of twenty-one missions—branched off the coast to head up over the mountains toward Santa Barbara.

The missions, founded between 1769 and 1823 by Franciscans to pros-elytize, assimilate, and control Native Californians in this far northwestern edge of Spanish territory, were instrumental in the colonization of Alta California. Native Californians were often forced to live in or around the mission settlements and used as workers; the Spanish called them "neo-phytes" or *reducidos*. This profoundly disrupted their traditional way of life and brought horrific abuses and oppression.[2] It is a matter of debate whether this chapel "served the Indians"; but it was certainly the site of a na-tive Chumash labor camp in the first decades of the nineteenth century. From here workers dug clay from Red Mountain across the river, and built a seven-mile adobe and stone aqueduct to steer water from the Ventura River to the Mission.[3]

During the Mexican colonial period (1820–1848), the missions were secularized (San Buenaventura in 1836) and went into decline. Around the Asistencia Santa Gertrudis, a small village grew, consisting of Chumash families, probably survivors of mission life or refugees whose traditional lands had been occupied by settlers. The chapel was within sight of a syca-more tree that had long been sacred to valley Chumash.[4] The traditional Chumash *aps* (brush huts) inspired Mexican settlers to call the site Casi-tas ("little houses"). The name survives on the local landscape—a town, a road, a dam, a lake—but its origins would not be known by most valley residents today.

The historical plaque says nothing about this small native village.[5] But multiple reports by late nineteenth- and early twentieth-century settlers at-test that Chumash families farmed by the river, having planted significant

2. See Castillo, *Cross of Thorns;* Cordero, "Missionized California Indian Futures."

3. See information at https://www.vcrma.org/mission-aqueduct; for pictures, see http://quarriesandbeyond.org/states/ca/structures/ca-ventura_mission_2.html.

4. Leidos, "Wind Sycamore." Yve Chavez argues that, even as the Franciscans were trying to wean the Chumash off "pagan" ways, the latter were appropriating the former's spaces to continue traditional ceremonies ("Indigenous Artists," 80–87).

5. Nor does the Wikipedia site, though it mentions Spanish relocations to the site after fires, pirate raids, and earthquakes on the coast (https://en.wikipedia.org/wiki/Santa_Gertrudis_Asistencia). Anthropologist John Johnson confirms that after secu-larization, "the Indian community was organized around the mission *ranchería* and a series of small farmsteads located along the lower Ventura River" ("Chumash Indians after Secularization," 144).

fruit orchards around the Asistencia, and sold produce to Ventura.[6] A *diseño* (Mexican plot map) used in an 1847 land-claim dispute over Rancho Cañada Larga shows the Asistencia, and testimony in the case indicates there were Chumash living there at that time. One source stated that in 1861, a former Mission *alcalde* and Chief of Mission Indians in the area claimed he had forty subjects at the Cañada. A 1932 book on Ventura history claims the chapel was used and occupied by Chumash families as late as 1868, well into the American period—remarkable given the awful fate of most Indigenous Californians after statehood.[7] By 1881, however, white settlers reported that the Chapel was in ruins, its roof tiles having been torn off and used for flooring in a house in Ventura, and the site no longer inhabited. Shortly thereafter the remains of the Asistencia were plowed under by Salmon Weldon and the land put into apricots, then citrus, then beans (a nearby canyon bears his name).

In 1965, the lost site of the Asistencia was rediscovered by Cañada Larga ranch foreman Mike Pulido while plowing the bean field. It underwent an emergency archaeological salvage excavation in the spring of 1966 because of a planned freeway extension. Significant Indigenous artifacts were found in and below the Asistencia period layers that testified to the profound change in Chumash lifeways as a result of colonization. In January 1968, the remains of the dig were buried in a pit (possibly near or under the historical marker), and the site paved over by the new highway. The native story was effectively disappeared, reduced to a place name whose origins were obscure and one sentimentalized sentence on a plaque put up by the Native Daughters of the Golden West.[8]

Mike Pulido's son is Ched's barber, and it was from him that we first heard about the deeper history of the site. Mike Jr.'s wife, Carol, is a local Chumash cultural officer, who as a young woman took part in the Asistencia dig. She's been teaching us about her people in this area, and points out that the 1968 destruction of the historic site could never happen today, thanks to slow but steady improvement in federal cultural remains legislation, fought for by Indigenous advocates over the last several decades. Another local Chumash elder has stood with us at the site and whispered about ghostly presences in abandoned ranch houses and trees nearby.

6. The following historical details are gleaned from the report of the 1966 excavation: Greenwood and Browne, "Chapel of Santa Gertrudis."

7. See Madley, *American Genocide.*

8. A "fraternal and patriotic organization founded in 1886 on the principles of Love of Home, Devotion to the Flag, Veneration of the Pioneers and Faith in the Existence of God" (https://www.ndgw.org/, para. 1).

Since learning this history, with the blessing of these elders, we've "adopted" the Asistencia site which so mystified us years earlier, keeping it clean of trash and planting and tending native species after the 2017 Thomas Fire burned everything but the stone memorial. We've noticed that a few others, unknown to us, continue to leave offerings and mementos there too. On the fiftieth anniversary of the freeway's destruction of the site we held a commemoration, and published a piece in the local paper about it. We've started celebrating the Feast of St. Gertrude (November 16) at the memorial. With Carol and other local Chumash we're still trying to figure out how to tell the fuller story publicly—just one modest step in our journey to discover what restorative solidarity means in the watershed where we have settled.

This monument, and the suppressed history buried beneath it, represents one tiny, almost hidden, yet fully illustrative example of the long and sordid legacy of settler displacement of Indigenous peoples and their stories. "Served the Indians?" Not likely. "In the early days?" A strictly settler timeline. This process of erasure and settler overwriting has occurred in virtually every square mile of North America, whether enshrined on sanitizing historical markers or not. Powerful national myths of conquest and "progress" continue to clear-cut the cultural and historical landscape. This devising and dismembering of people and place reaches even into an obscure corner of a small county like ours. So *here* we work to decolonize memory—because the Asistencia is a haunting.

1B. "YOU WILL NEVER BE ALONE": HAUNTINGS SEEKING HEALING

The best way to approach the notion of haunting in our colonized landscapes and histories is through words allegedly spoken by Chief Sealth, a revered leader of Duwamish and Suquamish tribes in Puget Sound, to the governor of the Washington Territory in the mid-1850s at the site of present-day Seattle:

> Every part of this country is sacred to my people. Every hillside, every valley, every plain and grove has been hallowed by some fond memory or some sad experience of my tribe . . . their deep fastness at eventide grow shadowy with the presence of dusky spirits. And when the last red man shall have perished from the earth and his memory among white men shall have become a myth, these shores shall swarm with the invisible dead of my tribe. And when your children's children shall think themselves alone in the field, the store, the shop, upon the highway or in the

silence of the woods, they will not be alone. . . At night, when the
streets of your cities and villages shall be silent, and you think
them deserted, they will throng with the returning hosts that
once filled and still love this beautiful land. The white man will
never be alone . . .

These lines, attributed to Sealth by Henry A. Smith in an 1887 newspaper article, not only speak of the land as haunted; this now-renowned
oration has also haunted settler consciousness ever since. This holds even
if the words weren't actually Sealth's, but the interpolation (or even partial
invention) of Smith three decades later.[9] Because, if the latter, they *directly*
reveal a haunted settler consciousness being projected onto a "noble Indian"
at a fraught historical moment just prior to the "closing of the American
frontier" (to use Frederick Jackson Turner's imperialist phrase).[10]

Avery Gordon asserts that "haunting is a constituent element of modern social life . . . a generalizable social phenomenon of great import. To
study social life one must confront the ghostly aspects of it."[11] Her work has
tried to understand

> modern forms of dispossession, exploitation and repression
> and their concrete impacts on the people most affected by them
> and on our shared conditions of living . . . [particularly] racial
> capitalism and the determining role of monopolistic and mili-
> taristic state violence . . . Haunting is one way in which abusive
> systems of power make themselves known and their impacts felt
> in everyday life, especially when they are supposedly over and
> done with (slavery, for instance) or when their oppressive nature
> is continuously denied (as in free labor or national security).
> Haunting is not the same as being exploited, traumatized, or
> oppressed, although it usually involves these experiences or is

9. Smith, an early settler in the Seattle area, published his account of the speech in
The Seattle Sunday Star on October 29, 1887 (see text at http://perolofdk.com/chiefs4.
htm). Though still widely reproduced as the words of Sealth, there is a continuing debate over its authenticity; the argument against its historicity is summarized by Clark,
"Thus Spoke Chief Seattle."

10. Other "Indigenous vows of haunting" from the same period and with similarly
hazy provenances echo Sealth's themes and continue to circulate in settler culture. For
example, the so-called "Curse of Chief Tenaya" (in response to the killing of his son
by the Mariposa Batallion in Yosemite, California in 1851) allegedly states: "Yes, sir,
American, my spirit will make trouble for you and your people . . . I will not leave my
home, but be with the spirits among the rocks, the water-falls, in the rivers and in the
winds; wheresoever you go" (Brennen, "Yosemite's Haunted Canyon," para. 5). See also
Boyd and Thrush, *Phantom Past, Indigenous Presence*.

11. Gordon, *Ghostly Matters*, 7.

produced by them. What's distinctive about haunting is that it is an animated state in which a repressed or unresolved social violence is making itself known, sometimes very directly, sometimes more obliquely.[12]

Unangax̂ scholar Eve Tuck and California artist C. Ree apply this notion specifically to

> genocide, desecration, poxed-blankets, rape, humiliation . . . Settler colonialism is the management of those who have been made killable, once and future ghosts—those that had been destroyed, but also those that are generated in every generation . . . Social life, settler colonialism, and haunting are inextricably bound; each ensures there are always more ghosts to return.[13]

But can we "heal" hauntings of histories, places, and consciousness? Gordon has more recently emphasized how reckoning with ghosts can mobilize movements of resistance and healing. Haunting "always registers the harm inflicted or the loss sustained by a social violence done in the past or being done in the present"; but unlike trauma, "it is distinctive for producing a something-to-be-done." This, she asserts, is the concept's main value: as a way of animating "individual, social, or political movement and change."[14] Indeed, two recent powerful social movements—the Indigenous-led resistance to the Keystone XL pipeline project at Standing Rock, North Dakota, and Black Lives Matter activism in response to continuing police killings of African Americans—can be seen in part as expressions of unresolved social violence "making itself known." Indigenous and Black scholars, artists, and activists have begun creatively mapping the hauntings of communal narratives and occupied landscapes.[15] And local grassroots initiatives by people of conscience are trying to heal haunted histories, notable examples being the efforts of two of our mentors. Rev. Lawrence Hart has re-commemorated massacre sites from nineteenth-century "Indian Wars" and organized for the repatriation of Native remains. Episcopal leader Catherine Meeks has led prayerful pilgrimages of remembering and repentance to twentieth-century lynching sites in Georgia.[16]

12. Gordon, *Ghostly Matters*, xv.

13. Tuck and Ree, "Glossary of Haunting," 642. For more on Eve Tuck, whose work figures significantly in this book, see http://www.evetuck.com/bio.

14. Gordon, "Some Thoughts on Haunting and Futurity," 2–3.

15. See for example: 2bears, "Mythologies of an [Un]dead Indian"; Freeman, "Indigenous Hauntings in Settler-Colonial Spaces"; Martens and Robertson, "How the Soil Remembers Plantation Slavery."

16. On Hart, see Enns and Myers, *Ambassadors of Reconciliation*, 2:121–33. On

Still, denial is the primary way settler culture handles these ghosts. Arguing from a psychological perspective, settler Canadians Scott Kouri and Hans Skott-Myhre maintain that the "settler unconscious" produces

> both a mythical subject free of the disruptive and forbidden activities engaged in during the extensive historical conquest of Indigenous peoples (European, African, Asian, and North American) and a mythical event horizon that obscures and eviscerates memory, producing the settler as innocent and desiring of democracy, fullness, and opportunity . . . We, as settlers, must not know, in any existential or phenomenological sense, the price we have exacted from the land, from the Other, or from our own desire . . . Under such a foreclosure of knowledge, the settler must believe that history is in the past and that any and all harm, trauma, and associated accountability has no contemporary actuality.[17]

As a result, they continue, settlers are "literally sick at heart and soul," making it difficult "to look at each other or ourselves without weariness, and this weariness extends to all those we encounter as other."[18] They conclude that deconstructing such "transcendent denial" requires an alternative to

> the horizon of a subject free of history and geography. Avoiding the pain, shame, anger, and guilt that constitutes the settler unconscious is inadequate to our current state of affairs. We need a new unconscious . . . capable of founding a subjectivity of increased relationality. To endure this undoing will require us to be vulnerable and to relate with accountability to Indigenous peoples, to our Indigenous friends, as we experience and work to dismantle ongoing colonialism together.[19]

A discipleship of decolonization embraces this demanding work.

Our LBS approach has grown out of study (both formal and informal), extended conversations with our communities, and workshopping this process with groups around North America. We hope this book can be a resource for mapping how ghosts inhabit both the *geographies* in which we settlers dwell (Landlines) and the *genealogies* we carry in our bones (Bloodlines), as well as for exploring how we can promote healing

---

Meeks, see Hiskey, "Pilgrims Bear Witness," and below 7B.

17. Kouri and Skott-Myhre, "Catastrophe," 3. See more on this as "moves to innocence" below 6C.

18. Kouri and Skott-Myhre, "Catastrophe," 7.

19. Kouri and Skott-Myhre, "Catastrophe," 14.

and justice by drawing on *generative* wisdom traditions of resistance and renewal (Songlines).

~

Gordon asserts that hauntings are "neither premodern superstition nor individual psychosis."[20] We think a poignant passage from Luke's Gospel addresses this phenomenon in terms of "unclean spirits" engaged by Jesus of Nazareth. The Gospels portray him unmasking such spirits, sometimes as political "occupying powers" (as in the case of the "Legion" who locks down a subject among the dead in Mark 5:1–20), and sometimes as personal forces of "possession" (as in the case of a silencing spirit that renders a young boy unable to speak or hear in Mark 9:17–29).[21]

A strange parable speaks to the complex layers of inward and outward haunting that must be peeled away in decolonizing work:

> When the unclean spirit has gone out of a person, it wanders through waterless regions looking for a resting place, but not finding any, it says, "I will return to my house from which I came." When it comes, it finds it swept and put in order. Then it goes and brings seven other spirits more evil than itself, and they enter and live there; and the last state of that person is worse than the first. (Luke 11:24–26)

This admittedly sounds weird to modern ears, but not to traditional cultures. The archetypal Jewish number seven—that traditional symbol of Sabbath and liberation—is used here to describe a geography of terror, indicating the gravity, power, and permeation of the pathology being described.[22]

We think this parable articulates the profound truth that underneath every symptom are deeper issues, beyond every mountain of injustice are seven more. It strikes us as a trenchant diagnosis of the psycho-social legacy of "possession/occupation" that arises from colonization, inflicting both inheritor-beneficiaries and victim-survivors. No sooner have we reckoned with one layer of haunting than seven more are revealed beneath it, like peeling the proverbial onion. The disease—in our psyches and spirits, our communities and culture, and our public life and institutions—is that deep.

---

20. Gordon, *Ghostly Matters*, 7.

21. See Myers et al., *Say to This Mountain*, 55–63 and 108–15.

22. The symbol resonates with other mystical traditions as well, such as seven chakras, the seven heavens of the Qur'an, or Thomas Merton's "seven story mountain" (see Crabtree, "Mystical Number Seven").

This is why the work commended in this book seems so daunting or disturbing to settlers of privilege, and why we avoid it at every turn.

Central to the vocation of Jesus of Nazareth was his work as a healer. But the Gospels insist he wasn't a *socializing* physician who patches people up so they can carry on with the status quo. Rather he understood that the real problems went deeper than symptoms; he was a radical doctor who sought out the roots of our ghostly dis-ease. This is symbolically articulated in his efforts to restore vision to those who do not see clearly.[23] Jesus offered strong medicine to treat the external oppression and internal psychosis of empire. This is why his healings were *always* disruptive of the status quo, and often earned him the ire of the authorities. He was surrounded by many who didn't understand what was wrong, especially people in power who insisted there were no fatal flaws in their social-political-religious system.

To his critics, Jesus famously retorted: "Those who are well have no need of a physician, but those who are sick. I have come to call not the righteous but sinners to repentance" (Luke 5:31–32). This dictum expresses a double truth that lies at the heart of why and how we are engaging settler colonialism in this book:

1. We will not seek healing until and unless we recognize *we* are sick, especially those of us who are privileged within a sick system.

2. The cure is found in the shared struggle to turn our pathological personal and political history around, because it's killing all of us.

The Greek term *metanoia* (5:32) means to change fundamental direction. It is usually translated "repentance," a term which in spiritualized Christian circles today has become utterly domesticated and sometimes damaging (powerful medicine that is mishandled can become toxic; see more below 6D). However, if we instead recognize the lethality of our disease (to borrow from Twelve-Step language) and turn to a Power greater than our own, we can turn our individual and communal history around in the service of wholeness and justice, and heal our haunted bodies and body politic. We long for faith communities to become places that nurture the courage to peel the settler colonial onion seven layers down, fueled by the prophetic hope intoned by Malachi that a day is coming when the Creator will burn the works of injustice to its roots, "until the sun of righteousness rises, with healing in its wings" (Mal 4:2).

---

23. The story of Bartimaeus in Mark 10:45–52, for example, is a paradigmatic tale of discipleship in which a marginalized "blind man" gives up what little he has just so he might see (see Myers et al., *Say to This Mountain*, 133–34). This is the trope under which we do our work at Bartimaeus Cooperative Ministries* (below 8B).

1C. TAKING INVENTORY: AN INDUCTIVE AND NARRATIVE APPROACH

Thirty-five years ago, Audre Lorde challenged people to break the many layers of silence imposed upon and internalized by them: "Your silence will not protect you," she warned. "What are the words you do not yet have? What do you need to say? What are the tyrannies you swallow day by day and attempt to make your own, until you will sicken and die of them, still in silence?"[24] Though addressed to people of color, her urgent query also pertains to white settlers who have been more subjects than objects of colonization. It may be that *our* humanity has been the most suppressed of all: white supremacist doctrines, policies, and leadership, argues Ruby Sales, keep "ordinary white people in a state of chronic mental chaos and devoid of self-esteem."[25]

The Italian Communist philosopher Antonio Gramsci knew about silencing. Much of his work as a public intellectual focused on how ruling interests control hearts and minds in capitalist societies through cultural hegemony and ideology rather than violence (though he also experienced the bitter edge of direct State suppression).[26] In his *Prison Notebooks,* Gramsci offered this stunning insight:

> The starting-point of critical elaboration is the consciousness of what one really is, and is "knowing thyself" as a product of the historical processes to date, which has deposited in you an infinity of traces, without leaving an inventory.[27]

For settlers committed to the work of decolonization, Gramsci's imperative is an important complement to Lorde's: a key part of doing our own work is to understand how we are products of "historical processes."

This is a task settlers studiously avoid. The "traces" are within and around us; it is the "inventory" that has been disappeared by a white culture awash in entitlement and historical ambivalence. Australian historian Henry Reynolds expressed the pain of unknowing in his 1999 book, *Why Weren't We Told*? Canadians Vincent Jungkunz and Julie White call it an

---

24. Lorde, *Sister Outsider,* 41–42.

25. "White rulers . . . use the Lie of Whiteness to hide class and other differences . . . a severe and dehumanizing form of spiritual and historical ethnic cleansing and dismemory which leaves White people devoid of an authentic self or healthy egos except what their abusers give them" (Sales, "Guardians of Whiteness," paras. 2, 5).

26. Gramsci was arrested in 1926 by Mussolini's fascist regime; at his trial the prosecutor vowed: "We must stop this brain from functioning." Gramsci died in captivity eleven years later at age forty-six. (Hoare and Smith, "Introduction to Gramsci," lxxxix.)

27. Gramsci, *Selections from the Prison Notebooks,* 324.

"epistemology of ignorance."[28] And Frances Swyripa asserts that the settler "luxury of forgetting" and "the absolution of amnesia" makes us afraid of our own past and "of the contention it invites."[29] We find the term "agnosia" to be a compelling and concise diagnosis, and explore it further below (6C).[30]

Illiteracy regarding our collective past of settler colonialism is rationalized through ideologies of Progress that focus on the future, conveniently detached from any form of historical accountability.[31] With no inventory, we erase behind ourselves any traces of a genocidal past. It is an "ethical and political necessity," argue Kouri and Skott-Myhre, for settlers to challenge this "self-serving forgetting of the entangled agency of one's history. . .with that of the displaced Native/colonized subject."[32]

We trace such "entanglements" in this project through communal narratives.[33] The Storylines within and around us are constructed by many trajectories, including family lore, local legends, established community accounts, "official" history, and group or national myths. They are imprinted onto our psyche through family tradition; race, class, and regional socialization; the education system; and media culture, both popular and corporate. Our Storylines can be precious—as are many of those related in this book—but also problematic insofar as they derogate, distort, or disappear people and places.

Working with Storylines is a strategy for breaking through two of the most common (and often unconscious) excuses settlers use to avoid decolonization work. One is *abstraction*: we imagine colonization is only about impersonal historical forces that are too complicated for us to deal with. The other is *exoneration*: we insist these issues do not require us to take responsibility, that they belong "to the past" from which we are conveniently disconnected and to which we are therefore unaccountable. In contrast, our process starts with the presupposition that colonization shapes us

28. Jungkunz and White, "Ignorance, Innocence, and Democratic Responsibility," 436.

29. Swyripa, *Storied Landscapes*, 44.

30. Vimalassery et al., "Introduction," 1.

31. In Wes Howard-Brook and Anthony Gwyther's concise summary: "This future orientation finds classic expression in the notion of 'progress' . . . the master metaphor that has made it imperative that Western society define the direction of its culture as 'growth' and 'expansion' . . . It is understood that it is in the future that our present problems will be resolved. An example is how we assume that virtually all of our crises will be fixed by future technological advances" (*Unveiling Empire*, 123).

32. Kouri and Skott-Myhre, "Catastrophe," 1, citing Alan Lawson's work. The principle of *ignorantia juris non excusat* (ignorance of the law is no excuse) is an analogy here cautioning us against our presumptions of innocence (below 6C).

33. See Mehl-Madrona, *Narrative Medicine*.

each and all, and that its consequences can and must be engaged personally and politically.

We overcome abstraction by making each individual settler the subject of the LBS process: everyone has lived in places, has some sort of family/communal context (whether blood-related or not), and draws on sources of inspiration. We are each shaped by multiple Storylines, as suggested by my narrative braids in the introduction: big (Mennonite migrations) and small (adopted cousins), personal (interviewing my Grandma Margreta) and political (the Russian Revolution). This book invites you to identify intimate threads in your own familial experience (whether you are a first- or tenth-generation settler), and to examine how these threads are woven into bigger narratives of how and why North America was colonized.

Rather than beginning with broad social and historical analysis, then, we advocate apprehending the past *inductively* through the particularities of our communal narratives. In fact, all the themes of "official" history (e.g., war or economic boom and bust) and all issues of public justice (e.g., racism or economic disparity) inevitably show up in our own Storylines. We're just not used to looking for those connections (which is part of settler privilege). Moreover, they are often obscured by silences (part of settler denial), but also by euphemism, since our narratives are invariably inhabited by tales of heroism and exceptionalism.

This inductive approach is both *accessible* (probing our own family stories doesn't require lots of secondary reading or theory, though that can help) and *involving* (we are each deeply entangled in colonization's past and present). LBS goals are thus:

1. to understand critically and conscientiously the Storylines (both inspiring and dysfunctional) we carry in our hearts, minds, bodies, and communities, and how they shape our identity and practice, so we can place them in the service of restorative solidarity; and

2. to learn Storylines that have been silenced, both our own and those of Indigenous and other marginalized peoples, especially in the places we inhabit.

Settler consciousness has been formed both by what we putatively know and by what we don't. It is our conviction that exploring Storylines while informed by issues of justice, trauma, and responsibility can nurture personal healing and build capacity for social movements of decolonization.

1D. DIS-ILLUSIONMENT: RE-VISING AND RE-MEMBERING

Nelson Johnson, cofounder of the Greensboro Truth and Community Reconciliation Project,* speaks of how public lies about a common history are a poison that seeps into the groundwater of culture, making everyone sick.[34] The further back the generative lie, the deeper the toxins dwell. This is an ancient lament, intoned for example by the Hebrew prophets Ezekiel and Jeremiah concerning "a proverb circulating in the land of Israel: 'The parents have eaten sour grapes, and the children's teeth are set on edge'" (Jer 31:29; Ezek 18:2). We speak of the narratives of settler colonialism as *devised* (perpetuating lies and half-truths) and *dismembered* (excluding stories and traditions of and about Indigenous and other marginalized peoples). Consequently, our twofold task is to *re-vise* (literally, look again at) and to *re-member*. This is the process we call *dis-illusionment*, and it is key to the work of detoxing "aquifers of colonization" and restoring health to the whole community.

Devised metanarratives function to legitimate the colonial project. The most obvious example is the tired but persistent old trope that "Columbus discovered America." This has functioned for centuries to reinforce European presumption enshrined in the notorious Doctrine of Discovery. The powerful and lethal myth of *terra nullius* imagines that the lands to which *conquistadores*, explorers, and settlers came were "uninhabited," and thus "there for the taking."[35] This ideological tapestry was woven by late-medieval European rulers, its warp and weft consisting of entitlement, white supremacy, and naked assertions of sovereignty.[36] This conceit arrogantly centered the "discoverer," objectified the "discovered," and rationalized the deepest two layers of the colonial project: the destruction of Indigenous cultures and peoples, and the violent removal of millions of Africans to the Americas in the trans-Atlantic slave trade.[37] After more than a half millennium of incalculable oppression, this mendacious fabric is beginning to unravel, symbolized in popular efforts in the U.S. to change commemorations

34. Enns and Myers, *Ambassadors of Reconciliation,* 2:133–49; below 8B.

35. Miller, *Discovering Indigenous Lands*; Cocker, *Rivers of Blood, Rivers of Gold.* Historian Sandra Beardsall points out that some scholars suggest *nullius* initially meant "empty" in the sense that the land was not owned by any Christian prince; Indigenous people were understood to be part of nature and had no stake (email correspondence with authors, May 5, 2020).

36. See Sanders's *Lost Tribes and Promised Lands.*

37. See e.g., Stannard, *American Holocaust,* and Baptist, *Half Has Never Been Told.* Many Indigenous people were also enslaved; see Reséndez, *Other Slavery.*

of Columbus Day to Indigenous Peoples Day (below 7D). Yet the discourse of discovery continues to wield widespread cultural power and persuasion, and still determines the politics and economics of resource extraction around the globe, perpetuating the grim colonial legacy of displacing traditional peoples and destroying their lands.[38]

Devised narratives persist in popular history through what Travis Wysote and Erin Morton call "white settler tautology—something that seems true by the very nature of its repetition and logical irrefutability in white settler histories, stories, and laws."[39] For example, some Mennonite immigrants embraced the common pioneer trope that "we came to this land and made it better." We will look at how European immigrants are pressured to assimilate into such "orthodoxies" of settler exceptionalism, and encouraged to shrug off their own past and shed their ethnicity (below 5B, C). We descendants become alienated from our heritage, rendering us cultural orphans, which makes us even more vulnerable to the devised identity of whiteness.

Merle Fossum and Marilyn Mason's articulation of family and social "shame systems" can also illuminate the social psychology of settler culture. This "self-sustaining, multigenerational system of interaction with a cast of characters who are (or were in their lifetime) loyal to a set of rules and injunctions demanding control, perfectionism, blame and denial" results in "an inability to distinguish between healthy guilt and paralyzing shame."[40] Fossum and Mason describe ways in which those in the system adopt masks to hide their shame, including:

i)   adopting a fairy-tale identity;

ii) disconnecting or escaping from one's identity;

iii) macho or fatalistic attitudes; and/or

iv) adopting a veneer of niceness or piety.

This accurately diagnoses settler myths of superiority and innocence (below 6C). Decolonizing discipleship seeks to move from shame to "healthy guilt," or what we call response-ability: a commitment to repair past harms and restore justice in our shared present (below 6D).

To heal and defect from this system involves intentional efforts to recover from multiple settler disorders:

- socio-historical ignorance (what we've been socialized not to know);

38. Chronicled by LaDuke, *All Our Relations*.

39. Wysote and Morton, "'Depth of the Plough,'" 479.

40. Cited and explored in Myers, *Who Will Roll Away the Stone?*, 91–92.

- cultural illiteracy (what we've been socialized not to learn);
- emotional disassociation (what we've been socialized not to care about); and
- credulity (what we've been socialized to believe).

The discipline of re-membering seeks to recover stories that have been disappeared by the dominant culture, dismembering whole communities from the body politic. Thus the settler story of Saskatchewan begins with the arrival of European homesteaders, yet as Candace Savage writes, "of the prairies' longer past and its deep reservoirs of stories of indigenous people we do not hear a single word."[41] We need instead to probe the silences of our own settler narratives, as well as learn a more complete and honest history of the lands in which we have settled.

Savage calls this the work of "historical stratigraphy," filling in the "gaps that exist between the received version of the settlement story and the lived reality."[42] I recall, for example, how as a young adult I drove by signs to Whitecap Reserve in Saskatchewan, but never *saw* it; that space was invisible to me. Then I met Harley Eagle, a restorative justice colleague and Dakota-Saulteaux who grew up at Whitecap.[43] We discovered we were only a year apart and had attended the same high school in Saskatoon—but I never saw him either. This book concentrates on re-membering two "gaps" that have characterized my community's narratives: regarding Indigenous peoples, and gendered experience. My family history books highlight how Catherine the Great invited Mennonites to settle the steppes of Russia/ Ukraine in the late 1700s—but make no mention of the Nogai and Cossack peoples (traditional inhabitants of the region) being forcibly removed by the Tsarina just prior to my ancestors arrival.[44] Similarly, those books say little about how the Canadian government made land available to Mennonite settlers that had been taken from Indigenous bands on the prairies (below 5B–D). My community also struggles with a patriarchal culture that tends to discount women's experiences, especially around stories of sexual assault (below 3D). Such silences handicap our capacity to transact traumas—both our own and those of others.

---

41. Savage, *Geography of Blood,* 36.
42. Savage, *Geography of Blood,* 58.
43. See Enns and Myers, *Ambassadors of Reconciliation,* 2:37–44.
44. See below 3D, n. 75.

1E. ARCHAEOLOGY AND CARTOGRAPHY

A popular metaphor for doing work around white privilege is Peggy McIntosh's "invisible knapsack."[45] For white settlers, this knapsack is full of: unearned privileges; socialized ignorance about histories of racism and inequity; self-justifying distortions and myths, both personal and political; moral injury; and, for some of us, unexamined trauma. We carry this prosthetic unconsciously, so accustomed to its weight that it feels like a part of our body. It goes with us wherever and however we travel—until and unless we engage in the difficult, intentional work of taking it off and unpacking it. In our LBS model this involves critically examining the stories we have been told about how we arrived in North America and who we displaced (Landlines); bringing to consciousness what we carry in our bones (Bloodlines); and discovering resources to give us courage to change (Songlines).

During one of my first LBS workshops, while talking about invisible knapsacks a participant objected that this kind of deep identity work wasn't addressing the urgency of "all the burning buildings" of this historical moment. Another participant responded: "If we *don't* do this work, we will be running into burning buildings with knapsacks full of gasoline and blow the whole thing up!" This is a powerful caution to settler activists who presume our own good intentions: we must recognize how we carry the very contradictions we seek to resolve. The work of emptying our knapsacks may at first feel like "losing" parts of ourselves, but ultimately it "lightens" our load so that we can walk more faithfully toward restorative solidarity.

We offer a second metaphor: digging into our settler Storylines is analogous to an archaeologist trying to read potsherds, in this case, fragments of our own ancestry. We typically only know pieces of our family and communal stories—what was thought "worthy" to record or pass down orally—and even less about their social and historical contexts. So we face many of the archaeologist's dilemmas. For one, our potsherds have often been moved out of their original setting, disconnected from other artifacts that might tell a fuller story. These pieces lie in generational and geographic strata that also need to be understood. For another, we may be digging in unwelcome territory—running into family resistance, going against the grain of local history, or encountering our own sadness or paralysis from what we learn. Our workshop participants have struggled to piece together fragments of their family stories, frustrated both by how and what they *do* know, and why and what they *don't* know about past and present. In particular, the

45. McIntosh, "White Privilege," 10–12.

silences weigh heavily. For all its difficulty, however, this work has the power to change how we see things.

Those whose ancestors were brought forcibly to North America face significantly different and more difficult exhuming work, given the violent suppression, obfuscation, and erasure of Black family and cultural history by centuries of chattel slavery. In a writing workshop in the fall of 2019, our co-facilitator pulled out a large sheet of paper with her genealogy charted on it, and said, "I want to acknowledge having all of this information is part of my white privilege." Two young African American women nodded vigorously, later sharing with us their deep sadness at not having any details of when or from where their ancestors came.

Still, some Black writers have persevered. Alex Haley's groundbreaking *Roots: The Saga of an American Family* (1976) provides an exemplary illustration of the power of this work and its public consequences. At the end of his riveting, almost 900-page tome, Haley describes the hard work of twelve years of research, interviews, and sifting through archives, trying to piece together seven generations of his forebears. His reconstructed story—though contested by some scholars—had a watershed impact. It "tapped deeply into the black American hunger for an African ancestral home that had been ravaged by centuries of slavery and racial dislocation," Michael Eric Dyson wrote, and also "prodded white America to reject the racial amnesia that fed its moral immaturity and its racial irresponsibility." Dyson concludes: "*Roots* was a soulful reminder that unless we grappled with the past, we would be forever saddled by its deadening liabilities"; it also "provided a touchstone for alternative history" (*Roots* was published during the U.S. bicentennial).[46]

More recently journalist Deborah Barfield Berry, on assignment to cover the 400th commemoration of the first slave ship to English-speaking America in 1619, traveled to Angola where she dramatically discovered her *own* roots. She encourages African Americans, for whom "the search for family roots can seem out of reach," to persist:

> For years, the census didn't even name them. They were simply listed as slaves or "free colored." Despite those challenges, more African Americans have launched searches, turning to DNA tests, musty court records, and libraries, hungry for information . . . Experts agree chromosomes tell only part of the story . . .

46. From Dyson's Introduction to *Roots*, ix–x. On the controversy, see Dugdale, "Roots of the Problem."

Interviewing elders is key to capturing family history "so it's not stuck in some attic somewhere."[47]

Genie Milgrom, while going through her mother's things, found a collection of recipes recorded and handed down by generations of women in her family. A Cuban-American raised Roman Catholic, Milgrom followed the trail of these old recipes (some dating back to Inquisition-era Spain and Portugal) to discover her hidden heritage as a crypto-Jew.[48] We believe all of us who are not native to North America can animate powerful changes of consciousness and practice by doing our own roots work, thereby helping to broaden that "alternative history" in order to make possible a different future.

Our LBS work herein will take place in two parts. Part I explores where settlers came *from*—an "archaeology" of our origins. We look at how our immigrant histories reflect (and were impacted by) larger patterns of conquest and colonization. This is crucial work for settlers old and new, especially in the U.S. where we are still coming to terms with what it means to be a nation of immigrants.[49] It is important that we who are citizens now re-member the realities of how and why people emigrate today, and working with our own immigrant stories helps us do that. Questions we investigate include: What lands did our ancestors leave and why, and how might those landscapes be imprinted on our souls? What circumstances did they face, how were they moved around by larger patterns of colonial "push and pull" (including forced displacement), and/or what privileges or advantages did they enjoy? What were the stories our ancestors came *with*, including experiences of loss and trauma, and how do we carry these in our bones? What Songlines of resilience and goodness influenced and sustained our people's migrations?

Part II explores where and how we/our ancestors came *to* North America—a "cartography" of settlement. This includes learning the histories and stories of the land(s) where we and our people settled, and how our settlement (and re-settlements) impacted (and continue to impact) local Indigenous peoples and other marginalized communities. Were our immigrant ancestors complicit in traumatizing events for others (e.g., Indigenous displacement, slave-owning, class oppression)? Were they used as

47. Berry, "I Was Writing," paras. 25, 26, 41, 37.

48. Milgrom, *My 15 Grandmothers*.

49. Trump administration policies are, for example, predicated on the perception that immigrants are a threat to our common life, despite the fact that in 1910 (the good old days according to the president) the percentage of foreign-born in the U.S. was actually *higher* than it is today. (Radford, "Key Findings about U.S. Immigrants.") See discussion of these issues in Myers and Colwell, *Our God Is Undocumented*.

pawns in the larger colonial project? Who did they befriend or ignore? Do we know how they acquired land in their new country and when and how they become "white?"

If our own mobility has taken us elsewhere in North America from the place(s) our ancestors settled—likely the case for most readers—what is our relationship to the place where we live now as "re-settlers?" How might we "reinhabit" our homeplaces, attentive to the demands of restorative solidarity for its native peoples (past and present, placed or displaced) and for the land itself? What will it take to heal the hauntings through which colonization "occupies" our places and "possesses" our peoples and spirits? What resources of wisdom and power—from Scripture to song to social movement history—remind us how to be human, and cut against the grain of our settler socialization? How can Songlines help us decolonize the landscapes and stories that shape *and* constrain us? How have they either compelled us to stay on beloved land or to travel to another place to learn how to be a "response-able" settler there?

This archaeological and cartographic approach to identity formation through Storylines examines how our individual and communal narratives are woven through and between Landlines, Bloodlines, and Songlines, in order to understand their gifts and dysfunctions. It's often complicated, and that's the point: to overturn simple settler stories (which are always partially devised and dismembered). For example, aspects of my Mennonite immigration story fit the archetypal narrative of leaving the old country under duress, arriving poor in the new land, "pulling ourselves up by our bootstraps," and through hard work and faithfulness achieving prosperity. There is some truth in this, but as a simple story it overlooks: privileges we were given on arrival (or even guaranteed before immigration); who we displaced; and our assimilation into the unearned benefits of white privilege in the racialized societies of the U.S. and Canada. Indeed, our long history of Anabaptist dissent against systems of domination was blunted by these arrangements, which eroded much of our distinctiveness (below 2D). Such losses are not uncommon for immigrant descendants with a dissident history such as Jews, Irish, or French Huguenots (below 6B).

At the same time, my Mennonite ancestors endured significant episodes of violence and dispossession. Therefore we look also at trauma that stretches intergenerationally. This may find points of resonance for non-European immigrants and Indigenous peoples. And European settlers brought more trauma to North America than their narratives typically admit, not least the pain and disruption of leaving a home place forever. Naming inherited trauma is an important part of Bloodlines work, because while metabolized trauma can *animate* empathy and solidarity, untransacted trauma can *impede* it (below 3C).

When settlers probe our family stories and communal or national histories, we not only run into frustrating walls of silence or unknowing. We also inevitably uncover uncomfortable or awful things from which we would dissociate. It is always a danger, Donna Haraway reminds us, that in reckoning with a "troubled" legacy we can slip into "disengaged denunciations rather than attentive practices of thought, love, rage and care."[50] But this work is about reparation, not blame, and about owning, not dismissing our past. Righteous distancing from our ancestors, like romanticizing them, simply represent opposite swings on the shame pendulum of depression and grandiosity. In fact, who our people *were* is who we still *are* in important respects. More than we realize, we are the products of the stories we carry and often reproduce unconsciously. It is better to understand this work as picking up where our progenitors left off, coming to terms with what was done and addressing that which was left undone.

It is our conviction that the inventory-taking advocated in this book is crucial to healing our haunted histories. Our work is to recognize the "traces" of white supremacy within and around us, and to journey toward a dis-illusioned identity that can animate practices of solidarity and justice. We hope these pages will help the reader build moral imagination, spiritual resilience, and political courage for a discipleship of decolonization.

---

50. Haraway, *Staying with the Trouble*, 56.

PART I

Archaeology
Excavating Storylines of Displacement, Trauma, and Resilience

> Uprootedness is by far the most dangerous malady to which human societies are exposed, for it is a self-propagating one. For people who are really uprooted there remain only two possible sorts of behaviour: either to fall into a spiritual lethargy resembling death, like the majority of the slaves in the days of the Roman Empire, or to hurl themselves into some form of activity necessarily designed to uproot, often by the most violent methods, those who are not yet uprooted . . .
>
> —Simone Weil[51]

THE FIRST HALF OF this book entails the difficult and often painful work of excavating and encountering our immigrant history to understand the spiritual lethargy and uprooting behavior of settler colonialism. To deal with the "most dangerous malady" of rootlessness we must face where our people came *from*, why and how they came, and what they carried (and we carry still). We use the verb *excavate* because so much of that legacy has been buried (often intentionally so), dismembered, or devised in order to erase traumas endured and inflicted. We use the term *encounter* because this is not about head knowledge, but an engagement of mind and heart, body and soul, self and society.

---

51. Weil, *Need for Roots,* 44.

These chapters are about re-membering and re-vising our Landlines, Bloodlines, and Songlines of origin. As we uncover the roots of our cultures, places, and stories—fragmentary and coded though they may be—we will better be able to reconstruct a dis-illusioned narrative that will encourage and equip us to encounter afresh the land and peoples we came *to* (part II).

Figure 13: Casa Anna Schulz Mural, panel 3 (depicting Anna feeding home invaders in 1918 and Margreta peering down from attic). Artist: Dimitri Kadiev (used with permission). Photo: Chris Wight (used with permission).

CHAPTER 2

Landlines I

Where Our Immigrant Ancestors Walked from

> [White people] are in effect still trapped in a history which they
> do not understand and until they understand it, they cannot be
> released from it.
>
> —James Baldwin[1]

2A. PILGRIMAGE TO UKRAINE, 2010

IN OCTOBER 2010, MY oldest sister, Janet Enns Regier, and I set off on a
long-awaited pilgrimage to southern Ukraine. We would retrace the steps of
our ancestors, and explore their history of prosperity and suffering, as part
of a Mennonite Heritage Tour. "How will this generation know who they
are and where they are going," my dad had written a decade earlier, "if they
don't know from whence they came?"[2]

Midway through the main itinerary, on the auspicious date of
10/10/10, Janet and I took a side trip to the former Mennonite village of Osterwick, where our maternal *grossmama* Margreta once lived. Driving up to

1. Baldwin, "Letter to My Nephew," para. 8.

2. From Beno Enns's preface to a family history book he curated with his brother-
in-law (Enns and Baergen, *Family of Franz and Katharina Enns*, iii): "I believe it is very
important," he continued, "to leave our children a map of where we have come from,
how we lived and how we dealt with our problems and struggles . . . how our God has
been with us, leading our parents out of the *Zerrissenheit*."

the *Schulz Fabrik* we could see it had once been an impressive factory, with intricate brickwork around the windows and an archway through which horse and buggy could enter the compound. To the left was our great-great grandparents' home, and beyond that the house where Grandma Margreta grew up. Making our way on foot toward the latter, we were disappointed to find it surrounded by a ten-foot barbed wire fence. Tatiana, our Ukrainian guide, warned us not to go in: "Very bad dogs!" We had indeed seen some vicious guard dogs over the previous days, so I whistled and hollered. When no dogs appeared—and cognizant that we would likely never be here again—we slithered on our backs through the mud and under the fence, Tatiana remaining on the other side, shaking her head.

It appeared no one currently lived there, and since the back door of the house was ajar we made our way in. Straight ahead was a staircase. We picked our way up rickety steps, and when the last few were missing altogether we stretched out on our bellies, straining to see the second floor. It was nothing like the grand room we had been told about as children. The roof and most of the floor were gone, burned (we learned later) a few years earlier when a homeless man perished in a fire he'd started to keep warm. As we gazed into the blackened shell of what had once been the heart of a thriving Mennonite household, I felt the weight of what happened here almost a century earlier.

Mennonites emerged as the most prominent strand of the Anabaptist movement, the radical wing of the Reformation in Switzerland and the Netherlands.[3] Anabaptists were generally committed to a rigorous separation of church and state, faith as discipleship, simple living, and a refusal to bear the sword. Their break from magisterial Christendom was symbolized by their practice of adult baptism, and for this they were heavily persecuted by both Catholic and nascent Protestant authorities. During the 1530s, Menno Simons (*Simonszoon* in Frisian), a former Catholic priest, became a prominent leader in the movement. Mennonites endured displacement and fierce opposition, often marked as people without citizenship status who could not own property or live in cities. By the seventeenth century, many had left Switzerland and the Netherlands; some immigrated to the American colonies and eastern Canada in the 1700s, while others settled in Prussia.

The late eighteenth century saw a major migration of Prussian Mennonites to southern Ukraine, where they were invited by Catherine the Great, Tsarina of Russia, because of their reputation as hardworking farmers who had been successful at cultivating marginal lands.[4] Catherine granted them

3. See Weaver, *Becoming Anabaptist,* and Estep, *Anabaptist Story.*
4. A summary of this migrant trajectory is at https://en.wikipedia.org/wiki/

religious freedom, including exemption from military service, in exchange for pioneering the steppe lands of Southern Ukraine and later Russia; in the process they displaced indigenous inhabitants (below 3D, footnotes 75 and 76). My people come from this wing of the Mennonite movement, as did historian Roger Epp, who summarizes: "From Friesland and Gröningen in northern Europe, to the Vistula Delta, to southern Russia, my Mennonite ancestors lived as stateless, migratory people at the privilege of rulers who desired them for their agrarian skills and economic prowess."[5]

Once settled in Ukraine and Russia, they flourished for almost 150 years in relatively autonomous German-speaking villages (see Figure 05). In the last decade of the nineteenth century, my Schulz family built a factory in Osterwick that employed more than 100 workers and manufactured farm equipment that was used all over Russia. But around the turn of the century problems arose across the country. Government policies forbidding subdivision of farmland led to a burgeoning landless population, including some Mennonites who ended up as servants on estates of wealthy co-religionists. These disparities, as well as religious and cultural disputes, led many to leave for Canada and the U.S. in the 1870s (below 3D, 5C).

The growing prosperity of Mennonite villages also contrasted starkly with the poverty of Russian peasants (liberated from serfdom only in the 1870s), as well as with the emerging urban industrial working class. Profound inequalities between landed gentry (including Mennonites) and the landless poor energized strong political opposition movements, which launched an unsuccessful revolutionary coup in 1905. World War I further exacerbated social and economic tensions throughout the archaic Tsarist regime.[6] These came to a head in the October Revolution of 1917, led by Vladimir Lenin and the Bolsheviks. After the Tsarists were overthrown, three years of civil war ensued throughout Russia and Ukraine, where fighting raged between three armed forces: the Red Army of the Bolsheviks; the White Army of Tsarist supporters (backed by the West); and irregular but formidable Ukrainian nationalist and anarchist fighters. Mennonite villages were hit hard during these years because of antipathy toward their German language, culture, and sympathies; their material prosperity; and the fact that as pacifists they rarely fought back.

Chortitza_Colony.

5. Epp, *We Are All Treaty People*, 96.

6. In August 1917, some 200 delegates representing various settlements came together in the All Russian Mennonite Congress. Educated professionals (over half of whom were landowners) talked about the crisis of landless peasants and debated issues of land reform, nationalization, and distribution to the poor. But this deliberation was too little too late; see Epp, *Mennonites in Canada, 1920–1940*.

Growing up I learned to fear the name Nestor Makhno. A Ukrainian peasant, Makhno had worked as a youth on a Mennonite farm.[7] At age seventeen, he was arrested for anarchist political activity, and spent ten grueling years in a Moscow jail. Freed during the 1917 revolution, Makhno returned to his home village of Gulai Polye in the heart of Southern Ukraine, and proximate to many Mennonite villages. There he emerged as a leader of peasant dissatisfaction. In the course of the civil war, he built the most successful anarchist army in history. The Makhnovists fought brilliant guerilla campaigns, and often redistributed wealth throughout Ukrainian villages. But they were often irrationally brutal. In a six-week period between late October and early December 1919, they murdered more than 800 Mennonites.[8]

The most notorious incident occurred at Eichenfeld, a small Mennonite village, about fifteen miles north of Osterwick. One night in October 1919, Makhnovist forces massacred seventy-five people and raped many girls and women, while local Ukrainian peasants plundered property.[9] According to historian Sean Patterson, class antagonism was the driving force of this violence, exacerbated by "actions on both sides of the Ukrainian-Mennonite divide," including:

> initial attacks by local bandit groups; the embrace of the Austro-German occupation and then the White army by the Mennonites; the establishment of the *Selbstschutz* [Mennonite self-defense unit] and the Eichenfeld unit's attack on the local soviet; the robbery, harassment, hostage-taking and abuse of civilian Mennonites by the Reds and the Makhnovists; the violent rhetoric of Makhno; and the land hunger and gross social inequalities facing Ukraine at the time.[10]

This is a history whose moral high ground is fiercely contested by both anarchists and Mennonites.[11] But it is also intensely personal for my family.

7. Peters, *Nestor Makhno*, 32.

8. Patterson, "Eichenfeld Massacre," 157.

9. Dyck et al., *Nestor Makhno and the Eichenfeld Massacre*, 26, 46, 105, 115. We discuss rape as a war crime below at 3D.

10. Patterson, "Eichenfeld Massacre," 168. For more on the *Selbstschutz* see n. 13 below.

11. For example, independent anarchist scholar Wayne Foster writes: "There is little prospect of imminent rapprochement between Mennonite and Makhnovist histories of the Russian Civil War. Makhnovist historians will need to abandon the fairy tale of unfailingly firm-but-fair revolutionary chivalry and acknowledge the undeserved violence endured by some Mennonites . . . The latter will need to abandon the myth of the Mennonite community's special martyrdom" ("Makhnovists and the Mennonites,"

During this period, Makhnovists frequently commandeered Mennonite estates as temporary headquarters. This is what brought the war right into my maternal Great-grandmother Anna's home. In 1918, she was forty-eight years old, with six children; her husband had died three years previously, leaving her sole owner of the family's successful factory. In April, she and her family were forced to flee their home by "robber bands" (as Mennonites referred to anarchist insurgents). For three weeks Anna and her children stayed at *Zachariasfeld,* also a wealthy estate several hours from Osterwick, which had been established by three of her brothers.[12] Six months later, the anarchists came to *Zachariasfeld.* This story, as recounted in my Great-grandfather Isaak Zacharias's memoir, relates how, as his niece Mariechen was being taken by the bandits, shots were fired by her brother, wounding the leader of their band. The family learned of the anarchist's death and a resulting order "that all small and large estates should be surrounded by 75 men, all guns should be confiscated . . . and no one should be permitted to enter or leave."[13] That night, the Zacharias families, after much deliberation, decided to leave *Zachariasfeld* forever. At three in the morning they fled back to the Schulz estate, then overflowing with "thirty people or more."[14]

---

para. 43). Foster is less sympathetic to Mennonites in this story, but probably fair in his assessment of our community, which he describes as comprised of "a mix of characters":

> They were landowners who earned more than whole villages. They were landless peasants, *anwohner,* who fought for the revolution. They were estate managers who whipped their workers but adored their sons. They were women who had the generosity of spirit to nurse those sick and dying Makhnovists who occupied their homes . . . They were pious Christians who resisted all military service. They were militia men who wept in church and begged forgiveness for the lives they'd taken. They were girls who lived in fear of rape . . . They were victims buried in mass graves. They were poor farmers in isolated villages caught in a war they didn't understand. They were proud patriarchs. They were soldiers who killed for the counter-revolution. They were pacifists. ("Makhnovists and the Mennonites," paras. 44, 45.)

12. Zacharias, *Meine Lebensgeschichte,* 27.

13. Zacharias, *Meine Lebensgeschichte,* 31. As this tale attests, Mennonite men occasionally felt compelled to use hunting rifles to defend their families. In summer 1918, under the leadership of Peter Van Kampen, some 200 young men from various Mennonite settlements served in the *Selbstschutz;* some were trained by and received weapons from Austro-German forces. This attempt at self-defense was regretted and renounced by many community leaders. See Toews, "Origins and Activities of the Mennonite *Selbstschutz."*

14. Gerbrandt, *Remembering the Schulzes,* 47. For Great-grandfather Isaak this was "the terrible time of misery . . . plundering, robbing, murdering. We slept in granaries covered with wheat, and I only mention the murder of friends in passing so that the

A month later, during Christmas 1918, anarchist soldiers approached the *Schulz Fabrik*.[15] The Mennonite males over the age of twelve fled into the nearby forest, while my fourteen-year old Grandma Margreta and her sister and five girl cousins were hidden in the attic. Great-grandmother Anna and her youngest boy, Bill, faced the soldiers alone, and for two weeks she "hosted" these invaders in the great room, the ruins of which my sister and I now gazed upon.

In the face of terror, Anna practiced hospitality: feeding, clothing, and nursing soldiers' wounds and fevers, and coping with their drunkenness, crude language, and gestures. But what else happened? Though difficult to believe, the story passed down in our family is that none of the women were sexually assaulted, because "the bandits were careful not to harm the people whom they needed to supply them with food."[16] The soldiers finally left the *Schulz Fabrik*, but months later returned and expropriated all of the estate's remaining resources and horses.[17] Somehow Anna kept her family alive through ten ensuing years of civil war, terror, and deprivation, finally escaping to Canada in 1927.

This was the traumatic tale my Grandma Margreta struggled to speak into my recorder when I was thirteen.

As Janet and I lay on our stomachs viewing the burnt-out remains of that room, I imagined my teenage grandmother listening through the attic floorboards as her mother served these peasant soldiers. When we finally made our way back down the stairs, legs wobbly and hearts throbbing, I was filled with questions. How did our female ancestors endure this ordeal? How did the males feel having to abandon them to save their own lives? How were these decisions made? And when the survivors finally left their homeland and escaped to Canada, forsaking their 150-year-old labor building a "Mennonite Commonwealth," what psychological baggage did they carry with them?

---

younger generations are cognizant of the horrors" (Zacharias, *Meine Lebensgeschichte*, 29).

15. Though another source dates these events in Christmas 1919, I prioritize the testimony of my Great-grandfather Isaak Zacharias. It is hardly surprising that victims' retrospective narratives are unclear about dates amidst multiple traumas.

16. Gerbrandt, *Remembering the Schulzes*, 47.

17. Zacharias, *Meine Lebensgeschichte*, 37. The memoir relates how his sister Maria [Zacharias] Friesen and family were not so fortunate at their home a few months later: "Around Pentecost [1919] they were held up by a band, driven into the cellar, and there sister Maria with the children—Isaak, Margareta, Tina and grandchild—were shot. W. J. Friesen saved himself by jumping through a window into the garden. D. J. Friesen hid himself with a small son on the loft of the big cow stable and wasn't found" (33).

2B. RE-MEMBERING DISMEMBERED IMMIGRANT HISTORIES

Landlines are both *placed stories* and *stories of place*. Part I of this volume explores where our settler ancestors came *from*, and how; part II where they came *to*, and how. Here we focus on our immigrant histories, whether generations back or recently, interpreting these narratives in the context of larger patterns of conquest and colonization (no matter which side of that equation one's people were on). For some, mobility was voluntary, for others compulsory. This part of Landlines work recollects the social, geo-political, and ecological characteristics of our family's former home place(s), as well as the circumstances of leaving (whether opportunistic, under duress, or forced).

Many North American settlers know only fragments of their immigrant roots, and some nothing at all. There are practical reasons for this: traditions and memories fade over many generations; geographical mobility scatters material legacies; and cultural atrophy undermines curiosity about, and literacy in, one's roots. But there are also relentless ideological forces that undermine immigrant identity, among which three deserve special mention. Here our analysis focuses on the U.S., where these factors are far more acute, but each is found in Canada in less dramatic form despite its stronger ethos of multiculturalism.

First and foremost, the pressures on immigrants to assimilate discourage cultural distinctiveness. In the U.S., these pressures have differed in style from the eighteenth century (Ben Franklin's complaint about too many German settlers in the colonies) to the present (English-only statutes), but not in function. Their purpose has always been to push new arrivals to *adapt* to dominant colonial cultural ways and to *adopt* its language, identities, and values. For those of European ancestry (or those who can "pass"), there is also the lure of gaining white privilege by conforming to white norms.

A second factor is the complex relationship between immigration and race/class hierarchies. The "tree" of U.S. settler identity is a strange mix of immigrant roots and anti-immigrant branches. From our inception as a nation, becoming "American" has entailed not only jettisoning former ways of knowing and being, but also being suspicious of immigrants coming *after* us, especially those of different linguistic, socioeconomic, and national origins. While this would seem to be a counterintuitive form of settler self-contempt, there are two powerful forces at work in this "othering":

- One is the color line, long established by the system of chattel slavery and Jim Crow in the U.S., a racial hierarchy that white and white-passing settlers (of all nationalities) are encouraged to internalize. This is why, over the last two centuries, immigrants of color—from nineteenth- century Chinese to twenty-first-century Syrians—have been consistently resisted and scapegoated by most "citizens."

- The other force is the mythography of middle-class prosperity that is mapped onto the American Dream, which teaches both fear and incrimination of poor folk (and often working-class people as well), who are perceived as unable or unwilling to conform to the Dream. How can one otherwise explain a family (or a president!) that on one hand *idealizes* an immigrant great-great-grandfather arriving in New York "with only ten dollars in his pockets" and eventually prospering; yet on the other, with no hint of irony, *demonizes* Central Americans crossing the border into Los Angeles today with only the clothes on their backs?

Racial and class myths of superiority drive many settlers to try to "close the door" of opportunity behind their own immigrant generation (except for additional family members).

A third factor is the future-orientation of modernism. Even if settlers *do* know something of our heritage, many of us are just not that interested in exploring it at any depth, because we've been socialized to believe the past is largely irrelevant to our future. Indeed, the former was overcome in the interests of the latter. During the era of Manifest Destiny, this exclusive focus on the future was key to underwriting settler innocence. Similarly, today's instantly gratifying technologies and "trending now" obsessions socialize us to believe there is little social or professional benefit to curating our immigrant identity and literacy. We don't see how our immigrant ambivalence orphans us, nor do we understand the Faustian bargain settler culture made by continually erasing the inconvenient history of colonization behind us in order to secure our role as noble protagonists in our story (below 6C).

These are some of the key political and personal ways in which settlers—of all ethnicities, but especially we of European descent—are socially formed to shrug off our immigrant past.[18] Such forces conspire to discourage us from maintaining—and once lost, from seeking to rehabilitate—immigrant identities and stories. The result is we know more about, and relate more intimately to, the devised narrative of "being American" than that of our own family past. This constructed ignorance not only alienates us from our own heritage; it also represents a consequential barrier to engaging

---

18. For further discussion of these issues see Myers and Colwell, *Our God Is Undocumented,* especially the introduction and Appendix II, upon which some parts of this chapter are based.

immigrant and Indigenous justice today, as we have seen dramatically during the Trump administration.

But we settlers *didn't* just magically appear here, and we *do* have responsibilities to the history of which we and our people were and are a part. Kouri and Skott-Myhre remind us: "Undoing foundational myths is settlers' first task in producing ourselves as ethical subjects."[19] They rightly name the fiction that we aren't connected to an immigrant past, people, and place as the foundation of all subsequent denials. From there it is easy to proceed to shed (and thereby exonerate ourselves from) the entire history of colonization and its toxic legacy. As James Baldwin put it, "To accept one's past—one's history—is not the same thing as drowning in it; it is learning how to use it. An invented past can never be used; it cracks and crumbles under the pressures of life like clay in a season of drought."[20]

Landlines work starts by tracing our settler lineage: where our people came from, and how, and why. To be sure, genealogies get complicated very quickly, with many lines and often multiple ethnicities. The work I do in this book looks at all four of my grandparental lines, because they were all part of the same wave of refugees from the Soviet Union in the 1920s (see family tree, Figures 08 and 09). However, we recommend you begin by tracing just *one* ancestral line, back to the immigrant generation if possible. Choose either the family line for which you have the most information, or the one in which you are most interested. Continue to work with this line through Bloodlines and Songlines. When you have exhausted all you know—and become more practiced at sleuthing—carry the work forward with other parts of your family tree. If you cannot find any information about any immigrant ancestor (not uncommon among settler families who have been in North America for many generations), then go back as far as you can, looking especially for ethnic traces. Again, if you are adopted, you can work with either your birth or adopted family genealogy or both.

As we've noted, for many of us much familial lore has been lost, suppressed, or dismissed. Research will often seem like a forensic examination of fragmentary evidence or an archaeological reading of potsherds. That is why we call this process "re-membering": the labor of recovering what has been dismembered by the ravages of time, mobility and ideological de-formation.[21] But each fragment is important, representing a piece of the puzzle,

19. Kouri and Skott-Myhre, "Catastrophe," 14; see above 1A.

20. Baldwin, *Fire Next Time*, 368. Though Baldwin was addressing African Americans, he believed understanding history was the key to liberation for both whites and Blacks.

21. This wordplay is different from our use of "remem-bearing" in chapter 3, which has to do more specifically with how we carry traumatic memory.

and none of us will ever have *all* the pieces (see tools below E). Though not all evidence we gather from family lore is of equal historical reliability, at the inquiry stage there are no right or wrong fragments. Indeed, moral judgments and filtering works against knowing the truth of who we were and are. And we underline again: what we do *not* know is as important as what we do know, and requires equal attention and reflection. Hauntings inhabit silences as well as testimonies.

Our workshops' participants have responded across the spectrum. In a 2018 group, for example, only two of twelve participants could name a great-great-grandparent; none spoke that person's native tongue. Some related partial genealogies, others specific tales (if often without much context). We heard statements such as:

- "I have heard they came on the Mayflower, but I don't know where they first settled."
- "I have no idea when or how my ancestors got here."
- "I don't know how my ancestors got land in the Midwest in the 1860s— was it the Homestead Act?"
- "We are all euro-mutts! It doesn't matter where we came from; only what we *become*."

This last generalizing confession is just another way to ignore the past and relieve ourselves of this work.

In another group, two participants had almost identical stories about an immigrant ancestor coming over "as a stowaway in a barrel." Both related it with incredulous laughter, though without any supporting detail. This trope is not uncommon, and may simply function as a metaphor for undocumented immigration. Yet what if such a tale were true, as we know it was for certain slaves escaping to freedom?[22] How does one survive such a journey? Who put them in the barrel, and how were they released? And most importantly, why were they forced to travel this way? Whether literally true or not, this scenario encodes trauma. Encountering this type of lore in our family narratives invites us to press beyond the laughter, because such "jokes" usually function(ed) to mask discomfort or pain.

In our experience, once people start digging—asking questions of parents and older relatives, visiting places of family legends, leaning into both tall tales and poignant facts—they are consistently surprised by how it opens up deeper curiosity within them. The work of re-membering

---

22. See for example Levine, *Henry's Freedom Box*, and Brown, *Narrative of the Life of Henry Box Brown*.

immigrant family history often feels like putting parts of our selves back together—even when we didn't know they were missing.

2C. HOW WERE OUR PEOPLE MOVED? PUSH AND PULL FACTORS

Why did our ancestors leave their home places? Most people do not easily abandon land, homes, and family, forsaking the place of their community's story and where their people were born and buried. Immigration is rarely like embarking on a grand adventure (even if characterized as such in retrospect). To be sure, for some migrants the promise of social or political freedoms or "available" natural resources (for nineteenth-century Europeans especially land, gold, and forests) afforded an opportunity for self-determination. This allowed them to shed stultifying constraints or animosities and make their lives afresh. But for most, deracinating relocation to unknown lands half a world away was full of loss, uncertainty, and risk, and prior to the twentieth century, usually entailed permanent separation from kin and culture.

Larger forces typically pushed and/or pulled our people to make the long, difficult journey to North America, including war, economic hardship, conquest, or enslavement. Though we use the broad term *immigrant* throughout this book, we acknowledge that not all circumstances of uprooting are equivalent. We suggest here four basic types that distinguish differences in the social power of the migrant, and place them along a spectrum of volition (willingness and ability to move from a home country to another) from greatest to least:

- A *colonist* is part of a political and/or economic project of occupation and expropriation of "foreign" land by a colonizing power. They are the economic or military vanguard of conquest and settlement (e.g., explorers, militia, tradespeople, resource extractors, government officials, families under government contract, and in some cases missionaries). Colonists are in some sense consciously participating in the project of subduing, exploiting, clearing, and repopulating, and are often rewarded for their labors with payment or grants of land or title.

- An *opportunist's* migration involves some degree of political and/or economic mobility, privilege, and agency. It sometimes includes official subsidies or incentives to move from "old" country to "new." This is often characteristic of secondary and subsequent waves of migrants under a colonization project. Opportunists migrate for land, work (including today professional opportunity), education, family, and even adventure.

- *Distressed immigrants* are pushed or pulled by forces beyond their control (usually political but sometime environmental) to leave home for somewhere else in order to survive; improve viability; attain religious, political, or cultural freedoms; and/or reunite with family.

- *Forced relocation* is when political or economic forces kidnap, traffic, or otherwise drive people across borders through war, ethnic cleansing, and slavery. (Indigenous peoples experience this frequently through dispossession by the settler state.)

Many people of racial or economic privilege today have ancestral emigration stories characterized by the first two types, whereas the latter two remain the reality of all poor migrants. My move from Canada to the U.S. was opportunist, whereas my grandparents' migration reflected the third and fourth types.

Landlines work seeks to understand the structural forces that impel immigration from generation to generation, which will help demythologize our family narratives. Throughout the last five centuries the political winds of conquest and settlement, and the global economic currents of boom and bust, have pushed and pulled people like great tides—if not across borders, then around a country's landscape (from rural to urban areas, or from job to job).[23] Below is a brief review of six important structural forces (as you read, keep your own family history of immigration or displacement in mind):

1) *War.* Over the last half century alone one can trace immigration patterns to the U.S. (and to some extent Canada) directly to the impact of American policies toward "sending" countries. For example, U.S. military intervention in the Dominican Republic brought some 60,000 Dominicans to the U.S. in the 1960s. The war in Indochina drove tens of thousands of Southeast Asians as refugees in the 1970s. A decade of U.S.-sponsored counterinsurgency warfare in the 1980s in Central America did the same for hundreds of thousands of Salvadorans, Nicaraguans, and Guatemalans. Over the last quarter century, U.S. interventions in the Arab world have increased those populations here. Similarly, the Russian Civil War displaced most of my grandparents' generation.

---

23. The following is an abbreviated summary of Myers and Colwell, *Our God Is Undocumented*, 9–15.

2) *Colonization.* For half a millennium European powers have been possessing, and their opportunist migrants occupying, countless lands and peoples around the world. Over the last 100 years, however, waves of "reverse migration" have ensued, in which impoverished people from colonized places are pushed and pulled toward rich nations because of political and economic exploitation. Cuban émigré Miguel de la Torre argues Latin Americans coming to the U.S. today, for example, are simply following the trail of riches stolen from their lands centuries ago.[24] In my story, the political forces of social upheaval in one part of the world (Russia) pushed, and colonial strategies of frontier settlement in another part (Canada) pulled, my Mennonite community.

3) *Economics.* This includes policies (such as tariffs, capital flight, or international financing of debt); resource extraction (mining or logging that destroys Indigenous habitats); industrial production (e.g., African Americans fleeing the Jim Crow South to work in factories in the North, eastern Europeans recruited for automobile production in Detroit, or Mexicans pushed into *maquiladores*); and commodity distribution and consumption (trade wars or fashion trends manipulating markets). Economic disparities fueled both voluntary migration by and violent displacement of Mennonites.

4) *Racial politics.* U.S. immigration policy throughout history has fluctuated dramatically, often in reaction to the above three factors. For example, during the railroad boom of the 1860s–70s, Chinese contract laborers were actively recruited, but when the "railroad bubble" burst in 1882, the Chinese Exclusion law was passed. Similarly, Mexican workers were actively sought due to a World War I labor shortage; a half million were then deported during the Depression of the 1930s. Mexican agricultural workers were again recruited during World War II through the *bracero* program, only to be deported in the Eisenhower administration's "Operation Wetback." Mennonites coming from Russia were impacted by fluctuating Canadian immigration policies, but also by popular antipathy toward pacifists during both world wars: "Mennonites flock to church while our boys fight," complained some, "don't conform to Canadian school laws" and "bring unsanitary habits and Asiatic diseases."[25]

5) *Social conflicts.* These include issues of land shortage, wealth disparity, and religious or ethnic differences within or between communities. All

24. De La Torre, *Trails of Hope and Terror*, ch. 1.
25. Anderson, *Settling Saskatchewan*, 120.

three were factors for Mennonite colonies in Russia, causing 12,000 to leave for North America between 1873 and 1882 (see 3D).

6) *Environmental issues.* Historically, drought, earthquakes, or flooding have forced people to move. Today we must include climate crisis, responsible for an increasing number of refugees fleeing sea-rise and extreme weather events.[26]

A critical understanding of how these forces impacted our ancestors helps us de-romanticize immigration legacies, as well as attend to issues of justice among the displaced today. While most of those just listed tend to be push factors, we also need to comprehend *pull* factors, such as the availability of free or cheap land to settlers (as a result of genocidal clearings); the desire to be reunited with already-migrated relatives; or the promise of religious or cultural freedoms. For example, many of the migrations of my Mennonite ancestors over the last three centuries were predicated on negotiated agreements regarding military exemption and cultural autonomy with the receiving country.

Some immigrants move as an extended family or community; others as a lone family or individual. Some have resources to travel first-class; others smuggle themselves aboard a ship, train, or truck headed to their hoped-for destination. Some have immigration documents or sponsorship; many have neither (white settlers should remember that most of their immigrant ancestors were undocumented in the modern sense). Some arrive without complication; others must survive illness, violence, or political shifts that close borders they are trying to cross (exiting, transiting, or entering). Some migrants are guaranteed a job or grant of land in the new country; others arrive penniless, indentured or encumbered by travel debt. Some resume the same class and political privileges they enjoyed in their homeland; others escape marginalization only to encounter the same in North America. And we must repeatedly remember that some come voluntarily, others under servitude. These differences are consequential for generations; to forget, erase, deny, or conflate them only obscures how they continue to affect our personal and political lives.

In this book I refer to my grandparents as "refugees," and their experience conforms to Merriam-Webster's generic definition of "a person who flees to a foreign country or power to escape danger or persecution." But they were relatively advantaged refugees: they had enough resources to procure documents (though with great difficulty) and to manage travel; and they benefited from outside aid and advocacy. Mennonites leaned heavily on

---

26. Climate change is first an economic, social, and political phenomenon of the "Platationocene" under capitalism. See Myers, "Nature against Empire."

their tradition of mutual aid and communal solidarity during my grandparents' generation. A commission was sent from Ukraine to North America in the summer of 1920 to alert co-religionists to the calamitous impact of civil war and revolution in Russia. Representatives of diverse Mennonite conferences in North America in turn organized to respond to the crisis, giving birth to the Mennonite Central Committee* (MCC).[27] From 1922 to 1925, MCC provided 25,000 people a day in Ukraine with rations, and sent farm equipment to Mennonite villages to replace horses that had been stolen or confiscated during the war, at a cost of some $1.2 million.[28]

As starvation and violence continued, Russian Mennonites sent a delegation to investigate immigration and settlement possibilities in Mexico, the U.S., and Canada. Canada, with its desire to settle the "frontier lands" of Saskatchewan, opened its doors to the prospective immigrants. On May 17, 1922, a Mennonite Board of Colonization was organized to support Russian Mennonites trying to get to Canada.[29] In June, that Board entered into a contract with the Canadian Pacific Railway's Department of Colonization and Development to transport Mennonites from Russia to Canada on a credit basis. My grandparents were among those who were aided by this communal project, both in departure and arrival.

2D. LOVES, LOSSES, BAGGAGE

Whatever the circumstances of immigration, every migrant leaves behind who, where, and what shaped them—in most cases forever (at least prior to the last half century). With the exception of intergenerational refugees— landless or stateless persons whose repeated experience of displacement have prevented any geographic identity from being established—immigrants leave behind home *places*. Even in contexts of extreme violence, oppression and/or privation, it is excruciating to decide to leave one's "hearth."[30] It is

27. In fall of 1920, the first three MCC workers were sent to deliver aid in Ukraine and Turkey. Clayton Kratz was in the village of Halbstadt in the Molotschna Colony when it was overrun by the Red Army, and never heard from again. It was another year before official permission was received from the Soviet government for MCC to begin relief work.

28. Smith, *Smith's Story of the Mennonites*, 318–20.

29. See below n. 39 for discussion of travel debt. David Toews was chairperson of this new organization, and his tireless labor earned him the moniker "Mennonite Moses" (see Harder, *David Toews Was Here, 1870–1947*).

30. It is germane that the Old English *heorth* (of West Germanic origin, related to Dutch *haard* and German *Herd*) is so close to the Old English *heorte* ("heart," of Germanic origin and related to Dutch *hart* and German *Herz*).

to wrestle with two powerful pulls: fleeing due to fear (thus conceding loss of home and/or land), or staying in hopes that things will get better (thus risking loss of life or freedom). For most people in most circumstances, migrating feels less like a choice than a perceived necessity for survival or betterment. Historically, few immigrants uprooted without regret—though in our hyper-modern era of globalized mobility this is changing among those with economic means.

Leaving home was certainly fraught for my ancestors. My mother's grandfather, Isaak Zacharias, described his experience of the early days of the Russian Civil War as a "shifting of bearable and unbearable days."[31] But in 1923, he could bear the violence no longer: "Bowed and with profound sorrow, we humbly implored God's gracious help and support during our flight, and so we said farewell on our knees to our dear home."[32] My father's father, Franz Enns—even after the horrors his family endured (below 3A)— saved the title to family farms confiscated during this period; after escaping to Canada he still imagined he might go back and reclaim his land. Indeed, many Russian Mennonites believed the situation would eventually get better. After the severe violence of 1918 to 1921, and the typhus epidemic and famine in 1922, the Soviet New Economic Policy eventually restored a sense of normalcy, especially for land and business owners, enough that some Mennonites chose to stay. However, beginning in 1930, the collectivization policy and Stalinist repression of the intelligentsia affected our communities profoundly. The artificially induced famine of 1933 killed millions; as a reflection of the desperation of that period, even graves became contested territory. My Great-great-grandfather Schulz's grave was dug up by people looking for gold rings.[33] On the other hand, Ukrainian neighbors protected Mennonite graves (see below 4B). All Mennonites who made the difficult choice to remain in Russia suffered, without exception.

Immigrants like my ancestors are forced not only to abandon lifetimes (or generations) of investment in farms and businesses, they also leave behind community and loved ones. My Great-grandfather Isaak Zacharias wrote poignantly about his family's departure:

> Like many of the others, Mama and I went out of our dear home village on foot, in order to say farewell to many friends and acquaintances . . . The large group of departing emigrants created a great commotion in the village. The procession went slowly forwards. A crying, wailing, ear-deafening outcry; parting from

---

31. Zacharias, *Meine Lebensgeschichte*, 29.

32. Zacharias, *Meine Lebensgeschichte*, 32.

33. Gerbrandt, *Remembering the Schulzes*, 30.

one's birthplace is sorrowful and pain gives rise to sighs, groans,
weeping and screaming . . . After the trunks, crates, suitcases
were put on the assigned wagons, the saying of farewells began
again on this last departure from the dear and native Chortitza.
Many relatives, as well as good friends, came to say good-bye,
among them our dear and respected elder Isaak Dyck, who left
behind in each wagon a note with his blessing . . . "God's angel
go with you" . . . A farewell service was planned [at the train
station] but one decided and was satisfied to remain still, quiet
and create no public upheaval, for we all knew well the oppressive time we were in. And so it happened that we left Chortitza
quietly, although with much weeping and sobbing. Later we
heard that a commissar intended to roll a large stone in front of
the locomotive in order to delay departure but he couldn't bear
the sad farewells and returned home without accomplishing his
wicked intention.[34]

Nineteen-year-old Margreta Schulz, my grandma, who five years
earlier had endured the home invasion, was in this group watching her
cousins, aunts, and uncles depart. Also leaving was Heinrich Toews, whom
she was courting. My Aunt Irma [Toews] Gerbrandt later wrote: "We still
have the pressed flowers kept all these years by our mother and given to
her by Heinrich, which he had picked for her at the station just before the
train left Chortitza to take him to Canada. The two kept up a very romantic correspondence."[35] Margreta's family stayed in Chortitza another four
years, but when they migrated in 1927 they left behind her sister Anna, her
brother-in-law, and two nephews (this Great-aunt Anna's harrowing journey is described below at 3D). Similarly, my paternal grandpa, Franz Enns,
who also immigrated in 1927 with his wife and two sons, departed without
his parents and siblings, many of whom ended up in Siberian work camps
under Stalin (below 3A).

The immigration journey itself also takes a toll, from the drama of
departure to the difficulties of transit to the uncertainties of arrival. In political contexts of turmoil and duress, procuring travel papers is problematic (or impossible), which can result in family members being left behind.
When my paternal grandparents, Katharina and Franz Enns, decided in
1926 to make their way to Canada, they sold their remaining possessions

34. Zacharias, *Meine Lebensgeschichte*, 45. Their journey ended at another train station in Rosthern, Saskatchewan, where they were greeted with another outpouring of
emotion (see below 4A).

35. Gerbrandt, *Remembering the Schulzes,* 136. A year after Grandma Margreta's
arrival in Saskatchewan, she and Heinrich were married.

and moved to Davlekanovo (about thirty miles southwest of Ufa, near the Russian Ural Mountains), hoping to process their paperwork quickly, but their exit visas were mysteriously cancelled. They had the resources to hire a lawyer to help them, but it still took a year of living in limbo before they got the needed documents to leave.

The travel from there was dangerous and taxing. Thousands of Mennonites were boarded on to boxcars at the Lichtenau train station in Ukraine (see chapter 3, mural panel four). Women sewed money and geröstete Zwieback (twice baked, dehydrated buns) into their clothes to sustain the family on the journey. They knew that during the six-to-ten-day trip to the Latvian border their trains would be searched repeatedly by soldiers who would confiscate possessions and cash—or worse, take their military-aged sons. When they passed through the Red Gate at the Sebesh station on the Soviet Union-Latvian border, they wept for joy (below 4A). Yet they still had to pass medical exams to be allowed on a ship from Riga to England through the Baltic Sea (those who failed the exam were detained for treatment). In England there were more exams. A quarter of the refugees were held back as medically unfit (including obesity and birth defects); for many of these it took years to make it to Canada.[36] Those who passed inspection boarded a Canadian Pacific Railway liner for a six-to-ten-day sail to New Brunswick or Quebec, after which a long train trip finally brought them to the prairies. This was a very rough journey for Grandma Katharina, who was pregnant with my Uncle Peter and had two small sons to care for. By the time they reached Saskatchewan, many had been stripped of all possessions, food, and money. My Great-grandfather Isaak's journal indicates he had only $32 Canadian upon arrival.[37] As a general rule, the fewer physical belongings refugees are able to bring with them, the more psychological baggage they carry.

Many distressed immigrants also bear crippling debt from their journey. Today undocumented migrants pay exorbitant fees to coyotes to facilitate their passage across the southern U.S. border.[38] My grandparents, like two-thirds of Rußländer immigrants to Canada, shouldered a Reiseschuld (travel debt).[39] Indebtedness disadvantages new immigrants economically:

36. Enns and Baergen, Family of Franz and Katharina Enns, 6–7.

37. Gerbrandt, Remembering the Schulzes, 50. This would be the equivalent of less than $500 CND today.

38. See e.g., Kulish, "What It Costs."

39. Over 21,000 Mennonites were brought to Canada under these contracts. The total credit extended by the Canadian Pacific Railroad in an agreement brokered by David Toews, a tough and strategic negotiator on behalf of Rußländer refugees, amounted to almost 2 million dollars (Epp, Mennonites in Canada, 1920–1940, 383–84). While the Reiseschuld enabled thousands to migrate from Ukraine/Russia, there was also strong

it makes them more vulnerable to exploitation as workers desperate to pay off obligations; and can also instill a sense of dependency or political domestication.

Another issue is how immigrants can bring with them the "baggage" of their own prejudices and conflicts. For example, my work with the U.S. Office of Refugee Resettlement in the early 1990s exposed me to the tensions that existed between different cultural groups coming from the same country or region, who had been settled together and were perceived by the dominant culture as unitary (i.e., between Salvadorans and Nicaraguans or Hmong and Cambodians). There are also class or religious differences, as was the case with internecine rivalries between distinct waves of Mennonites immigrating to Canada between 1870 and 1930.[40] Then there are issues of acculturation, as immigrants settle in with their customary practices (from cuisine to child-rearing to economic exchange). Assimilated neighbors often perceive these with hostility, as do official institutions such as schools or hospitals. Thus, newcomers must make a myriad of adjustments to a novel social universe, and in the process they inevitably question how much to keep of their own culture. Over time, alienation from the dominant society can manifest through depression, mental illness, abuse, addiction, and family fracturing. But such first-generation challenges often get lost as assimilation takes hold and memory fades, such that descendants underestimate the toll of the immigration experience—particularly if the wear and tear of that adaptation disappears beneath heroic retrospective narratives.

2E. QUERIES FOR YOUR IMMIGRANT PAST

We again recommend you start with just one strand of your family line about which you have the most information concerning an immigrant ancestor. List country of origin, when and where he or she came to North America, and the location and dates of each generation's birth, including subsequent migrations. Here are two examples: from my family and from Ched's:

---

opposition to it by some Canadian Mennonites, arising from a strong antipathy toward credit. Many *Russländer* were plagued for years by the debt burden; others did not feel responsible for repayment (which embarrassed Canadian church leadership). With half the debt still unpaid by 1939, Mennonite churches collected or assumed debt payment, and it was "paid in full by November 1946" (Hamm, *Continuity and Change*, 92).

40. There were three main waves of Mennonite immigrants to Canada from Russia and Ukraine: those coming during the 1870s were called *Kanadier*; those during the 1920s were referred to as *Russländer*; those arriving after World War II are referred to herein as Soviet Mennonites; see 3D.

Elaine's Toews Family Line

Anna [Zacharias] Schulz (maternal great-grandmother)
    Born: 1871, Osterwick, Ukraine
    Migrated: 1926, to Saskatchewan, Canada
    Died: 1950, Saskatoon, SK

Margreta [Schulz] Toews (maternal grandmother)
    Born: 1904, Osterwick, Ukraine
    Migrated: 1926, to Saskatchewan, Canada
    Died: 1984, Rosthern, SK

Margaret [Toews] Enns (mother)
    Born: 1933, Dundurn, SK
    Died: 2011, Rosthern, SK

Elaine Enns
    Born: 1967, Saskatoon, SK
    Migrated: 1989, to Fresno, CA, USA
    Resident: Oak View, CA

Ched's Guerena Family Line

Francisco Mendoza (paternal great-great-grandfather)
    Born: 1827, Azore Islands, Portugal
    Migrated: 1848, to Sonora, California via Veracruz, Mexico
    Died: 1918, Sonora, CA

María Rosario Mendoza de Guerena (paternal great-grandmother)
    Born: 1863, Sonora, CA
    Died: 1942, San Francisco, CA

Ynez Belle Guerena de Myers (paternal grandmother)
    Born: 1887, Sonora, CA
    Died: 1970, Pasadena, CA

Edward Allan Myers (father)
    Born: 1923, San Francisco, CA
    Died: 1991, Laguna Niguel, CA

Ched Myers
    Born: 1955, Pasadena, CA
    Resident: Oak View, CA

The family line you identify becomes your primary "text" for researching the questions below.

When we do this work with groups we post a large world map on the wall and invite participants to trace their identified ancestor's migration path (writing on the map the departure/arrival locations, dates, and which generation), using either yarn or markers. The resulting patterns form a dramatic visualization, and this map is a point of reference throughout the workshop as we uncover dimensions of privilege and displacement. This emphasis upon the particularities of our people's place(s) of origin and settlement gives us a "genealogy of Landlines" as well as of Bloodlines; both are essential to this work.

Obviously your most important sources are family members and community historians and genealogists. Don't wait to interview elder relatives, because many stories die with them! Be transparent with your interviewees about what and why you are interested in their stories, and how you will use the information. Because this is sacred work, informal but intentional, we suggest opening with a simple ritual: offering gifts, lighting a candle, reciting a prayer or song (together if possible), and arranging family pictures into a small altar. Food and drink always provide social lubrication. We encourage the use of video or audio recording, as well as careful note-taking, all of which should be predicated by asking for your interviewees' consent. Do not prejudge what details are important; seemingly obscure pieces of the puzzle may provide important keys later on.

Here are the kinds of basic questions that will help you construct your immigrant social history from fragmentary family data:

1. What kind of land(s) or cities did your immigrant ancestors leave? Invite interviewees to describe in as much detail as they can those homeplaces, including topology, ecology, and built environments in which they (or their ancestors) dwelled. Did they exhibit similar geographic characteristics to the place(s) to which they immigrated? (If you ever make a pilgrimage to the place your ancestors came from, see if you "recognize" the land.)

2. How many generations had lived in that original homeplace? What earlier migrations had brought them there? How and why?

3. What were the primary tongues your immigrant ancestors spoke in their country of origin?

4. What was the class stratum of your ancestors: poor/peasant; working-class; middle-class; landed gentry; other?

5. Was their immigration voluntary, involuntary, or forced? What were the larger push (e.g., war, famine, landlessness, or unemployment) and pull factors (e.g., family reunification, economic opportunity, religious freedom) that impelled migration?

6. What political forces of boom or bust, poverty or affluence, discrimination or social violence, shaped their movements during that historical period?

7. Were your ancestors advantaged or marginalized during their immigrant journey (did they travel as stowaways or in suites? was the journey merely long or was it dangerous?)? Did they come as a large family or community, or individually?

8. Did they have immigration (or legal) documents? Were they promised land or work when they got to their new country?

9. If they incurred travel debt, how was it paid off?

10. Who did your immigrant ancestors leave behind, and what property, homes, and livelihoods? Why did other family or community members stay? Did they remain connected?

Ask your sources where and how they learned what they are relaying to you. Who told them the stories? Were they passed down orally or written down somewhere? Pay attention to *how* their narratives are told: What is transmitted through jokes or heroic lore? What is dismissed? What brings up emotion? Where are the silences?

After gathering these stories it is time for critical interrogation of these family immigrant narratives. How have these accounts been influenced and shaped by nineteenth- (or twentieth- or twenty-first) century race, class, sexuality, and/or gender myths, frames and interpretations? Henry Giroux writes:

> Critical reading is especially important at a time when ignorance has more political currency than historical memory, moral witnessing, and thinking itself. The need to think critically becomes particularly important in a society that appears to become increasingly amnesiac—a country in which forms of historical, political and moral forgetting are not only willfully practiced but also celebrated.[41]

Yet even as we cast a critical, decolonizing eye on our own family legacy, it is important to keep in mind that our ancestors were as captive to the social and cultural realities of their times as we are in ours. Adopting a self-righteousness of hindsight only distances us from what we carry in our bones, undermines our "way to wholeness," and exonerates us from political responsibility to make things right today. Even if our immigrant progenitors may have benefitted from their settlement in a colonial state, they were

41. Giroux, "Terror of the Unforeseen," para. 20.

also victimized by its deracinating gravitational forces and dehumanizing imperatives. They carried invisible baggage: cultural, psychic, and spiritual costs of displacement and disorientation, loss, and trauma. This arc of immigrant trauma reaches forward across generations to us, a matter we now turn to explore in chapter 3.

Figure 14: Casa Anna Schulz Mural, panel 4 (depicting Mennonite refugees at Lichtenau Train Station, Ukraine, 1923, and Menno Simons holding Bible with "Love your enemies" in Greek and German). Artist: Dimitri Kadiev (used with permission). Photo: Chris Wight (used with permission).

CHAPTER 3

Bloodlines I

"Remem-bearing"

> The *Remembearers* . . . [are] those who have the traumatic
> event registered in their consciousness without actually having
> experienced it themselves: the second circle of witnesses to the
> violent experience.
>
> —Lotem Giladi and Terece Bell[1]

3A. *ZERRISSENHEIT*

In the summer of 2019, brimming with questions provoked by this project,
Ched and I traveled to Alberta and Saskatchewan to interview elderly aunts
and uncles of my Enns clan. The first of our seven conversations was in
Calgary with ninety-two-year-old Peter Enns, the third of nine siblings and
the first born in Canada. Peter's failing health had pushed us to make this
trip, and it was a holy time; he passed just two weeks later. As he spoke of
his parents, Peter was overwhelmed by emotion at several points. Similar
tearful interludes punctuated most of our subsequent interviews with these
normally taciturn elders—often they would be unable to continue speaking
for several moments. This confirmed to us that this generation has carried

---

1. Giladi and Bell, "Protective Factors for Intergenerational Transmission of Trauma," 384 (italics theirs).

the weight of what *Russländer* Mennonites call the *Zerrissenheit* ("time of being torn apart").

Franz Enns (1891–1971), my paternal grandfather, and his wife Katharina were, like my maternal Toews grandparents, among the 22,000 refugees from the Russian Revolution and civil war who escaped to Canada. Franz was born to Johann and Helene at Wiesenfeld in Ukraine, an extended part of the Mennonite mother colony of Chortitza. When Franz was three years old (1894), his parents moved on horseback to the Ufa region of Russia, 1,900 kilometers north and east, pushed by lack of land for their growing family. Part of the first wave of Mennonite settlers in Ufa, Johann and Helene developed a successful farm estate they named *Johanneshof*. But the next two decades saw increasing social unrest in Russia, culminating with the Revolution of 1917. When several local landowners were shot by peasant rebels demanding money in 1918, Johann and Helene fled to the nearby city of Davlekanovo, leaving twenty-seven-year-old Franz and his younger sister Anna to manage the estate.

My Grandpa Franz later recalled that in 1920, with "murder and execution the order of the day,"

> the Communists arrived at *Johanneshof* and took everything—
> the livestock, the farm machinery, the grain, and all contents
> of the house, even the farm hands. My sister and I were each
> allowed to take a bed, a chair and a table for the two of us, then
> we were ordered to leave. Where we were to go was none of their
> concern.[2]

The two fled to their sister Helene's home nearby, but the Communists soon expropriated that as well. Anna went to be with their parents in Davlekanovo, but Franz had to go into hiding because the authorities discovered that Franz had been hiding grain at *Johanneshof* (see more below 4A). He escaped on horseback in the middle of the night, riding some 400 miles south to "disappear" among other Mennonite colonies.

Some months later, Franz returned to the Ufa area, staying with his brother Peter. His father Johann died of a stroke in Davlekanovo in January 1921. Franz rented land to farm, but "times were bad . . . people were starving because all the grain had been confiscated."[3] In October 1921, Franz married Katharina Fast, and they lived at brother Johann's farm in Golyschewo, about fifteen miles north of Davlekanovo. Franz and Katharina built a cabin nearby made of logs hauled from thirty miles away, with a "roof

---

2. Mierau and Reimer, *Sojourners*, 73.

3. Quotes in this paragraph are from Franz's account recorded in Mierau and Reimer, *Sojourners*, 73–76.

made with straw dipped in clay." There, despite losing their first child at six months old, "with fresh courage [we] started to farm again." But economic difficulties under the new Soviet regime continued. After two of Franz's brothers (Peter and Bernhard) migrated to Mexico, Franz and Katharina also decided to leave. They "sold everything at auction," and after numerous bureaucratic delays, they and their two young boys (with Katharina pregnant) procured paperwork and departed for Canada in March, 1927. On April 1, they arrived at St. John, New Brunswick, and made it by train to Rosthern, Saskatchewan in the summer. In September, they "were informed by the Resettlement Board about a farm being sold in the Glidden area. My father-in-law and I . . . bought the whole farm."

Though Katharina's parents and siblings also made it to Canada, only two of Franz's siblings did. The rest endured continued oppression, exile, and death under Stalin's Soviet Union. Franz's mother Helene (along with her youngest daughter, Greta) moved back to Ukraine to live with relatives; Helene passed in 1931. A review of Franz's eight siblings (in birth order, not including three who died in infancy) will suffice as a grim portrait of the *Zerrissenheit*:[4]

- *Johann (1881–1933):* His farm in Golyschewo was confiscated by Soviet authorities in 1929, the family driven off their farm with only the clothes on their backs. Johann was imprisoned for two years, released only because of illness, dying shortly thereafter at age fifty-two. His family eventually ended up in Siberia.

- *Peter (1883–1964):* Because of the turmoil he and his family abandoned their farm in 1925. They managed to sell off farm animals and equipment, and immigrated to Guanajuato, Mexico to join his brother Bernhard (below), and then to Winnipeg, Canada.

- *Bernhard (1886–1965):* He was conscripted into the Tsarist Forestry Service from 1908 to 1911, then again from 1914 to 1917. During the Revolution, although he was Chairman of Golyschewo, officers of the Red Army commandeered his house and his family was forced to move into one room. After his land was confiscated by the Soviet government, he sold what he could at auction and immigrated with family in 1924 to Guanajuato, Mexico, later joined by brother Peter. After two years building a farm there, they judged the political situation too unstable and moved to Manitoba, Canada. En route, wife Elizabeth [Dueck] gave birth on the train; the baby died three days later.

4. Longer accounts of each Enns sibling can be found in Mierau and Reimer, *Sojourners.*

- *Agatha* (1889–1969): She married Johann Rempel in 1910 and lived in Golyschewo, developing a farm and cheese factory. When the Soviet New Economic Policy ended in 1929, all village lands were expropriated and incorporated into the state-run collective farm.[5] After years of moving around, they finally settled near Omsk, Siberia. Johann was arrested in 1941 and died in prison after being forced to stand in icy water following a flood. Agatha died in Siberia. Their children were drafted into work armies during World War II.[6]

- *Helene* (1893–1969): She married Heinrich Mierau in 1913, and they lived at *Johanneshof*. After its confiscation, they took over brother Bernhard's farm when he left, until it was confiscated in 1928. They moved consecutively to four different Mennonite colonies, ending up in Grodowka (Hrodivka), Ukraine, where Heinrich worked in a coalmine. In 1936, Heinrich was expelled without explanation from the mine, and the family left for Mennonite settlements near Omsk. The KGB Soviet secret police arrested their eldest son Johann in 1937, who was never seen again. Helene and Heinrich were assigned to different cities in Siberian work camps during World War II. Eventually they were reunited in Solnzewka, where they lived out their days.

- *Katharina* (1894–1982): She moved to Davlekanovo when the family was forced off their farm. She married her younger sister Anna's widower (Jacob Enns, below), and in 1930 moved to the Molotschna Mennonite colony. Her husband Jacob was arrested in the late 1930s and never heard from again. Katharina endured hardships and deprivations, and was eventually evacuated to Siberia, where she died at eighty-eight.

- *Anna* (1896–1929): She stayed with her brother Franz to manage *Johanneshof* until 1920, when they were forced off the farm with nothing. She married Johann Fast, who died the day their only child Johanna was born. She then married Jacob Enns, but Anna died in 1929 (no details how or why).

---

5. This policy, though initially beneficial for some Mennonite farms and factories, terminated with the liquidation of all private enterprise. Taxes were so high that formerly affluent farmers could not pay and were deported as *kulaks* to the forests of the north; poorer farmers were encouraged to form collectives. Golyschewo village was turned into a *smychka* collective farm, whose base was the former *Johanneshof* (Mierau and Reimer, *Sojourners*, 67, 107).

6. After Germany invaded Russia in 1941, people of German background living in Russia were conscripted into work armies, typically suffering barbaric conditions (see Polian, *Against Their Will*).

- *Greta* (1900–1957): She moved with her mother to Memrik in the Molotschna colony in Ukraine. There she worked as a domestic servant, and married Heinrich Epp, who nine months later was arrested by the KGB in front of the children. She worked on a state farm until October 3, 1941. As the war front neared, she and all residents of German ancestry were given one night to pack and prepare food, then put on trains for a grueling three-month journey to Kazakhstan, Siberia.[7] After the war, she learned that Heinrich had died in prison in 1941. She worked to prove that he had not been convicted of wrongdoing, and was eventually granted a pension. Her daughter Hilda didn't return home until 1953, after ten years away in a work army. Greta died in 1957. Her children were able to immigrate to Germany in the late 1970s.[8]

In sum, each member of my Grandpa Franz's immediate family was dispossessed and displaced in the years following the Revolution. Those who remained in Russia or Ukraine endured arrests, disappearances, and relocations. *Zerrissenheit.*

It is little wonder that my Enns aunts and uncles all characterized their father Franz as "stern." I was four years old when he died, so I have little memory of him, except for his watchful, quiet presence from a big chair in the living room. My dad describes his mother Katharina [Fast] Enns as "the epitome of hard work, love, and patience." He would often tell how when he was a little boy, sick with rheumatic fever, she would take care of him all night, even in the middle of harvest. She comforted him by singing German lullabies, then continued her work during the day feeding the hungry work crew.[9] I remember my *Grossmama* Katharina as kind and gentle, and a wonderful cook (as a child I marveled, watching her at the kitchen counter rolling and cutting long noodles for delicious chicken noodle soup, or baking

7. Mierau and Reimer, *Sojourners*, 129–30. The Lichtenau train station in Ukraine was where many Mennonites in the 1920s had boarded for Moscow on the first leg of their migrant trip to North America. In the 1940s, however, Mennonites like Greta were rounded up and forced onto trains headed east (the opposite direction). With many men already having disappeared in the middle of the night, these families knew if they tried to flee they would be shot. So they got onto cattle cars, on which they lived en route to Siberia. On Janet's and my 2010 pilgrimage (above 2A) our group held a memorial service at this still-operating train station; we heard about the painful history and sang *Nun Danket Alle Gott*, concluding with a moment of silence that was eerily broken by an arriving train.

8. A thirteenth "sibling," Heinrich Klassen, whose mother died at his birth, was raised in the Enns household, and fled with family in 1918 from *Johanneshof*. He immigrated to Canada in October 1928.

9. Enns and Baergen, *Family of Franz and Katharina Enns*, 155.

pereschkie, a scrumptious Christmas cookie). She died when I was fourteen, and only recently did I learn that she also carried hauntings.

Though *Grossmama* Katharina's siblings and parents made it to Canada—with the exception of three who died as children, and Jakob, who passed at fifteen—none of her aunts, uncles, or cousins did. My Aunt Irene, Katharina's only daughter, told me her mom saw soldiers hold a gun to her husband Franz's head on three different occasions.[10] Katharina's oldest sister, Maria, suffered from some form of mental disorder. "They said she had a broken heart and a nervous breakdown when she left her love in Russia," my Uncle Jake wrote, "and never recovered from it."[11] In Grandma Katharina's later years in Saskatoon, after Grandpa Franz died, she struggled with hallucinations. She sometimes saw Russian soldiers sitting in her living room threatening to take her back to Russia, or heard their menacing phone calls in the middle of the night.

The *Zerrissenheit* traumatized an entire generation.[12] But when, as a child, I would inquire about this, my grandparents spoke only about the vast abundance and beauty of Ukraine and Russia, shielding me from their pain. Then, in my senior year at Rosthern Junior College (a Mennonite high school), our teacher brought in *Zerrissenheit* survivors to speak about their experiences. As I began to realize what the *Russländer* generation had endured, I wondered how they had processed so much fear, violence, and loss, and about what wounds they carried.

Many of these questions remain unanswered—and my grandparents' generation is long gone. But my generation carries their legacy in our bones, if often unawares. There was a poignant moment in one of our interviews during summer 2019. My cousin Alvin—the oldest son of Jake, who was the oldest son of Franz Enns—had been sitting quietly as we discussed how Grandpa Franz had refused to talk about what happened in Russia. Suddenly Alvin sat up, eyes full of tears, and said solemnly: "Just before he died, Grandpa told me the whole story. I guess it was because I was the first grandchild." He halted, beginning to weep. "But I just can't recall it all. Why didn't I write it down?" I felt his pain deeply. This book is in part my attempt to come to terms with the *Zerrissenheit* and its legacy, and to live into a call, planted in me decades ago, to become a "Remem-bearer."

10. Conversation, August 12, 2019.

11. Enns and Baergen, *Family of Franz and Katharina Enns*, 106. Also in Fast, *Grandson Remembers*, 8.

12. Walter Sawatsky has written about how it shaped Mennonite theologies of martyrdom ("Dying for What Faith?").

3B. SOCIAL, SOMATIC, AND PSYCHIC INHERITANCES

This chapter explores questions of what we have inherited, biologically and psychically, and how we carry it. We do not use "Bloodlines" narrowly as genealogical lineage only, but broadly to include particularities of family and group socialization: *our embodied story.*[13] It includes what we are born into (place; racial, ethnic, and gender formation; social status; cultural traditions); how we were taught to be a part of a family and community; the stories we were told (and retell) about who our people were and are; and legacies we have inherited, both painful and proud.

In our hyper-modern, urbanized society that disconnects us from land and alienates us from community and tradition, it is counterintuitive to delve into one's origins. Most of us in North America do not grow up in families who are literate in their own story, much less cultural heritage. Instead we are surrounded by consumerism and the high mythologies of Progress. It is challenging, therefore, to find the time, resources, and desire to research one's Bloodlines. If we do tackle the task, we can be stymied by fragmentary and missing data, complicated family genealogies, and un-contextualized tales of dubious veracity. It is easy to become paralyzed by multiple faint trails leading off into the trackless wilderness of a murky past.

Nor are our family stories simple. My Bloodlines present initially as a relatively intact community of German-speaking, Russian Mennonites on the Canadian prairies. Yet it is a story full of contradictions. I inherited both the racial privileges *and* brokenness of whiteness, the strengths of my Anabaptist faith tradition *and* the wounds of intergenerational trauma. Similarly, Ched lives with white privilege, but his heritage too is one of loss and alienation. A fifth-generation Californian, his paternal grandmother was *Californio* (Mexican Californian), a side of the family that lost language and culture through U.S. colonization and subsequent assimilation and discrimination.[14] Colleagues Sue Park Hur and Hyun Hur, with whom I've co-facilitated LBS workshops, are first-generation Korean-American immigrants. They carry intergenerational trauma from the Korean War (and the resulting division of their homeland and families), but also face the pressures of "model minority" Asian stereotypes in contemporary U.S. society. Navigating complex histories of both victimization and privilege demands critical mindfulness of personal and political patterns of power—something difficult to maintain in the face of fractured and often romanticized family traditions.

13. We remind readers who are adopted that you can work with your biological family, or your adoptive one, or both.

14. See Myers and Colwell, *Our God Is Undocumented,* 193–200.

Here we focus on how trauma lodges in our Bloodlines and how our people talk about it—or don't.[15] The conceptual frame and semantics of trauma have moved from the margins to the center of popular discourse over the last quarter century, and become an academic discipline. Because it is used throughout this book, but also misused in everyday language, trauma is important to define. Etymologically, the noun derives from the ancient Greek *trauma*, meaning "wound or damage" (*trau-* is from the root *tere-* "to rub or turn," with derivatives referring to twisting or piercing). It appeared in the 1690s for "physical wound" in medical Latin. In English, the sense of "psychic wound or unpleasant experience causing abnormal stress" dates from 1894. Some today analogize trauma as the wound *underneath* the flesh, the inner scarring that lasts long after surface injuries have mended.

We find theologian David Carr's definition useful: "Trauma is an over-whelming, haunting experience of disaster so explosive in its impact that it cannot be directly encountered, and influences an individual and group's behavior and memory in indirect ways."[16] Too many people today trivialize the term by using it to describe driving in heavy traffic or navigating an annoying bureaucracy. We use trauma herein to refer to the psychological, emotional, and spiritual damage resulting from experiences and systems of war, torture, slavery, oppression, rape, and genocide. While painful individual losses such as divorce, illness, or bereavement can certainly be traumatic, we will focus on acts and structures of dehumanization that victimize both persons and communities, leaving wounds in both bodies and the body politic.

Each of us are repositories for both the courage and trauma of our ancestors, whether they were victims or perpetrators of injustice, or both. This is why we all do well to identify, understand, and engage our Bloodlines. But this work is *essential* for settlers committed to restorative solidarity today. It is difficult labor, taking us into the intersections of the personal and political, familial and communal, old identities and new ones, past and present. It requires reckoning with silences, breaking family taboos, decoding distorted narratives, and coming to terms with loss.

Studying trauma is urgent work for at least four reasons. One is the toxic political moment we are facing in the U.S. Over a decade ago, Adele Stan

---

15. Later (6E) we will discuss the related but distinct phenomenon of moral injury, the psychosis of dominant group complicity in systems of oppression.

16. Carr, *Holy Resilience*, 7.

wrote an essay entitled "America the Traumatized," in which she claimed
that the first decade after the new millennium saw a string of public political events that "challenged our sense of national identity," including
"the 2000 election, 9/11, Enron and WorldCom, Afghanistan, Iraq on a
lie, Abu Ghraib, the Patriot Act, Guantánamo, Katrina and near economic
collapse."[17] She continues:

> In America today, it seems we all have a touch of post-traumatic
> stress disorder, as evidenced by our increasingly vitriolic po-
> litical environment, where reality is denied and histrionics
> run riot. Anger, we're told, is the natural reaction to trauma; in
> people with PTSD [post-traumatic stress disorder], anger is out
> of control. By that measure, the millennial decade has brought
> us PTSD politics . . . [which] have moved beyond the bounds of
> extreme partisanship into the realm of mental illness.

Her prescient analysis predates the Trumpian phenomenon by several election cycles, but anticipated its politics of polarization and denial.
Stan continues:

> Rooted in denial, the doctrine of American exceptionalism edits
> out of the American story the sins against humanity that created
> our nation: the genocide of the people who were here before the
> Europeans came, and the building of the nation on the backs of
> involuntary laborers who were tortured, abused and even killed
> for their trouble. Once you ditch that, it becomes easier to look
> past the other unpleasant realities of our history, be it our neo-
> colonialism throughout the world, which helped to build our
> economy, or the enduring practices of racism and sexism.

Stan's conclusion echoes our opening comments about haunting
(above 1B): "Denial almost invariably leads to trauma, when on one day,
or in one decade, the decay that denial fostered summons home the demons set loose through willful ignorance to do their fright dance before
one's very eyes."

Canada has its own expressions of this current drift: the policies of
the Harper government and the ideological turn of the current Conservative Party; xenophobia and anti-Islamic legislation in Quebec; continued
scapegoating of Indigenous peoples; right-wing politics in Alberta and
Saskatchewan; the functional segregation of African Canadians in Nova
Scotia and elsewhere since their arrival on the underground railroad; mass

17. The following quotes are from Stan, "America the Traumatized," paras. 8, 4, 5, 7.

shootings (Montreal, Toronto, and most recently Truro, Nova Scotia); and the epidemic rate of violence against Indigenous women and girls.

But the roots of all this lie in a longstanding culture of historical amnesia committed to suppressing—sometimes implicitly, often overtly—our traumatic and traumatizing past. So a second reason why this work is crucial is how both U.S. and Canadian body politics are riddled with untransacted historic trauma. During the 1992 Columbus Quincentenary in the U.S., Ched summarized this problem, arguing that settlers must

> dredge up the ghosts of Columbus and Cortés, Custer and Calley, not because we can change *their* historical behavior, but because otherwise we cannot change *our own*. If we do not, we will keep reproducing the illusions and violence of that history through repetition compulsion. But it is also the case—both psychology and politics teach us this—that we will simply be unable to hear the pain of others, or to build new alliances of solidarity with them, if we are not in touch with our own pain . . . Buried in our own legacies are both stories of collusion and collision with empire. But somewhere in there are stories of primal trauma, [and] they are the most suppressed . . . [Maori activist scholar] Donna Awatere . . . believes that for European immigrants, original trauma lay in the disconnection from their roots. Only a people severed from their own land and culture, she contends, could turn around and so systematically disinherit Indigenous peoples from theirs. We must . . .inquire into these primal traumas and their relationship to the conquest of this continent if we want to break their power over us.[18]

A third, pressing reason is we have a responsibility to communities, families, and individuals impacted by contemporary trauma. Each war the U.S. fights or sponsors or arms translates into tens of thousands of cases of PTSD for soldiers and civilians and their progeny. Similar damage is being wrought by other continuing horrors at home and abroad: from the displacement of refugees to ethnic suppression; from corporate pillaging of Indigenous lands (such as Canadian Tar Sands development and pipelines) to the deepening economic divide between rich and poor; and from human trafficking to the sexual predations of the powerful. Survivors of these violations have to deal with trauma's ongoing footprints. Even as we combat the social and political conditions that generate these new traumas, we must accompany those struggling to heal, and support emerging trauma therapies.

---

18. Myers, *Who Will Roll Away the Stone?*, 132–33 (italics his).

A fourth reason is theological: trauma and memory lie at the foundation of the Judeo-Christian scriptural tradition. David Carr's recent *Holy Resilience: The Bible's Traumatic Origins* argues that most of these ancient narratives emerged from histories of displacement, violence, and oppression. The Scriptures "both of Judaism and of Christianity are a written deposit of centuries of suffering, and communal resilience," which "helped these communities endure catastrophe, rather than be devastated by it." These texts, he writes, "present suffering as part of a broader story of redemption. In complicated ways, each tradition depicts catastrophe as a path forward."[19] We who are middle-class Christians need to be reminded the biblical testimonies were generated not by the privileged, but by marginalized and oppressed people trying to survive violent circumstances. We believe these traditions can help us face our own traumatized landscapes.

In sum, trauma is woven through North American culture, from deep scriptural memories, through the history of colonization, to the present political moment. Our denial of this damaged and damaging legacy hinders our ability to heal, and undergirds policies and practices that continue to inflict new traumas on others. The future of our societies and our biosphere depends on our willingness and ability to break this cycle by *healing these hauntings*.

3C. RECKONING WITH TRAUMA ACROSS GENERATIONS

Trauma studies is a dynamic, emerging field. Over the last two decades, much research has focused on the intergenerational transmission of trauma in a wide range of cultural groups and communities who have experienced war, slavery, genocide, and other political violence. Maria Yellow Horse Brave Heart (Hunkpapa/Oglala Lakota) has developed theory and therapies by and for Indigenous people in North America. She writes: "Historical trauma is cumulative emotional and psychological wounding over the lifespan and across generations, emanating from massive group trauma . . . The historical trauma response is a constellation of features in reaction to massive group trauma."[20] Joy DeGruy's *Post Traumatic Slave Syndrome* explores

19. Carr, *Holy Resilience*, 6, 3. Mark Brett's recent *Political Trauma and Healing* also applies the biblical understanding of trauma from Israel's displacements to contemporary debates around decolonialization, especially in the Australian context.

20. Brave Heart, "Return to the Sacred Path," 4–5 (we recommend this presentation as an overview of her journey into the exemplary work of the Takini Institute*). See also Brave Heart et al., "Women Finding the Way"; Brave Heart, "Historical Trauma Response among Natives"; Brave Heart et al., "Historical Trauma among Indigenous

the etiology of adaptive survival behaviors in African American communities throughout the U.S. and the diaspora. She focuses on the consequences of centuries of chattel slavery and multigenerational oppression of Africans and their descendants, as well as continuing injustices.[21]

PTSD describes a syndrome in which a survivor is unable to banish violent events from their mind and soul, arising regardless of whether responses to threat were "fight," "flight" or "freeze."[22] Rachel Yehuda, Professor of Psychiatry and Neuroscience at New York's Mount Sinai Hospital, has been studying the biology of PTSD since the late 1980s, primarily with Holocaust survivors. She notes the following symptoms: nightmares, flashbacks, panic attacks, heart palpitations, severe physiological disturbances, and avoiding certain persons, places, or events that trigger memories.[23] Yehuda also found the offspring of parents with PTSD, when exposed to their *own* traumas, displayed an unusually high rate of psychiatric disorders.[24] She further observed that trauma caused by intensely personal violations (such as sexual assault, torture, or military combat) is far more likely to cause PTSD than, for example, a natural disaster. She is also trying to understand why "most exposed persons do not develop PTSD, or if they do. . . recover from it quickly."[25]

Sociologist Pamela Sugiman, daughter of Japanese Canadians who were dispossessed and interned after the bombing of Pearl Harbor, was not herself incarcerated. However, "the pain of that experience . . .is etched in my memory. It has become an integral part of my existence, as well as the defining moment in my own family's history."[26] Education scholar Riham Azizeldin wonders whether and how the human body acts as an archive for trauma, and thus also a compass for narrating our stories; somatic therapies are exploring these notions.[27]

Peoples of the Americas"; and Brave Heart, "*Oyate Ptayela.*"

21. DeGruy, *Post Traumatic Slave Syndrome.*

22. Carolyn Yoder notes that a freeze response "traps the intense trauma energy in the nervous system. If it is not discharged or integrated within a few days or weeks, this constriction of energy is believed to be what produces common trauma reactions later" (*Little Book of Trauma Healing,* 20). Cathy Carter Snell found a freeze response in approximately half of the sexual assault victims she encountered ("Psychological Effects of Trauma"). See also 4B, n. 15.

23. Yehuda, "Clinical Relevance of Biologic Findings in PTSD."

24. Yehuda, "Biological Factors Associated with Susceptibility," 34–39. See also Khazan, "Inherited Trauma Shapes Your Health."

25. Yehuda, "Clinical Relevance of Biologic Findings in PTSD," 124.

26. Sugiman, "Passing Time, Moving Memories," 52.

27. Azizeldin, "Do Human Bodies Act as Archives of Trauma?" See Stanek, "Bridging Past and Present."

Studies are finding trauma can be passed down through both nature and nurture: biologically and epigenetically, as well as through family systems and communal narratives. Here are four current trajectories of research concerning how trauma symptoms can transmit across generations:

1. *The role of cortisol.* A common factor among Holocaust descendants was low levels of cortisol.[28] Exposure to stress triggers an immediate cascade of biological responses in the amygdala (the part of the brain that assesses threat). The hypothalamic-pituitary-adrenal (HPA) axis is activated as the adrenal gland releases powerful stress hormones, including cortisol and adrenaline.[29] These give the body the resources to "fight or flee," but as Dutch psychiatrist Bessel Van der Kolk notes, researchers have discovered

> traumatized people keep secreting large amounts of stress hormones long after the actual danger has passed . . . Ideally our stress hormone system should provide a lightning-fast response to threat, but then quickly return us to equilibrium. In PTSD patients, however, the stress hormone system fails at this balancing act . . . Instead the continued secretion of stress hormones is expressed as agitation and panic and, in the long term, wreaks havoc on a person's health.[30]

Yehuda shows that if the body is unable to successfully shut down these reactions after the threat has passed, an over-sensitized HPA axis can result in lower cortisol levels.[31] An inability to produce cortisol in sufficient amounts may lead to the development of PTSD when faced with another stressor.[32] Van der Kolk describes how, after three years, cortisol levels went down in abused girls who had shut down and

28. Yehuda et al., "Posttraumatic Stress Disorder Characteristics of Holocaust Survivors," 841–43.

29. Yehuda, "Clinical Relevance of Biologic Findings in PTSD," 123–33; see also Van der Kolk, *Body Keeps the Score*, 61.

30. In Van der Kolk, *Body Keeps the Score*, 30.

31. Yehuda, "Biology of Posttraumatic Stress Disorder," 41–46.

32. Yehuda, "Biological Factors Associated with Susceptibility," 34–39. One of Yehuda's studies looked at women in their third trimester of pregnancy who were exposed to the 2001 World Trade Tower attacks. She found that both mothers *and their infants* had lower cortisol levels, the latter's cortisol levels thus likely altered *in utero* (Yehuda et al., "Transgenerational Effects of Posttraumatic Stress Disorder in Babies" 4115–18). This is important when we consider our female ancestors who experienced trauma while pregnant.

became numb, no longer reacting to distress by, for example, taking protective action.[33]

2. *Epigenetics*. This is a relatively new field of study. According to Natan Kellermann, who studies Holocaust trauma, epigenetics is typically defined as the study of heritable changes in gene expression that are not due to changes in the underlying DNA sequence. These "often occur as a result of environmental stress or major emotional trauma, and would then leave certain marks on the chemical coating, or methylation, of the chromosomes. The coating becomes a sort of 'memory' of the cell and since all cells in our body carry this kind of memory, it becomes a constant physical reminder of past events; our own and those of our parents, grandparents and beyond."[34] Alterations to the chemical coating of chromosomes have been found in survivors of life-threatening experiences such as war, torture, or famine. Progeny thus can carry a physiological footprint of the trauma.[35]

3. *Family socialization*. A third trajectory of study explores how trauma is transmitted through nonbiological avenues such as parenting styles and family systems. For example, a study of survivors of the Khmer Rouge killing fields in Cambodia found that role-reversed parenting was a recurring symptom.[36] When a parent looks to a child to meet the adult's needs of intimacy, comfort, or play, and the child attempts to meet those needs, this can lead to anxiety in the child. Similarly, Yehuda found that offspring of Holocaust survivors could be more vulnerable to developing PTSD just by witnessing their parents' chronic PTSD; some experienced symptoms just from *hearing* about Holocaust-related events.[37] A study of Kosovar survivors of war and ethnic cleansing found that children's depressive symptoms were significantly related to their fathers' mental health.[38]

Rachel Lev-Wiesel of the University of Haifa suggests trauma is passed down as a family legacy *whether or not* survivors speak about it.[39] I observed both in my interviews with descendants of *Russländers*, who noted that some of their parents or grandparents refused to speak

33. Van der Kolk, *Body Keeps the Score*, 162.

34. Kellermann, "Epigenetic Transmission," 34.

35. Yehuda and Bierer, "Relevance of Epigenetics to PTSD,".

36. Field et al., "Parental Styles."

37. Yehuda et al., "Phenomenology & Psychobiology."

38. Schick et al., "Trauma, Mental Health, and Intergenerational Associations."

39. Lev-Wiesel, "Intergenerational Transmission of Trauma across Three Generations."

about what they had endured, while others told such unfiltered and graphic stories that they as children experienced significant trauma just listening to them. Some of my interviewees described how their traumatized mothers were unable to bond with them. One described his mother sitting at the table during meals with tears streaming down her cheeks, but his father ignored it so the children did too. Another said: "My mother and I never bonded, there was very little intimacy. She had two 'nervous breakdowns' (as they then called it). Mother felt so badly about herself that she passed this on to all of her children; we all struggle with feeling inferior."[40] Another reported, "When I was a child, I got a full dose, and Mom's stories were not subtle; as she got older the stories were even more recurrent and unfiltered." Two interviewees related similar experiences of waking up to the sound of their parents' screams as they suffered from nightmares. "Mom's childhood was as real to us as our own," one said; "it felt as though the Russians were at our front door." Another related: "My grandmother was often teased at birthday parties because when balloons were popped, she would cry and wonder aloud if the Russians were coming. Seventy years in Canada and the traumatic response never went away!"[41] As I've noted above, my Grandma Katharina experienced similar symptoms.

4. *Communal narratives.* Trauma is also passed down through a group's broader stories about itself, both what is told and what is absent. We examine this in the next section (D).

These studies indicate there are a variety of ways in which trauma can pass from generation to generation.

In my *Russländer* community, Lynda Klassen Reynolds has investigated the psychological effects of trauma. A significant percentage of her first-generation immigrant respondents spoke about witnessing the arrest or murder of a family member or loved one; seeing their home destroyed; and/or living in fear under the Soviet security apparatus. There is no doubt they were traumatized.[42] But Reynolds also interviewed second- and third-generation subjects, and compared their scores against the norms of the

40. These comments are from *Russländer* Focus Group interviews by Elaine Enns, Saskatoon, Saskatchewan, June 25, 2014.

41. Email correspondence with Elaine Enns, August 25, 2014.

42. There is also sociological evidence: *Russländers* had to pay "a 5-cent-a-month-per immigrant fee for the care of mental patients to prevent their deportation" from Canada (Epp, *Mennonite Exodus*, 211). In 1931, there were sixty-one *Russländers* "sick with the nerves" in public mental institutions (Epp, *Mennonites in Canada, 1920–1940,* 418).

Minnesota Multiphasic Personality Inventory-II. She found that *each* of the three generations exhibited significantly higher-than-normal levels of anxiety, depression, and other mental illness, such as psychasthenia (a psychological disorder characterized by phobias, obsessions, compulsions, or excessive paranoia).[43]

Inherited trauma has likely been an important factor impacting mental health among prairie Mennonites (our battle with anxiety, hypervigilance, an inability to express emotions and show intimacy, as well as our explosive anger came up in all of my Focus Groups). But here our concern goes beyond trauma as victimization (a common approach of current studies). For formerly oppressed settler communities that are now privileged and prosperous, such as mine, does untransacted trauma complicate our ability to work in solidarity with Indigenous neighbors struggling with injustice now? Is therapist Carolyn Yoder right that Mennonite pain is still "so great [that] we are blind to how we harm or oppress others?"[44]

3D. "TOO AWFUL TO TALK ABOUT": SILENCES IN COMMUNAL NARRATIVES

Communities shape and pass down stories about themselves through both "official" and grassroots narratives. These function to entertain, instruct, preserve legacy, and maintain identity. But publicly traded settler histories typically suffer from dismissal, distortion, and deception in order to portray the essentially moral character or heroism of the "protagonists." This can also happen in more intimate, community-curated traditions such as mine. Here we focus on the thorny problem of *omission*.

Historian Marlene Epp contends that for Jews and Mennonites—both historically persecuted communities—"the memory of history is a religious duty."[45] The issue for my community is not *whether* our story is important, but *how* we narrate it. An important vehicle of transmission is the family history book (our family has no less than seven). I am grateful for the meticulous work of my parents, aunts, and uncles in preserving and making accessible stories and pictures of our journey over the past century. Indeed, their tireless and faithful work has profoundly shaped me and this project. Nevertheless, what is left out of these narratives can be problematic.

---

43. Reynolds, "The Aftermath of Trauma," 67, 70, 76.

44. Yoder, "European Anabaptist History and Current Reconciliation Efforts," 98. See below discussion of "fictimization" (6Cvii).

45. Epp, "Memory of Violence," 62.

Omission is important to reckon with because of the complex relationship between trauma and silence. Avoiding recall can be appropriate and even necessary following traumatic events, especially if dangers still exist. Indeed survival may depend on one's ability *not* to succumb to the hyper-arousal stimulated by traumatic memories. As our colleague Rev. Russ Daye puts it:

> Repression and the creation of narratives that minimize the impact of traumatic events may actually aid immediate survival, especially where perpetrators are still present. There may be real danger of provoking further violation if truth is shared through narratives that do justice to the "facts." But the tragic irony is that these strategies of repression become terrible psychic prisons once a community or individual has passed through the acute phase and has re-established life in a context of greater safety. By then the ghosts of traumatizing events are stored away and victims know they cannot be released without suffering great psychic pain or even destabilization.[46]

Victims of violence often resist discussing a painful past. My grandparents' generation faced terrible choices during the *Zerrissenheit*. As soldiers approached their villages or estates, men had either to flee (thus leaving women alone to face intruders) or stay to face death (my Grandpa Franz witnessed several neighbors being executed). How were such excruciating decisions made? Whether forced to watch the violation of a loved one or learning about it later after fleeing, these men surely suffered from powerlessness, grief, and rage, perhaps even questioning their deeply held convictions about nonresistance. Similarly, Mennonites who made it out of Russia left loved ones behind, and thus struggled with survivors' guilt. Some downplayed their own traumatic experiences by comparing them to their relatives' grim fate.[47] We should empathize with those who want to suppress painful memories for their own sanity, and protect others (particularly children) by keeping their ghosts locked inside them.[48] But there is a cost to this.

What is more problematic is when traumatic events or testimonies are *edited out* of a communal narrative in order to shore up self-perceptions of

---

46. Email correspondence with authors, May 15, 2020. See Daye, *Political Forgiveness.*

47. Epp discusses this in terms of post-World War II immigrants in *Women without Men*, 55.

48. For example, in Sandra Birdsell's novel *The Russländer*, the protagonist Katya delays telling the story of her family's murder until she is widowed "lest the spirits of the story pollute the air" (220).

morality, strength, or prestige. Here we will look at three specific patterns of omission in my community.

The constraints of sanctioned or sanitized communal narratives. In the course of my interviews with some fifty descendants of *Kanadier, Russländer,* and Soviet Mennonites, it struck me how often participants seemed anxious not to diverge from the stories found in their family books. One noted afterward how some in the group were "looking back and forth in their books to make sure they would have the right wording, trying to present a certain picture. We want to carry on the myth, and not go into the place of pain."[49] Several older women responded to my questions by reading directly out of their books, and when I asked about controversial matters such as gendered violence, I was met with polite refusal. This reluctance (or inability) to depart from the communal "canon" perhaps indicates a psychological distancing from the pain of the real history. It made it more difficult to engage participants with how they might be existentially carrying trauma. In the guise of honoring our history can we become too distanced from it? Can reverence lead to disassociation?

Robert Zacharias raises another aspect of "narrative orthodoxy" in his discussion of how historical fiction can construct and constrain communal memory and identity. He shows how Canadian Mennonite novels of the second half of the twentieth century often focused on the demise of the Mennonite Commonwealth in Russia, and how their popularity turned the *Russländer* experience into a mythic origin story for the entire Canadian Mennonite community, overshadowing both earlier and later migrations from Russia.[50] But the narrative arc of "order, chaos, and flight" found in these novels avoids complicated and contradictory aspects of this legacy, such as the fate of the 80,000 Mennonites left behind after the 1920s migrations, or the contested political and historical context of the Canadian prairies into which these Mennonite immigrants settled.[51]

A related concern is how communal narratives can become domesticated. As Marlene Epp puts it, "The tendency to sanitize written life stories dictates against a literal telling of traumatic personal experience."[52] A

---

49. Interview by Elaine Enns, Saskatoon, Saskatchewan, June 26, 2014.

50. Zacharias, *Rewriting the Break Event,* 13. See also Sawatsky, "Dying for What Faith?," 36. Conversations with my interviewees confirmed that more Canadian Mennonites learn about their ancestors through such novels than from academic history.

51. See below 5C. A few Canadian Mennonite-heritage novelists *have* addressed some of these problematic pieces, including Al Reimer's *My Harp Is Turned to Mourning,* Rudy Wiebe's *Peace Shall Destroy Many,* and Sandra Birdsell's *The Russländer* and *Return of the Day.*

52. Epp, "Memory of Violence," 61.

Rassländer interviewee told me that while writing up her mother's stories she "just cleaned them up a bit, made them nice."[53] Another confirmed this impulse: "We just want to remember certain things. We leave out details because our history needs to be a nice story; we create a certain kind of history to legitimize our situation today."[54]

The gender gap in our testimonies. My Mennonite community continues to struggle with a patriarchal culture that discounts women's experiences. This is particularly acute when it comes to sexual violence, past and present.[55] *Rassländer* narratives of the *Zerrissenheit* highlight male suffering over that of females. Accounts of violence endured (e.g., murder, disappearance, or robbery) in Russia largely omit (or allude to only obliquely) "shameful" episodes such as rape. Were men who fled, or were killed, maintaining their commitment to pacifism considered exemplary, while women who survived sexual assault labored under the shadow of shame and silence?

Rape as a weapon of war has been all too common across time and space.[56] Russian Mennonite women also endured this during "The Great Trek" (when they made arduous journeys out of Russia during World War II). Russian soldiers, writes Marlene Epp, often rationalized sexual assault as spontaneous retribution for German atrocities during Hitler's occupation of Soviet territory. There is evidence that it was systematically incited, and may have been "unofficial" military policy.[57] Some women sought out a protector so as to be violated by only one man. Repatriated Soviet Mennonite women continued to fear random and brutal sexual attacks until as late as 1947. To avoid this, some would sleep in cramped closets all night, or disguise themselves as boys or as elderly when they worked in the fields.[58]

But androcentric Mennonite narratives tended to ignore or downplay these realities. For example, firsthand accounts by *Rassländer* survivors of the 1919 Eichenfeld Massacre describe in great detail the dismemberment, torture, and murder of individual men, and even movements of Makhno's

53. *Rassländer* Focus Group, interview by Elaine Enns, Saskatoon, Saskatchewan, June 25, 2014

54. Interview by Elaine Enns, Saskatoon, Saskatchewan, June 26, 2014

55. Though here we focus on immigrant histories, breaking silence around sexual abuse at Mennonite academic institutions and within the church is also a contemporary struggle (see http://www.ourstoriesuntold.com, and Roberts et al., *Recovering from the Anabaptist Vision,* 11–13, 47, 97–99).

56. See definition by the United Nations and its agencies at https://www.ohchr.org/en/newsevents/pages/rapeweaponwar.aspx. For current work in response, see Dr. Denis Mukwege Foundation.*

57. Epp, "Memory of Violence," 60.

58. Epp, *Women without Men,* 61.

troops. Yet the few references to sexual assault occur only in generalized, euphemistic comments such as "virtually every girl fell victim to the ruthless hands of these devils in human form."[59] Similarly, Marlene Epp, who in her groundbreaking work, *Women without Men,* brought to light dramatic stories of the Great Trek, shows how their experiences were largely overshadowed by those of men who had lost their lives under Stalin. The latter's stories "fit" the Mennonite theology of martyrdom in ways that female survivors of rape did not.[60] Moreover, many Canadian Mennonites believed those repatriated back to the Soviet Union suffered a fate worse than sexual assault. The tragic result is we don't learn about the remarkable physical, emotional, and spiritual courage of these women. Quite the contrary: some male Mennonite leaders in Canada assumed mental health issues among refugee survivors of the Great Trek were somehow linked to lack of faith and even "moral compromise."[61] Elsie Neufeld laments how an undiagnosed condition that left her grandmother catatonic for months at a time was perceived by many church folk to be *Seelenkrankheit*—that is, the result of unconfessed sin.[62]

Patriarchal power dynamics and perceptions of shame surrounding sexual assault meant such stories received little attention in our community, and that victims were often stripped of their willingness and/or ability to tell their stories. Stigma, as well as the pain of recounting the horror, caused many women to suppress their own experiences. Their testimonies detailed other adversities, but studiously avoided speaking about rape. Marlene Epp lists five common evasions:

- Deflecting: "It is too enormous to begin to describe";

- Depersonalizing by using more abstract narrative;

- Referring to consequences rather than the assault itself (e.g., "girls who were too young and women who were too old" were having babies);

- Narrators who were most likely raped switching from first- to third-person in the middle of their story;

59. Dyck et al., *Nestor Makhno and the Eichenfeld Massacre,* 46. See also Epp, *Mennonites in Canada, 1920–1940,* 476, and Patterson, "Eichenfeld Massacre."

60. Epp, *Women without Men,* 58–60. Another reason for the silence, Epp points out, may have been that male survivors who practiced nonresistance in the face of their women's rape may have felt humiliated: "husbands and fathers of rape victims [had] their masculinity . . . taken away" (Epp, "Memory of Violence," 75).

61. See Krahn, "Lifespan and Intergenerational Legacies of Soviet Oppression"; Neufeld, "Madness in One Family's Journey," and Wiebe, "Living on the Iceberg," 90–91, which looks at the dangers of silencing stories among survivors of trauma.

62. Neufeld, "Madness in One Family's Journey," 14.

- Telling the story of other women rather than one's own.[63]

Such patterns were evidenced among *Russländers* as well. "Women and even twelve-year old girls were raped, manhandled in a variety of ways and infected with venereal diseases," wrote Helena Harder Martens, "but I and my sisters (thanks be to God) did not fall into these devilish hands."[64] In Linda Reynolds's study of sixty-seven *Russländer* women, a significant percentage spoke about experiences of arrest, murder, displacement, and fear, but not one admitted to being raped—though half of the respondents indicated they knew someone who was.[65]

My *Russländer* descendant interviewees also struggled to decode family testimonies despite recognizing that the likelihood of sexual violence was, as one participant put it, "pretty high in the 1920s."[66] One admitted: "Rape never came up because it wasn't appropriate to talk about. It was a hidden thing, but there were certainly children who were the result of rape."[67] Another deduced that her mother must have been raped based on her behavior and attitude towards sex. A third heard her father speculate about his mother's rape. Four others acknowledged that sexual assault was widespread, and recalled anecdotes of girls being hidden in attics or haylofts, or crawling out of a window to get away from soldiers.[68] "My grandparents were reticent to speak of things," said a participant, "but my dad's older brother managed to get some information. But . . . a lot of people don't want to hear him talk about what he learned. These stories are somehow shameful or secret."[69] Another volunteered:

> My mom said she knows that women were raped, but none of my great-aunts or my grandmothers were . . . at least not that she knows of . . . The oldest child in a friend's family is a half sibling, but their mom has never talked about why or how that came about. My friend believes her mother was raped.[70]

---

63. Epp, *Women without Men,* 59–60.

64. Cited in Dyck et al., *Nestor Makhno and the Eichenfeld Massacre,* 68.

65. Reynolds, "Aftermath of Trauma," 68–69.

66. Interview by Elaine Enns, Saskatoon, Saskatchewan, July 10, 2014.

67. Interview by Elaine Enns, Rosthern, Saskatchewan, June 16, 2014.

68. *Russländer* Focus Group, interview by Elaine Enns, Saskatoon, Saskatchewan, June 25, 2014.

69. *Russländer* Focus Group, interview by Elaine Enns, Saskatoon, Saskatchewan, June 25, 2014.

70. Small group interview by Elaine Enns, Tiefengrund, Saskatchewan, July 17, 2014.

One interviewee wondered aloud why her father's skin was so dark. We do not know how many children were born of rape during either the *Zerrissenheit* or Great Trek, as there has been no academic research on that subject.

The silencing of women was broader than just topics of sexual violence; their voices were often absent from communal historical accounts. My Grandma Margreta's oldest sister—my Great-aunt Anna Schulz, who was hidden in the attic with her during the home invasion in Christmas 1918 (above 2A)—was one who escaped the Soviet Union during World War II, only to be captured and returned. She was the only sibling who did not migrate to Canada with her parents in 1927, having married Peter Kroeger in 1921. Peter, a skilled tool manufacturer, was in 1937 "taken away by Communists, even though he did nothing wrong," and died of a heart attack somewhere "in exile" in 1942.[71] Great-aunt Anna fled to Germany in 1943 with her youngest son Harry, but was eventually overtaken and arrested by advancing Soviet soldiers near Berlin. She and other Soviet citizens were forcibly repatriated, taken to northern Siberia by cattle cars and open barges. There, in a wintery wilderness, these women and children had to construct the barracks in which they would dwell. Subjected to hard labor and scarce resources, in 1950 Harry died at age twenty of tuberculosis and starvation.[72] Great-aunt Anna migrated to Winnipeg in 1960, one of the first Mennonites allowed to leave the U.S.S.R. after Stalin. Yet she never spoke of these multiple traumatic events. "We will talk about that someday," she told her older son Arthur, whom she had not seen for sixteen years. "But," he lamented, "we never did."[73]

The experiences of so many women, one of my interviewees summarized, were "just too awful to talk about." But when victims are not allowed to tell and process their violations in safe settings, it only deepens the trauma, forcing it to fester within.

The inconvenient evidence that our people were complicit, too. A third consequential silence in settler Mennonite communal narratives is the way our people were entangled in events that traumatized others, such as settler displacements. My family history books highlight how Catherine the Great invited Mennonites to farm the steppes of Ukraine in the 1780s, and

71. Gerbrandt, *Remembering the Schulzes,* 109–10.

72. Zacharias, *Wilhelm Zacharias and Descendants,* 349.

73. Gerbrandt, *Remembering the Schulzes,* 114–19. Arthur spent World War II in Germany, then migrated to Canada in 1959. My sister Janet, who has fond memories of *Tante* Anna, wonders: "How could she be such a gentle, loving person after all she went through?" (Email correspondence with authors, May 15, 2020).

how they negotiated certain privileges from the Tsarina.[74] No mention, however, is made of the fact that Nogai and Cossack peoples—traditional inhabitants of the steppes—who just prior to my ancestors arriving had mounted a significant resistance to forced removal by Catherine's military. This was brutally suppressed, referred to by the Nogai as "the weeping of the steppes."[75] A century later, my great-grandparents Johann and Helene Enns moved up to settle in the Ufa region of Russia, where the indigenous nomadic Bashkir had earlier been forced to give up nomadic life under the pressure of Russian settlers and colonial policy.[76]

The same pattern would be repeated in Canada, when late nineteenth-century Mennonite settlers from West Prussia, Manitoba, and the U.S. procured land in Saskatchewan that had just been taken by the federal government from Cree tribes. Historian Frank H. Epp points out that

74. After fleeing persecution in the Low Countries during the mid-sixteenth century, Dutch Mennonites found varying degrees of tolerance and freedom in the Vistula delta of Prussia. Though they never achieved full citizenship status during their two centuries there, Mennonites did "negotiate numerous charter privileges which counteracted discriminatory laws or government orders" (Ens, *Subjects or Citizens?*, 5). This established a pattern whereby Mennonite leaders sought religious toleration not by constitutional means, but through special *Privilegia* from a reigning monarch. They negotiated a twenty-point *Privilegium* with Catherine, which included complete freedom of religious practice, exemption from military service "for all time," and complete autonomy "forever" for Mennonite immigrants and their descendants. In 1870, however, Czar Alexander II ended the "eternal" Mennonite *Privilegium*, a major factor pushing thousands of Mennonites to immigrate to North America.

75. Urry, who describes the Nogai as transhumant pastoralists, notes that in the 1790s "the selection of land for the Mennonites involved further removal of the Nogai." The Mennonite village of Lindenau, for example, was the site of a Nogai settlement that had been evacuated by Catherine, resulting in subsequent tensions between Nogai and Mennonites (*None but the Saints*, 96, 107). In 1783, after the liquidation of the Crimean Khanate, Russian authorities planned to relocate the Nogai to an area between the Volga and the Urals. But the Nogai refused to leave the Kuban area, an uprising that saw some 7,000 Nogai warriors killed and 1,000 captured, not counting women and children (today considered an act of genocide). Most Nogai finally acceded to the Russian Empire in exchange for not being removed; some moved to the Caspian coast, where many descendants live today. The Dzhemboyluk and Yedisan Hordes, however, moved to the Molochna River region where Mennonites were being settled. See Suleimenov, "Weeping in the Steppe."

76. In 1552, the area was first conquered by Russians, and Ufa was founded in 1574 to begin colonization. This led to many Bashkir uprisings which were harshly repressed (see https://www.britannica.com/topic/Bashkir). Neufeld et al. describe the pull that drew Mennonites such as the Ennses from south to north at the end of the nineteenth century: "At the time any and all settlers were free to purchase land. It was cheaper than that in the colonies of South Russia" (*Ufa*, 20).

> In some ways Canada faced a problem similar, albeit not quite
> as acute, to that of Catherine of Russia a century earlier. Unless
> permanent agricultural settlers were brought in the nomadic
> native indigenous to the area . . . would make nation-building
> difficult if not impossible. The part which Mennonites played in
> the Canadian domestication program, first in Manitoba then in
> Saskatchewan. . . was essential to the national policy.[77]

Sociologist Leo Driedger sums up the dilemma in both countries:
"Each time when the hunters and trappers had been cleared away, the Mennonites moved in. It was a struggle between the food gatherers and the food
growers—the hunters and the farmers. The Mennonites were part of the
farming invasion."[78]

Yet not a whisper of any of this in our family books. Frank H. Epp
adds: "As is common among prosperous societies, the Mennonites were not
much aware of their privileged position and the extent to which wealth was
derived from the land, freely given or easily purchased, as well as from the
servile labor in an abundant supply. Instead they remembered their own
erstwhile poverty and how hard they had worked and consequently how
much God has blessed them."[79] This alludes to another issue rarely talked
about in our communal narratives: the growing wealth disparity within
Mennonite colonies in Eastern Europe. James Urry, in *None but the Saints:
The Transformation of Mennonite Life in Russia, 1789–1889,* discusses how
the inequality among Mennonites in Prussia was eventually reproduced in
Russia. By 1860, over half of the Mennonite community in Ukraine was
landless living as renters, sharecroppers, or laborers for other Mennonite
farmers. In 1863, 150 poor Mennonites signed a petition to "distribute all
remaining reserve and surplus land among the landless," only to be intimi-
dated by some wealthy Mennonites, who bribed officials to take no action.
Mennonites migrating from Ukraine and Russia to Canada in the latter half
of the nineteenth century (*Kanadier*) left in part because of this growing
wealth disparity within their colonies (as well as theological and cultural

---

77. Epp, *Mennonites in Canada, 1786–1920,* 305. The Canadian government aggressively wooed Mennonite colonists, who in turn negotiated a *Privilegium* that included
free land grants after three years' residence and blocks of land reserved exclusively for
Mennonite settlement. See Ens, *Subjects or Citizens?,* 3–5, 22–31, and Schwinghamer,
"'Problem Is a Vexing One.'"

78. Driedger, "Louis Riel and the Mennonite Invasion," 6. Steve Heinrichs, Director of Indigenous Relations for Mennonite Church Canada, points out that Mennonite
agrarian settlement of traditional hunting and trapping lands continues today in the
boreal forests of Treaty 8 territory.

79. Epp, *Mennonites in Canada, 1920–1940,* 142.

disputes). This struggle spawned a legacy of bitterness and mistrust between *Kanadier* and *Russländer* immigrants that is still whispered about today among Canadian Mennonites.[80]

Even more acute was disparity between Mennonite and other estate-owners and the Ukrainian and Russian peasants. Widespread poverty and authoritarian rule were driving the country inexorably toward crisis at the turn of the twentieth century, leading eventually to the Bolshevik Revolution in 1917. Absent in our communal narrative, however, is how so many of the terrors visited upon Mennonite communities during the *Zerrissenheit* came at the hand of disaffected workers and peasant neighbors. Frank H. Epp summarizes: "Immense wealth and Mennonite neglect, if not exploitation of the Russian peasant, made them immediate and quite understandable targets of such aggression."[81] Once Soviet policies of land collectivization began, large estates—including those of Mennonites such as the Enns's—were targeted first.[82]

I recall as a teenager asking my dad *why* our people had experienced so much violence. He stated simply: "We got too rich in Russia." That terse phrase stuck with me, and I have spent much of the last decade trying to exegete it.

3E. QUERIES FOR EXCAVATING BURIED STORIES

The greatest challenge of Bloodlines work is to keep interrogating both silencing and sanitization in our communal narratives. This can be painful. I too am sometimes reluctant to transmit the whole truth of traumatic events in my tellings. For example, ten years ago I was talking with a restorative justice colleague (herself a victim of a home invasion years earlier) about the story of my Grandma Margreta's experience in Ukraine as it had been passed down in my family. I told it as a compelling story of women's strength and courage, imagining my Great-grandmother Anna announcing to the soldiers: "There will be no violence in this house!" My colleague looked at me with sadness in her eyes; "Elaine, it is pretty unlikely that sexual violence *didn't* happen." I was stopped short, and burst into tears. How does

80. Urry, *None but the Saints*, 59, 99, 201–13. See also Epp, *Mennonites in Canada, 1920–1940*, 414–21.

81. Epp, *Mennonites in Canada, 1920–1940*, 144.

82. Though agricultural collectivization had been encouraged since the Revolution, we were surprised to read that in 1928, toward the end of the New Economic Policy, "hardly more than one percent of the arable land was cultivated by collectives" (Kenez, *History of the Soviet Union*, 85). This suggests only the wealthiest landowners were targeted for confiscation in the first decade of Communist rule.

one integrate horrors in handling intimate family stories? And *that* is not as difficult as raising issues of complicity in one's own community!

Nevertheless, we must pay close attention to patterns of omission because they exacerbate trauma. This is the consensus of four researchers whose work has informed ours (and all of whom, tellingly, focus on experiences of women). Pamela Sugiman cautions that a dominant story typically doesn't acknowledge how social power, such as age, gender, and social class, shapes people's vocalization of their own experiences.[83] Educational psychologist Erin Seaton adds that power dynamics within a tight-knit community impact what stories or perspectives are "recognized, valued, dismissed, or damned."[84] Marlene Epp shows how master narratives structure meaning but also mask particularities of individual situations, especially those of women.[85] And Elizabeth Krahn warns how silencing "unacceptable" narratives, or perpetuating stories that shame or blame, can be especially damaging to those who are rendered invisible or suspect.[86] This is the personal and political truth: narratives that silence individual, group, or communal contradictions will not help us heal from hauntings.

To attend to our Bloodlines is to step into the vocation of being Re-mem-bearers of our ancestors' trauma, whether they were victims or perpetrators of violence, or, as is often the case with immigrants-become-settlers, both. We carry this past in our bones, so bringing it to consciousness—ours and that of others in our community—is crucial. Sigmund Freud famously gave an intrapsychic rationale: what remains lodged in our unconscious generates repetition-compulsion. And philosopher-historian George Santayana later reiterated this dictum as a political ultimatum: those who cannot remember the past are condemned to repeat it.[87]

Again, ours is a double task: working through omissions, and assessing stories to which we do have access. Like the proverbial archaeologist, we are working with fragments, circumstantial or indirect evidence, even dubious sources. We have to read between lines, imagine what our communal narratives might not want to tell, and decode obfuscated testimonies. In this critical approach, we must remain empathetic to narratives of violation, and keep in mind that victims often have memory gaps or difficulty recalling details precisely as a result of the trauma. If we are able to exhume buried

---

83. Sugiman, "Passing Time, Moving Memories," 56.

84. Seaton, "Common Knowledge," 295.

85. Epp, *Women without Men*, 63.

86. A community mental health worker, Krahn describes how individual identity can be overshadowed by a collective one ("Lifespan and Intergenerational Legacies of Soviet Oppression").

87. Santayana, *Life of Reason*, 284.

stories, we must do so respectfully. What is ours to bring to light? What might the impact be on our families and communities?

The same is true of how we handle what we *do* know. Sugiman reminds us that personal memories and assumptions are a source alongside family letters or interviews or secondary studies, and discourages "accusations of faulty or distorted memory," or objectifying stories simply as "sources of data."[88] Remem-bearers must also be vigilant about what Robert Zacharias calls the "appropriation of particular traumas by those who did not experience them."[89] Seaton shows how peers or researchers can reconstruct a victim's story through the lens of their own biases in ways that "contradict, cover over, dismiss or challenge" the victim's own account.[90] Those of us intending to be advocates and allies inevitably filter these stories through *our* interpretative interests. I acknowledge this as an ever-present challenge for me in this book. We can only try to be respectful and avoid exploitation, taking care neither to exaggerate nor understate the damage our ancestors endured—or inflicted.

These cautions should not discourage us from Bloodlines work. Engage with courage and curiosity your family and community stories. The first step is to determine what sources are available to you. Beyond your immediate family lore may lie a distant relative who has done some genealogical or historical work; such folks are often eager to share material (though their perspective on it may differ dramatically). Family books, letters, diaries, or other texts—if they exist—are often scattered throughout the extended family, and sometimes reside in local museums or with researchers. It takes persistence and assertiveness to find these pieces of the puzzle. Secondary sources, from historical studies to novels, are an important and often necessary way to learn about the broader context of your peoples' history.[91] Visits to places where your immigrant ancestors came from, or where they first settled, are invaluable, as my experience testifies.

But most of us rely on oral traditions of family, friends, and neighbors, sometimes only whispers. A first step is to start cataloguing favorite tales

88. Sugiman, "Passing Time, Moving Memories," 58.

89. Zacharias, *Break Event*, 146.

90. Seaton, "Common Knowledge," 303.

91. For example, one of my interviewee's grandparents was a survivor of the Eichenfeld massacre: "My grandparents only talked about the happy times in Russia, but what has informed me the best is reading *The Russländer* by Sandra Birdsell. For the first time I realized this is what my family went through, and after I read it, I had a number of conversations with my mom, who confirmed this is what our family experienced" (Russländer Focus Group, interview by Elaine Enns, Saskatoon, Saskatchewan, June 25, 2014).

that still circulate, recording them without prejudice (the critical decoding comes later). Multiple sources for such stories provide variation in version and perspective. When there is laughter or a joke, probe deeper: Dark humor typically functions as a mask for pain or loss. Then comes the task of interviewing people, which can take place both formally and informally. Personal testimony is rich and humanizing, as well as partial and partisan. Some may not completely trust what they know or heard, and you can simply note that. Above all it is important to try to create a space where people can safely recount stories, especially regarding traumatic events, with no fear of judgment or challenge to their memories.

Here is a partial checklist of things to look for:

1. What stories are told easily and often, and with what affect in both storyteller and listener? Are there aspects of stories that are *not* included in particular tellings or by certain people or sources?

2. What stories have been silenced, dismissed, denied, or covered up in your ancestral narratives, and what feelings does that stir in you?

3. How are women and sexual minorities portrayed? Does gendered violence or discrimination get addressed? Are such stories suppressed in your communal narrative (accounts of both pain and loss, and of courage and cunning)?

4. Who tends to be portrayed as heroes or villains in communal tales, and how?

5. Are there any fictional or academic historical accounts of your larger community's story?

6. Do you see footprints of intergenerational trauma or unresolved historic pain in your family or community (e.g., early death, depression, anxiety)? How does it get articulated or manifested?

7. What are ways your people may have been complicit in—or challenged—events or systems that traumatized others (e.g., displacement of Indigenous peoples, the slave trade, class oppression)? How are such matters processed or erased in your family story? (We will continue to raise this important issue in later chapters.)

8. How do *you* carry intergenerational pain, loss, shame, or pride?

Bloodlines work can sometimes feel like doing surgery on living flesh. Exploring your family and community traditions requires care. But ultimately, *bearing* family and community memory, especially regarding trauma, means trying to make sense of these traditions, not simply passing them on uncritically or timidly as mere artifacts or curios. A discipleship of decolonization invites us to "reread" our peoples' stories mindfully, and to revise them compassionately, through our commitment to healing and restorative solidarity.

Figure 15: Casa Anna Schulz Mural, panel 2 (depicting Franz Enns bending rifles at *Johanneshof*, Ufa, Russia, 1918). Artist: Dimitri Kadiev (used with permission). Photo: Chris Wight (used with permission).

CHAPTER 4

Songlines I
Traditions of Resilience

> I seek to solicit each of you into the subversion of spiritual
> silence. I want you to join me in honoring the vision that has
> helped to shape your life.
>
> —Steven Charleston[1]

4A. VISION OF GIFTS, 2005

DURING 2004 WE EXPERIENCED many losses: the death of my father and
my mother's rapid decline into Alzheimer's, and our own personal health
struggles. Throughout the year I attempted a daily practice of gratitude, acknowledging all of the goodness in my life. But I was relieved on December
31 to close out the year.

A few nights later, as I was falling asleep, I entered that thin place between consciousness and slumber. I saw myself sitting in front of a basket
full of gifts, packages large and small wrapped in burnished gold paper with
shiny ribbons. I was overwhelmed by this abundance. (After all, I grew up in
a Mennonite household where frugality was a catechism in distinguishing
want from need. I was often embarrassed about how few Christmas gifts I

---

1. Charleston, *Four Vision Quests of Jesus*, 37. Charleston is a Choctaw elder and
former Episcopal bishop; we highly recommend this beautiful short book that reads the
Jesus story through a compelling Indigenous lens.

received compared to my friends; one year I even made up presents to im-
press them, a ruse that was soon discovered, to my chagrin!) I tried to pick
up the basket, but it was too large and overflowing. So I sat down and pulled
a bundle into my lap. As I tugged at the ribbon, the paper fell away, and suddenly I was surrounded by my parents and their parents and their parents.
They were smiling and reaching towards me with love and encouragement.

I awoke to darkness. For a long time I basked in a deep sense of awe,
thanksgiving, and assurance. A few days later I described this experience to
an elder Quaker friend with a mystical bent. "You had a vision," she said in
a matter-of-fact tone. "Pay attention to it."

During a Passover celebration with Jewish friends that spring, we sang
Dayenu, and afterwards reflected together on the question: "What really is
enough?" Immediately my vision came to mind, but I was hesitant to talk
about it openly, fearing it would be dismissed. Steven Charleston asks, "Do
we acknowledge that we have had a vision, or keep it to ourselves?"[2] I
didn't yet have the courage to share it. Indeed, it took five years to embrace
it fully. Its meaning was confirmed to me during my trip to Ukraine: this
basket of gifts represents my Songlines.

The Mennonite faith was for my ancestors, and remains for me, a central Songline. Much of that tradition was and is expressed through music.
We are a singing people, skilled at four-part harmony (with or without instrumental accompaniment). *Nun Danket Alle Gott* ("Now Thank We All
Our God") holds a special place in our musical canon, having been sung
with great emotion at the bookends of our *Russländer* migration. After the
Zachariases and other Mennonite families passed through the Red Gate in
1923—praying their way through the final inspection at the border between
Russia and Latvia on a train heading west to freedom (above 2D)—this
beloved hymn spontaneously "burst from every breast" in cathartic relief,
as Great-grandfather Isaak put it. "What had been so fervently and passion-
ately wished for," he wrote, had been realized: "We have escaped the Russian
hell and can breathe freely and confidently. What a feeling of happiness . . .
not to be so terribly afraid of people."[3] Later thousands of people gathered
at the Rosthern, Saskatchewan train station to meet these *Russländers*. According to a *Saskatoon Star Phoenix* reporter:

> A great hush fell upon the assembled thousands, and to the ears
> of the Canadian came a soft, slow chant. . . . a musical expres-
> sion of the great tragedy and heartbreak. Then the Canadian
> Mennonites took up the song and the tone increased in volume,

2. Charleston, *Four Vision Quests of Jesus*, 34.

3. Zacharias, *Meine Lebensgeschichte*, 46. See above, ch. 3, n. 7.

growing deeper and fuller, until the melody was pouring forth in several thousand throats.[4]

Despite lingering mistrust between these previous and new immigrants, they honored each other's pain, resilience, and faith by singing this same hymn to and with each other.[5]

Music was our backbone for generations. My *Grosspapa* Franz was a *Vorsänger* in Russia, the church music leader who would pick the starting note and tempo for a hymn. I imagine him lining out the beginning fifth (*do-so*), then the full chord (*do-mi-so-mi-do*) so congregants could find the four-part harmony. In a tradition deeply proficient at a capella musicality, his was an esteemed and solemn position. Due to trauma, he did not sing much after arriving in Canada. But when my dad contracted rheumatic fever as a young boy and could not go outside, Grandpa Franz comforted him by giving him a xylophone (an extravagant gift during the Depression). My oldest Uncle Jake chuckled as he relayed the story: "Your dad was just a little guy, but loved to play tunes on that xylophone; they even had him play in church one time!"[6] As an adult, my dad loved nothing better than to rouse us out of bed on Christmas morning by blasting Handel's *Messiah* on the downstairs stereo.

The power of communal singing filled my childhood. All of us children took music lessons and sang in the church choir. I majored in music performance in college, and sang professionally for a short while. As in-laws joined our family, we continued to sing together with delight, making up songs for weddings and other important occasions. Today in California I lead Taize services, and still feel happiest when I am singing.

Music was the heart of that visionary basket of gifts. My most important Songline remains song itself.

4B. WHAT CARRIED US THROUGH

Songlines are the narratives, cultural practices, and ceremonies that sustain and transform individuals and communities. They are stories of conviction we seek to live by, and which motivate us in the work of justice and decolonization, consoling our suffering and inspiring us to end the suffering of others. Songlines inspire and empower us to resist and transform situations of oppression, guide us in healing past and present wounds, and remind us how

4. Brown, cited in Epp, *Mennonites in Canada, 1920–1940*, 172.

5. The earlier wave of Mennonite migrants had broken with their co-religionists in Ukraine two generations earlier for religious and economic reasons (see above 3D). Still, many *Kanadier* families took destitute *Russländer* into their homes upon arrival.

6. Conversation with Elaine Enns, Carrot River, October 2012.

to be human. These traditions are many and diversely expressed, and every community has them. In this book we focus mainly on two strands: those articulated through religious faith, and through the testimonies of social movements for humanization—and especially the intersection of the two.

Movements for justice and inclusion have always been generated and sustained by Songlines: the promises and visions of Scripture; the hymnody of freedom; the witness of leaders young and old. In the U.S. this can be most clearly seen in the prophetic traditions of the Black church in song, proclamation, and action.[7] But there have been many other noble expressions in North America: Indigenous ghost dancing and Quaker silence; evangelical abolitionists and Baptist social gospelers; Methodist labor activism and Catholic Worker service to the poor. In this chapter we will focus on traditions that guided my immigrant forebears, helping them survive trauma and embrace decency though settlers in an unjust colonial state. In chapter 7, we will look at strands that animate our efforts toward decolonization today.

Songlines enable us to believe collective change is possible. As inhabitants of empire, we are everywhere surrounded by the dominant and dominating narratives of the powerful and the privileged that legitimize the status quo of poverty and affluenza, racism and supremacy. In the U.S. those who would follow gospel values have always had to contend with strong gravitational forces of alienation and apostasy: the pull of eighteenth-century "City on a Hill" ideologies of exceptionalism; the power of the nineteenth-century civil religion of Manifest Destiny; the demands of twentieth-century imperial wars and corporate extractivism; and the seduction of twenty-first-century consumer fetishism that colonizes our desires and the distractions of media saturation and infotainment. Without a grounding in, and constant reorientation by, older and wiser Songlines, it is impossible to navigate such fierce competition for our hearts and minds.

In our discourse, Songlines refer not to *any* myth or metaphor, but to those that serve the cause of personal and political liberation. They are necessary for both those under oppressive systems and for those of us seeking to defect from our privilege within those systems. For settlers, Songlines often stand in tension with inherited Landlines and Bloodlines, especially as they call us to defect from our family, race, class, or gender socialization.[8] Our received settler Storylines are partially or significantly dysfunctional,

7. For good overviews, see Harding, *There Is a River*; Cone, *Spirituals and the Blues*; Hopkins and Cummings,, *Cut Loose Your Stammering Tongue*; West, *Prophesy Deliverance!* See below 7B.

8. On defection from oppressive systems, see Myers, *Who Will Roll Away the Stone?*, 176.

destructive and dehumanizing, especially heroic tales of ethnic superiority (resuscitated today in Trumpian fantasies of "Making America Great Again"). Settlers need storied traditions that help us transcend, critique, and transform ethnocentric Bloodlines and entitled Landlines. Some we need to learn from communities that have struggled historically against colonialism. Others we must discover hidden in our own stories, because for us these are the most subversive of all.

Settler communal narratives are informed and shaped by a mix of humanizing Songlines and colonizing half-truths. For example, as Mennonites we took pride in our "separation" from the colonial state, yet we enjoyed certain *Privilegia* from secular authorities at key points in our migrations, especially land grants in both Ukraine and Canada. Mennonites escaping marginalization in Western Europe were used by Catherine the Great as a "buffer class" to help Russia colonize the steppes, in the process disenfranchising indigenous Nogai and Cossack peoples (above 3D; a similar pattern was repeated in the migration of my ancestors to Canada, below 5C). Yet there were many commendable aspects of the Mennonite "Commonwealth" that grew up along the Dnieper River in Ukraine.

For example, a 1914 plot map of Osterwick and Kronsthal villages, Ukraine (Figure 16), shows how each similar-sized property had access to river or ditch irrigation, suggesting an equitable social architecture.[9] Community conflicts were resolved without resorting to policing, and agricultural abundance had been achieved. Yet as some prospered, including my maternal great-grandparents, economic stratification marginalized others of their own kin, not to mention local peasant workers. These patterns of disparity contributed to the social turmoil that culminated in the Russian Revolution, spelling the end of this Commonwealth experiment. As a descendant of this legacy, my task is to affirm and learn from their significant achievements without overly idealizing them.

Language was and is a Songline tradition for my family's Mennonite identity, though not without ambiguity. My forebears in Ukraine lived for 150 years in semi-autonomous communities that remained German-speaking (both vernacular *Plautdietsch* and High German). As just noted, German hymns brought them through the bitter times of the *Zerrissenheit*, and in Canada, High German was unquestionably the language of church. Though Mennonite loyalties to German culture were sometimes problematic (see below 6Cv), in Canada German-speaking immigrants endured hostility throughout both World Wars.

---

9. Map in Schroeder and Huebert, *Mennonite Historical Atlas*, 24. A more detailed map is in Gerbrandt, *Remembering the Schulzes*, 15.

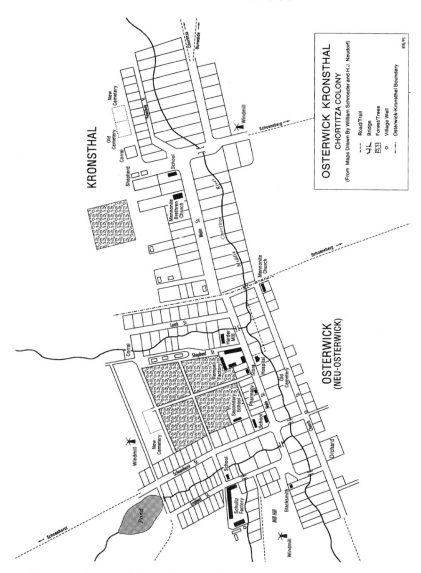

Figure 16: Plot map of Osterwick-Kronsthal village, Chortitza Colony, ca. 1914.
Mennonite Historical Atlas, 24 (used with permission).

We must always keep in mind that language can be either used to preserve culture and identity *or* to suppress it. For immigrant communities, maintaining one's native tongue is a keystone practice for resisting cultural assimilation (below 6B).[10] German remained the language of most

10. On loss of our German language, see below 6B; on Indigenous language suppression and revitalization, see below 7D.

Canadian Prairie Mennonite churches through the 1950s. Though my bi-lingual parents helped found a primarily English-speaking church in 1963, weekly hymnody included singing in German. When I was between ages five and fourteen, I attended *Deutsche Schule* with my siblings and church friends every Saturday. We spoke only German, played games, and put on an annual Christmas celebration that included folk traditions such as carol-ing and making a big gingerbread house. I spoke to my grandparents in High German, and as teenagers at our Mennonite high school we used Low-German phrases to ask each other out on dates ("*Wirst du spazierengehen mitt mir?*" "Will you go for a walk and talk with me?"). We laughed heartily at Low-German jokes we heard from our parents, even if we did not com-pletely understand them. Such efforts to maintain linguistic traditions in a bicultural immigrant community were healthy, but for us there was also a dark side. Implicit attitudes of German superiority worked synergistically with European hegemony in Canadian society, helping pave the way for us to "become white" (below 6B).

The central Songline of my ancestors was "being church." Mennonites suffered multiple episodes of persecution, forced migration, and communal resettlement over four centuries because of their fierce fidelity to the Ana-baptist faith, which was criminalized as "anti-social" and heretical by Euro-pean Christendom. Their experiments in collectivist economics, egalitarian social models, and resistance to state conscription predated both socialist and anarchist movements by centuries, and planted seeds of the modern separation of church and state.[11] Their dissident form of Christian disciple-ship brought considerable trouble from the authorities, but their holistic embodiment of community sustained them.

Mental health workers have studied how religious practices can pro-mote resilience in a variety of ways.[12] Disciplines of prayer, Scripture study, contemplation, and altruism help preserve healthy cortisol levels. Worship provides space for lament and joy, and invites members to confess and forgive. Faith can help make meaning out of trauma, and social solidarity rebuilds trust. Receiving and offering mutual aid is another vital factor in maintaining community viability. We recognize religious upbringings can be dysfunctional, and churches are still far from being free of patriarchy and abuse. But for my *Russländer* community, church played an important role in holding and healing our personal and collective intergenerational trauma.

11. See Myers, *Who Will Roll Away the Stone?*, 363, and sources cited there.

12. Brewer-Smyth and Koenig, "Could Spirituality and Religion Promote Stress Resilience?"

Here are key church practices that nurtured my progenitors, and that I too embrace:

1. *Community singing:* Mennonites not only express their devotion through joining their voices in song; we also are *playful* together in making music. As children in worship, my friends and I would take turns during hymns singing each voice part—soprano, alto, tenor, and bass. Music is also an acceptable way to express ecstasy in our repressed northern European culture!

2. *Service:* Founder Menno Simons famously enjoined his followers to acts of altruism.[13] Mennonites take great pride in their contemporary tradition of service and relief through organizations like Mennonite Central Committee* and Mennonite Disaster Service.* My parents were deeply involved in refugee resettlement, and regularly brought migrants from around the world to our dining room table, many of whom became friends of our family (I particularly recall Aschalew and Abebe from Ethiopia doting on me as a little girl). This exposure was certainly part of what led me, after graduating from college, to seek work that addressed injustice. Mennonite Voluntary Service* prompted my move from Saskatoon at age twenty-one for an assignment with the Victim Offender Reconciliation Program* in Fresno, CA, which launched my vocation in restorative justice.

3. *Mutual aid:* There is a long tradition of Mennonite communities sharing labor and resources with each other to survive and promote equity, part of a larger pattern of aid societies among immigrants.[14] Though the Gilded Age saw increasing internal economic disparities among *Russländer,* when crisis hit during the Russian Revolution and civil war, practices of mutual aid reemerged as co-religionists housed, clothed, and fed each other, and fled, migrated, and settled together.[15] It is fair to say there has been a steady undercurrent of tension among Mennonites between the "socialistic" tendencies of traditional mutual

---

13. See Lewis, "Take into Account All that Menno Wrote."

14. See Nolt, "Formal Mutual Aid Structures among American Mennonites and Brethren." For good definitions, see https://wiki.p2pfoundation.net/Mutual_Aid_Societies, and Pëtr Kropotkin's classic, *Mutual Aid.*

15. Such practices have been identified in recent trauma studies as a "tend and befriend" response to threat. Twentieth-century "fight or flight" studies were conducted only on men; it was simply assumed women responded in these same ways. Current research, however, shows the release of oxytocin in women facing danger mobilizes a response that "tends" by looking after the young and "befriends" by supporting and protecting one another (Taylor et al., "Biobehavioral Responses to Stress in Females,").

aid and the culture of capitalist self-sufficiency.[16] Still, my family's local church practiced grassroots mutual aid as a matter of course.

4. *Table fellowship*: Many Mennonite households linger over meals, sharing stories of family members and friends. (Ched calls this practice in my family, with both bemusement and envy, an "ongoing exercise of orally mapping the extended village.") Essential to this table fellowship were (and to some extent still are) traditional foods such as *borscht, holubschi, kotletten, zwieback,* and *platz*. Our family meal table had two major functions:

- *It embodied values of inclusion and abundance.* Not only did refugees from different parts of the world often join us, on any Sunday I knew I could invite over friends who happened to be in church for a delicious, bountiful meal. My mom had a particular genius for finding enough on hand to feed whoever would show up, carrying on the tradition of her grandmother. Mom's sense of hospitality was renowned and revered in our extended community.

- *It was a space for instruction as a child, and remembering as an adult.* After I moved away to California, meals during visits home were a time to update me on relatives and friends, ensuring I remained woven into the communal tapestry.

5. *Preserving one's story:* As noted, many *Russländer* descendants wrote memoirs or family history books. These acts of testimony and meaning-making were clearly therapeutic for families who endured significant trauma. And even if these documents weren't always able or willing to tell the whole story (above 3D), they remain a tremendous gift to descendants. Mennonites have also generated a disproportionately large corpus of scholarly and popular literature (such as historical novels) concerning our various settlements and migrations. This fierce commitment to chronicle our own history is undoubtedly a longstanding response to Christendom's efforts to erase the Anabaptist movement over the centuries, and today it helps us mitigate the culture of amnesia in North American settler colonialism.

6. *A communal center:* Each of the aunts and uncles I interviewed repeated the refrain that, growing up, "church was at the center of our lives." It was an expression of culture through language, food, music, and dance, and a place where Mennonite conviction and identity as

---

16. For example, Mennonite mutual aid has been institutionalized into more conventional insurance enterprises over the last half century (Rogalsky, "Mutual Aid or Financial Institution?").

a minority people was built and nurtured. Church was also a space for older women to assert leadership through groups like Ladies' Aid and sewing circles.[17] As a child I was at church at least four times a week, and one of my fondest memories was of community dances. In the small towns of Dundurn and Hanley, my extended maternal family and friends would gather to dance polkas, the Butterfly, and the Fox Trot, and to sing and play music. These were magical nights full of laughter and delight where relatives expertly played the accordion, guitar, mandolin, and fiddle. My home church would host socials in local gymnasiums where we square danced and ate together. Communal dancing would now be recognized as an expression of somatic healing (see below 8E).

I delight in seeing some of these traditions survive in the next generation behind me; but others are atrophying through assimilation driven by the fragmenting pressures of capitalism, secularist modernity, and "whiteness" (below 6B). My elderly aunts and uncles recognize this too, lamenting that "church was more important to us than it is now." As with so many Catholics and Jews, many Mennonites today retain identity more through household habits than faith practices. This book is one of the ways I am trying to respond to the challenge of preserving and renewing traditions of my ancestors that can support a contemporary Anabaptist discipleship of decolonization.

For millennia, Indigenous peoples have been sustained by their traditional knowledge, culture, and spiritualities. These vary widely among tribes across North America, but include song, prayer, music, dance, sweat lodges, smudging, teachings of the medicine wheel, and use of herbs, roots, and plants.[18] With the brutal suppression of these teachings and ceremonies throughout the history of settler colonialism, native communities know about loss—but also about reclamation and renewal in spite of the odds.[19] Many traditions have survived and continue to provide healing and strength, including "native diets, rituals that greet the seasons and the harvests, ceremonies, and the use of native plants for healing purposes [that]

---

17. Marlene Epp describes how "ladies auxiliaries" functioned within the patriarchal Mennonite denomination as a "parallel church" in which women could exercise agency in mission and charitable work, performing roles otherwise closed to them. The sewing circle was "a veritable battleground for the emancipation of Mennonite women," as well as a space of emotional support and de-isolation (*Mennonite Women in Canada*, 154–60).

18. See Martin, *Land Looks after Us*.

19. See Battiste, *Reclaiming Indigenous Voice and Vision*.

have been used to promote health by living in harmony with the earth."[20] In the last two generations there has been a resurgence of Indigenous practices in schools, communities, and even the criminal justice system (below 7D). Unfortunately, this renaissance is hampered by settler cultural appropriation, a contemporary form of colonization.[21]

Indigenous communities have long understood the most primal Songline is nature herself.[22] Settler colonial culture, on the other hand, with its commodification of land and exploitation of nature, has been largely deaf to the earth's voice. But there are notable exceptions, from nineteenth-century Utopian communities and Transcendentalists to twentieth-century environmental writer-activists such as Rachel Carson and Wendell Berry. Agrarian spirituality, though quite different than Indigenous notions of the Earth as "relative," characterized many settler small farmers prior to industrialized agriculture, and has enjoyed a renaissance in the last generation, from permaculture to eco-psychology. My grandparents did not have as romantic a view of the land as we do today—having experienced the hardships of subsistence farming—but they certainly embodied a spirituality of land-tending. My mom would often relay tales about her father's joy of swimming in the Dnieper River, and the bountiful, delicious watermelons grown in the loamy soil along its banks. As my Grandpa Franz wrote on numerous occasions: "With the Lord's blessing, I harvested a good crop."[23] My Uncle Jake, though retired from farming, "still likes to go and help in the fields. That's where I feel closest to my God."[24]

While serial displacements repeatedly disrupted my ancestors' attachment to specific lands, they became adept at finding landscapes in their new country that resonated with those they'd left. My Grandpa Franz moved his family to Carrot River, Saskatchewan to farm at almost the exact latitude he'd left in Ufa, Russia. I glimpsed this for myself during our 2019 Ukraine pilgrimage when Janet and I stepped out of the van at the site of a former Mennonite village. Beholding a vast, open prairie, endless blue sky, and rich dark earth, we exclaimed to each other: "This looks just like Tiefengrund!" (where Janet now lives).

20. Koithan and Farrell, "Indigenous Native American Healing Traditions," 478.

21. See below 6Cx and various articles at https://unsettlingamerica.wordpress.com/tag/cultural-appropriation/.

22. See Friesen and Heinrichs, *Quest for Respect*.

23. Mierau and Reimer, *Sojourners*, 73. See also Kaufman, *Drama of a Rural Community's Life Cycle*.

24. Mierau and Reimer, *Sojourners*, 78.

Traditional spiritualties of many kinds have functioned as Songlines for past human flourishing and survival. With some revisioning they can and must continue to do so in our work of decolonization.

4C. "RIGHT NOW WE HAVE MANY TEARS . . . " EXHUMING SUBVERSIVE STORIES

For us the strongest counter-tradition to the self-aggrandizing narratives of Western settler colonialism are found in the Jewish and Christian Scriptures, which the religious "majority" *purports* to revere. Biblical stories of liberation arose from the ancient imperial periphery, not its center, and thus have always sat uneasily with the managers of power. The most obvious example in American history was how slave-holder religion silenced and marginalized prophetic texts that yearned for freedom and demanded justice, while the faith of the enslaved kept those visions alive.[25] The "unsettling" story of exodus enshrined in the Jewish liturgy of Passover has animated social movements of resistance to oppression across millennia.[26] We also find biblical stories of women's noncooperation with violence: Shiprah and Puah, Abigail and Esther, Mary and Priscilla.[27] The Gospels depict Jesus' organizing among the poor, and the early church's struggle against the Roman Empire.[28] These texts have not lost their power to contest domination, and in our opinion remain a key resource for faith-rooted decolonization movements. They are our *most* important Songline tradition.

In addition there have been robust traditions that venerate the faithful throughout the history of the church in stories and iconography of saints.[29] In that vein, a special place has been held for those killed in service of the gospel, expressed by early Anabaptists through the *Martyrs' Mirror*.[30] A copy of this tome, with its elaborate illustrations of torture, was always on my family coffee table, and as a child I would pore over it with equal parts reverence, horror, and fascination. Profiles of individuals who have

25. See e.g., Goatley, *Were You There?*; Wilson-Hartgrove, *Reconstructing the Gospel*.

26. See e.g., Walzer, *Exodus and Revolution*.

27. See e.g., Hollyday, *Clothed with the Sun*, and Winter, *WomanWisdom, WomanWord,* and *WomanWitness,* lovely studies in the witness of biblical women.

28. See e.g., Myers et al., *Say to This Mountain,* and Horsley, *Paul and Empire*. For an annotated bibliography of biblical studies in this vein, see Dykstra and Myers, *Liberating Biblical Study*, 223–45.

29. See e.g., Ellsberg, *All Saints,* and *Blessed among All Women*.

30. Edited by Thieleman Van Bragt and published in 1659. But the influence of this martyrology has not always been positive (see Roth, "Complex Legacy of the Martyrs Mirror").

embodied exemplary discipleship—"biography as theology"—is another important Songline resource.[31]

Communities also embody such examples. Black and Brown expressions of church in North America and beyond represent ways of metabolizing Christian faith that stand in tension with colonial societies.[32] Songlines of past nonconformity fire faithful imagination toward new movements of resistance and renewal within a compromised Christendom. Settlers need to learn stories of oppressed communities who have struggled for liberation—but we must practice *apprenticeship* to these traditions, not *appropriation* of them. We are deeply grateful to mentors Murphy Davis and Eduard Loring of the Open Door Community* for how they challenged and resourced us to live into an identity as "disciples of Jesus in the tradition of Martin Luther King," much as Franciscans, Methodists, or Mennonites did with their namesakes.[33]

Yet settlers cannot rely *only* on stories of other people's movements of faith and justice. Doing our own work also means discovering and claiming Songlines of conversion, solidarity, and redemption in *our* communal stories and ethnic histories. In digging into the soil of my ancestral narrative I have indeed found accounts of peaceableness from my grandparents' generation in Ukraine and Russia, some of which I've related herein. We have tried to honor these Songlines through several intentional steps. In 2008, we decided that since I was a Canadian living in California—Ched's homeland for five generations—he should formally join my clan. So at my home church in Saskatoon, our venerable old pastor Vern Ratzlaff, who had married us and buried my parents, laid his bony hands on Ched, welcoming him into the Mennonite denomination. My pilgrimage to Ukraine was another effort to honor my ancestors.

A third step to seek equilibrium between "my people, Ched's place" occurred in 2012 as part of a sabbatary celebration of our seventh year in the Ventura River watershed. In the tradition of the Catholic Worker movement, we named our home after a movement hero: my great-grandmother. "Casa Anna Schulz" was christened during a July Fourth "Interdependence Day" celebration as a center for discipleship education and organizing. We asked itinerant muralist Dimitri Kadiev to paint a mural on our patio wall that would depict stories of my forebears. After studying old family photographs

31. See McClendon *Biography as Theology*. McClendon, Ched's theological mentor, helped instigate the (re)turn toward narrative over that last half century.

32. See e.g., Douglas, *Black Christ*; Hendricks, *Universe Bends toward Justice*; Charleston and Robinson, *Coming Full Circle*; and Romero, *Brown Church*.

33. More below 7B. Myers and Enns, *Ambassadors of Reconciliation I,* reads key New Testament texts through a Kingian lens.

we'd given him, Dimitri designed the magnificent mural depicted in this book (for full description see 7A). The process of its composition and community execution during our summer ecojustice Institute was deeply satisfying.[34] This compelling visual testimony to the Landlines, Bloodlines, and Songlines of my people serves now as both a teaching tool with visitors and a focal point of memory for us.

In panel two of this mural stands my Grandpa Franz Enns (pictured at the beginning of this chapter) bending rifles, another sacred family story-cum-Songline passed down through my father. The context of this story is Red and White armies fighting for control during the Russian Civil War, raiding farms to support their efforts, confiscating land, grain, and horses. As mentioned (above 3A), my Grandpa Franz and his younger sister Anna had been left alone to manage *Johanneshof* as their parents fled to Davlekanovo. Just twenty-eight years old and not yet married, Grandpa Franz bought four big hounds in an effort to deter the "bandits," but the dogs were simply shot the next time they returned. In 1919, the battle line between the armies ran directly through *Johanneshof*, the front shifting back and forth as one army advanced and the other retreated. At one point the White Army had to make a hasty withdrawal, and in order to run faster, soldiers hid their rifles in one of Grandpa Franz's straw stacks.

Later that afternoon one of the hired men found the rifles and reported it to Franz. This was a very dangerous situation, since some of his workers were Bolshevik informers. Grandpa Franz carefully gathered and counted the rifles and put them in the shop. That night, when everyone was asleep, he snuck back to the shop and bent each rifle barrel just slightly, so that it could not be aimed to kill.[35] The next day he brought the rifles to the Red Army, making him a hero in the eyes of the local Bolsheviks (who did not perceive they were useless). Several weeks later, Mennonite men from the district were arrested, including Grandpa Franz, and taken to Bolshevik headquarters for interrogation. As they were being lined up, the officer who had received the rifles from Grandpa Franz walked into the room. Upon seeing Franz, he ordered his release—but all of the other men arrested that day were disappeared and never seen again.

The constant confiscation of resources continued, leaving farms nearly destitute. There was an outdoor shower on *Johanneshof* farmyard, with a large pit underneath to capture water so it would not spill onto the yard. During winter 1919, Grandpa Franz hid four hundred pounds of wheat

---

34. See a video about the painting of and information about this mural at: https://www.bcm-net.org/about/casa-anna-schulz.

35. For a contemporary story of decommissioning guns, see RAW Tools: Forging Peace, Disarming Hearts.*

in the cavity underneath the shower. Later, after the Bolsheviks had taken over *Johanneshof*, the weather turned unexpectedly warm, and some soldiers took a shower. The seed started to ferment, and the grate began to rise. Grandpa Franz, hiding out nearby with his sister, had to flee. "With a horse and cart borrowed from my brother-in-law Peter, I left in the dark of night," he recounted; "I fled first to Neu Samara Colony and then to Orenburg, about four hundred miles away. There I stayed for several months, until I received word that the danger seemed to be over."[36]

Though I have no writings from my grandmothers, there are stories of Mennonite women also practicing nonviolent ingenuity as they faced invading soldiers after their men had fled. They hid their children; facilitated each other's escapes; and even did battle with bureaucrats, as related in a favorite tale of my Aunt Irene. Frustrated by interminable waits in Russian government offices for immigration paperwork to be processed, mothers began refusing to change their babies' diapers in the waiting room. "They stunk up the place in hopes of moving the visa process along!"[37]

And there are moving accounts of kindness shown to our people, one of which we encountered during our pilgrimage in Ukraine. At Schoenfeld, a village our Great-great-grandfather Enns helped found in 1869, an elderly Ukrainian peasant woman we met pointed to a family cemetery plot in the yard next to hers. She told us that an Enns family had lived there before the Revolution. "They were good people," she said through our translator, then gestured toward a low-lying area about a hundred meters from us. "Look there." We made our way through the bushes, snagging our clothes and stumbling on uneven ground, finally discovering what she was referring to in a small clearing hidden by the brush. A number of tombstones had been dumped there, covered now by a tangle of weeds and small trees. Searching and scraping, we found two with the name Enns. One read: *"Janseits schwindet, Jede Traenen, Treue wird sich, wiedersehen* ("Right now, we have many tears, those that are true will see each other again"). The woman later explained that during the Stalin years Ukrainian neighbors had hauled the huge gravestones away from the cemetery and hid them in the bushes so that Soviet workers would not take them to use in building. These Ukrainians—despite their extreme poverty and suffering under Stalin's regime—had respected their Mennonite neighbors enough to make this tremendous effort to preserve their burial dignity. This was a powerful and poignant Songline

36. Mierau and Reimer, *Sojourners*, 73.

37. Irene (Enns) Baergen, conversation with Elaine Enns, Saskatoon, Saskatchewan, March 29, 2006.

for us, and inspires Ched and me to learn how to honor the human and cultural remains of Chumash departed in the lands on which we now dwell.

4D. "HANDS THAT HELD US": GENEALOGIES OF FAITH

On Mother's Day 2015, I preached at my home church in Saskatoon, Nutana Park Mennonite, which my parents had helped found in 1963. It was the first time I'd been in that sanctuary since my mom's funeral three years earlier. In her honor I wore the dress she had on at our wedding there in 1999. I was in town for my graduation from a Doctor of Ministry program at St. Andrew's College, and some of the interviewees from my research were in the congregation. Wanting to honor the women who bore and raised us, taught us and held us, I decided to address the importance *and* marginalization of female voices in our Mennonite tradition (see above 3D).

I reflected on a selection of passages from the epistles of 1 and 2 Timothy, which open an interesting window into the life of the second-generation church:

> I remind you to rekindle the gift of God that is within you through the laying on of my hands; for God did not give us a spirit of cowardice, but rather of power and love and self-discipline . . . (1 Tim 1:6–7)

> Do not neglect the gift that is in you, which was given to you through prophecy with the laying on of hands by the elders. (1 Tim 4:14)

> I am reminded of your sincere faith, a faith that lived first in your grandmother Lois and your mother Eunice and now, I am persuaded, lives in you. (2 Tim 1:5)

> Continue in what you have learned and firmly believed, knowing from whom you learned it, and how from childhood you have known the sacred writings that are able to instruct you for salvation through faith in Christ. (2 Tim 3:14–15)

The apostle Paul is here portrayed reminding his younger missionary associate of his nurture and mentoring by women, commending the many ways Timothy had been spiritually formed and educated by his grandmother and mother. In the context of this ancient patriarchal society, such public acknowledgment and acclaim was countercultural. Given that Paul had rabbinic training (Acts 22:3), it is startling that he centers the sacred education his mentee received from these women.

I like to imagine Eunice and Lois holding baby Timothy, singing him lullabies that had come from his ancestors Miriam, Deborah, and Mary, recounting tales of his people's strength and persistence.[38] The Timothy texts have provided encouragement to me, reminding me of how the genealogy of faith is constructed through passing on Songline stories of survival and flourishing, service and compassion, resistance and refusal. They concern, but also transcend, our Bloodlines; they narrate both far-away Landlines and the local landscapes we inhabit. Their transmission is best preserved by communities of conviction and purpose, passed on through songs, testimonies, and patient instruction in a living tradition. This process is most reliable when overseen by the hands and hearts of elders, who steward memory and values. The culture of communal transmission is universal to traditional societies across time and space, however diverse in expression. It is also atrophying under the deforming influences of individualism, mobility, historical amnesia, and tradition-dismissal under capitalism.

I am profoundly grateful to have been raised in a community considered "defective" from the perspective of modernity, which practiced such transmission, and especially for the women whose hands have held and helped me, and passed on stories of our people. My mom and Aunts Irma and Irene have been Remem-bearers. So is Vickie Dyck, a drama teacher at my high school who had us perform a reader's theatre rendition of Barbara Claassen Smucker's young adult novel *Days of Terror* about the *Zerrissenheit*. And so are women who have broken silencings at great cost. In my restorative justice work with victims and offenders I've learned that healing is more likely to come when we are able to tell our *whole* story, including the parts we are ashamed of, or would like to forget. Because even traumatic stories can turn into Songlines as we move on the journey from being victims (or perpetrators) to survivors to healers.

In the course of pursuing this project over the last decade, I have repeatedly encountered the deep desire of women in my community to do the hard work of facing past and present pain and injustice among ourselves and others. I have been given new eyes to see women elders—including many in my home congregation—who demonstrate the power, love, and self-discipline about which Paul spoke. I "know from whom I learned" our genealogy of faith, those who taught me the Songlines of Scripture and who laid hands on me, "rekindling the gifts" I glimpsed in my mystical vision-basket.

---

38. Hollyday, *Clothed with the Sun*, 135.

4E. QUERIES FOR NURTURING COUNTER-NARRATIVES

There are many wellsprings from which you can draw to identify Songlines in your family and community: place and nature; religion and culture; stories of ethnic identity and survival. Remember to pay attention not only to *what* you know, but also *how* you know it, and how Songlines were transmitted in your community.

1. Which Songlines did you learn in your family, and at what age(s)?

2. Which ones are from life in your ancestors' country of origin, and which from the immigrant experience?

3. What faith tradition(s) did your ancestors practice, and what spiritual impacts did immigration have?

4. What spaces of your community (workplace, church, school, or dance-hall) stewarded Songlines traditions, and in what forms?

5. Which Songlines are in danger of being lost, and why? What might you do to help preserve and strengthen such traditions?

6. What family stories narrate courage, compassion, and conscience? Do they evoke heroism or humility? Is there adequate social and historical context associated with the telling, or have they morphed into individualistic or moralistic tales?

7. Are you able to tease out troubling aspects of settler denial or dysfunction that might be woven into otherwise liberating Songlines? How might these stories be critically revised?

8. What are examples of resilience in your community? Of solidarity with other peoples, especially those who were marginalized?

9. What ethnic expressions have been retained in the transmission of Songlines?

10. How did/do ancestral Songlines stand in tension with race/class/gender socialization or expectations, then and now?

11. What exemplary individuals or social movements were inspirational to your ancestors and family?

12. Where are hidden stories of grassroots goodness and neighborliness?

13. Are there Songlines you would like to strengthen or even recontextualize for your life today?

It is important that settlers get to *this* part of doing our own work. Many of our Songlines date to "before we became white" (below 6B), and will require considerable digging. Others have become so compromised by domestication (including by churches) that they are hard to recognize or reclaim. Nevertheless, the fragments are there in greater number and significance than we might imagine. Piecing together this puzzle is as important to our healing as deconstructing settler fantasies.

Moreover, Songlines are an antidote to the temptation to be hypercritical of our settler forbears. A presumed moral superiority of hindsight, through which we would disassociate from their complicity, cannot exonerate us from our own.[39] As we said at the outset, the line between "us" and "them" is not a firewall. We carry the trauma and contradictions of our ancestors, but also their traces of courage and ingenuity. Honoring ways our people acted decently by practicing solidarity, mutual aid, and friendship—often the hardest stories to hold onto in the settler historical record—helps us recover our full humanity.

The night before my fiftieth birthday I had another vision. I felt clearly instructed to go to Wheeler Gorge, deep in North Matilija Creek Canyon, far from the cacophony of built environments. I had a strong sense that this place would guide me in the next chapter of my life. I went there the following day and sat quietly for hours by the thrum of a small, flowing stream, praying and meditating under a thick summer canopy of alder, sycamore, and oak. I was cloistered with toyon, ceanothus, and sticky monkey flower, breathing in the aroma of sage and artemisia, delighting in the soft air and birdsong. This has become a regular discipline since, though disrupted for a year by the Thomas Fire which devastated our watershed and closed the Gorge. Here I listen to the land to which I have come on my settler journey, Storylines we explore in part II.

---

39. This is a self-defeating strategy of white fragility, which we flagged at the end of chapter 1 and will explore further below 6C. This work is about complexifying, not pejorative distancing, about deconstructing white supremacy but also about identity re-formation for a decolonial future.

Figure 17: Chumash arborglyph, Tajiguas Canyon near Santa Barbara, CA, 1974.
Photo: William Myers (used with permission).

Theological Interlude
Two Biblical Warning Tales

IN THE LATE SIXTIES and early seventies, a gaggle of families from Ched's suburban Los Angeles neighborhood used to go camping over Thanksgiving on the Gaviota Coast northwest of Santa Barbara. It was, and remains, one of the last relatively undeveloped areas of chaparral habitat left in coastal southern California—and the heart of Chumash country. His time among those oak-studded canyons and pristine beaches made a huge psychic imprint on his adolescent consciousness, connecting him more to his sense of place as a fifth-generation Californian than any other experience.

His dad, Allan, loved to explore remote historic areas of the state, perhaps because his mother, Ynez Guerena, was *Californio* (Mexican Californian families who predated statehood). So the group of families often camped in Tajiguas Canyon—the former site, Ched learned much later, of the Chumash village of *taxiwa* (or *tehaja).* One year Allan called Ched's attention to an old coast live oak not far from their campsite. It was adorned with an arborglyph, probably dating to the early 1800s and thought to be a Chumash rendering of a neophyte (someone taken into the mission system) receiving communion from a Spanish padre.[1] At the time, there was no conversation between Ched and his dad about the history behind this image. The "Indian Tree," as they called it, was simply a curiosity (Ched's oldest brother took the photo at left, Figure 17). We doubt this tree exists any longer, nor would we be able to find out, since the canyon is now a private trophy ranch.

As a fourth grader, Ched dutifully built a model from soap, sugar cubes, and wooden sticks of one of the twenty-one Franciscan missions that dot the Pacific coast from San Diego to Sonoma. But this exercise, standard

---

1. For a detailed discussion of Chumash arborglyphs, see Saint-Onge et al., "Archaeoastronomical Implications of a Northern Chumash Arborglyph."

still in the California public school curriculum, was wholly devoid of context, and he was too young for critical consciousness.[2] The Indian Tree was Ched's first exposure, as an already-alienated teenager growing up in an unchurched home, to the heavy footprint of missionary colonizing history in this bioregion. And that fading photo, which has hung on his walls for forty years, always haunted him.

In the second half of this book we look at how our settler ancestors came to North America, and their (and our) relationship with and impact on Indigenous peoples living here. We don't discuss the role of missionary institutions and ideologies that helped drive, legitimate, and underwrite European colonization; this complicated and important part of the wider settler story is beyond the scope of this book. But the theological convictions underlying our project do not allow us to pass over the subject without comment.[3] This interlude offers two reflections, each shaped around an unsettling biblical text, concerning this fraught legacy. To reiterate Nikki Sanchez's dictum, this history is not the fault of contemporary Christians, but it is absolutely our responsibility (above 1A).

A. CHRISTIAN MISSION "DISROBED": THE ROAD NOT TAKEN (LUKE 9:1-6)

> When the Missionaries arrived, we natives had the land and they had the Bible. They taught us how to pray with our eyes closed. When we opened them, they had the land and we had the Bible.[4]
>
> —Jomo Kenyatta

Most would-be "progressive" settler Christians today prefer to disassociate from the painful, half-millennium-long history of missionary entanglements with colonization. We are not, however, exonerated by such

---

2. "If you grew up in California," wrote Chris Clarke in 2016, "you probably learned most of what you know about the history of California Indians while you were in fourth grade . . . California Indians still vanish from mention in the newer fourth-grade curricula by the time of the Gold Rush. They're relegated to the past tense." (Clarke, "Untold History," paras. 1, 4).

3. For the most part Mennonites did not participate in efforts to missionize Indigenous communities in North America, but see Heinrichs, "Confessing the Past." On diverse Native responses to missionary presence on the prairies, see Beaucage and LaRoque, "Two Faces of the New Jerusalem." Chris Budden's *Following Jesus in Invaded Space* explores an Australian model of decolonizing theology.

4. Now a famous adage often attributed to Desmond Tutu, it was reported in Walker, *Certain Curve of Horn*, 144. See also Achebe, *Things Fall Apart*.

a "move to innocence" (see below 6Cviii). Our society was fundamentally shaped by intimate collusion between churches and empire—regardless of whether or not one calls oneself a Christian. Many settler privileges are rooted in this legacy. To exercise "response-ability" we must resist the temptation simply to ignore this history (as conservatives do) or denounce it (as liberals do). Restorative solidarity requires going to the roots of this dis-ease in our tradition.

Jesus' so-called "Missionary Instructions" as recorded in Luke's Gospel, which we examine below, should haunt the conscience of Christendom. Their essence is: "Whichever house you enter, stay there, and leave from there" (Luke 9:4). Had Christians observed these straightforward guidelines for how to live among other peoples and places, the history of the world would be profoundly different. Jesus could not have been clearer or more unequivocal in his marching orders, as we'll shortly show. But for the most part, our ancestors in the faith ignored them. Consequently, a bitter legacy of domination and genocide has been tattooed like an arborglyph on every land around this wide world.[5]

Because the history of Christian missions is long and complex, we want to qualify the above generalizations by making four preliminary observations. First, it is important to acknowledge that the spread of Christianity across time (two millennia), space (the entire globe) and cultures (almost none untouched) hasn't *always* and *everywhere* been synonymous with colonization. If we assume a simplistic story we miss significant episodes in which the gospel spread organically and peaceably, and often *not* through the agency of white folk.[6]

Second, it is equally crucial to recognize that all too ubiquitously over the last 500 years Christian missions *did* fuse cross and sword, conversion and conquest, evangelization and subjugation. Because of this apostasy, the history of contact between Indigenous and settler cultures in the Americas has been characterized by the latter's duplicity and violations, right up to the present.

Third, Christianity, since its inception, has been intrinsically mission-driven. The first disciples took up Jesus' annunciation of God's kingdom as an alternative to the Roman Empire, a vision of grace, social equality, mutual aid, and healing. This message of liberation and wholeness spread rapidly among those who suffered under Rome's slave-based, extractive economy. It was a subversive mission with real costs, as reflected in Luke's

5. A good overview is Tinker, *Missionary Conquest.*

6. See e.g., portraits of Indigenous missionaries Samson Occom (Mohegan), William Apess (Pequot), and George Copway (Ojibway) in Peyer, *Tutor'd Mind,* and the more detailed study in Gura, *Life of William Apess.* See also Andrews, *Native Apostles.*

portrait of the apostle Paul in Acts, who confesses: "The Holy Spirit testifies to me in every city that imprisonment and persecutions are waiting for me. But I do not count my life of any value to myself, if only I may . . . testify to the *good news* (Gk. *euangelion*) of God's grace" (Acts 20:23–24).

The movement's use of the Greek term *euangelion*, appropriated from the lexicon of Roman propaganda, was polemical and pointedly political. Caesar's public relations machine boasted that the *Pax Romana* brought *euangelia* to the world, for which every city in the Eastern Empire was obliged to keep a festival, where sacrifices were offered on behalf of the emperor's "grace." Imperial media proclaimed this myth everywhere, including on everyday coins such as the *denarius* that circulated in first-century Palestine. It depicted the goddess *Providentia* holding a globe in her right hand, symbolizing world-sovereignty. Inscribed in Latin: *AETERNITAS,* Rome's hegemony forever. The early church's counter *euangelion* challenged this political cosmology, announcing the restoration of God's sovereignty through Christ the "Lord" (Caesar's title). Picking a fight in this war of myths is why evangelists like Paul landed in jail.

What began as a grassroots mission from *below* for liberation *from* empire, however, began to change, especially after the adoption of Christianity by Emperor Constantine in the fourth century CE. Increasingly it became a project of imperial *conquest* from *above* in the name of a now-institutionalized church.[7] A millennium later, in late-medieval Europe, Christendom's mission of hegemonic expansion began to be fused with powerful mythologies of ethnic superiority, codified in papal *pronuncimientos* that articulated a Doctrine of Discovery.[8] Of the many white supremacist conceits that followed, perhaps none was more consequential than the notion that the Europeans' arrival on other shores represented a religious epiphany—of enlightenment for "pagan" inhabitants, and of entitlement for Christian subjugators.[9] This ideology drove a long history of missions-as-conquest, with which most modern churches have yet fully to come to terms, notwithstanding denominational "missions moratoria" over the last half century.[10]

7. For an overview, see e.g., Odahl, *Constantine and the Christian Empire.*

8. See Sanders, *Lost Tribes and Promised Lands;* Williams, *American Indian in Western Legal Thought;* and Newcomb, *Pagans in the Promised Land.*

9. This is archetypally captured in Joshua Shaw's Manifest Destiny-era painting "Coming of the White Man" (1850), which depicts Indigenous people blinded by, and cowering before, a sunrise that brings a European tall ship from the east; above them fly geese (representing "naturalistic" migration patterns). See it at https://www.csub.edu/~gsantos/img0105.html.

10. Global movements of independence from colonial rule in the mid-twentieth century and the growing indigenization of many Third World churches led mainstream North Atlantic denominations to rethink the missionary legacy and vocation, and in

Fourth, we must also acknowledge Christianity is not the *only* missionary movement historically, nor should mission be seen as inherently religious. "Mission" can be defined generically as convictional and critical engagement with the world by those with a vibrant vision of how that world can be changed. Consider, for example, the following transformative missionary-type movements over the last two centuries, all but the third of which were wholly, or in part, secular:

- abolitionists and civil rights activists working to end slavery and segregation;

- labor activists organizing for worker-enfranchisement and equity;

- the Ghost Dance movement of the 1890s, led by a prophet who called native people to defy the government's attempts to disappear their culture and to re-ground themselves in the old ways;[11]

- revolutionary struggles against colonial regimes throughout the Third World; and

- feminists educating and organizing for gender equality.

These and other social movements have spread their perspectives with evangelical fervor, often through classic "churchly" tactics such as cajoling, moral shaming, apocalyptic warnings, or itinerant proselytizing.

Other examples of secular missionizing are far less sanguine. For example, states have for centuries aggressively spread a "gospel" of military triumphalism, mobilizing prejudice and xenophobia to recruit civilians to become soldiers. Here it's worth taking a close look at another example from the colonial project in the U.S. With secularization in the late nineteenth century, ideologies of discovery morphed into doctrines of Progress and Manifest Destiny, as depicted in John Gast's well-known 1872 painting (Figure 18).[12]

---

the early 1970s the World Council of Churches called for a moratorium. As Paul Verghese, East Indian theologian and former associate general secretary of the WCC, put it in 1974: "Today it is economic imperialism or neocolonialism that is the pattern of missions," which he called "the greatest enemy of the gospel" (Goodwin, *Eclipse in Mission*, 7). The moratorium caused yet another split between mainstream churches and evangelicals (for many of whom "soul-winning" remains central).

11. See e.g., Mooney, *Ghost-Dance Religion*; Smoak, *Ghost Dances and Identity*.

12. See more examples of similar art at Truettner, *West as America*.

Figure 18: *American Progress*, oil painting by John Gast, 1872. Public domain (Autry Museum of the West, Los Angeles, CA). Image source: https://commons. wikimedia.org/wiki/File:American_Progress_(John_Gast_painting).jpg#file.

Originally a recruiting poster issued shortly after completion of the U.S. transcontinental railroad in 1869, it sought to assure settlers in the east that it was "safe" to move to the far west. It unabashedly celebrates the inexorable march of white domination across a prairie-centric continent, tellingly led by a militia member, who is followed closely by resource extractors and then farmers (foreground). Westward transport dominates the middle of the composition, heading toward the Pacific (upper left): a covered wagon (and in the far distance a wagon train), a Pony Express rider, a stagecoach, and no less than three locomotives, as merchant ships ply the Mississippi River (far right). The sun rises behind them while Indigenous people, together with bison and bear, flee into the darkness (left). The symbolism is firmly secular: that's not an angel at the center of the painting, but an image of "Columbia" (the feminized version of Columbus), presented as the mythic goddess of liberty and the personification of America. She lays telegraph wire with her left hand, in her right is a "School Book" (*not* a Bible)! Such settler art glorifying conquest and colonization was ubiquitous in the nineteenth century, and still adorns many public buildings around the U.S. today.[13]

13. For example, our colleague Jim Bear Jacobs has drawn attention to the racist nature of murals at the Minnesota State Capitol (see https://healingmnstories.wordpress.

But missionary-style Manifest Destiny persists today, as U.S. corpora-tions roam the globe in search of resources to extract and markets to domi-nate, evangelistically promising economic growth and capitalist "fixes" to local social problems. One could argue the archetypal twenty-first-century American corporate representative abroad has fewer scruples about exploit-ing people and land than the most ethnocentric nineteenth-century Chris-tian missionary!

Powerful social movements, then, are usually missionary, for good or for ill. The critical ethical questions are therefore:

- mission for *what*?
- *how* is the mission embodied?
- with *whom* and *where*?
- and most importantly, to *whose benefit*?

For any great social cause (religious or secular), pressing a strong cri-tique and a "good news" alternative is one thing. *Imposing* a problem analy-sis and its solution—especially by military, economic, or cultural force—is quite another. The moral crux is whether a missionary vocation can remain structurally and ideologically free of the politics of domination—and Chris-tian movements are not alone in having failed this test.

The ancient key for avoiding missionary oppression, according to Je-sus' original instructions to his followers, is the ethos of *hospitality*—given and received. The perverted gospel of colonization was (and still is) predi-cated upon colonization of the gospel: the (often theologically elaborate) ways churches ignore, suppress, or rationalize away Jesus' clear directives. Given the focus of this book and our own faith convictions, it is necessary to revisit these roots to understand where we Christians went so wrong.

Luke underlines the importance of Jesus' missionary orders by reporting them twice: in the commissioning of the Twelve (Luke 9:1–6) and again in the (more elaborate) sending of the Seventy (10:1–20). We'll examine the shorter version, laid out here as a chiasm:

---

com/capitol-art/). A statue of Columbus and Queen Isabella standing in the middle of the Rotunda at the California State Capitol was the target of native activists in 2018 in a Poor Peoples Campaign action* in which we took part (see Dickman, "Protesters of Christopher Columbus 'Genocide' Climb Statue").

A Jesus called the twelve together and gave them power and authority over all demons and to cure diseases, and sent them out
to proclaim the kingdom of God and to heal.

  B He said to them, "Take nothing for your journey, no staff,
  nor bag, nor bread, nor money—not even an extra tunic.

    C Whatever house you enter, stay there, and leave from
    there.

  B' Wherever they do not welcome you, as you are leaving that
  town shake the dust off your feet as a testimony against
  them."

A' They departed and went through the villages, bringing the
good news and curing diseases everywhere.

—Luke 9:1–6 (NRSV)

Let's look at how this passage speaks to the critical questions just posed.
What: The purpose of Jesus' mission was twofold. He "empowered"
his disciples to:

i) proclaim an alternative sociopolitical order called the kingdom of God; and

ii) heal (Greek *therapeuein*) people oppressed by the demonic
and by disease.

Each practice is iterated in verses 1 and 6, framing the passage for
emphasis (A, A'), and identified as "good news." Since every human society
contains elements of both political oppression and personal illness, a mission that organizes and advocates for freedom, justice, and health would
seem to resonate with universal moral values.

How: The significance of the first instruction (9:3) cannot be overstated: "Don't carry your baggage into your host community." This is not
just about traveling light; it's about going vulnerably. Forbidding staff and
bag means missionaries are not in control. Jesus' rhetoric alludes (by way of
contrast) to the old story of David, who famously approached the foreigner
Goliath with a *staff* and a *bag* full of five stones—in other words to do battle
(1 Sam 17:40). Too often in Western history, missionary baggage was wea-
ponized, since the ultimate goal was not liberation, but domination; not to
heal, but to usurp. Similarly, the directive to travel without bread and money
refers to the means of sustenance on the road. *Not* to be self-sufficient makes
travelers dependent upon their hosts, who thus retain the upper hand.

The counsel to possess only one tunic is interesting. A "change of
clothes" would have been a rare luxury among peasant Middle Easterners.

Moreover, in Luke 3:11, John the Baptist exhorts: "If you have two coats, give one to the poor." Presumably, Jesus is ensuring that missionaries have already distributed their surplus. We might further extrapolate that a limited wardrobe means that over time they will eventually need to adopt the local style of dress! Traditions of dress matter: they are a way of either fitting in or remaining apart; of cultural imposition or adaptation. European Christian missionaries almost always got this backward. Not only did they bring trunks full of their own culture; they also imposed this baggage, including their costumes, on their native hosts. This is illustrated by the well-known image (Figure 19) of the eight-year-old Cree Thomas Moore Keesick before and after his enrollment in Regina Indian Residential School, Saskatchewan, a keystone of colonial policies of forced assimilation.[14] How different things would have been had Christians practiced a "disrobed" mission: naked (so to speak) and unashamed!

Figure 19: Thomas Moore Keesick before and after his enrollment in Regina Indian Residential School, SK. Undated archival photo from an 1896 Department of Indian Affairs annual report.

14. This photo is found, with helpful analysis, at https://sites.google.com/a/hdsb.ca/gwss-chc2d/unit-1-1914-1929/7-how-did-residential-schools-impact-native-canadians. See also Benjoe, "Thomas Moore Keesick More Than Just a Face," and Brady and Hiltz, "Archaeology of an Image." See also Niessen, *Shattering the Silence,* and below 5C and 7C.

With whom and where: The middle of Jesus' three instructions concern the missionary's responses toward "welcoming" spaces (9:4). We should note that the phrase "whichever house you might enter" (Greek *heis ēn an oikian eiselthēte*) connotes a conditional or contingent prospect—something that cannot be assumed, much less demanded. Luke's Jesus then underlines two crucial and contrasting imperatives regarding the guest's positionality:

- "stay in that place. . ." (Gk *ekei menete*, meaning to "remain, abide, or continue on");
- ". . .and leave from there" (Gk *exerchesthe*, which could be translated "and be gone").

This sentiment is expanded in Luke's longer version: "Remain in the same house, eating and drinking whatever they provide . . . Do not move about from house to house. Whenever you enter a town and its people welcome you, eat what is set before you" (Luke 10:7–8). In other words, don't move around looking for a better deal, don't demand special treatment, and eat locally and gratefully (stated twice).

The missionary remains a guest, whose task is to understand the new place and people, which as anyone who has lived cross-culturally knows, can take a long time! Being hosted is the opposite of a colonizing settlement, because eventually the missionary *leaves*. That these instructions were taken seriously is indicated by the narratives of Paul's missionary itineration in Acts and his own epistles. Should the missionary be invited to stay permanently—though Jesus does not include this prospect, nor did Paul "settle" in the places he missionized—it is on the terms of the host community. The tenure as guest presumably trains missionaries how to enculturate into the local way of life, so that the good news might indigenize.

All of this is predicated, however, on finding locals willing to provide more than "passing through" hospitality, and Jesus realistically assumes there will be places where this is *not* the case (9:5). Since this is everywhere a distinct possibility, a final simple instruction is included: if you are unwelcome, leave. Don't retaliate, don't force yourself on the locals, and don't take over their country! Move on. The ritual of shaking off the dust from one's feet is a symbolic gesture that is important to Luke (it also appears several times in Acts).[15] In Luke 10:11, Jesus describes it as a form of protest, associating it with the story of Sodom, whose primal sin was lack of hospitality to strangers (contrary to how most Christians understand that old tale).[16] This

15. Paul leaves Iconium (Acts 13:51) and later Corinth (18:6) in such fashion, though the same gesture is used *against* him by his Jerusalem opponents (21:23).

16. In Genesis 19, the Sodomites refuse and then abuse the very angels Abraham

confirms inhospitality as a serious problem, especially for missionaries. But all one can do is point it out. If people don't have ears to hear good news—providing of course that the missionary's telling and showing of the gospel is credible and respectful—then try elsewhere. Done and dusted, as it were.

European missionaries on Turtle Island almost always initially encountered generous hospitality from Indigenous peoples they met; indeed, welcoming strangers was and is endemic to traditional cultures everywhere. Settler societies in North America, claims Roger Epp, were "founded on an act of sharing that is almost unimaginable in its generosity—not only land but food, agricultural techniques, practical knowledge, and trade routes."[17] But Indigenous hospitality was very soon abused by the guests, who as double agents of both church and colonial powers pursued objectives more suited to conquest than to community.

At the center of the chiastic structure of Jesus' teaching in Luke 9:1–6 is the command to respect one's host by learning how to live within the limits of their hospitality, and knowing when to leave. How different history would have been had Christians practiced "unsettling" styles of mission: embodying the good news of healing and liberation and then moving on. Instead we are haunted by the oft-repeated lament of African leader Jomo Kenyatta cited above. Our missionary ancestors too often tolerated or even promoted policies of "killing and taking possession"—an ancient formula of domination illustrated in a second biblical object lesson.

B. NABOTH'S *NAHALA*: A TALE OF TWO QUEENS

> The story of Naboth is an old one, but it is repeated every day.
>
> —St. Ambrose, *De Nabuthae*[18]

Queen Lili'uokalani (1838–1917), the last Constitutional monarch of the sovereign nation of Hawai'i, was deposed in 1893 in a *putsch* engineered by a coalition of white settler missionaries, traders, and plantation owners. They had been scheming for fifteen years to prompt the U.S. to annex Hawai'i, just as American settlers in Mexican California had done a half century earlier. A heartbreaking appeal was penned by the Indigenous queen as she languished under house arrest, concluding her open letter to "honest Americans," whose consciences she hoped to awaken after their nation's colonial takeover of her homeland:

---

and Sarah had welcomed in Genesis 18.

17. Epp, *We Are All Treaty People*, 133 (citing James Tully).

18. See below n. 38.

Oh honest Americans, as Christians hear me for my downtrod-
den people! . . . Quite as warmly as you love your country, so
they love theirs. With all your goodly possessions, covering a
territory so immense that there yet remain parts unexplored . . .
do not covet the little vineyard of Naboth's, so far from your
shores, lest the punishment of Ahab fall upon you, if not in your
day, in that of your children.[19]

Lili'uokalani, a devout Christian, was invoking the story of Naboth's
Vineyard, an ancient tale that features a very different queen: the infamous
Jezebel (see below). It narrates the struggle between powerful interests who
expropriate land for profit and the people *of* that land who are displaced or
disappeared. These two queens represent different sides of the colonizing
project throughout history: Indigenous peoples are dispossessed of land
and resources by militarily powerful settlers who mask their violence with
the rhetoric of nobility, tactics of deception, and false covenants.

Captain James Cook came to the Hawaiian Islands in 1778 (shortly
after the advent of Spanish settlers in California). New England Congre-
gational missionaries followed in 1820, and with their pejorative view of
native culture, set about instilling their blend of Puritan morals and capitalist values.[20] Over the next half century these families and their descendants
became wealthy, able to buy land, launch businesses, establish plantations,
and influence the Hawaiian native aristocracy. This colonizing trend was
challenged during David Kalākaua's reign (1874–1891), which tried to reverse *haole* (white) domination of the Hawaiian economy and government,
and vowed to restore waning native rights. As a result, the "Missionary Party" and other foreigners who favored annexation to the U.S. grew increasingly hostile to Kalākaua, and in 1887 formed a group called the Hawaiian
League. On July 1, a local militia of Americans backed by the League forced
Kalākaua to sign a new constitution at gunpoint. Nicknamed the "Bayonet
Constitution," it removed much of the king's executive power and deprived
most Indigenous Hawaiians of their voting rights.[21]

Upon Kalākaua's death in January, 1891, Lili'uokalani became the first
Hawaiian female monarch. Shortly thereafter she responded to petitions
from Hawaiians to abrogate the Bayonet Constitution, and began drafting a
new one that would restore power to the republican monarchy and voting

19. Liliuokalani, *Hawaii's Story by Hawaii's Queen*, 373.

20. See Munger, "Civilizers or Conquerors?," and Kuykendall, *Hawaiian Kingdom, 1778–1854*, 100–16.

21. See a good summary at https://hawaiiankingdom.org/blog/the-1887-bayonet-constitution-the-beginning-of-the-insurgency/; for a full account, see Dougherty, *To Steal a Kingdom*.

rights to disenfranchised Hawaiians and Asians. This became the proximate cause for the American overthrow of the kingdom, as foreign businessmen claimed Lili'uokalani had "virtually abdicated" by challenging the 1887 Constitution. On January 14, 1893, a group calling itself the "Committee of Safety" implemented plans to depose the queen and secure annexation by the U.S. Two days later, U.S. Marines came ashore in Honolulu Harbor under "orders of neutrality," yet effectively forced the queen (who had no standing military) to step down the next day. She agreed to *temporarily* relinquish her throne in order to avoid loss of life. "I do," Lili'uokalani pronounced, "under this protest, and impelled by said forces, yield my authority until such time as the Government of the U.S. shall, upon the facts being presented to it, undo the action of its representative and reinstate me in the authority which I claim as the constitutional sovereign of the Hawaiian Islands."[22]

The settler colonial machine moved swiftly. A provisional government composed of European and American businessmen was instituted until a U.S. take-over could be achieved (large plantation owners, heavily dependent on low-wage workers, favored annexation rather than statehood so as not to be subject to U.S. labor laws). On February 1, the American "ambassador" proclaimed Hawai'i to be a protectorate of the U.S., which a *New York Times* headline decried as the "Political Crime of the Century."[23] In Washington, President Grover Cleveland commissioned an investigation, which concluded that the overthrow of Lili'uokalani was illegal and that U.S. diplomats and troops had acted inappropriately. Congress responded with a rival investigation which in February 1894 found all parties not guilty— with the exception of the queen! On July 4, 1894, a Republic of Hawaii was proclaimed. Sanford Dole, a plantation mogul and longtime opponent of the monarchy, was appointed president. It was immediately recognized by the U.S. as a protectorate.

Lili'uokalani was arrested in January 1895 after a failed attempt to restore her to power led by Robert William Kalanihiapo Wilcox.[24] She was sentenced to five years of hard labor in prison by a military tribunal and fined $5,000, later commuted to house arrest at 'Iolani Palace. There she began work on her autobiography and wrote poetry and songs, most famously

22. Dougherty, *To Steal a Kingdom*, 169.

23. Siler, "Queen and the Clevelands," para. 5. See her detailed study, *Lost Kingdom*. Malia Boyd's review notes: "Siler underscores another bitter footnote to the story: while [contemporary] Hawaiians vie for political recognition that may never come, many descendants of those who profited . . . remain some of the state's wealthiest and most influential landholders" ("Other Side of Paradise," para. 9).

24. The queen denied knowledge of this plan at her trial; for more, see Starr, "Robert Wilcox and the Revolution of 1895."

"Aloha Oe," still sung around the world today. She abdicated her throne in exchange for the release of (and commutation of death sentences on) her jailed supporters, and spent the rest of her life protesting the theft of Hawaiian sovereignty and land.

In 1898—the height of the Gilded Age—Hawai'i became an incorporated territory of the U.S., the final chapter in the three-century westward march of American settler colonialism. The islands immediately became the launching pad for the expansion of that project into an international empire, as a strategic way-station for the U.S. Navy to Asia. During the ensuing Spanish-American War in the Philippines, the U.S. took control of more than a million acres of Crown land in Hawai'i. That same year Lili'uokalani published *Hawaii's Story*, which closes with the haunting of Naboth cited above.

Lili'uokalani embraced this scriptural tale as a Songline, a "remembearing" of colonial dispossession and the promise of divine justice. She understood it as a call to the prophetic faith of Elijah to expose and resist the Ahabs of this world, and closed her memoir with a theological warning to the American public. "Be not deceived, God is not mocked," the queen cautioned:

> The people to whom your fathers told of the living God, and taught to call "Father," and whom the sons now seek to despoil and destroy, are crying aloud to Him in their time of trouble; and He will keep His promise, and will listen to the voices of His Hawaiian children lamenting for their homes.[25]

Lili'uokalani was holding American Protestantism's missionary project accountable to a God who hears the groans of the oppressed (Exod 3). Her testimony retains the power to animate our political imagination for decolonization more than a century later. But to understand and honor her witness, we must explore the story to which she appeals as an archetypal parable of empire vs. indigeneity.

∼

First Kings 21 (see Appendix II for full text) is a relatively free-standing narrative unit inserted into the Deuteronomic history of the Omrid dynasty. Its canonical placement suggests its ancient standing as a revered cautionary tale from the Elijah cycle. The story pits the famously apostate Israelite King Ahab and his Sidonian Queen Jezebel against the traditional landowner and protagonist Naboth. Hebrew Bible scholar Ellen Davis rightly calls this "an

---

25. Liliuokalani, *Hawaii's Story*, 373–74. On ecclesial and governmental reparations in 1993, see below 7D.

emblematic tale of two economic systems or cultures in conflict, each with a different principle of land tenure."[26] Most contemporary readers, socialized as we are into the culture of real estate deals and state exercise of eminent domain, see no problem with Ahab's proposition. From our settler vantage point, the king appears to make a generous offer (21:2), while Naboth's unequivocal refusal seems unreasonable (v. 3). But from an Indigenous perspective, the struggle between Naboth's ancestral land-stewardship and Ahab's royal land-grab represents a perennial, and vastly asymmetrical contest, portrayed here in grim parody.

The setting is germane (v. 1): the Jezreel Valley was then (and still is today) the agricultural heartland of Israel. Ahab doesn't live in a house, but a "palace," a term the Bible usually reserves for foreign kings (and it is just his winter residence!). Naboth, on the other hand, is from the traditional agrarian class. The key to understanding his perspective lies in the Hebrew term *nahala* (v. 3). Poorly translated as "possession" or "inheritance," it rather connotes a sense of ancestral stewardship of land that is understood as a gift from the Creator, its use contingent upon an intergenerationally enduring covenant relationship. Tellingly, there is no appropriate word in English that expresses such a meaning (having developed alongside the rise of capitalism). Our attitudes toward land—long shaped by ideologies of ownership and "productivity"—make it difficult for us to comprehend *nahala* as a relationship free of commodification. The only line Naboth speaks in the entire story articulates concisely his Indigenous cosmology: the land does not belong to him, he belongs to the land (v. 3).

Davis points out that Naboth's objection is predicated on the theological notion of impurity (*halila*): to sell the land would *defile* him. In a few strokes the biblical storyteller has captured the incommensurability of two ways of life that has defined the history of civilization. Lili'uokalani invoked this story because it narrates the essential conflict between an aggressive political-legal culture based upon an ideology of land possession and one in which there is *no word for land ownership*. The former has prevailed historically and globally by force of arms, followed by economic and legal appropriation, from Ahab to Canadian and American settler states. A 1911 U.S. Department of the Interior advertisement depicts this succinctly (Figure 20).[27]

The biblical tale has its own social context. The expanding power of the Omrid regime brought an intensification of land expropriation and

26. Davis, *Scripture, Culture and Agriculture,* 111; Davis's reading of this text is illuminating.

27. The poster portrays Not Afraid of Pawnee (Yankton Sioux tribe), and indicates the average prices of tribal lands per acre. Image at http://www.californiaindianeducation.org/indian_land/for_sale/.

centralized command economics to early Iron Age Israel. Ahab (ca. 870–850 BCE) aligned by marriage with Canaanite elites (thus the narrative's "casting of Phoenician Jezebel as villainess").[28] Their "foreign and domestic policies . . . were enriching for the elite but difficult or disastrous for small farmers," writes Davis, and "required the appropriation and redistribution of food commodities on a large scale, and thus of the conversion of Israel's economy from one focused on local subsistence to a state-controlled economy designed to generate surpluses of the key crops."[29] Traditional smallholders were compelled to grow for export in a system controlled by urban managers, or were forced off the land by debt or tribute burdens. The result was the disenfranchisement of traditional subsistence agriculture, destruction of village life, inequality of wealth, and degradation of local ecosystems. These impacts are all too familiar to native people in modernity, from Lili'uokalani to contemporary Cree communities in northern Alberta facing the largest extraction project on earth at the Tar Sands.[30]

The rise of socioeconomic disparity in ancient Israel provoked two waves of prophetic protest enshrined in the Hebrew Bible: Elijah and Elisha in the ninth century BCE, and Amos, Hosea, Isaiah, and Micah in the eighth. These dissidents railed against the ruling class while reasserting Sabbath covenants to try to preserve the old agrarian system of mutual aid and equity in the face of elite "structural adjustments."[31] The Naboth story lies at the roots of this prophetic tradition.

The plot commences with an account of the sinister royal conspiracy to seize what Naboth refuses to sell (vv. 4–16). This was not a provincial dispute over eminent domain, but a political power play through which Ahab attempted to break agrarian pockets of resistance to his growing royal hegemony.[32] This may have been why he moved his winter palace into the Jezreel Valley (v. 1); this was not unlike putting a settler fort in the heart of Indian Territory in the nineteenth century, or a U.S. military base in the middle of tribal areas of Afghanistan today. The ancient tale captures the

28. Rentería, "Elijah/Elisha Stories," 91.

29. Davis, *Scripture, Culture and Agriculture*,113.

30. See summary by the Indigenous Environmental Network* at https://www.ienearth.org/what-we-do/tar-sands/.

31. For a popular summary, see Myers, *Biblical Vision of Sabbath Economics.*

32. Davis suggests Ahab's desire for a "vegetable garden" (21:2) was a ruse, given the much higher value of an established vineyard. His actual purpose was "to expropriate Naboth's vineyard and produce wine, first for his own table, and then for the export economy" (*Scripture, Culture and Agriculture,* 112). Lavish displays of wealth, she notes, were strategies through which elites maintained power, secured trade deals, formed political alliances, and bought off potential opponents.

continuing story of empire: resources that can't be accessed by persuasion (or market seduction) will be taken by force.

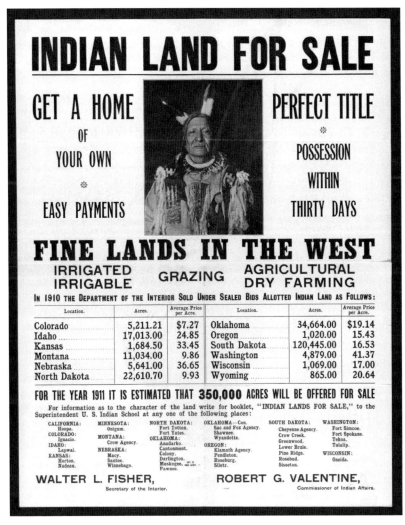

Figure 20: Indian Land for Sale poster, U.S. Department of the Interior broadside, 1911. Photo is of Not Afraid of Pawnee (Yankton Sioux); advertisement indicates average prices of tribal lands per acre. Image at Library of Congress website: https://www.loc.gov/item/2015657622/.

Naboth, a recalcitrant traditionalist like Liliʻuokalani, refuses to sell out, a stance recounted three times by his incredulous and outraged antagonists (vv. 4, 6, 13). Unable to co-opt Naboth, the regime sets about eliminating him. Jezebel becomes the main actor in this sordid plot, while Ahab is portrayed as a sulking little boy who can't get what he wants. "Are you exercising sovereignty or not?" she taunts (v. 7). This unflattering portrait has all the elements of a political cartoon; in fact, Ahab was a powerful warrior and stern ruler who lost few battles and brooked no opposition. The Bible is full of such political satire and dark caricature, traditionally a rhetorical weapon of the disenfranchised.[33] Jezebel's underhanded dealings are, for example, echoed later in the Gospel parody of a drunken Herod conscripting women to help murder the inconvenient prophet John the Baptist (Mark 6:17–28); and again in Jesus's trial before the Jerusalem authorities, convicted by false witnesses.[34]

The Phoenician queen, agent of the nearby powerful and aggressive city-states of Tyre and Sidon, knows how to break native resistance. Naboth is brought in on trumped-up charges, his refusal to sell characterized as a "curse" on the king (vv. 8–10).[35] The local village assembly of elders, of which Naboth was a member, is turned against him, doubtless by granting favors to those who cooperated with the conspiracy. This is part of the archetypal story: divide, then conquer. Local leaders collaborate with the regime so as not to share Naboth's fate, only to end up losing their way of life, too.

The narrative depicts the worst kind of political and moral behavior. This plot to murder an innocent man is:

- veiled in the piety of a public fast;
- engineered by false witnesses (perhaps the worst sin in all of Torah); and
- couched in terms of blasphemy against God *and the king* (as if the two were equivalent!).

Nevertheless, the despicable plan—which makes a mockery of sacred ritual, community deliberation, and theological confession all at once—is dutifully carried out, the careful repetition of each detail meant to underline its depravity (vv. 11–13). The depressing finality of Naboth's demise and land foreclosure is again reiterated three times (vv. 14–16).

But just as the king is about to take legal possession of the land he covets, a Songline suddenly opens a new chapter in the resistance with an intervention by a wilderness prophet (vv. 17–29). Elijah has already skirmished repeatedly with Ahab (1 Kgs 17–19), and has gone into hiding for fear of his life (18:3–4). Moreover, Jezebel, called by the narrator "the killer of the prophets of Israel," has a standing vendetta against Elijah (19:2). Despite

33. On parody as a subversive strategy, see Scott, *Weapons of the Weak,* 137–57. Also Weisman, *Political Satire in the Bible.*

34. See Myers, *Binding the Strong Man,* 214–17 and 369–38.

35. Judith Todd interprets this strategy as accusing Naboth of "reneging on a deal" ("Pre-Deuteronomistic Elijah Cycle," 33).

the obvious dangers of confronting these rulers with their public crimes, their assault on the traditional way of life in Jezreel is so egregious that the beleaguered prophet rousts himself once more to speak truth to power.

Elijah pronounces a divine double indictment (21:19): murder and expropriation, again repeated three times in the narrative (vv. 15, 16, 19). This is surely the most concise definition of settler colonialism's crimes across history. The king rightly understands the prophet to be his enemy: "Ah, *you* again!" he laments wearily (v. 20a). Elijah's retort is sharply ironic, accusing the one whose land policies are creating debt slaves across the latifundial-ized economic landscape of having sold *himself* into slavery to his Phoeni-cian overlords (v. 20b).[36] The eventual result of oppressive politics will be reciprocal violence: the power of death is contagious. Elijah describes the murderer's fate in graphic detail (vv. 21–24).

The epilogue (vv. 25–29) is also instructive to settler readers. After reiterating that "there was no one as evil as Ahab," the narrator reports his surprising response to Elijah's indictment: the king "tore his clothes and put sackcloth over his bare flesh, and fasted" (v. 27). Is this unlikely repentance part of the political cartoon? This depends upon how we interpret God's explanation to Elijah, which closes the story: "Have you seen how Ahab has humbled himself before me? . . . I will not bring the disaster in his days; but in his son's days I will bring the disaster on his house" (v. 29). It articulates an important dialectal realism we often find in biblical narratives: personal efforts to "turn around" are meaningful, even among the powerful, but by themselves they do not change political systems. Ahab's penitence—notably there is no mention of any change in Jezebel's character—can at most only postpone the collapse of his regime, which his own policies make inevitable. As narrated later in 2 Kings 9, the Omrid dynasty indeed expires in the next generation.[37] As for Jezebel, her sons bleed to death on the very ground of Naboth's vineyard, and the queen herself is thrown out of a palace window by her own attendants (another cartoon; 2 Kgs 9:30–37). The violence of colonization's "murder and dispossession" ultimately consumes its perpe-trators: divine judgment as historical consequence.

36. "Latifundialization in social scientific literature is generally defined as the pro-cess of land accumulation . . . in the hands of a few wealthy landowners to the depriva-tion of the peasantry" (Premnath, "Latifundialization and Isaiah 5.8–10," 49). The great Abraham Heschel points out that, ironically, "the charge falsely brought against Naboth and for which he was condemned . . . could now have been brought rightly against Elijah" (*Prophets II*, 259).

37. For conflicting archaeological evidence about the Omrides, see https://en.wikipedia.org/wiki/Omrides.

A millennium and a half before Liliʻuokalani, Saint Ambrose, Archbishop of Milan, similarly invoked Naboth's legacy to protest injustice. *De Nabuthae* was written in the last decades of the fourth century CE. This was just two generations after the Christian church had made its fateful deal with Constantine, after which it would be colonized by the Roman Empire almost beyond recognition. Its opening lines are a lament that echoes down the corridor of ages, as if Ambrose was summarizing the countless acts of genocide and dispossession that empires had and would inflict on people of the land:

> The story of Naboth is an old one, but it is repeated every day. Who among the rich does not daily covet others' goods? Who among the wealthy does not make every effort to drive the poor person out from his little plot and turn the needy out from the boundaries of his ancestral fields? Who is satisfied with what is his? What rich person's thoughts are not preoccupied with his neighbor's possessions?
>
> It is not one Ahab who was born, therefore, but—what is worse—Ahab is born every day, and never does he die as far as this world is concerned. For each one who dies there are many others who rise up; there are more who steal property than who lose it. It is not one poor man, Naboth, who was slain; every day Naboth is struck down, every day the poor man is slain.[38]

These searing words confirm the biblical story as an enduring warning parable about all who "kill" traditional people and "take possession" of their *nahala*, "every day" of our history.

～

These two warning tales from our deep religious past—the radical teaching of Jesus regarding missionary behavior and the ghost of Naboth—ought to trouble us North American Christians. The virulent legacy of colonizing missions explains why so many justice-seeking people today, Indigenous and other, have shaken the dust from *their* feet in protest of Western Christianity. The great task facing us, and the future of gospel mission, is to be accountable to—not evasive of—this dysfunctional inheritance. We can yet heed the witness of Mother Liliʻuokalani, and heal this haunted history through practices of reschooling, restorative solidarity, and reparation.[39]

---

38. Ambrose, *De Nabuthae*. Full text can be found at https://hymnsandchants.com/Texts/Sermons/Ambrose/OnNaboth.htm.

39. See below chapter 8. For more biblical reflections in the vein of this interlude,

Can we Christians reimagine a "disrobed" and "unsettling" style of mission focused *only* on healing and liberation? Can we stand in solidarity with the descendants of Naboth? Or will our efforts seem too little and too late in a world facing global ultimatums—the ecological consequences of the social systems we have inherited—such as climate catastrophe and viral pandemics, both of which affect the poor first and worst? The good news at the roots of our faith holds that new beginnings *are* possible when we acknowledge the end of our civilizational presumptions. Jesus *still* calls us to "repent" (that is, to "turn around" our personal and political histories) here and now (Mark 1:14–15; below, 6D).

The soul of Jezebel inhabits many of our rulers today: those who bulldoze oil pipelines over the bodies of Water Protectors at Standing Rock and engineer coups in places like Bolivia for resources like lithium, determined to colonize the remotest reaches of creation. But the voice of Elijah lives too, challenging the children of settler colonialism to make things right, or face the inevitable consequences. Indeed, Elijah, like Jesus, is notoriously "undead" in the biblical testimony. His legacy hovers in a fiery chariot over our history like an unresolved chord (see 2 Kgs 2). He beckons us to speak truth to the Ahabs within and around us, and to stand with Naboth's spiritual descendants in the ongoing struggle for justice and repatriation. It was this Elijah that Jesus summoned as he hung upon a Roman cross (Mark 15:35). In his resurrection, the Nazarene similarly carried on his insurrection, despite empire's attempts to disappear it.

The only way to resolve the hauntings of Ahab is to take up the mantles of Elijah and Jesus. Elisha continued the tradition of prophetic and healing mission (2 Kgs 2:13–15). So did Peter, James, and John (Mark 1:16–20). So did Lili'uokalani. So can we, by embracing a discipleship of decolonization, whose landscape we explore in the second half of this book.

see Heinrichs, *Unsettling the Word*. In that volume, Ched "re-places" Mark's story of Jesus' baptism into the Ventura River Watershed in the mid-nineteenth century with Chumash characters (Myers, "Shaman Appeared in Ventura").

PART II

Cartography

Re-Vising Storylines of Settlement,
Assimilation, and Dissidence

> Nothing of the past five hundred years was inevitable. Every raised fist and brandished weapon was a choice . . . The decision to censor the Native truth was a choice. The decision to manipulate the knowledge of American history was a choice . . . With my relations around me, I go into mourning—but I go angry, alive, listening, learning, remembering . . . I do not vanish. I do not forget. I will not let you forget.
>
> —Wendy Rose, 1992[40]

All immigrants carry with them Landlines, Bloodlines, and Songlines, to places new to them that hold old stories of land and people. Culturally healthy ways to adapt to and adopt a "country not one's own" include:

- attending to the protocols of receiving hospitality, including seeking permission and terms from hosts;

- endeavoring to understand and embrace the responsibilities of being a guest, and, if invited to stay, becoming a good neighbor, including learning the sustainable lifeways of those whose tenure precedes us; and

- being continually engaged with the traditions of one's hosts, respecting and maintaining space for them.

---

40. Rose, "For Some, It's a Time of Mourning," 3–4, a piece written for the 1992 Columbus Quincentenary. See http://nativeamerican-authors.com/rose.html).

Things go quite differently, however, if the inward and outward narratives driving newcomers are primarily ones of colonization, or of opportunity, or even of sheer survival (for those pushed and pulled by dislocating forces, see above 2C). Neither entitled settlers nor distressed immigrants are likely to pay attention to the older "strata" of already-inhabited landscape under our feet, especially if we are not required or taught to do so. This is especially true when our socialization promotes ideologies of supremacy; defines opportunity as self-advancement (and even self-reinvention); and compels quick assimilation into the dominant socioeconomic and cultural codes of settler society. These forces shaped how many migrant Europeans came to North America and how we stayed, while waves of immigrant "others" (poorer and darker-complected) have been "managed" by the settler state through segregated housing, low-wage labor, and criminalization.

Our settler ancestors too often ignored the Indigenous past and present of the places to which they came, while looking for every occasion to gain access and title to Native land and resources. They (and we) were taught not to know or care about what preceded us on Turtle Island, and to "help ourselves" (in both meanings of that phrase). Christians have yet to come to terms with how profoundly we violated Jesus' instructions for how to proclaim and live the gospel as guests. As citizens we have not reckoned with our complicity in the ancient crimes of "killing and dispossessing" Naboth while ignoring voices like that of Lili'uokalani (above Interlude). Progenitors who "took possession" and prospered have passed on material and social advantages to us, directly or indirectly.

But the haunting persists, despite every public policy or private habit of Indigenous erasure. This is because, as Wendy Rose (Hopi/Miwok) reminds us, Native communities do not vanish, do not forget, and will not let us forget.[41] In the wise council of Poet Laureate Maya Angelou (cited at the beginning of this book), settlers must find the courage to face the "wrenching pain" of our history, not because we can "unlive" it, but in order that we do not *continue* to live it. To settler Christians, we commend the healing way of decolonizing discipleship: revisiting how our people settled (Landlines II); reversing the "*agnosia*" and assimilation perpetuated in our families and communities (Bloodlines II); living as dissidents determined to make things right (Songlines II); and embracing restorative solidarity by redistributing wealth, land, and power (chapter 8). To these tasks of "mapping and remapping" we turn in part II.

41. See for example Waziyatawin, *In the Footsteps of Our Ancestors.*

Figure 21: "Grandmother Oak," near Santa Ana Creek, Ventura River Watershed, CA, 2014. Photo: Tim Nafziger (used with permission).

CHAPTER 5

Landlines II
Where We Walked into

> Crazy Horse, it says in my American Heritage, was "killed while
> resisting arrest." Lies can make you crazy faster than anything
> else. This is not the first lie I have discovered in the dictionary,
> but I wish it was the last. What would the last lie look like? How
> would it feel? Would we miss lies if we didn't have them? Living
> with lies is a shattering experience. The dictionary tells us the
> root for craze is *krasa*, Old Norse meaning "to shatter." This is
> not a lie.
>
> —Christina Pacosz[1]

5A. TWO RIVERS RUN THROUGH ME

Two rivers flow through my soul, pulsing alongside the genetic currents
of my ancestors.

One is the mighty South Saskatchewan (Cree, *kisiskāciwani*, "swiftly
flowing river"). Along with its northern sister it drains most of the central
Canadian prairies, an area of almost 4,000 square miles, the largest inland
delta in North America (see above Figure 06). With headwaters in the
Rocky Mountains of Alberta (North) and Montana (South) respectively, the

---

1. Pacosz, *Some Winded, Wild Beast*, 95. See more at Myers and Enns, "Healing
from the 'Lies That Make Us Crazy.'"

two Saskatchewan rivers join east of present-day Prince Albert in Saskatchewan, and drain into Lake Winnipeg (Cree, *win-nipi*, "of the muddy water")
in Manitoba (Cree *manitou-wapow*, Ojibwa *manidoobaa*, both meaning
"straits of the Great Spirit").

The South Saskatchewan bisects the heart of Saskatoon, and as a teenager in summer I would swim and play in it (though forbidden because of
dangerous undertow).[2] Its mesmerizing flow, its reflections of wild light-
ning storms or fall colors, are imprinted on my soul as *home*. So too is the
memory of many walks with my parents along its banks (which have been
preserved as public space by the City of Saskatoon). This river runs through
my inner landscape, alongside other imprints from my bioregion: the dancing northern lights and the ghostly call of loons; the magic of fireflies and
the luminous harvest moon; the smell of autumn and the feel of grain flowing through my hands; the stillness of falling snow.

There are, however, stories carried by the South Saskatchewan of which
I am ignorant, farther down in its currents and far older than my memories. At our 2019 Bartimaeus Institute, Mohican activist and pastor Jim
Bear Jacobs told us: "Westerners tend to steward their narratives through
texts. Indigenous cultures, in contrast, understand our sacred stories to be
embedded in the land itself. The land holds the stories, which is why we
must learn to listen to it."[3] The Saskatchewan River Valley holds countless
songs and testaments of First Nations peoples who have lived there over
millennia, including the Siksika, Piikani, Kainai, Dakota, Stoney Nakoda,
Cree, Assiniboine, and Tsuut'ina. They managed the resources of the rivers
(which provided fish, waterfowl, and transportation), the long grass prairies
(habitat for birds and animals), and surrounding boreal forest (wood for
shelter, fire, and instruments, as well as medicine, berries, and roots). The
stories of their older, symbiotic way of being human remain in the soil and
the river's currents. Do settlers have ears to hear *these* stories, and do we
have the stamina to dive into the deadly undertow of colonization's narratives also held by this river?

Growing up I could not imagine moving away from the Saskatchewan
River watershed. But at eighteen I left for college in Winnipeg, and after

2. Upstream of Saskatoon, the Gardiner Dam was constructed in 1967, one of the
largest embankment dams in the world, regulating the South Saskatchewan's flow. Because of warm effluent discharged by the city, the river no longer completely ices over
in winter. The dam was opposed by many Indigenous groups, and a sacred rock was
knowingly destroyed during construction (see Dawson, "Buffalo Child Stone Rediscovered in Lake Diefenbaker").

3. Jacobs leads Healing Minnesota Stories,* bringing people to Indigenous sacred
sites to feel their pain and power (see O'Loughlin, "Sacred Sites Tours," and Bowling,
"American Indian Storytelling Project").

graduating in 1989 moved far away to Fresno, California. I lived there for
a decade, first working with Mennonite Voluntary Service* at a Victim
Offender Reconciliation project,* then completing a graduate program in
Theology and Peacemaking at a local seminary, then teaching restorative
justice at Fresno Pacific University. In 1999, when Ched and I were married,
I relocated to Los Angeles, continuing my restorative justice work under
Bartimaeus Cooperative Ministries.* In 2005, we (and BCM) moved to the
Ventura River watershed, nestled at the northern end of the southern Cali-
fornia coastal bioregion. For the last fifteen years we have lived and worked
beside the Ventura River, midway down its short sixteen-mile course, in the
little blue-collar, unincorporated town of Oak View (pop. 4,000).

The Ventura River watershed could not be more unlike the vast Saskatchewan River system of the prairies. The basin of the Ventura River covers only 230 square miles, with more than a 6,000-foot elevation fall from
mountains to ocean. The South Saskatchewan is wide, steady, and powerful
(captured in a neo-impressionist rendition that hangs on our living room
wall painted by Meghan Driedger Krause, a young Saskatchewan artist).
The Ventura, by contrast, is a seasonal, "braided river" that meanders and
regularly shifts its course, celebrated in Robert Valiente-Neighbours' etch-
ing that graces the cover of this book.[4] It has no recorded Chumash name.[5]

The Ventura's headwaters rise in the western Transverse Ranges, some
of the youngest and most tectonically active mountains in North America. It
empties through an estuary into the Pacific just west of the city after which
it is named (see above Figure 07). The watercourse corridor is a complex
riparian and tableland mix of forested savannah and understory, chaparral
and alluvial scrubland. It supports a diverse array of habitats from freshwa-
ter marshes to coastal sagelands. The river originally flowed perennially for
much of its length, and we listen longingly to local old-timers who speak
of when it was brimming with steelhead trout and birdlife.[6] Typically now
it is dry two-thirds of the year, compromised by agricultural drawdown
and suburban encroachment. It is congested by an obsolete dam at the
foot of the mountains (plans for removal long stymied by bureaucracy and

4. See Patoway, "Stunning Beauty of Braided Rivers."

5. Local Chumash scholar Matthew Vestuto explained this to us during a cultural
tour of the watershed on August 31, 2019 (the thirtieth anniversary of my arrival in
California): "We didn't name rivers. The term for river is 'ut'am. I guess you knew by
proximity or context which river was being discussed—there's only two of them in these
parts!" River, city, and county were named by settlers at Mission San Buenaventura (St.
Bonaventure), the ninth of twenty-one Franciscan missions that formed the backbone
of Spanish colonization in Alta California between 1770 and 1820.

6. See Beller et al., "Historical Ecology," 123–61.

politics); channelized and bermed for flood control in stretches (including in front of our home); and diminished by diversion into the reservoir just over the hill from us.[7] For all this, however, the Ventura is more intact than most seasonal streams in arid and overdeveloped southern California.

The river has two very different faces. For most of the year it flows only underground, the riverbed a mossy matte created by nitrogen-rich manure and fertilizer-laden runoff from orchards and ranches.[8] The few remaining steelhead—subjects of halting local, state, and federal restoration efforts—struggle to summer over in shaded pools, which we anxiously watch shrink and sometimes disappear in fall.[9] But *if* intense winter rains come from the west (courtesy of "Pineapple Express" atmospheric rivers), the Ventura roars. For these brief, celebrated periods, the river exhibits a fierce power that can carry mature trees like toothpicks, transport huge boulders down-stream, erode acres of riverbank, and sometimes lap the bottom of the little bridge below our home. We locals keep constant vigil throughout the rainy season to see if the river is flowing; inured to drought, we compulsively track rainfall statistics. Come spring, the river's channelets have changed, and we must find new pools to vigil over, ever fretting about the habitat of box turtles, kingfishers, snowy egrets, and great blue herons. We mark the seasons by these different expressions of our river, whose moods often impact our own.

Like Saskatchewan, our Ventura landscape is haunted by Indigenous memory and settler amnesia. Flowing underground with the river are sto-ries of millennia of Chumash habitation in villages on or near its shifting banks *(mat'iłha* and *šomas),* back amidst oak savannas *(sulukukay* and *kašomšomoy),* along its foothill tributaries *(sitoptopo'* and *awhay'),* and at its mouth *(šišolop/mitsqanaqan'* and *kamexmey').*[10] The river also remembers how—over the course of a mere seventy-five years after the founding of San Buenaventura Mission in 1782—Chumash communities were almost com-pletely wiped out by successive waves of Spanish, Mexican, and American colonization. Today the Indigenous presence, like the river itself, has been reduced to a trickle by settler occupation.[11] The river cuts through these

7. Lake Casitas, built in the late 1950s, serves as the primary water source for our watershed, affording us water sovereignty (independent of imported water by the state grid), though this may change with continuing drought cycles and development.

8. See Jenkin, "Manure Problem."

9. See Jenkin, "Recovering Ventura River Steelhead."

10. Thanks to Matthew Vestuto for the transcription of village place names. See also King, "Names and Locations of Historic Chumash Villages."

11. Chronicled in Hurtado, *Indian Survival on the California Frontier.*

layers of history, exposing, if we have eyes to see, a stratigraphy tortured by the tectonic pressures of empire.

From the study where we write this book we look out over the river bed. On its far side, majestic live oaks dot rolling hillsides. Upstream we soak in the hot springs of Matilija Canyon, once the site of a thriving Chumash village.[12] Above this we hike Murrieta Trail, where legendary *Californio bandido* Joaquin Murrieta allegedly took refuge in the early 1850s.[13] Downstream at Foster Park we've held Farm Church footwashing liturgies in the river on Maundy Thursday. The river mouth at the Pacific Ocean is precious to us for different reasons. Ched surfs there, just offshore of the site of *kamexmey'*, a nineteenth-century Chumash village (see below, footnote 82). It is his most contemplative place and practice, communing with seals, dolphins, pelicans, and cormorants, moving with off-clock-and-calendar rhythms of wind and tides, swell, and weather. For me the ocean is the closest analogue to the prairies: stretching to the horizon, sun shining on glistening waves as it does on fields of wheat.

Two rivers run through me. I am apprenticing myself to both beloved watersheds and the stories they hold, that I might better exercise responseability for a more just inhabitation going forward.

5B. "LIES MAKE US CRAZY": ORIGIN STORIES

Lies, wrote Polish American settler Christina Pacosz, make us crazy. The first-century church, under the shadow of the Roman Empire, understood Christian discipleship as a primal struggle against lies:

> Do not lie to one another, seeing that you have stripped off the
> old self with its practices and have clothed yourselves with the
> new self, which is being renewed in knowledge according to the
> image of its Creator. (Col 3:9–10)

This ancient epistle exhorted early followers of the crucified Christ not to internalize imperial fictions, nor to reproduce them in their communities

12. Matilija is a Chumash name of uncertain meaning; a famous poppy bears this name (which we cultivate in our yard, along with many other chaparral natives). Matilija's north and south forks converge to form the Ventura River.

13. The 1854 novel that launched the myth, *The Life and Adventures of Joaquín Murieta,* by Cherokee writer John Rollin Ridge/Yellowbird, was republished in 2018. Its excellent introduction by Hsuan Hsu summarizes how the story encoded the racialized violence of American colonization, well before it was appropriated into twentieth-century popular culture as Zorro and Batman ("Introduction," xv–xxx). For Ched's take on the Murrieta legend, see Myers, *Our God Is Undocumented,* 198–99.

(the lead Greek verb is *pseudomai*, "to falsify"). A determined defection from a culture of "fake news" was the key characteristic of a "renewed consciousness" grounded in the *imago Dei*. This is articulated through the baptismal metaphor (and ancient ritual) of stripping naked and donning new clothes.

The text continues: "In that renewal there is no longer Greek and Jew . . . slave and free . . ." (Col 3:11). This is a specific rejection of categorical distinctions or value-hierarchies between peoples, which is unmasked as the central lie of imperial slave economics and military policies, predicated upon notions of Roman superiority. Given these roots of the Christian movement, it is the bitterest of ironies that almost a millennium and a half later the Doctrine of Discovery was authored by popes and perpetuated by the highest legal and theological authorities of both Catholicism and Protestantism. This doctrine, reiterated and repackaged over the next five centuries by and for settler colonialism, provided the fundamental ideological and legal rationale for European conquest, land expropriation, enslavement, and destruction of peoples across the world.[14] North American settler churches have long internalized these mendacities, and healing requires that we stop "lying to one another" and face how this legacy has "shattered" us.

Settlers tend to live autonomously from our Indigenous neighbors, disinterested in the seniority of their tenure, ambivalent about their demands for justice, and unconscious of the huge footprint we have left over so short a time. If we wish to "reinhabit" the watersheds in which we reside, and forge respectful and restorative relationships with Native neighbors, we will have to abandon the privileges inherent in settler unknowing (below 6C) and embrace a double task.[15] First, we will need to build our literacy in Indigenous histories held by the land and peoples around us, as well as their continuing culture and lifeways. And second, we will need to re-vise our own narratives, which for so long have been devised and distorted by colonial supremacy.

∾

14. See Indigenous lawyer Steve Newcomb's *Pagans in the Promised Land*, summarized in his "Five Hundred Years of Injustice" (also documented in a film; see Wolfchild, *Doctrine of Discovery*). See also Williams, *American Indian in Western Legal Thought*; Burrell, "How the West Was Won"; and Charles and Rah, *Unsettling Truths*.

15. The notion of "reinhabiting one's watershed" comes from bioregionalist thought (see Myers, *Watershed Discipleship*, 7–9). We adapt it here to connote settlers "seeing again for the first time" aspects of the land on which we live, and building literacy in the ecology, history, and Indigenous cultures of our adopted places. See also Dahill, "'Unworthy of the Earth.'"

The history of our places should always begin at the beginning—which was *not* when our ancestors arrived. For example, if the span of human tenancy in the Saskatchewan River Valley were a twenty-four-hour clock, my Mennonite immigrant forebears would appear only in the last fifteen minutes. Nor should we perpetuate origin stories about Indigenous peoples that conveniently characterize them as merely "earlier" immigrants.[16] The prevailing "scientific" (and Euro-centric) view that humans first arrived in North America by walking across a frozen Bering Strait Land Bridge from Asia during the last Ice Age is now widely disputed by anthropologists and archaeologists—and has never been accepted by Indigenous communities.[17] The earliest radiocarbon-dated village site in Saskatchewan is at least 10,000 years old.[18] The earliest human remains yet found in *all* of the Americas (13,000 years old) were excavated in 1959 on Santa Rosa Island (*Wima'l*), off the coast of Ventura.[19] Neither of these artifacts from my two home watersheds cohere with the land bridge hypothesis.

Indigenous communities hold a wide variety of origin stories, but most narrate some sort of emergence or placement. "There are two general themes in tribal memories in North America about human beginnings," write Kidwell et al.; "people either emerged from below or were crafted from dirt or clay; or they dropped from the sky."[20] An example of the latter is taught by Norm Wesley of the Moose Cree First Nation: A man and woman agreed to go from the world above to the world below, and went to Spider to learn how to get down; but they didn't follow instructions, and fell into a great eagle nest, where they were rescued by wolverine and bear, who taught the couple how to live on Cree land.[21]

16. An example is conservative politician Tom Flanagan's *First Nations? Second Thoughts,* which refers to Indigenous peoples as "Siberian-Canadians." These earlier immigrants, he asserts, were then necessarily eclipsed by technologically and politically superior European colonizers, who made better use of the land (cited in Epp, *We Are All Treaty People,* 124). Such white supremacist sentiments are being freshly reimagined by ideologues in the Trump era.

17. For example, hearths excavated in 1949 in Texas were radiocarbon-dated to be more than 37,000 years old (see Crook and Harris, "Pleistocene Campsite Near Lewisville, Texas"). For an overview of how the conventional theory is in flux, see Worral, "When, How Did the First Americans Arrive?" For critiques and Indigenous alternatives, see Deloria, *Evolution, Creationism, and Other Modern Myths,* and Thomas, *Skull Wars.*

18. See Waiser, "Saskatchewan's Oldest Graveyard Is Ancient," and Epp and Jones, "Prehistory, Southern Saskatchewan."

19. See Johnson, "Arlington Man."

20. Kidwell et al., *Native American Theology,* 37. For examples, see Hampton and Chun, *Creation and Other Stories.*

21. Hear it at https://www.youtube.com/watch?v=Qn0zJ1QH2Zc.

One Chumash tradition reflects the former theme, as told by Barbare-
ño-Ventureño tribal chair Julie Tumamait-Stenslie. Earth Mother *Huta-
sh* buried the seeds of a magical plant on *Limuw* ("in the sea," now known
as Santa Cruz Island). Men and women sprang full-grown from the plant
and inhabited the islands in the Santa Barbara Channel, eventually walking
a "Rainbow Bridge" to get to the mainland.[22] When Indigenous stories do
speak of migration, it is in response to what the land allows, such as a need
to move because of drought, or climate cooling, or following the bison. One
does *not* find stories of migration for purposes of conquest or entitlement.

About forty miles south of Opwashemoe Chakatinaw/Stoney Knoll,
Saskatchewan (see preface), Wanuskewin Heritage Park sits above where Opimihaw Creek meets the South Saskatchewan River. Opimihaw Valley contains "at least fourteen pre-contact archaeological sites, including a medicine
wheel, tipi rings, rock cairns, campsites and bison kills."[23] Beginning some
6,000 years ago, after the receding of ice, virtually every Indigenous group
across the Great Plains visited this location. According to Wanuskewin archaeologists and elders, they came "to hunt bison, gather food and herbs, and
escape the winter winds . . . This site was a place of worship and celebration,
of renewal with the natural world and of a deep spirituality."[24] One doesn't
need to romanticize Indigenous societies (which weren't innocent of war,
slavery, or enmity) to acknowledge that they lived on the land for millennia
in sustainable cultures with viable economies, trade, diplomatic relationships,
complex social structures, sophisticated ceremonies, and highly developed
health care and relational justice practices.

The functional etiological myth of European colonization, in contrast, is about leaving one's homeland and settling in "an-othered" one.
This despite the fact that our scriptural traditions of creation *also* clearly
narrate emergence: the first human (Heb. *'adam*) is formed from the hu-
mus (*adamah*), and placed in a habitat with which they are invited to live
symbiotically (Gen 2). It is not difficult to see how an identity shaped by a
settler metanarrative of "sacred migration from Old World to New" would
generate (and legitimate) practices of displacement. Thus the advent of the
European represented the "beginning of the end" for traditional lifeways on

22. See a text of, or hear Julie tell, the story in Eidt, "Chumash Story." She points out
the Chumash universe consists of three worlds: "the upper, held up by a giant eagle, the
middle, held up by giant snakes, and a lower world" (email correspondence with authors,
June 6, 2020). Recent anthropological research confirms the Chumash were the original
human inhabitants of our bioregion (see e.g., Gamble, *Chumash World*, 6).

23. At https://www.historicplaces.ca/en/rep-reg/place-lieu.aspx?id=2725, para. 1.
See Kylie, "Connecting to 6,000 Years of History."

24. Quoted at https://wanuskewin.com/our-story/the-land/.

Turtle Island, replaced by a socially and ecologically unsustainable agricultural-industrial society that may not last another century.

∾

Figure 22: Rupert's Land grant by King Charles II to Hudson's Bay Company, 1670. Map at: https://en.wikipedia.org/wiki/Rupert%27s_Land#/media/File:Ruperts_land.svg (used with permission).

In 1670, the Hudson's Bay Company (HBC) was granted by *fiat* of England's King Charles II a charter over a stunningly vast territory defined by the watersheds of all rivers and streams flowing into Hudson Bay (Figure 22). This was a bold deployment of the Doctrine of Discovery's "principle of contiguity."[25] The private estate of "Rupert's Land" (named for the king's royal cousin) stretched from the Atlantic Ocean to the Rocky Mountains,

25. Contiguity stipulated that colonizers who "discovered" a river mouth could claim hegemony over the entire watershed of that river. This was later used by the U.S. to claim huge domains of the Mississippi and Columbia River drainages (see Friesen, "Great Commission," 33–35).

and from the prairies to the Arctic Circles, encompassing nearly a third of present-day Canada. For 200 years, the HBC operated a commercial monopoly throughout this territory, setting up a strategic network of trading forts which doubled as colonial outposts.

Trade focused initially on animal hides and pelts (including of species that are extinct today). Prior to 1670, it is estimated that up to 60 million bison roamed the Great Plains of North America; by 1880, their population had been reduced to 325 animals.[26] The settler destruction of the bison aimed to undermine the culture and economy of Indigenous tribes who depended on them. The "foundation for agricultural settlement was being laid in wholesale carnage," writes Candace Savage; yet settlers typically "pass over this tragedy with phrases like 'after the buffalo disappeared' or 'when the buffalo vanished' as if the animals had wandered off peacefully in the great beyond."[27]

In July 1691, English fur trader Henry Kelsey became the first recorded European to come into the Saskatchewan valley, led by Cree guides and following their foot trails (this was prior to the advent of the horse on the prairies). Like all early foreign explorers, Kelsey's navigation relied on the deep literacy of lands and waters developed by Native communities over millennia, and he survived only because of *their* technologies and economy.[28] Kelsey's group ascended the Saskatchewan River by canoe, then turned up the Carrot River, where Kelsey became the first white man into the aspen parklands of the prairies (Figure 23).[29] Celebrated in settler histories as the first European to see "great store of buffalo" and "silver-haired grizzlies," Kelsey's primary mission was actually to colonize. Over the following decades he was key to that expanding project, appointed in 1718 by the British as Governor of all Hudson's Bay settlements.

Some 250 years later, my father's people, refugees from a Russian horror, settled outside the town of Carrot River to farm. As a child, our family visited our many Enns relatives there at Christmas and summer. But we never visited nearby Cree communities at the Shoal Lake or Red Earth First Nation Reserves along the Carrot, and were oblivious to how that river carries the story of Kelsey's inauguration of the settler domination of Saskatchewan.

26. See Heath, "Bison."

27. Savage, *Geography of Blood,* 88–91.

28. For overviews, see e.g., Dickason, *Canada's First Nations;* Binnema, *Common and Contested Ground;* Carter, *Aboriginal People and Colonizers of Western Canada to 1900.*

29. Map from Meyer and Russell, "'Through the Woods,'" 164. See also Irland, "What the River Knows." On Kelsey, see https://en.wikipedia.org/wiki/Henry_Kelsey.

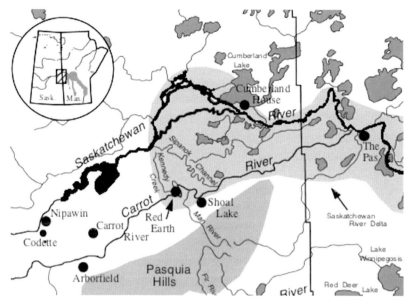

Figure 23: Map showing the Carrot River, along which the Henry Kelsey expedition
traveled (guided by Cree scouts) to enter the Saskatchewan River Valley, 1691.
Found at Meyer and Russell, "Through the Woods" (used with permission).

5C. RE-VISING DEVISED SETTLER HISTORIES

Not far from Stoney Knoll is the Rosthern/Laird area, where my brother-in-
law Rob's grandparents were among the first Mennonite settlers. My sister Janet taught for many years at a predominantly Indigenous elementary school
at nearby Duck Lake. Over the years, Janet and Rob have helped Ched and
me learn local history through walking and driving tours, including a canoe
trip to Batoche, the center of Cree and Métis resistance to English colonization in the 1880s. Our paddle down the South Saskatchewan on a beautiful summer afternoon was slow and contemplative, bald eagles circling
overhead. We meandered with the current past willow-thatched high banks
riddled with nests of bank swallows and little sand islands teeming with
riparian life. After several hours we arrived at Batoche on the east bank of
the river, founded in 1872 as a Métis settlement. A Francophone and Roman
Catholic community, it was organized around a river-lot system similar to
what Mennonites had designed in Ukraine, where each parcel had access to
the water (see above Figure 16). Batoche was the focal point of Métis leader
Louis Riel's dissident Provisional Government of Saskatchewan, organized

to prevent further dispossession of Métis, such as had occurred a few years earlier in Manitoba.[30] The May 1885 Battle of Batoche spelled the defeat of Riel's uprising, the last armed insurgency against Canadian hegemony.[31]

Though pivotal to both regional and national identity, the Northwest Resistance is still not widely understood by my community. Its dramatic events occurred less than a decade prior to the arrival of the first Mennonite settlers, yet there is little evidence that they understood the importance or implications of the Métis struggle for land justice. The bullet holes that still remain at Batoche National Historic Site, especially obvious in the front wall of the church, are a haunting with which I must reckon. The pain held by the waters we paddled I must learn to feel.

In school I learned that Canada had been "kinder" to its Native peoples compared to the U.S., as evidenced by the relative lack of "Indian wars." The realities of nineteenth-century government policies in Canada tell a different story, however. In addition to duplicitous treaty-making, which we'll look at below (E), two genocidal policies took an enormous toll on Indigenous peoples.[32]

One was the Indian Act of 1876. The Canadian Parliament gave sweeping powers to the federal government over Indigenous identity, political structures, governance, cultural practices, and education.[33] The act defined Indigenous people as wards of the state, even as the government was still negotiating treaties with individual First Nations! It also restricted or criminalized many cultural practices and dramatically reduced traditional hunting and fishing rights. Bob Joseph (Gwawaenuk) summarizes: "The Indian

---

30. On the designation Métis, see above preface n. 4. In 1867, British Colonial control of Canada stretched only as far west as Ontario; nothing north and west had been surveyed. Many Métis settled in the Red River area, around present-day Winnipeg. In 1870, this settlement was unilaterally transferred to the Canadian government, sparking an uprising led by Riel and creation of a Métis provisional government. This led to a negotiated creation of Manitoba as a province under Canadian confederation, but the government soon forced Riel into exile. Disadvantaged under the new arrangement, many Métis moved farther west to Saskatchewan, where they would try again to assert autonomy under Riel. The Northwest Resistance of 1885 "began as a peaceful citizen's protest against government inefficiency," but ended in tragedy for which the "federal government must bear most of the responsibility" (Friesen, *Canadian Prairies*, 228). For more, see Driedger, "Native Rebellion and Mennonite Invasion," and https://indigenouspeoplesatlasofcanada.ca/article/red-river-resistance/.

31. Above, Prologue. See historical summary at https://indigenouspeoplesatlasofcanada.ca/article/1885-northwest-resistance/.

32. For a comprehensive study, see Daschuk, *Clearing the Plains*.

33. See Hanson, "Indian Act."

Act imposed great personal and cultural tragedy on First Nations, many of which continue to affect communities, families and individuals today."[34]

The second deadly policy was Indian Residential Schools (IRS). Beginning in the 1830s, the colonial government looked to churches to take the lead on education initiatives to "civilize" Indigenous children. Methodist minister and educational reformer Egerton Ryerson is widely acknowledged as the architect of the IRS system, which began operating widely in Canada after 1880.[35] For more than a century, Indigenous children were taken from their families and held captive in sometimes distant schools, where many were abused emotionally, physically, and sexually. The genocidal nature of the IRS project is captured in a famous declaration in 1920 by Duncan Campbell Scott (Canadian Deputy Superintendent of Indian Affairs, 1913–1932), announcing his policy to make school attendance mandatory: "Our objective is to continue until there is not a single Indian in Canada that has not been absorbed into the body politic and there is no Indian question, and no Indian Department."[36] More than 130 schools operated in Canada, where First Nation, Inuit, and Métis children were forced to conform to European lifeways. The last to be shuttered (in 1996!) was Gordon IRS in Punnichy, Saskatchewan, two hours southeast of where I grew up. The devastating impact of IRS policies and practices—in both Canada and the U.S.—on Indigenous health, welfare, and cultural sovereignty simply cannot be overstated.[37]

These policies shaped the context into which my Mennonite immigrant forebears walked. And we were not as aloof from the fray as we like to imagine. On July 1, 1873, a Canadian immigration agent brought four Mennonite delegates from Russia to explore possible settlement in the Red River area of Manitoba. The government was offering "exemption from military service and included a free grant of 160 acres of the best land in Manitoba, or in any other part of the Northwest Territory [which then

34. Joseph, "21 Things You May Not Have Known about the Indian Act."

35. Ryerson was a champion of public education, and worked with Mississauga/Ojibwe leader Peter Jones developing the schools model, but they wrongly believed these would be self-governing within a generation (see https://en.wikipedia.org/wiki/Egerton_Ryerson#Common_School_Bill_of_1846). See also Miller, "Residential Schools in Canada."

36. King, *Inconvenient Indian*, 72. See also Regan, *Unsettling the Settler Within*. For survivors' accounts, see Starblanket, *Suffer the Little Children*.

37. An historic Truth and Reconciliation Commission in Canada (http://www.trc.ca/) took place from 2008 to 2015, and issued a remarkable report with Calls to Action for all sectors of Canadian society to come to terms with the IRS legacy, including churches; see more below 7C. For the parallel U.S. history, see Little, "How Boarding Schools Tried to 'Kill the Indian.'"

included Saskatchewan and Alberta], to persons over the age of 21."[38] Historian Ted Regehr writes about what happened next at Whitehorse Plains (west of Winnipeg):

> Indians and Métis . . . were justifiably concerned that a major influx of new agricultural settlers would seriously disrupt and probably destroy their traditional way of life . . . Métis intercepted and harassed the new arrivals with verbal threats . . . Much alarmed, the land-seekers sought refuge at House's Hotel (a crude local hostelry) while their agent stood guard at the door with a loaded shotgun . . . The Lieutenant-Governor . . . ordered the local military forces to the trouble spot . . . [which] quickly dispersed the Métis and arrested several of their leaders. This was the inauspicious beginning of Mennonite agricultural settlement in western Canada . . . Although the Whitehorse Plains incident was frightening, the local government was supportive and the federal government, eager to attract more agricultural settlers to the West, granted all the political and religious concessions they asked for.[39]

Benefitting from armed state intervention problematizes Mennonite narratives of innocence. The fact is, our people were deeply entangled in the colonization of the Canadian prairies from the outset.

Mennonites, as "priority immigrants," profited from government grants of land for farming that had previously been the territory of Indigenous and Métis communities, first in Manitoba and again a generation later in Saskatchewan.[40] Often the Canadian Pacific Railroad acted as middleman, brokering large tracts of surplus land.[41] For the Canadian government,

---

38. For background of the Mennonite delegation, see Guenter, *Hague-Osler Mennonite Reserve, 1895–1995*, 13–15.

39. Regehr, "Mennonites and the New Jerusalem," 109–10.

40. The Dominion Lands Act of 1872 "entitled a settler to secure entry to a quarter-section of land on payment of a ten-dollar fee. A homesteader could obtain an adjoining quarter-section and could purchase it at a price set by government"; there was also a "hamlet or village" clause that allowed settlers to settle together, which suited Mennonites (Smillie, *Visions of the New Jerusalem*, 2–3). Mennonites from Ukraine also settled in the Dakota Territories, as narrated in Roy Kaufman's recent *The Drama of a Rural Community's Life Cycle*, which offers parallel reflections on his Landlines, Bloodlines, and Songlines.

41. See Driedger, "Native Rebellion and Mennonite Invasion," 298. "Under the initial contract with the Canadian government to build the railway, the CPR was granted 25 million acres . . . [and] began an intense campaign to bring immigrants to Canada . . . Immigrants were often sold a package that included passage on a CP ship, travel on a CP train and land sold by the CP railway" (https://en.wikipedia.org/wiki/Canadian_Pacific_Railway#CPR_and_the_settlement_of_western_Canada). See also Redekop,

Frank H. Epp points out, "Mennonites were only a means to an end. The real purpose was to fill the prairies with a united Canadian society, which would prove the possibility of prosperous settlement there and, simultaneously, domesticate the lands in the face of Indian and Métis rebellion and discourage any American incursion, peaceful or otherwise."[42]

The other arm of Canada's domestication strategy for the prairies was focused on Indigenous communities, which were pressured to abandon traditional lifeways and adopt agriculture. Yet official policies undermined Indigenous farming efforts at every turn, while advantaging those of settlers. Métis writer Chelsea Vowel summarizes the deceit:

> Many reserves were located in areas not suited to farming, and many grain seeds and farming implements promised to First Nations never materialized . . . However, even with these impediments, farming was at first very successful in a number of First Nations communities.[43]

When some Indigenous groups, using a collective model of dry farming, began large-scale export of produce, it became clear the government did not want them to succeed in cash-crop markets.[44]

Vowel summarizes three policies of restriction:

- *Severality*: Reserve farmland was divided into 40-acre plots and no one farmer could own more than 160 acres. The intention was to promote "individualism," directly undermining successful collective efforts. Also, any "left over" land could be surrendered and made available for sale to nonnatives.

- *Peasant farming*: "Experts" were sent in to teach Native farmers, to reduce output to subsistence levels, essentially just enough to support a single family. Thus expensive large-scale machinery would be unnecessary.

- *Pass and permit system*: These restricted the ability of First Nations peoples to leave the reserve, as well as severely curtailing their ability to sell their products or purchase farming implements.

Mennonite Displacement of Indigenous Peoples.

42. Epp, *Mennonites in Canada, 1786–1920*, 209.

43. Vowel, "Undermined at Every Turn," para. 18. See also, Carter, *Lost Harvests*.

44. Friesen, *Canadian Prairies*, 159.

Vowel concludes: "These systems ensured that aboriginal farmers could not compete with non-aboriginal farmers," while creating economic dependence on reserves as a form of social control.[45]

Only seven years after the Northwest Resistance, and just twenty miles from its center in Batoche, a small group of families from Manitoba, West Prussia, and the U.S. became the first Mennonite settlers in the Saskatchewan Valley in 1892. They initially lived in railroad cars at the CPR line's end in Rosthern, where the arrival of the railroad promised to open up agricultural markets for new settler farmers. Mennonite sociologist Leo Driedger writes that Old Colony Mennonites who settled in a government-created reserve at Hague-Osler in 1895 sometimes characterized the Métis pejoratively as "lazy farmers of mixed Indian blood"; the newcomers "never really were aware of these people and their bitter feelings." Driedger himself grew up in the area, "yet had never seen the French settlement there until forty years later . . . Mennonite invaders were often not cognizant of their role in making earlier residents homeless . . . and looked upon them with disrespect and condescension."[46]

In 1894, Mennonites made requests to the government for additional tracts of land in the Saskatchewan Valley, the last of which included the Young Chippewayan reserve granted under Treaty 6.[47] In 1885, the Department of Indian Affairs had begun withholding treaty payments for Young Chippewayans, who the government (erroneously) suspected of having participated in the Northwest Resistance. By 1888, the Department no longer identified Young Chippewayans as a separate band, and a decade later opened their land to Mennonites (and then to Lutherans and others). This injustice continues to impact all these communities (below 6A).

45. Vowel, "Undermined at Every Turn," para. 24; summarized policies, para. 20.

46. Driedger, "Native Rebellion and Mennonite Invasion," 299.

47. Guenter, *Hague-Osler Mennonite Reserve*, 29. See above Prologue. A document from the Minister of the Interior dated December 24, 1894 states: "it has been represented to him, on behalf of the Mennonites Settlers in Manitoba, that their two Reserves in that Province are now overcrowded . . . in order to meet the growing needs of their families, and to encourage the settlement of their fellow-countrymen in Canada, it becomes necessary for them to ask the Government to establish a reservation for them from lands in the Prince Albert District . . . It is now their intention to assist with their own means their fellow-countrymen, in Europe and elsewhere, to remove to and settle upon the tract now applied for . . . The efforts of the Mennonites to induce the immigration of their friends in Europe and elsewhere to the North West should be encouraged, and to do this it is necessary to give the intending settlers an assurance that they will be enabled to carry out the principles of their Social System . . . by obtaining entries for contiguous lands" (Committee of the Honorable the Privy Council, Canadian Superintendent General of Indian Affairs, Department of the Interior "Report of the Committee . . . 23rd January, 1895").

Prior to the turn of the century, the establishment of farming communities on the Canadian Prairies went slowly, in part because Hudson's Bay Company and the Canadian Pacific Railway withheld so much arable land for their purposes of profitable speculation. But the government continued aggressively to encourage settlement.[48] In the first three decades of the twentieth century, prairie population increased sixfold to 2.4 million (during which time Canadian production of wheat increased tenfold).[49] By 1930, almost 20,000 Mennonites and more than 12,000 Lutherans had immigrated to Canada, roughly a third of each group settling in Saskatchewan.[50]

My grandparents were among those advantaged by Canadian settlement policies for farmers during this period of immigration. In preparation for the *Russländer* influx, the Mennonite Board of Colonization established a Land Commission that began appraising available land.[51] With this help my maternal Great-grandfather Isaak Zacharias was able to establish a farm at Dundurn, Saskatchewan shortly after their arrival in 1923.[52] My paternal grandparents, Franz and Katharina Enns, arrived in Rosthern, Saskatchewan in spring 1927. In September they were "informed through the Resettlement Board about a farm being sold in the Glidden area. My father-in-law and I went there and bought the whole farm, including seven quarters of land, livestock and implements. The price was high, but we did not have to make a down payment."[53]

To be sure, the settlement experiences of these generations were not without significant difficulties. Between 1927 and 1933—the height of the decimating Dust Bowl across North America—my Enns grandparents endured serial crop failures from frost, hailstorms, and drought in Glidden. The family having grown to seven children, Grandpa Franz went to investigate a Mennonite reserve to the northeast that had been founded in Carrot River in 1908. He was impressed with the local church, and through Mennonite connections was able to purchase land. In 1933, they resettled there,

48. Francis and Palmer, *Prairie West,* 239.

49. Friesen, *Canadian Prairies,* 242.

50. Anderson, *Settling Saskatchewan,* 120.

51. Anderson, *Settling Saskatchewan,* 120.

52. The Mennonite Settlement Board purchased twenty large farms for *Russländer* in Hanley and Dundurn (Anderson, *Settling Saskatchewan,* 125). My great-grandmother Anna Schulz arrived with her family in 1927; my grandparents, Heinrich Toews and Margreta Schulz, were finally reunited and married a year later (Gerbrandt, *Remembering the Schulzes,* 88).

53. Mierau and Reimer, *Sojourners,* 74.

with the help of government-provided boxcars.[54] Part of the attraction was that Carrot River's latitudinal geolocation is only one degree different from Davlekanovo, Russia, where the Ennses had farmed before emigrating, so they were successful using similar farming methods. But it was challenging for my Grandma Katharina to move 325 miles away from her family in Glidden; she didn't see them again for seven years.

Russländers who had not been farmers before arriving in Canada, such as my maternal Grandpa Heinrich Toews, struggled economically in the new country.[55] Many also faced pressures to pay off their travel debt acquired under the immigration contracts with the CPR (above 2D, footnote 39). My maternal Great-uncle George Zacharias related how family members "of working age had to go to work because the transportation debt had to be paid." He added:

> Teenagers were not allowed to continue their education as they needed to find work as soon as they arrived in Canada. Even those who had a good education could not effectively make use of it because of the language barrier and lack of money and resources.[56]

Because of such financial pressures, Marlene Epp writes, many families in rural areas "sent their daughters, some as young as thirteen years old, to nearby cities to fill the high demand for domestic workers." Mennonite girls were highly sought after as domestics because of their lack of "'defiance' or class-conscious resistance to exploitative treatment on the part of employers."[57] These young women sent most of their earnings home to support their families, to help pay off the travel debt, and to aid family members left behind in "the misery and persecution" of Russia.[58] Epp documents how these girls commonly endured fifteen-hour workdays with only three afternoons off a month. They were often treated as servants, allowed to enter the dining room only when summoned. They ate meals alone, slept in the basement, and entered the house by the back door. Domestics in private homes always faced the possibility of sexual harassment or assault.[59]

---

54. Mierau and Reimer, *Sojourners*, 74–75. According to my Uncle Jake, Franz arrived at the Carrot River congregation on a Sunday morning and saw "the church full of young people and decided *this* is where they would move." Interview by authors, Carrot River, August 2019.

55. Gerbrandt, *Remembering the Schulzes*, 88.

56. Zacharias, *Wilhelm Zacharias and Descendants*, 553–54.

57. Epp, *Mennonite Women in Canada*, 42–43.

58. Zacharias, *Wilhelm Zacharias and Descendants*, 554.

59. Epp documents several situations of abuse, though most went unreported

In light of these common experiences, it was painful for me to discover in my family history book the terse phrase that my twenty-three year old Grandma Margreta, shortly after arriving in Canada, "found housework in the City of Saskatoon."[60] Newly arrived in a strange country, she was grateful to have left the tumult of Russia behind, and joyful at being reunited with her beloved Heinrich and extended family. I imagine her happiness, however, was disrupted by the need to work alone as a servant in a stranger's home, where she knew neither the language, customs, or even the kinds of meals she was required to prepare. The thirty-mile distance from home was not commutable, intensifying her isolation. She had likely never worked alone before, since household chores were always shared with her mother and sisters, typically accompanied by laughter, storytelling, or commiserating.

Like most immigrants, then, Mennonites had to navigate many challenges: linguistic and cultural barriers; securing work and housing; financial viability and paying off debt; helping children adjust; starting or continuing education; curating community gathering spaces; dealing with prejudice and ridicule; and healing from traumas endured. As hard-pressed newcomers trying to start farms in a strange land, it is not surprising they did not seek to engage their Indigenous neighbors. But this precluded them from learning how to be guests on this land and adapt to it.

Moreover, *Russländer* brought with them a history of ambivalence toward Indigenous peoples, whom colonizing powers had invited them to replace in Europe, a scenario repeated in Canada. Nor was there anything in "*Englische*" culture (how German-speaking Mennonites referred to dominant white Canadian society) that encouraged or equipped immigrants to build relationships with Native communities. Quite the opposite: there were structural disincentives (such as an existing social architecture of segregation), and plenty of opportunities to absorb the anti-Indigenous prejudices that prevailed at all levels of settler society.

Our *Russländer* communal narratives tend to stress the immigrant generation's great fortitude: both how they survived horrors in Russia and how they worked hard to prosper in Canada. And there is much there to commend. Rarely spoken of, however, are the advantages that often automatically accrued to European newcomers, the government agricultural and land policies from which Mennonites benefitted, and the religious and cultural *Privelegia* they negotiated.[61] Do we consider how our imported

---

(*Mennonite Women in Canada*, 43–50).

60. Zacharias, *Wilhelm Zacharias and Descendants*, 378.

61. The *Privilegium* of 1873 offered by the Dominion of Canada to Russian Mennonites included land, military exemption, and private schools. As noted, migrating Mennonites have had a long history of negotiating agreements with receiving countries;

and adopted prejudices contributed to the marginalization of Indigenous communities in their own land, and how they still do so today (below 6B)? Luke Gascho, retired professor in the Sustainability and Environmental Education Department at Goshen College, reminds us: "All these examples of disconnection from Indigenous peoples are repeated by white settlers across the continent. We are each called to unpack them in our own story and location."[62]

5D. HOW HAVE WE REMAINED? DISPARITIES, DEGRADATIONS, RE-SETTLEMENTS

In Landlines I, we looked at "how our people were moved" in migration; here we examine how we descendants of these settlers have "stayed," and the impacts of our tenure. The Enns family built a successful farm in Carrot River, which is operated by my cousins today. Relatives still attend the church where my paternal Uncle Frank long served as assistant pastor. My maternal Zacharias family helped establish the *Nordheimer Mennoniten Gemeinde* in the Hanley-Dundurn area of Saskatchewan, where extended relations remain. And Mennonite families still live and farm on land taken from the Young Chippewayans at Opwashemoe Chakatinaw/Stoney Knoll. Indigenous communities in the Saskatchewan Valley, in contrast, have endured an immeasurably different experience over the last century.

As a landless band, Young Chippewayans have been forced to inhabit other reserves, mostly outside of Prince Albert and North Battleford, Saskatchewan. In 1972, Albert Snake, then Chief of the Young Chippewayan band, requested the Minister of the Interior to review their land claim. Snake insisted again that it was desperate hunger (not opportunism) that originally drove his people off their small government-allotted plot in the 1880s, as he had asserted some two decades earlier:

> I was about nine years old when my Grandfather Chippewayan, the chief, advised his people to leave their reserve for the winter . . . because he was afraid they would have nothing to eat . . . They were not getting provisions as promised by the treaty . . . There was no sign of any coming when we left our reserve.[63]

---

for a list of *Privelegia* signed with more than a dozen nations between 1557 and 1957, see Crous and Ens, "Privileges." See above 3C n. 74.

62. Email correspondence with authors, May 14, 2020.

63. Albert Snake interview with Harry Michael, Sandy Lake Indian Reserve, February 12, 1955 (transcript in Leonard Doell Archives, Mennonite Central Committee, Saskatoon).

This claim was rejected by the government even as it was developing a federal policy concerning other Indigenous claims. This led to Young Chippewayan protests during the 1976 centenary commemoration of Treaty 6 (see discussion below 6A). In 1993, they again petitioned the federal Indian Claims Commission, which the following year ruled that the claimants were not a band under the Indian Act, and therefore not entitled to submit a specific claim.[64] Nevertheless, Young Chippewayans continue to work towards justice, focusing in recent years on genealogical research to prove continuous lineage from original band members.

Settler agricultural prosperity in the prairies today is predicated not only upon colonial land occupation, but also upon a political economy of industrial farming that has become dominant over the last half-century. Here we note just two of its negative impacts.

Land concentration. A 2015 study of farmland ownership in Saskatchewan describes increasing concentration in fewer (often corporate) hands, and the steady atrophy of small family farms.

> Broadly speaking, "land grabbing" refers to the twenty-first-century phenomenon wherein large tracts of farmland are bought up by investment funds, corporations, pension funds, sovereign wealth funds, and other private interests . . . The term deliberately politicizes large-scale land deals as a way of underlining their potential for dispossessing marginalized groups including small-scale farmers, pastoralists, and indigenous peoples . . . While the processes, politics, and consequences of large-scale land deals vary tremendously across social and geographical contexts, the common thread is a transfer of ownership and control of land and resources away from local communities and actors towards financial capital and corporate interests . . . [These trends] involve "willing sellers" and "willing buyers" in a capitalist land market. However, these transactions are made in a highly unequal playing field in which some actors (investors with tens or hundreds of millions of dollars at their disposal) have considerably more resources than others (family farmers).[65]

64. Bellegrade et al., "Young Chippewayan Inquiry." There are only fourteen federally recognized First Nations tribes in Saskatchewan despite the fact that the Federation of Sovereign Indian Nations represents seventy-four groups there (http://www.native-languages.org/saskatchewan.htm)!

65. Desmarais et al., "Land Grabbing and Land Concentration," 18–19. Study coauthor Nettie Wiebe is a Mennonite farmer, former professor of Elaine's at St. Andrew's College Saskatoon, and an active social justice advocate. These trends are tracked more broadly at https://www.farmlandgrab.org/.

The new corporate actors buying up farmland across the prairies include "public pension plans, investors and investment companies, farmer/investor hybrids, and large-scale farmers."[66]

The same study shows how "concentrated land ownership has meant a continuous decline in the number of farming families" since the 1930s. "Larger farms and fewer farm families mean that many rural communities are unable to sustain the services and institutions that require a critical mass of users to continue to operate. The steady erosion of schools, hospitals, churches, and post offices, as well as the closing of businesses, banks, and grain elevators creates a downward spiral, making it more difficult to continue to live in these communities." One farmer lamented to the study's authors: "There is an ongoing emptying of the countryside. Rural communities have been under duress ever since settlement, and what is going on is really part of a long process of de-settlement."[67]

We might more accurately characterize these pressures as a *re-colonization* of the prairies, with big capital now in the role formerly played by government in the redistribution of land. Small farmer descendants of homesteaders are themselves being displaced by market forces, following after the Indigenous peoples their forebears displaced a century ago. While some Mennonites in Saskatchewan are fighting these trends, others cooperate with and benefit from them.

Ecological degradation. The industrial agriculture which is driving land concentration has also sponsored environmentally disastrous practices in the three Prairie Provinces, which comprise almost 90 percent of Canada's arable farmland. Monocropping, use of genetically modified seed stock, Roundup-Ready farming, heavy use of herbicides and fossil-fuel-based fertilizers, and water draw-down are accelerating the double crisis of soil fertility loss and climate warming.[68] The World Wildlife Fund's *Plowprint Report 2018* opens with these warnings: "Temperate grassland ecosystems are the least protected biomes on the planet. Worldwide, these important habitats are being lost at an alarming rate . . . significantly impacting species . . . as well as the vital ecosystem services these grasslands provide—from carbon

---

66. Desmarais et al., "Land Grabbing and Land Concentration," 32; they map in rigorous detail these entities.

67. Desmarais et al., "Land Grabbing and Land Concentration," 38–39. Another professor friend, Dr. Cam Harder, specializes in pastoral care among distressed prairie family farmers (see http://www.circle-m.ca/links/), where suicides are a widespread problem. These trends exist in the U.S. Midwest as well (see Snell, "Suicide Is Rising among American Farmers").

68. See the prairie-specific study by Zlomislic, "Field of Dreams."

sequestration to water filtration."[69] In the same year, Nature Conservancy Canada called Canada's prairies "the world's most endangered ecosystem," with more than 70 percent already converted to monocropping, and notes that North America's Great Plains "have lost a greater proportion of intact grassland than the Brazilian Amazon has lost rainforest."[70]

Land monopolization and degradation are ethical issues in their own right, but they also represent a continuation of colonizing relations by the settler state, which began with the dispossession of Indigenous peoples. I wrestle with the questions: How often have we North American Mennonites (both rural and urban) cooperated with this project? And how does this cohere with Anabaptist visions for embodying an alternative to dominant society? A half-century ago, Mennonite sociologist Leo Driedger raised this very conundrum in a challenging article in the *Mennonite Quarterly Review* regarding the history of Mennonite settlers in the Canadian prairies. How, he asked,

> could the Mennonites cooperate with governments in gaining land for community-building, when their belief system often advocated separation of church and state . . .? Could nonresistant Mennonite minorities benefit from lands and protection secured by government through war and violence without again compromising one of their basic principles?[71]

Such hard questions grow more intense as we assimilate further into middle-class white culture with each generation (below 6B). They are directed to me and my community, but also to anyone who would face the contradictions between their moral traditions and how their people have remained on this land and prospered under settler colonialism.

~

The Ventura River watershed where Ched and I have "re-settled" (see below), and to which we are also accountable, has a parallel legacy of land inequity, environmental deterioration, and continuing dispossession. The local Chumash band here, like Young Chippewayans, is also landless and similarly unrecognized by the federal government.

The Chumash lived along the California coast between Malibu and San Luis Obispo for at least 13,000 years prior to European contact. They

69. See https://www.worldwildlife.org/projects/plowprint-report, para. 1

70. See Kraus, "Why Canada's Prairies," para. 5.

71. Driedger, "Native Rebellion and Mennonite Invasion," 300. See below, beginning of chapter 6.

developed a sustainable bioregional culture and economy centered on a symbiotic relationship with ocean, mountains, and oak chaparral.[72] Their sophisticated maritime technology, particularly the *tomol* (plank canoe), may have connections to ancient Polynesian seafarers.[73] Organized warfare appears to have been unknown prior to colonization by the Spanish in the late eighteenth century, whereas medical and horticultural practices were sophisticated.[74] Like prairie Cree, the Chumash were an ancient and resilient society.

In 1542–1543, Juan Rodríguez Cabrillo, a Portuguese soldier commissioned by the viceroy of New Spain to explore new routes to China and the mythical "Northwest Passage," sailed up the coast of California.[75] He anchored at Point Mugu (Chumash *muwu*) south of Ventura, and after brief explorations and skirmishes with local Native folk, he died from an injury on San Miguel Island in the Santa Barbara Channel. The Spanish crown did not follow up on his explorations, however, for more than two centuries, and then only because of fear of Russian and English "encroachment" on the Pacific coast. In 1769, Gaspar de Portolá (and the infamous Fr. Junipero Serra) led a land expedition from Loreto, Baja California, through present-day San Diego, up to the San Francisco Bay and back.[76] In San Diego the Franciscans inaugurated the Spanish colonial period in Alta California by establishing the first of twenty-one missions, which would eventually stretch up to Sonoma, north of San Francisco. The ninth of these missions was founded near the mouth of the San Buenaventura River in 1782. Sometime in the late 1790s or early 1800s the outlying Asistencia Santa Gertrudis was erected (above 1A).

72. Of the voluminous anthropological literature the most extensive overview is Lynn Gamble's 2008 book, *The Chumash World at European Contact*. More technical recent studies include Erlandson and Jones, *Catalysts to Complexity*; Arnold, *Foundations of Chumash Complexity*; and Altschul and Grenda, *Islanders & Mainlanders*. Popular introductions include Gibson, *Chumash*, and Miller, *Chumash*.

73. See Davidson, "Did Ancient Polynesians Visit California?"

74. Gamble, *Chumash World*, 6–10; Walker and Hudson, *Chumash Healing*; Timbrook, *Chumash Ethnobotany*.

75. Like most Europeans, Cabrillo believed California was an island (see Polk, *Island of California*) and, as with all early explorers, stood to profit from any trade or treasure in lands "discovered."

76. The Portolá expedition was chronicled in Crespí, *Description of Distant Roads*; it notes that the Spaniards first passed through Ventura on August 8, 1769. Fr. Serra's legacy has recently been the subject of fierce debate; on the one hand he was canonized in 2015 by Pope Francis; on the other, he has been sharply denounced for his treatment of Indigenous Californians (see Castillo, *Cross of Thorns*). After the police murder of George Floyd in May 2020, local protests (in which we participated) successfully called for the removal of Serra's statue from in front of Ventura's City Hall.

In California the colonization and missionizing of Indigenous peoples were explicitly fused. Elias Castillo's *A Cross of Thorns* chronicles the brutal capture, enslavement, forced labor, and punishment of Native Californians in the Mission system, where the death rate was appalling. Chumash/Ohlone scholar Jonathan Cordero, who has studied Native life at the Missions extensively, summarizes: "Approximately 85,000 Indians were baptized at the missions, but by the time the missions were secularized beginning in 1833 only 15,000 remained."[77] The majority of coastal Chumash had been brought into the Mission system by 1820. "Nearly two-thirds of all children born at the [San Buenaventura] Mission died within the first five years of life," write anthropologists Sally McLendon and John Johnson. By "1833–34, Chumash populations had been reduced to about fifteen percent of their estimated levels at the beginning of Spanish colonization."[78] There was only minor armed resistance, but the largest organized uprising in colonial California was the Chumash Revolt of 1824, impacting three missions.[79] But as their communities and habitats were devastated, Chumash survived either by assimilating or fleeing into California's interior.[80]

Mexico wrested independence from Spain in 1821, maintaining tenuous hold on the remote colony of Alta California. The Secularization Act of 1833 confiscated much mission land, including what was purportedly being held "in trust" for Indigenous communities by the padres. This was then redistributed, sold or given away by *Californio* governors in large grants to already-affluent *rancheros*-cum-cattle barons (nineteen land grants in Ventura alone). This led to further disenfranchisement of the Chumash, especially those socialized into the mission system.[81] By the time of American takeover, all Chumash had been removed from the Channel Islands (which were purposed for livestock ranching), and no mainland villages remained intact, though a few "reconstituted" communities struggled to continue more traditional ways of life.[82]

77. Cordero, "Missionized California Indian Futures," 63.

78. McLendon and Johnson, *Cultural Affiliation and Lineal Descent*, vi.

79. See Beebe and Senkewicz, "End of the 1824 Chumash Revolt," and Talaugon, "Four Things You Should Know." A Tongva female shaman planned a revolt in 1785 (see John, "Toypurina").

80. John Johnson writes that some Chumash settled "elsewhere in Hispanic California in places like Monterey, Los Angeles, and San Juan Capistrano. Others removed themselves as far as possible from European influence, settling among Yokuts and Kitanemuk Indians in the Tejon region of the Southern San Joaquin Valley." ("Chumash Indians after Secularization," 144.)

81. Overviewed in Johnson, "Chumash Indians after Secularization."

82. Bornemann and Gamble describe several such Chumash enclaves during the post-Mission, pre-American period. For example, near the mouth of the Ventura River,

In 1848, at the conclusion of the Mexican-American war, the U.S. Army of the West occupied Alta California, a process that had been well underway since the so-called "Bear Flag" revolt at the start of the war in the summer of 1846.[83] Under American rule, the fate of Indigenous people deteriorated precipitously as a result of genocidal policies and massacres, as Benjamin Madley has recently chronicled in *An American Genocide: The United States and the California Indian Catastrophe, 1846–1873*. Disease, alcohol, and the sexual exploitation of Indigenous women further devastated Native populations ("securing Indian children for indenture or outright sale was common in California from 1850 to 1863"[84]). Though the U.S. had agreed in the Treaty of Guadalupe Hidalgo to honor both Mexican and Native land grants, these were "deliberately ignored by Whites who were often able to wrest title to the land through their political connections, the Indian owner's unfamiliarity with American law and Native people's lack of access to legal advice."[85] In 1851, Congress approved the Land Claims Act with a "process for proving claims; land titles that couldn't be perfected within two years would pass to the federal government as public domain, available for homesteading"—a timeline, Leon Worden notes, that was impossible to meet for virtually all traditional land owners.[86]

"the village at *kamexmey'* and activities that were recorded there serve as testimony to the continued persistence of traditional religious and economic activities," including use of the *tomol* ("Resilience among Hunter-Gatherers in Southern California," 188). One of these displaced communities reconstituted at the Asistencia Santa Gertrudis (above 1A).

83. The short-lived settler *putsch*—similar to the one in Hawai'i fifty years later (see Interlude B)—was led by U.S. Captain John Fremont, who had "arrived in California at the head of a 60-man geographical survey. Fremont was supposed to be on a mission to locate the source of the Arkansas River, but he wasted little time in encouraging the local American settlers to carry out an uprising." (Andrews, "What Was the Bear Flag Revolt?")

84. Heizer, *Destruction of California Indians*, 219.

85. McLendon and Johnson, *Cultural Affiliation and Lineal Descent*, vi. See also Lightfoot, *Indians, Missionaries, and Merchants*.

86. Worden, "Treaty between the United States and the Indians," para. 2. See the expansive study of W. W. Robinson, *Land in California*. A local example is Rancho Ojai, 17,717 acres granted to Fernando Tico by Governor Juan Alvarado in 1837. Title to these lands wasn't perfected until December 22, 1870, when the U.S. granted a patent to the Mexican grantee; but Tico's family had already been forced to sell seventeen years earlier to Henry Carnee. In Santa Barbara, there was only one exception to this litany of dispossession: Maria Ygnacia, a Barbareño Chumash, executed several trust deeds to preserve her mission-granted property rights north of town for her heirs, who still inhabit that parcel (Johnson, "Chumash Indians after Secularization," 147). For a study of the contrasting Mexican and American systems, see Bastian, "Henry Wager Halleck, the *Californios*, and the Clash of Legal Cultures."

The town of San Buenaventura was incorporated in 1866, and the county officially split from Santa Barbara in 1873. When the Southern Pacific Railroad shortened the name to "Ventura" for its timetables, the rest of the Anglo community soon followed suit. By this time most land parcels had passed into white hands in this ranching and agricultural region, whose crops changed according to episodic drought. Real estate schemes went boom and bust. Chumash laborers were replaced by immigrants who were equally exploited and then marginalized, from Chinese in the 1880s to Indigenous Oaxacans today.[87] Today Ventura's landscape is marked by more than forty (hispanicized) Chumash names such as Hueneme, Topa Topa, Malibu, Lompoc, Pismo, Mugu, Piru, Castaic, Saticoy, Simi, and Ojai ('awhay', "moon"). The Chumash themselves, however, are not so visible; there are just a handful of descendants left in our watershed.[88] But they *have* survived the successive waves of Spanish, Mexican, and American colonization, and though Ventureño Chumash are still not federally recognized, leaders persist in the long, slow struggle to rebuild their language, ceremonies, identity, and roles as traditional stewards of this land.[89]

Ched and I live on soil which, like the Ventura River, holds these stories. We are "re-settlers" here. It is easy to problematize rural settlers farming on Cree land in Saskatchewan, because the genealogy of dispossession there is relatively simple. But we are just as compromised, as are suburban or urban property owners everywhere on Turtle Island. We re-settlers have moved around the landscape to live in various places for reasons of work, family, or personal preferences (though sometimes under duress). We presume our right and entitlement to do so, never considering whether we should ask for permission from Indigenous leaders in the places where we re-settle. In this way we perpetuate patterns begun by the first colonizers. As we said at the outset, the pathology of settler colonialism goes "seven layers deep."

It's been a challenge tracing the history of the ground under our feet in little, unincorporated Oak View. We bought our home from a descendant of

---

87. Two leading organizations working on contemporary immigration issues in Ventura County are the Central Coast Alliance United for a Sustainable Economy* and the Mixteco/Indigena Community Organizing Project.*

88. According to Johnson, "one family of documented three-quarter Chumash ancestry and another of half Chumash descent are still residents of Ventura county today" ("Chumash Indians after Secularization," 148). We are grateful for our relationship with both families.

89. See Cason, "Chumash Beliefs Defy Easy Labels." The Chumash are among some 245 landless bands in the U.S. "According to most recent census data, California is home to more people of Native American/Alaska Native heritage than any other state in the country. There are currently 109 federally recognized Indian tribes in California and 78 entities petitioning for recognition" (https://www.courts.ca.gov/3066.htm, para. 1).

mid-twentieth century homesteaders from the Midwest, who bought several adjacent plots and built small houses on this mesa above the river. Sharon, in her eighties, is part of that family and she grew up in the 400-square foot building we now use as our BCM office; she still lives next door. "My dad just saved money until he could buy more cinder blocks to build another room," she told us. From the 1930s on, Oak View slowly became a bedroom community for blue-collar workers in the oil fields down the valley; oil prospecting and production along the Ventura River has extracted more than a billion barrels over the last century. Before that our neighborhood was the site of fruit orchards (hence the street names Olive, Almond, and Apricot). Next to our home is the old route of a narrow gauge railroad spur (now a bike path) that brought Ojai produce down to Ventura packing houses from 1899 to 1968. In our yard we exhumed a large boulder on which Chinese and Japanese characters were carved, likely by workers constructing that railroad.

A few miles away, in a basin now depopulated by the Water District to protect the watershed around Lake Casitas, is relatively intact chaparral habitat. Shortly after moving here we found an oak tree hidden away there, possibly a half-millennium old, leaning over an unnamed seasonal brook with amazing vernal ponds. We prayed often under "Grandmother Oak," until she was destroyed by the climate-fueled Thomas Fire in December 2017.[90] The land around her, including what is now Oak View and Lake Casitas, was bought and subdivided in the 1870s by American entrepreneurs. Before that it was part of the 21,522-acre Rancho Santa Ana, granted by Mexican Governor Juan Alvarado to Crisogomo Ayala and Cosme Vanegas in 1837.[91] Prior to that it was part of Mission San Buenaventura's lands. And before colonization, the valley between Coyote and Santa Ana Creeks hosted two Chumash villages: *sulukukay* and *kašomšomoy*.[92] From the remains of Grandmother Oak one can see the ridge upon which, according to tradition, the "Rainbow Bridge" touched down.

It is our discipleship duty and desire to build our literacy in both our Ventura River watershed and my beloved Saskatchewan River Valley. We seek to know ever more deeply their pain and promise, and to help heal past and present dispossession, disparities, and degradations.

90. See Ched's lament "If an Ancient Cathedral Had Burned."

91. Vanegas was the son of a *poblador* of Los Angeles (a term referring to the forty-four original Spanish settlers and four soldiers who founded the Pueblo de Nuestra Señora la Reina de los Ángeles in 1781).

92. See Beck and Haase, *Historical Atlas of California*, 36; King, "Names and Locations of Historic Chumash Villages."

5E. COVENANTAL FAITH: BECOMING TREATY PEOPLE

"As long as the sun shines, grass grows and rivers flow." As noted in the Prologue, the graffiti of this famous treaty language in a back alley of the neighborhood in which I was raised expresses a haunting—"wronging the wrongs," as Eve Tuck puts it. It reminds us the trail of broken agreements made by the settler state with Indigenous peoples awaits a settler politics that will fully embrace what it means to honor or renew them. A key aspect of decolonization work, therefore, is to revisit treaties our ancestors made as solemn covenants with Creator, land, and people, and the commitments to which they obligate us. We must learn the history of treaty-*making* (or lack thereof) and *breaking* in order to be accountable for it.

Between 1701 and 1923, the British and later Canadian government signed seventy treaties with 364 First Nations. This process began in earnest after 1869, when the Hudson's Bay Company sold its vast holdings *back* to the British Crown, land which was then incorporated into the new Dominion of Canada. By 1874, in order to develop a system that would support private land ownership, "an international team of surveyors had marked the Canada-U.S. boundary," writes Candace Savage. "Soon thereafter, an invisible network of longitude and latitude began to extend north across the open prairie . . . assigning a numerical designation to every section and quarter-section."[93] Surveying was the harbinger of settler invasion, but in order to formally "open" the land the government set about negotiating treaties, which between 1870 and 1906 "effectively reduced First Nations territories to a network of fairly small reserves."[94]

Present-day Saskatchewan is covered by six numbered treaties between First Nations and the Crown, signed between 1874 and 1907 (Figure 24); there are a total of eleven numbered treaties. Treaty 6 is central to my story, covering most of the Saskatchewan River watershed. Indigenous signatories (twenty-nine bands in Saskatchewan alone) proceeded in good faith, trusting the queen's promises to provide food, clothing, medicine, education, agricultural technology, and most importantly, assurance of right relationships. But as historian Susan Neylan points out, "Homesteading policies (such as the 1872 Dominion Lands Act) were created even before treaties were signed, suggesting that expediency and opportunity trumped genuine regard for Indigenous land rights."[95] Bands that did not sign treaties were pressured to do so through starvation policies, and if they

93. Savage, *Geography of Blood*, 124.

94. Anderson, *Settling Saskatchewan*, 24.

95. Neylan, "Canada's Dark Side," para. 25.

continued to resist they were dispossessed, as illustrated in the tragic story
of the remarkable Cree chief *Mistahi-maskwa* (Big Bear).[96]

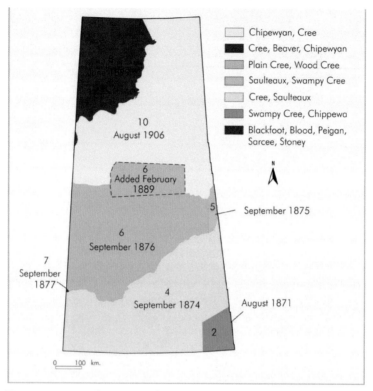

**Figure 24: Historical Treaties with First Nations in SK. Map by Canadian Plains
Research Center, found in *The Encyclopedia of Saskatchewan* (https://esask.
uregina.ca/entry/aboriginal_treaty_rights.jsp).**

Treaties remain Canada's law of the land today, and a primary point
of reference for many Indigenous leaders. The modern treaty era began in
1973 when the Supreme Court recognized Aboriginal rights for the first
time. This landmark decision led to development of the Comprehensive
Land Claims Policy and the first modern treaty: the 1975 James Bay and
Northern Québec Agreement.[97] Since then Canada has signed twenty-five
additional treaties (or comprehensive land claim agreements) with Indigenous groups, and continues to deal with demands that Aboriginal titles be

96. See Dempsey, *Big Bear*; Wiebe, *Temptations of Big Bear*; and Savage, *Geography
of Blood*, 133–50.

97. For the court decision, see https://scc-csc.lexum.com/scc-csc/scc-csc/en/
item/5113/index.do; also Turcotte, "James Bay and Northern Quebec Agreement."

respected.[98] These include "comprehensive claims," which concern indigenous rights of Métis, First Nations, and Inuit communities that did not sign earlier treaties; and also "specific claims" filed by First Nations regarding Canada's breach of official historic agreements. Despite all this, Native reserves are only 0.2 percent of Canada's land mass![99]

In California, the history of Chumash country was dramatically different. In 1850—amidst widespread settler massacres of Indigenous communities in northern California in part driven by "gold fever"—the U.S. Senate authorized three commissioners to negotiate treaties with the state's Indian tribes (mostly to secure Native secession of potentially gold-bearing lands).[100] Between April 1851 and August 1852, these commissioners, having arbitrarily divided California into eighteen regions, traveled the state "negotiating" treaties with random groups that rarely corresponded to actual tribal or clan groups.

Archaeologist Robert Heizer summarizes:

> Eighteen treaties were made but the Senate on July 8, 1852 refused to ratify them in executive session and ordered them filed under an injunction of secrecy which was not removed until January 18, 1905 . . .

> While there may have been some kind of communication, there is great probability that the literal wording of the treaties often was not, and indeed could not be, made intelligible to the Indians present . . .

> None of the Commissioners had any knowledge whatsoever of California Indians or their cultural practices, especially those regarding land ownership and use . . .

> The three Commissioners did not have the slightest idea of the actual extent of tribal lands of any group they met with. Their orders were to secure Indian land title to California, and they managed to do this to their satisfaction by making treaties with some Indians and then dividing all of California west of the Sierra-Cascade crest into eighteen unequal cession areas which, happily, quite covered the entire region . . .

98. See Albers, "Indigenous Land Claims"; Pitawanakwat, "Indigenous Treaty Rights."

99. See Manuel, *Unsettling Canada*.

100. Madley has documented these awful killings in detail in *An American Genocide*, 67–144, 173–288.

Taken all together, one cannot imagine a more poorly conceived, more inaccurate, less informed, and less democratic process.[101]

When these Treaties "re-emerged" in Congressional consciousness in the early twentieth century, minor funds were given to purchase the first of northern California's Indian *rancherias*.[102] Only the 1851 Treaty of Tejon involved Chumash signatories, though involving lands that lay well east of their traditional territory. But it too was never ratified, and through a particularly sordid history eventually passed into the private hands of California's Indian Commissioner![103] Like so many of California Native communities, the Chumash were thus left unprotected by any treaty agreement or land grant.

~

Indigenous communities have not forgotten the sins of both commission and omission in this lamentable legacy. In contrast, a keystone characteristic of settler "unknowing" (below 6C) is that we are illiterate and uninterested in treaty history, and thus harbor no sense of accountability to these covenants (or lack of them). Or we misunderstand them. "Treaties figure in the settler imagination in a number of problematic ways," writes Chris Hiller of the Canadian context:

101. Heizer, "Eighteen Unratified Treaties of 1851–1852," 1–5. This long article includes the long-hidden text of these treaties; a summary is found in Worden, "Treaty between the United States and the Indians." For a map of native California territories and the treaty areas, see http://calindianhistory.org/california-unratified-treaties-map/.

102. Miller, "Secret Treaties with California's Indians," 45. In California, *rancherias* refer to fifty-nine Indian settlements established by the U.S. government for survivors of the Indigenous population. See also Slagel, "Unfinished Justice."

103. In 1851, "the California Legislature didn't want anything or anyone to stand in the way of further immigration and exploitation of the natural resources. The federal government reorganized California Indian affairs under one overseer instead of three commissioners—namely, E. F. Beale. With no rights to the Tejon or any other land, Indians from as far away as the Owens Valley were brought to the Tejon (aka San Sebastian) Indian Reservation. But it was not to last. In 1858 . . . the U.S. government validated the old Mexican title to Rancho El Tejon and issued the patent in 1863. The patent relegated the reservation Indians to the status of squatters on someone else's property—and that someone was none other than the crafty E. F. Beale, who purchased the land from its Mexican-American owners for $21,000. The Indians were left to fend for themselves; some found work as ranch hands on Beale's eventual 300,000-acre spread while others returned to their ancestral homes to eke out a similar existence" (Worden, "Treaty between the United States and the Indians," para. 15).

1) as real estate deals "that extinguished the property rights of the original occupiers" and conveniently "eliminate[d] the legal impediment to settling Indigenous lands" . . .

2) as "special rights" for Indians—perks arising from antiquated agreements made in faraway and now largely irrelevant histories of early encounter, and allocated now by a magnanimous nation state;

3) as yet another self-reinforcing sign of Canada as the "benevolent peace-maker" nation, with its continued and defining generosity towards Indigenous people.[104]

Over the last two decades, however, this socialized ignorance has begun to change as a result of political organizing and education.

In 2003, Alberta political scientist (and prairie Mennonite) Roger Epp published a concise overview of problems and prospects for settler-Indigenous "reconciliation" in Canada in the wake of the government initiatives during the 1990s.[105] His trope "we are all Treaty people" has resonated widely in many parts of Canada, and is used now in schools and even some government circles.[106] Epp's analysis—important for the U.S. as well—shows how difficult this is for settlers, given the radically divergent worldviews of European Enlightenment social contract theory on one hand and the Indigenous ethos of relational covenant on the other. This includes differences "between liberal-individual and tribal-communal identities, between venerative and instrumental attitudes to language, between oral and written histories, between covenantal and contractual understanding of treaties."[107] Susan Neylan summarizes it this way: "What Indigenous people believed were nation-to-nation agreements of peace the Canadian government viewed as real estate deals intended to extinguish Indigenous claims to land ownership and designed to remove or restrict rights of access to resources."[108]

In 2015, Harry LaFond (whose Afterword graces this volume) gave us a small book entitled *Treaty Elders of Saskatchewan* that impacted us in

---

104. Hiller, "'No, Do You Know??,'" 382.

105. It is the title essay in Epp, *We Are All Treaty People*, 121–41.

106. Expressions can be found from universities (https://www.oise.utoronto.ca/abed101/we-are-all-treaty-people/) to elementary schools (https://www.canadashistory.ca/education/classroom-resources/we-are-all-treaty-people) to a provincial government (https://www.youtube.com/watch?v=TePIVr2bgCY). See commentary at McKenzie-Jones, "What Does 'We are All Treaty People' Mean?," and Corrigan, "We Are All Treaty People."

107. Epp, *We Are All Treaty People*, 126.

108. Neylan, "Canada's Dark Side," para. 23.

a big way. At the time, he was Executive Director of the Office of the Treaty Commissioner (OTC) Saskatchewan, the vocation of which is to "facilitate discussions about the meaning of the treaties and to work towards the implementation of their terms in a way that is consistent with the original spirit and intent of the treaties as it was, and is, understood by the parties."[109] The book is a remarkable collection of testimonies by Indigenous elders from each of the numbered treaty areas in Saskatchewan concerning their understanding of treaty-making. In reading them what was most instructive to us as Christian settlers was their fundamentally *theological* approach. "First Nations' first and foremost objective in the treaty-making process was to have the new peoples arriving in their territories recognize and affirm their continuing right to maintain, as peoples, the First Nations relationships with the Creator through the laws given to them," editors Harold Cardinal and Walter Hildebrandt write. "The starting point of discussions on treaties is their relationship to the Creator."[110]

It was assumed a similar orientation would be true for colonial representatives:

> Elders refer to the spiritual ceremonies conducted and spiritual symbols used by First Nations and the active participation of various Christian missionaries along with the Christian symbols utilized by the Crown in those negotiations to assert that both parties anchored their goals and objectives on the values and principles contained in the teachings of each of their own spiritual traditions.[111]

This, however, was hardly the case. At most, the Christian symbolism used by Crown negotiators was window dressing around their operative understandings of land possession and treaties as transactions akin to real estate deals. This asymmetry is particularly odious given the purported theological underpinnings of European colonization from fifteenth-century Doctrines of Discovery to nineteenth-century missionization.

---

109. Cardinal and Hildebrandt, *Treaty Elders of Saskatchewan*, vii. The OTC was created in 1989 and helped curate the "Treaty Land Entitlement Agreements between 28 First Nations and the Governments of Canada and Saskatchewan." Staff then documented historic accounts of treaty-making through academic studies, and traveled around the province soliciting "Elders to share some of their vast knowledge about the treaties in Saskatchewan," gathering oral testimonies in Dene, Nakoda, Saulteaux, and Cree languages "from the Elders who are the keepers of oral tradition and history" (vii–viii).

110. Cardinal and Hildebrandt, *Treaty Elders of Saskatchewan*, 6–7.

111. Cardinal and Hildebrandt, *Treaty Elders of Saskatchewan*, 6–7.

More striking still is the fact that Indigenous understandings of a "people-land-Creator" triad coheres with the biblical notion of covenant. The latter is seen in a poignant image from the book of Joshua, cited at the very beginning of this book:

> This stone shall be a witness against us; for it has heard all the words that the LORD spoke to us; therefore it shall be a witness against you, if you deal falsely with your God. (Josh 24:27)

This is an ancient example of how both written and oral covenant are witnessed not only by Creator and people, but by the land itself: cairns "hear" and can "testify." Indeed, sacred stones are prominent in the oldest biblical traditions. They animate Jacob's mystical dreams (Gen 28:11, 18) and are drawn up from the River Jordan to hold the memory of Israel's liberation movement (Josh 4). The Ten Commandments (Exod 31:18) and the entire Law (Deut 27:8) are etched in rock, and only "unhewn" stones can be used for a sacred altar (Exod 20:25). This tradition was invoked later by the "weeping prophet" Jesus of Nazareth in his insistence that if people are silent the "stones will cry out" (Luke 19:39–42, alluding to Hab 2:11). And it was a "keystone" conviction of the early church that "the stone the builders rejected has become the cornerstone" of renewal (Ps 118:22, Mark 12:10; see below 8E).

By the nineteenth century, however, these scriptural injunctions to a "triple covenant" with land, people, and Creator had been fully eclipsed in settler thinking by Enlightenment ideologies of autonomy and supremacy. Roger Epp concludes that such presumptions, coupled with the powerful and persistent "myth of *terra nullius*," continue to allow settlers to "live more comfortably, forgetfully, with the dirty little secret that the treaties were a one-time land swindle than with the possibility that they might mean something in perpetuity."[112] But the Saskatchewan Elders—and the Hebrew and Christian Scriptures—call us to reconsider covenant relationship so as to become Treaty People today.

Heather Ross, a Canadian diversity educator, summarizes two key Cree principles at play:

1. *kihci-asotamâtowin*, which means "sacred promises to one another, the treaty sovereigns sacred undertakings." . . . [W]hen the new comers entered into treaties, they entered into a covenant with First Nations people, which was made sacred by the smoking of the pipe. In doing so, it was understood that both parties were making an agreement, not

112. Epp, *We Are All Treaty People*, 133.

only with one another, but also with the Creator. Thus, the covenant was an enduring one, which could only be broken by the Creator . . .

2. *miyo-wîcehtowin*, meaning "getting along well with others, good relations, [and] expanding the circle." Becoming more knowledgeable about treaty history, and about current treaty issues promises to bring about a greater understanding of First Nations.[113]

The salient issue for settlers is whether we will take both the content and living spirit of treaty covenants seriously as part of *our* identity and relationship to the land on which we dwell, or continue to shrug them off as inconvenient, obsolete, or irrelevant. This is especially true for those of us whose Anabaptist ancestors "called themselves 'covenanters' (*Bundgenossen*)."[114]

Stacey LaForme, a band councilor for the Mississaugas of the Credit, puts the challenge succinctly: "To be a treaty person simply means to understand who you are, how you fit in the treaty process, to understand what you have to do to ensure that it works."[115] This has begun to register with some Mennonites and Lutherans in the Saskatchewan Valley, who are trying to become better Treaty People by supporting the ongoing Young Chippewayan land claim (see below 6A, Epilogue).[116]

Meanwhile, Ventura's small Chumash community, with benefit of neither treaty legacy nor federal recognition, is in a re-birthing phase of political and cultural identity re-formation. Our job as local settlers is to learn about, listen to, and support this process as we build relationships of restorative solidarity. Chumash scholar Matthew Vestuto took our local Farm Church community on tours of the Ventura River watershed, teaching us Chumash names of mountains, plants, and village sites. It is a different way of walking on this land: learning the stories it holds is a discipline settlers everywhere would do well to embrace. Only through such practices will we learn to become Treaty People—even on land without treaties.

113. Ross, "We Are All Treaty People," paras. 3, 4. She is quoting from Cardinal and Hildebrandt, *Treaty Elders of Saskatchewan*, 14, 25.

114. See Wenger, "Covenant Theology," which suggests early Anabaptists may have preceded magisterial Reformers in emphasizing covenant theology.

115. Turner, "What Does It Mean?," para. 16.

116. Bridges, "Saskatchewan's 'Landless Bands' Fight for Recognition, Reconciliation," para. 31. See Doell, "Report to Mennonite Central Committee Saskatchewan."

5F. QUERIES FOR REINHABITATION

The issues we've been posing here pertain to any and all places our people settled, from where our immigrant ancestors first landed to where we grew up and where we live now. Considering the settler and the Indigenous histories of multiple places can be complicated and time-consuming. This book concentrates on two watersheds essential to my story, in Saskatchewan and California. We recommend you start with *one* place relevant to your family story, preferably the one you know the most about. Preface your work with an introspective exercise, as I did at the beginning of this chapter: What landscapes are imprinted on your soul, and why? Because, as our friend, Canadian theater scholar Julie Salverson, puts it: "The question 'What ground do I stand on, and who am I standing here?' is a critical and possibly transformative one."[117]

The term *reinhabitation* has been employed by ecological social theory over the last half century to suggest a deeper engagement with a place: learning to live "within" it, not just "on top" of it, and to truly *belong* to one's bioregion and help restore damage wrought there by industrial capitalism.[118] We agree with David Greenwood that a "critical pedagogy of place" should link decolonization with reinhabitation.[119] He proposes the following questions for "place-based inquiry and action":

- What needs to be remembered?
- What needs to be recovered or restored?
- What needs to be conserved or maintained?
- What needs to be changed or transformed?
- What needs to be created?

We suggest these apply to how we relate to Indigenous cultures as well as to the land, and to a lived past as well as present.

Here are more queries for mapping your Landlines:

1. Where did your immigrant ancestors first land in North America, and did they settle far from there? Why did they settle where they did? Did the land have geographic characteristics similar to what they had left?

117. Salverson, "Loopings of Love and Rage," 35.

118. Gary Snyder was one of the early articulators of this eco-vision (see his 1976 "Reinhabitation"), emphasizing that settlers need to learn how to "re-place" themselves on the land from Indigenous peoples. See Messersmith-Glavin, "Between Social Ecology and Deep Ecology."

119. Greenwood, "Critical Theory of Place-Conscious Education," 96.

2. How soon did these ancestors acquire land or housing—if at all—and how were they impacted by opportunities or obstacles?

3. Did they benefit from direct or indirect subsidies, and if so, how were those advantages narrated to posterity?

4. What new forces of push and pull did they encounter once they settled?

5. How soon did they procure jobs and education, and under what conditions? What were the socioeconomic factors impinging upon the places they settled?

6. How important were social networks (including religion) and/or ethnic associations in determining the where/when/how of your ancestors' settlement and mobility?

7. Who did your immigrant ancestors befriend, and who were they suspicious of?

8. Who were the Indigenous people(s) of the area where your forebears settled, and what was happening to them as your people moved in?[120] Do you know any stories of settler-Indigenous encounters there?

9. What were local settler practices or official government policies that impacted local Native communities, including treaties (if any), agricultural or industrial development, and schooling? How can you learn the original spirit and intent of treaties in that area?

10. Did your predecessors exhibit much literacy or interest in Indigenous culture or history? If so, did they pass it on? Do you know the deep history of that area's first inhabitants, or their Creation stories?

11. Can you sketch a timeline of significant events in the colonization of the area your people settled from both Indigenous and settler perspectives (see above Figures 10 and 11)? How is that history (including notorious events such as massacres or environmental disasters) enshrined on the local landscape (i.e., by place names or monuments, and in what language)? What is *not* enshrined?

12. Can you find traces of entitlement in your family or communal narrative, e.g.:

   • *terra nullius* presumption ("there was no one doing anything with the land when we arrived");

   • superiority complexes ("we came here and made things better"); or

   • Manifest Destiny ideology ("it's just Progress")?

120. A helpful resource is the map at https://native-land.ca/.

13. How were prejudices toward Indigenous or other ethnic groups expressed, were they recognized as such, and how might you have internalized them (even unconsciously)?

14. What stories did you learn from your family about the place(s) you grew up? How were you taught to care for and love those places?

15. Is there anything you wish your community would have done (or not done) in retrospect?

16. What is missing from your family and communal Landlines stories in North America, and how are those silences justified? How might your people have contributed to the erasure of local Native people and undermined their survival?

Now explore similar queries regarding where you currently live:

1. How far is the place you currently live from where you were born or raised? From where your immigrant ancestors first settled? What caused your ancestors to move? Your family? How many times have you made significant geographic moves as an adult, and what personal or political forces have driven your "re-settlements?" How do these moves affect your sense of identity or home?

2. What is the culture and history of Indigenous peoples in your place of residence, and the current landscape of settler privilege and Indigenous struggle?

3. What relationships with Native people do you have, and how might you deepen and broaden these?

4. Do you live on treaty land or proximate to other forms of Indigenous sovereignty (reservations, tribal organizations, etc.)?

5. What practices might help you become more of a "Treaty person?" How might you affirm covenant even if official agreements were never made (or have been abrogated) with Indigenous communities of your area?

6. What are other practices you can explore to reinhabit your place more deeply as a decolonizing settler?

Landlines can either haunt us or liberate us. Wherever settlers dwell in North America is a human and ecological landscape *into* which we walked. If we remain aloof from the stories held by the land and its First Peoples, "the stones will witness against us," as the biblical Joshua warned. Conversely, to become a "reinhabitory citizen" of our place is to work diligently to understand how injustices have marked land and people, how violations persist, and how to heal them.

Figure 25: Student body of the German English Academy, Rosthern, SK, 1950 (includes both of Elaine's parents). Enns family archival photo.

CHAPTER 6

Bloodlines II

De-Assimilating

As a minority concerned about love and their neighbors, could [Mennonites] participate in the agricultural invasion of another minority which destroyed the livelihood and way of life of that minority without serious compromise of their beliefs?

—Leo Driedger[1]

6A. UNSETTLING SQUATTERS, 1976

"I feel like a refugee in my own country."

George Kingfisher, Young Chippewayan hereditary chief, was addressing students at Rosthern Junior College in April 2015.[2] For me, as the grandchild of refugees (and a graduate of RJC), his lament was particularly painful. Though Chief Kingfisher chose not to add that my people had benefitted directly from the historical erasure of his people (above 5C and D), he didn't need to. A half century before, Young Chippewayans had brought this inconvenient fact to the attention of my Mennonite community in a locally notorious episode that has both troubled and animated us since.

August 1976 brought a special edition of the annual "Treaty Days" commemoration at Fort Carlton, Saskatchewan. The fort was the site of

1. Driedger, "Native Rebellion and Mennonite Invasion," 300.
2. Schulz, "Students Learn about Indigenous Land Issues," para. 1.

the local Hudson's Bay Company trading post from 1795 until 1885; it was burned during the Northwest Resistance, and a replica fort rebuilt in 1967 as a National Historic Site. A big government-sponsored gala was in the works for the August centenary of the signing of Treaty 6. Months earlier, however, Federation of Saskatchewan Indian Nations Chief David Ahenakew had pronounced to the *Saskatchewan Indian* newspaper: "This anniversary represents one hundred years of broken promises."[3]

At the public event, Chief Rod Okemow of the Lucky Man band refused to accept a Treaty Medallion from Canadian Chief Justice Emmet Hall. Instead he spoke out on behalf of his and other landless band members:

> My band once numbered 872 people. Today there are 48 of us. We are scattered throughout this province, on different reserves, in cities, and living under conditions which "civilized" people would not tolerate . . . We too are civilized people, with a culture and a tradition, of monumental courage and perseverance, of great bravery and greater suffering . . . Men came from the Queen, they promised us land, housing, education, health care and treaty money . . . There is a litany of broken promises . . . through the years you offer respect, flags and medals, it is meaningless and empty for me and my people . . . My band is without a home. We are squatters on the reserves where we live, without a voice in the councils of those reserves, without land, without pride of place or possession, without future for the generations of our people who may survive . . . Men have come again from the Queen, I ask these men here today, if they will honour the Treaty signed by Chief Lucky Man . . .? We, who have no home, ask in the name and spirit of Treaty #6, that this treaty now be honoured, and our rights granted . . .[4]

Descendants of Young Chippewayans identified closely with these sentiments. After the official Treaty Days gathering, some decided to go to visit their historic land at Opwashemoe Chakatinaw/Stoney Knoll, which many had never seen (see Figure 26).[5] And they wanted to talk with local farmers about their landless situation.

---

3. Doell, "History of Mennonites and Natives," 1, (citing the *Saskatchewan Indian*, April 1976, 15). Ahenakew died in 2010 after a long career advocating for treaty rights (see https://www.cbc.ca/news/canada/saskatchewan/controversial-native-leader-ahenakew-dies-1.885292).

4. "Chief Rod Okemow Refuses Treaty Gifts," 38.

5. Map of 1898 addition to Hague Mennonite Reserve showing Young Chippewayan Reserve 107, including Stoney Knoll. Tiefengrund is where my sister Janet lives now.

As local historian Leonard Doell tells it, some forty persons approached several Mennonite farms, staying in the area for three days. Some felt threatened; one Mennonite told me that Native men had gone to people's doors with rifles, demanding that they "need to leave this land; it is ours!" Participant Sidney Fineday (from Sweetgrass Reserve, about eighty miles east, and son of a Young Chippewayan band member) insisted however they were unarmed and came in peace—though he did note that they told farmers to "take good care of this land, because soon it will go back to the Indians."[6]

These events stirred up both fear and prejudice within the Mennonite community. They also got the attention of the Conference of Mennonites in Canada, which hired Doell to research Young Chippewayan claims. A year later Doell delivered a report for the Conference's Native Ministries Program. He detailed the history of Treaty 6, and showed: the relentless pressure government representatives put on Indigenous leaders to sign; the chiefs' resistance and requests for fairness and assurances; and the conflicted role of missionaries. The report then overviewed Mennonite migrations to Saskatchewan and their impact on Indigenous peoples, focusing on the Stoney Knoll and Tiefengrund areas. It also raised difficult issues, such as Mennonites leasing Reserve land for farming. Doell concluded that despite some "parallel histories" of marginalization, "the Indian just cannot identify with the rich Mennonite farmers. The Mennonite has no time to relate because he is busy working, continually striving to attain more things. Not only has race become a barrier, but often economics as well."[7] Fifty years later, Doell's report remains one of the most thoughtful and comprehensive analyses of the issue.

But in August 1976, some in the local Mennonite community were awash with anxiety. A few complained that their children were coming home from school asking, "Are the Indians coming to take our land away?" A petition was circulated among the congregation of historic Tiefengrund Church demanding that neither the Conference of Mennonites nor Mennonite Central Committee get involved with the Stoney Knoll conflict. Some church members wanted to understand and reckon with Mennonite entanglement in Young Chippewayan landlessness, while others felt threatened and resolute in their land ownership. This divisive season opened painful fissures, some of which are still felt in the community today.

---

6. Doell relates these events in his subsequent report, "History of Mennonites and Natives," 32–33. There he states: "some Mennonites suggested . . . they would be willing to protect their land and property with guns if necessary"—a deeply ironic twist (armed pacifists vs. unarmed "militants!"). Doell reiterated this account in "1976 Treaty Six Commemoration," 2.

7. Doell, "History of Mennonites and Natives," 35. Parts of Doell's findings were published in "Young Chippewayan Indian Reserve No. 107."

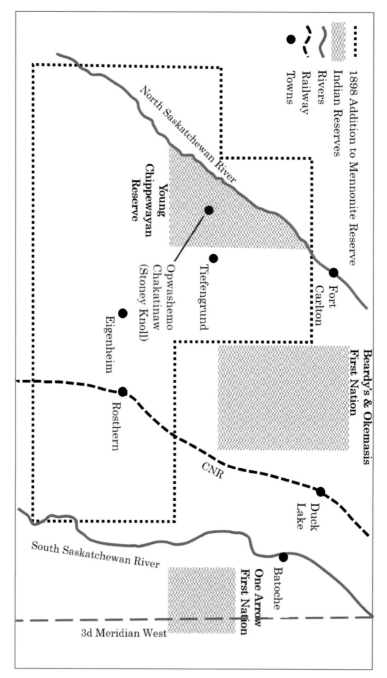

Figure 26: 1898 addition to Mennonite Hague Reserve (including Young
Chippewayan Reserve 107). Detail of map found in Ens, "Mennonite Relations with
Governments" (adaptation by Chris Wight).

The events of August 1976 surely expressed a haunting of a history in which settler "squatters" created Indigenous ones (to use Chief Okemow's word). In my 2014 doctoral research, interviewee Barb Froese (who, with husband Wilmer, owns land adjacent to Stoney Knoll today) confirmed this:

> I lived for years in fear. Our farm is at the bottom of the hill. I thought, one day we're going to see Teepees on top of that hill, and "they" are going to be occupying it, and it's going to come down to haunt us. There was [vandalism] on some of the yards, our light was shot out. We kept talking about how unfair this is, but about not wanting to get involved.[8]

But this pall began to lift in 2005 when Leonard Doell (then Indigenous Neighbors Coordinator for MCC Saskatchewan) got the Froeses to talk face to face with Young Chippewayan leaders Gary LaPlante and Chief Ben Weenie. These conversation resulted in what Barb called "beautiful, intimate times." Shortly thereafter, in 2006 (on the 130th-anniversary commemoration of the Treaty 6 signing), a Memorandum of Understanding was signed. It signaled a new chapter of partnership, to which we'll return in our conclusion.[9]

The unsettling legacy of Reserve 107 is personal for me. As previously mentioned, my sister and brother-in-law live just a few miles from Stoney Knoll. In 1894, Rob's great-grandparents emigrated from Prussia, among the first Mennonite settlers to the area. In the 1960s, Rob's parents bought a farm next to Beardy's and Okemasis Cree Nation (a Reserve established under Treaty 6), from whom Rob's dad rented additional land. In 1982, Janet and Rob moved onto this "Meadow Lane" farm and have lived there since.

Janet and Rob are both elementary school teachers, with a keen sense of local history and geography. Over the last twenty years they have shown us around the region on various tours: a Treaty Day celebration at Fort Carlton; the aforementioned canoe trip to Batoche to learn the story of the Northwest Resistance (above 5C); viewing the murals along Duck Lake's Main Street, especially of *Kisse-Manitou-Wayo*/Almighty Voice. We've attended occasional Sunday morning services at Tiefengrund Church, where three generations of Rob's ancestors are buried, and where his grandparents were the first couple to be married after the building was completed in 1910. Rob and Janet are committed to caring for the land: raising their own food and livestock (which they butcher on their yard); observing a Sabbath year

8. Tiefengrund Focus Group, interview by Elaine Enns, Carlton, Saskatchewan, June 23, 2014.

9. Below 8E. The story is depicted in an award-winning 2016 documentary film (https://www.reserve107thefilm.com/).

204 PART II: CARTOGRAPHY

practice (one year they ate only food grown in Saskatchewan); and experimenting with solar panels. Their second son operates a small organic market garden at Meadow Lane, selling his produce at the Farmers Market in Saskatoon ninety minutes away.

Still, my sister admits that as the next generation on this land, theirs has been a long, slow learning curve trying to figure out how to live in a good way with their Indigenous neighbors. "For many years we always went *west*, to the settler towns of Laird, Rosthern and Tiefengrund," she told me, "never *east* towards Beardy's."[10] A turning point came in 1995 when they took their four children for a sabbatical year to Port Hardy, British Columbi to teach in *Gwa'sala-'Nakwaxda'xw* School. Port Hardy is in the traditional territory of the Kwakiutl First Nation, on the northernmost tip of Vancouver Island, with a horrendous history of forced relocation and a long litany of broken promises from the Canadian government.[11] During this sojourn, Janet and Rob got to know survivors of residential schools ("children's prisons," as locals called them) and forged their first authentic friendships with Indigenous people. This immersion inspired them to commit to building relations with their Native neighbors in Saskatchewan. As is often the case with us settlers, it was a journey far away that pushed them to span distances of just a mile back home.[12]

In 2007, Janet began full-time teaching at Stobart Community School in Duck Lake, which serves students from Beardy's and Okemasis, wanting to get to know "this community to the east and north of us and to overcome the 'wall' between us." The student body is over 90 percent Métis and Indigenous, most of whom carry a strong, infectious pride in their families and traditions. Janet noted their community support for one another, and felt as a teacher she benefitted from a culture that encourages expressions of love and positive physical contact. "Children would run up to hug me at the beginning of each day!" she marveled, pointing out how different this was from other schools where she had previously taught. "Teaching mostly Indigenous kids at a public school near the reserve has opened up a whole new side of my connection to this land—and to our closest neighbors."[13]

10. Tiefengrund Focus Group, interview by Elaine Enns, Carlton, Saskatchewan, June 23, 2014.

11. See http://www.gwanak.info/about-us/history-vision, which describes the disastrous 1964 dislocation of the Gwa'sala and 'Nakwaxda'xw First Nations to Port Hardy.

12. Ched refers to this in his own similar journey, as "ap-proximation" (*Who Will Roll Away the Stone?*, 220–24).

13. Quotes in paragraph from Janet Enns Regier, phone interview, December 5, 2019.

Janet and Rob have gotten close with the Seesequasis family from Beardy's and Okemasis, and sometimes join them in sweats. On summer solstice 2014 they took me along. There were a dozen of us in the sweat lodge sitting closely, men and women on opposite sides. The drumming reverberated through my body, my spirit rising to the singing. My skin glistened with the bear oil we had rubbed "onto the places that need healing," and each time water hissed on the heated stones I delighted in the steamy blast. After an hour or so, Elder Herb bade each person in the circle to offer a brief reflection. Then the canvas flaps were thrown open and cool air rushed in. Feeling renewed, we all shared a potluck together in the Seesequasis home. It was a holy time, a glimmer of communion that seemed far removed from the "disturbance" of August 1976.

But Young Chippewayan leaders are *still* working to undo their disenfranchisement, and the Opwashemoe Chakatinaw/Stoney Knoll issue remains unresolved. The legal, economic, and moral tendrils of historic injustice run deep and wide. We settlers have much "turning around" to do yet, which is the focus of this chapter.

6B. HOW DID WE BECOME WHITE?

The continuing insularity of our settler communities represents a problematic social world of privilege, in which relationships with Indigenous people are entirely elective, and matters of Native justice rendered invisible or remote. The segregation of my family and community from our Indigenous neighbors was largely a function of our assimilation into the white Canadian mainstream. While not unique among European immigrant groups, it has come with a double cultural cost. On one hand, we lost opportunities to learn about and from Native communities. On the other, our own heritage atrophied, which we will focus on here.

Writing during the 1992 Columbus Quincentenary, the late Jeanie Wylie spoke of the U.S. as "a nation of Esaus":

> How many white Americans know their ancestry? How many can sing a song, say a prayer, bake the bread of their country/countries of origin? As important, how many know the positions their fore parents took in the struggles of their Native land? Did they fight for or against the monarchy? Did they support or reject ecclesial authority? . . . There is power in knowing these things. They offer a construct through which to consider the United States today. And most of us forfeited it. It was exchanged for employment at Ford Motor Company, or for

admission to the elite schools of the nation, or for the appear-
ance of upward mobility. Like Esau, we sold our inheritance for
a mess of pottage.[14]

The "strange journey from Ellis Island to the suburbs," as David Roediger puts it, has been explored in recent studies of Italian, Irish, and Jewish communities in the U.S..[15] Immigration and assimilation patterns are
historically different in Canada, with its comparatively small percentage of
undocumented migration, less widespread anti-immigrant prejudice, and
greater tolerance for multiculturalism. But many Canadians nevertheless
exhibit similar patterns of integration into whiteness.[16] Bloodlines work can
help all of us better understand how assimilation has distorted and disappeared our immigrant legacies and ethnic roots.

A parallel (if also distinct) assimilating trend holds for some non-
European immigrants as well, including Asian Americans, Arab Americans,
and even Latinx. Those willing and able to "climb the racial hierarchy" often
do so by defining themselves over and against the "otherness" of Black and
Indigenous communities and their histories of oppression under settler
colonialism.[17] As we acknowledged at the outset (above 1E), slavery and
its legacies in the U.S. make it almost impossible for many Black people
to trace their family histories back to African homelands. Yet because the
assimilation of people of African descent has historically been blocked by
the color line, Black consciousness of communal identity has remained relatively more intact—if constantly under attack by white supremacy. Lauret
Savoy's recent *Trace: Memory, History, Race, and the American Landscape*
(2016) took an approach similar to our LBS vectors, looking at the interaction between her people and their various places. Savoy "calls for an ethic
of place that acknowledges people who have been there before us, a sense
of their lingering presence evoked by the way the land around us has been
treated"—something we also endeavor to nurture in this book.[18]

Settlers of color will approach the problem of assimilation differently.
But for white folks it involves probing how our families became entangled in
structures and presumptions of privilege. This means understanding how,

14. Wylie, "Exchanging Birthrights," 5–6.

15. Roediger, *Working toward Whiteness*. See also Vellon, *Great Conspiracy against
Our Race*, and Ignatiev, *How the Irish Became White*.

16. See e.g., Griffith, "Building a Mosaic."

17. See e.g., Bhangal and Poon, "Are Asian Americans White?"; Ajrouch and Jamal,
"Assimilating to a White Identity"; and Levitz, "America Will Only Remain 'Majority
White' if Blacks Remain an Underclass."

18. Ballowe, "Review of *Trace* by Lauret Savoy," para. 6.

when, and why we "became white." Because whiteness is not an actual ethnic identity, but a social construct of supremacist settler colonialism.

∿

How, in just two generations, was my community of *Russländer* Mennonites transformed from German-speaking and (to some degree) culturally
separate to increasingly indistinct, middle-class, white Canadian? It seems
privileges that accrued from our European ethnicity, and from our growing
prosperity, have taken us far down the path of whiteness.[19] Here are five
trajectories of this process for us over the past century:

i. *Privilegia.* For more than four centuries Anabaptists endured a fraught
    relationship to dominant European institutions. As a "free" church
    professing dissident values such as pacifism, mutual aid, and adult
    baptism, our ancestors lived in tension with the state and its church
    (both Catholic and magisterial Protestant). At the same time, in or-
    der to survive disenfranchisement and frequent attempts at erasure,
    Mennonites became highly mobile, and in the process became adept
    at negotiating favorable terms with countries willing to accept (and
    use) them. In the Vistula Delta of Prussia, Mennonites were welcomed
    for their engineering and agrarian skills working marginal lands, and
    garnered "numerous charter privileges," which, according to Adolf
    Ens, "counter-acted discriminatory laws or government orders."[20]
    Subsequent Mennonite migrants negotiated a twenty-point *Privile-
    gium* with Catherine the Great of Russia in the 1770s, then again a
    century later with the queen of England in Canada. In both cases our
    people were used to help "open" land on colonial frontiers for settle-
    ment (above 3D). Acting as shrewd agents of our own migration was
    a nonviolent tactic of fleeing rather than fighting, yet our advocacy
    rarely included other oppressed communities or larger issues of social
    injustice. Mennonite immigrants were well versed at working with
    European systems and worldviews, and with *Privilegia* came an in-
    evitable degree of domestication under the ruling regime, a distinct
    pathway to assimilation.

ii. *Public schooling.* In 1873, the first wave of Russian Mennonite immi-
    grants negotiated a *Privilegium* with the Canadian government that

19. For a comprehensive overview of the sociological literature on this topic, published in 1977 amidst the second great wave of Mennonite assimilation in Canada, see
Smucker, *Sociology of Canadian Mennonites, Hutterites and Amish.*

20. Ens, *Subjects or Citizens?*, 5.

stipulated a right to educate their own children in their own traditions. But in the early twentieth century, public education became a key official strategy for assimilation into dominant Anglo society. This affected many communities, Indigenous and Métis, as well as Mennonite, Ukrainian, and others. Mennonites had resources to build their own schools so as to preserve their language (see next point). Prior to World War I, Mennonites in Manitoba and Saskatchewan were allowed to fund and maintain private schools; but afterward, with anti-German sentiment high, the provincial government forced their closure and required Mennonites to send their children to English-only public schools. Some Mennonites complied, but conservative communities resisted fiercely.[21] In 1919, Saskatchewan's School Ordinance forbade use of German during school hours, and tried to compel attendance at public schools through fines of $10 a month per child. Some families accrued large fines, and one person was imprisoned with a thirty-year sentence, but not one Old Colony Mennonite child went to public school.[22] When continued noncooperation became impossible during the 1920s, more than 7,000 Mennonites migrated to Latin America. Many of those Mennonites who did participate in public education went on to the graduate level (including almost everyone in my immediate family). Professional credentialing was predictably a major factor in our assimilation.

iii. *German language loss.* The German-English Academy was established in Rosthern, Saskatchewan by Mennonites in 1905 with a mission to: "protect the German language in the face of the developing public school system"; "train qualified Mennonite teachers"; "provide vocational training for farm boys who might not be able to access land"; and "provide Biblical and religious education."[23] Conscription issues during the First World War attracted more students, including

21. Bowen, "Resistance, Acquiescence and Accommodation," 554. Old Colony Mennonites, for example, regarded school as a key institution for teaching children religious values, and believed "if we send our children to public school, we are violating God's commands." Tactics of resistance included petitions, moving to remote areas outside of public school authority, and noncooperation with compulsory attendance. But some separatism was grounded in prejudice (i.e., not wanting their children to mix with Indians and Métis, claims that "English schools were dirty," and fears of sex education). In any case, mandatory public schools "dealt a severe blow to the community as children were exposed to worldly ways and their commitment to [traditional values] increasingly challenged" (569–73).

22. Anderson, *Settling Saskatchewan*, 143.

23. Epp, *Roots & Wings*, 15.

Mennonite draft dodgers from the U.S..[24] The influx of *Russländer* immigrants in the 1920s further boosted enrollment, leading to a strong teaching staff.[25] For three generations, everyone in my family attended the Academy (which changed its name to Rosthern Junior College in 1963, offering grades 10–12) as residential students: my parents, my siblings and their children, most of my relatives, and much of the prairie Mennonite community. RJC was key to language preservation for two generations: I grew up with *Deutsche Schule* at church on Saturdays, German hymnody in worship, and conversing with my grandparents and older relatives (above 4B). That said, many of my Carrot River cousins never learned to speak the "mother tongue," and *Deutsche Schule* was discontinued after my generation due to lack of interest. Already when I was at RJC, German was not taught as a requirement, and today is not offered at all![26] Language loss—and painfully, I have lost my childhood German—is widely recognized to be the biggest single factor in cultural assimilation.

iv. *Urbanization.* Through the second half of the twentieth century, agrarian prairie Mennonites were on an arc towards economic prosperity. Yet many became part of the wider nationwide sociological trend of migration to cities: a 2011 report showed that over half of all Canadian Mennonites now live in cities. This "shift from traditional rural communities to urban living has mirrored that of the general population."[27] Both my parents were part of this demographic transition. When my dad contracted severe rheumatic fever as a child in Carrot River, doctors advised him not to pursue farming. After graduating high school he moved to Saskatoon to pursue a Commerce degree, eventually becoming the assistant chief accountant at University Hospital. My maternal grandparents Heinrich and Margreta Toews defied expectations that *Russländer* immigrants should farm, and moved their young family to the city. My mom grew up in Saskatoon, and trained to be an advanced medical laboratory technologist before getting married.

24. Epp, *Roots & Wings*, 17.

25. In a different part of Saskatchewan in the 1920s, my Zacharias (maternal) immigrant ancestors helped establish the *Nordheimer Mennoniten Gemeinde* in the Hanley-Dundurn area, "that long made a consistent effort to maintain Mennonite traditions and the German language" (Anderson, *Settling Saskatchewan,* 126).

26. RJC continues to thrive today, though with fewer (and more diverse) residential and day students.

27. Epp and Driedger, "Mennonites," para. 10. See Driedger, "Changing Mennonite Family Roles."

Our home was suburban, though connections to farm life continued.[28] With so much of Mennonite tradition and culture historically tied to rural or small-village life, urbanization has inevitably been an assimilating force. And for those still on the land, technologies such as cell phones and the internet bring the urban world closer, while many elders retire in cities, towns, or regional centers to be closer to services.

v. *Intermarriage.* For minority communities, "marrying out" is another classic factor in assimilation. Traditionally, Mennonites worked to provide social opportunities for single young people to meet others from their community. Until the late 1950s, the most important guests at a wedding were the young single adults, who would get their food first and sit together in designated spots in hopes that coupling would develop. The vast majority of my parents' generation married Mennonites (as in Indigenous communities, we operated under strict protocols to prevent in-breeding). According to the 1981 Canadian census, only Jews among religious groups had higher rates of endogamy than Mennonites. Yet the latter's rate fell from 93 percent in 1921 to 61 percent in 1981.[29] This trend continued in my generation: half of my cousins married out, as did I. This shift has contributed to the atrophy of our community cohesion—though it has also opened Mennonite subcultures in North America to many diversities.[30]

Our Mennonite tradition unfortunately developed few resources (theological or otherwise) to help us exercise a "hermeneutic of suspicion" regarding the whiteness into which we were moving either unconsciously (as atrophy) *or* consciously (as aspiration).

Church is the one space where Mennonite identity has been most consistently retained and nurtured. My parents, married in 1955 at First Mennonite Church Saskatoon, helped found a new congregation on the south

28. My dad stayed in touch with his farming roots by helping his brothers with seeding and harvesting in Carrot River. At Janet and Rob's farm, their son, Jordon, earns his living as an organic truck gardener. My brother, Gordon, has worked in agriculture for his career, including organic farming and promoting food security and sovereignty regionally and internationally. My sister, Diane, and her husband, Peter, live just two blocks from where we grew up in suburban Saskatoon, yet they are avid gardeners and one of their daughters has married a farmer and moved onto the land. So while Mennonites may no longer be predominately rural, those roots are deep and persistent.

29. Neff and Kauffman, "Intermarriage," paras. 16, 17. But one of my uncles married an Anglican and another a Catholic!

30. This resonates with the changing demographics of the global Mennonite church, which is now majority non-European. Indeed, the biggest problem with our traditional "social cohesion" was the functional insularity it promoted.

side of the city in 1963. Nutana Park Mennonite (NPMC) was the backbone of our family's life, conducting baby dedications, baptisms, marriage ceremonies, and funerals. It is where Ched chose to be welcomed formally into the Mennonite faith. I will always be a child of this church, which taught me about faith, Scripture, justice, and community. Over the years, NPMC has also taken courageous steps to embrace God's radical love: hosting refugees; renouncing militarism; becoming the first Mennonite congregation in Canada to preside over the marriage of a gay couple; and recent efforts to join Indigenous neighbors in their campaigns for justice.[31] Insofar as our Mennonite churches incubate and resource an engaged discipleship, they remain the best "check" on our drift into whiteness.

I read recently where my maternal Great-uncle George Zacharias reminisced about the clothing he wore upon his arrival in Saskatchewan from Ukraine in 1923. "It must have appeared strange to the Canadian people to see our costumes. For example, the men and boys wore their shirts outside and over their pants and then fastened with a belt." He continued: "Unfortunately, much has been lost . . . [in] the changes that have taken place during the 72 years our people have enjoyed this new homeland of ours."[32] I am left with many questions about how we became so acceptable to the "English" Canadian society that once pathologized Mennonites. Why did so many of our farmers embrace industrial agriculture and its market-determinations of how we engage the land? When did we start taking commercial loans rather than relying on relational mutual aid economics?[33] How have we urbanites acclimated to consumerism, fashion, and mobility? Why do some U.S. Mennonite churches have the flag in their sanctuaries today? What have we lost in our drift from communal identities to individualist habits? And why are so many of my generation and the one following ambivalent about church? Above all, have we Mennonites, though an historic discipleship tradition, stopped wrestling with what it means to be "*in* the world but not *of* it?"

31. In 2015, co-pastors Anita Retzlaff and Patrick Preheim married two gay men (see Bergen, "Saskatoon Gay Couple 1st to Be Married in Mennonite Church").

32. Zacharias, *Wilhelm Zacharias and Descendants*, 553–54. Uncle George knew something about nonconformity, since he did not marry until he was well into his sixties.

33. One workshop participant at an MCC Canada Annual General Meeting in Winnipeg (September 18, 2014) shared how some Mennonites insist we "always purchased our land through fair and square deals." This reflects an embrace of market orthodoxy ("anonymous buyers and sellers"), while overlooking how early Mennonite settlers preferred to sell and buy from co-religionists on favorable terms (for example, my Grandpa Franz purchased land in Carrot River from my brother-in-law Rob's grandfather).

~

Deconstructing our Mennonite insularity has opened us up to a healthier social ecology of diversity. But there is no doubt the erosion of many of our communal values has facilitated our move into the façade of whiteness, which lies at the heart of settler colonialism. I worry about our accommodation to middle-class values and patterns today, given the continuing marginalization of Indigenous communities. After all, a century ago my ancestors found themselves on the wrong side of a social and economic divide in Ukraine/Russia, which spelled disaster. Bloodlines work invites us to interrogate our familial "integration" into dominant culture structures and patterns, to re-evaluate our ethnic identities, and to contest our assimilation.

In 1996, sociologist Stephen Murray published an important study of what he called "deassimilation": how various groups (ethnic, religious, sexual minorities, etc.) chose to resist social conformity by deliberately accentuating their distinctiveness.[34] Indeed, in recent decades throughout North America minority groups of all types have sought to differentiate themselves from the "mainstream." Expressions range from the personal (e.g., accentuating ethnic dress or style) to the political (i.e., celebrating identity through a public Cinco de Mayo festival or Gay Pride parade). This trend is empowered by identity politics and a growing acceptance of pluralism. It is especially synergistic with global movements of "devolutionary politics."[35] A significant example of this trajectory is "Indigenous Resurgence," which we'll look at below (7C).

White settlers trying to deconstruct their historic assimilation into the social project of settler colonialism have everything to learn from these efforts. For Mennonites, deassimilation resonates with our Anabaptist dissident origins.[36] But de-assimilating from whiteness is a process of disillusionment, *not* dis-association. Our task is to wrestle with a difficult

---

34. See Murray, *American Gay*. "Dissimilation" (the act of making or becoming unlike) would be the logical antonym, but it is used chiefly in phonetics and linguistics. Deassimilation had negative connotations for Jews under the Third Reich; it was used to "other" targeted groups, thus increasing their vulnerability. But a contemporary Jewish movement called "Deassimilation Education" uses the term positively (see Gringauz, "Young Jews Created an Online Community for Kvetching").

35. Devolutionary politics is when communities "reject artificial political boundaries and seek to regroup into more natural ethnic, linguistic, religious, or cultural domains" (Martin, "Devolutionism," 78; see also https://en.wikipedia.org/wiki/Devolution).

36. Ched has outlined an Anabaptist-inspired project for North American Christians he calls "defect-ive discipleship as an experiment in dis-continuity" (*Who Will Roll Away the Stone?*, 175–86).

dialectic: we must forget we are white, and mustn't ever forget we are white.[37] That is, on one hand, our whiteness is a toxic fiction, and we must reconstruct our identity based on reclaiming ethnicities, however hybrid. On the other hand, those of us who will nevertheless remain white-positioned in a white-dominant social system must continue to be cognizant and critical of all the problematic privileging this entails.

This lifelong reconstruction work needs to include three important explorations:

- How we evade our entanglement in white supremacy's dehumanization of others by taking refuge in "narratives of innocence" (below C);
- Understanding and addressing complicity (D); and
- Acknowledging *and feeling* moral injury: ways in which our socialization into settler colonialism has damaged our own humanity (E).

We'll examine each briefly as crucial components of our work of personal and political healing.

6C. FROM NARRATIVES OF INNOCENCE TO RESPONSE-ABILITY

In November 2019, I was sitting at the California Indigenous Genocide Conference in San Diego. It had been deeply enriching and disturbing. The day before, I'd conversed with Tamara Starblanket, a *Nehiyaw iskwew* (Cree woman) author and activist from Ahtahkakoop First Nation in Saskatchewan whose work I admired, and I had come back specifically to hear her plenary address. I was disappointed but not surprised that the audience was small, with only a few settlers scattered throughout. Tamara began describing her life in Saskatchewan and the impact of Indian Residential Schools on her family and community.[38] As her grim litany continued, and as she named patterns of settler silence and ambivalence regarding this legacy, discomfort began to rise in me. My whole being wanted to scream out, "*I am not like that!*" It was a familiar feeling—that deep sense of shame that drives us to clamor (if only internally) for personal exemption from such sweeping indictments, as we suddenly find ourselves conjuring algorithms of how complicated it all really is. And as activists we brandish our solidarity resumes to get a pass.

---

37. This is a play on the opening line of Pat Parker's 1978 poem "For the White Person Who Wants to Know How to Be My Friend."

38. See Starblanket, *Suffer the Little Children.*

In these inevitable moments of internal paralysis or dissociation, the challenge for settlers is to stay engaged and present, even as we pay attention to how we reflexively turn to strategies of defensiveness and denial. To battle an "unclean spirit" we must first recognize and name it (Luke 11:24–26; above 1B). Tuck and Yang have articulated what they call "settler moves to innocence," and we adapt their basic framework here.[39] These moves are attempts to convince ourselves we aren't *responsible* for (or to) the history and ongoing disaster of colonization. This imagined innocence, in turn, undermines our personal and political *ability-to-respond* (hence our use of the term "response-ability").

Our taxonomy below looks at ten strategies for securing innocence as they are deployed, respectively, by the politico-cultural "center," "right," and "left" of contemporary North American settler society (with some examples from my community). We begin with three moves that ubiquitously characterize the settler "silent majority":

i.   *"Agnosia" as willful ignorance.* An "epistemology of unknowing" (above 1C) is a typical presenting symptom of settler innocence. When it comes to past and present violations of colonization, we don't know, don't know what we don't know, and don't really care that we don't know. This condition has been diagnosed as "colonial agnosia":

> [T]he predominant lack of acknowledgment or engagement with the histories and contemporary relations of colonialism—especially with regard to the specificities of Indigenous peoples and colonial entanglements of differential racialization—is not simply a matter of collective amnesia or omission. The magnitude of this disavowal is not primarily a matter of a forgotten or hidden past, at least to the extent that forgetting might be viewed as a passive relation or a concealed past might suspend culpability. Instead, this ignorance—this act of ignoring—is aggressively made and reproduced, affectively invested and effectively distributed in ways that conform the social relations and economies of the here and now . . . attributing finality to events of conquest and dispossession.[40]

---

39. Tuck and Yang, "Decolonization Is Not a Metaphor." They are building on the work of feminist theorists (Mawhinney, "'Giving up the Ghost,'" and Fellows and Razack, "Race to Innocence"). For theological considerations see Dodd and Findley, *Innocence Uncovered.*

40. Vimalassery et al., "Introduction," 1. "Agnosia" is a medical term (an "inability to process sensory information"), but we find its metaphorical use concise and compelling.

Agnosia sets the boundaries of acceptable discourse in our educational and media systems. It also pervades our own family stories, making it difficult to discern whether "silences" we encounter there are the result of historical disappearance (above 3D) or the product of socialized unknowing.

In workshops we find that questions of where and how our ancestors settled (above chapter 5) provoke litanies of unknowing, sometimes accompanied by howls of protest: "How am *I* supposed to know these things?" But abiding by such boundaries of ignorance (real or perceived) functions to keep underwriting the half-millennium-old mendacity of *terra nullius*. Even if we acknowledge the preexistence of Indigenous peoples in the places we live, our practical ignorance of their lifeways, history, and survivance renders them nonexistent to us.[41] Our settler mobility keeps reinforcing agnosia: for example, when I moved to California, most local residents neither expected—nor were able to help—me to learn the Indigenous history beneath my feet.

ii. *Personal dissociation.* Personal detachment from history is a uniquely North American conceit of settler colonialism. This ahistoric individualism understands the self as a free-floating entity neither constrained nor advantaged by the past. The settler "I" is: unaccountable to a history which is not "my fault"; disinterested in how I continue to benefit from historic arrangements in the present; and concerned chiefly with my personal future. When hauntings or demands for responsibility *do* impinge upon our consciousness, we see no reason to revisit the past. The infamous dodge of Robert Walpole, Britain's first Prime Minister, persists in settler culture: better to "let sleeping dogs lie."[42]

One of my elder interviewees described with sadness how many in our community have become highly individualistic, especially in contrast to Indigenous peoples: "We've accepted a deeply held conservative position that each person is responsible. We don't have community responsibility . . . I can't depend on my family or the government.

---

41. See Epp, "'There Was No One Here When We Came.'"

42. An idiom going as far back as Chaucer in the fourteenth century ("It is nought good a slepyng hound to wake"), it informed Walpole's policies of "salutary neglect" toward the American colonies, which functioned to increase the flow of capital from their economies to England in the mid-eighteenth century. Among the "sleeping dogs" left unexamined were how Walpole's own fortune was made investing in the South Sea Company's trade in the New World's speculative market for slaves and exotic imports (see https://www.phrases.org.uk/meanings/let-sleeping-dogs-lie.html).

I need to do it myself, and I've done it! Why don't 'those people' get off their butts and do it too!"[43]

iii. *Inheritance without responsibility.* Related to the first two is accepting history as a *fait accompli.* We have merely "inherited" this history, and have no sense of accountability to it. The problem is the land on which we live was in the course of this history wrested from Indigenous peoples by force, swindle, theft, or duplicity. Many of us have inherited this very land as private property, whether as suburban homes, urban businesses, or rural farms. And most white settlers have gained some form of economic, social, and political advantages from this history, which continues in the contemporary disparities between settler prosperity and Indigenous marginalization. So to imagine our privilege is gained and maintained "unwittingly," says critical race scholar Zeus Leonardo, "is analogous to suggesting that a person could walk through life with other people stuffing money in to his or her pockets without any awareness or consent on the walker's part."[44]

These three moves to innocence are basic symptoms of what Dina Gilio-Whitaker calls "settler fragility": the "need to distance oneself from complicity," and "the inability to talk about unearned privilege."[45]

Straddling these "unknowing" strategies of the settler mainstream are contrary assertions of settler "knowing" that circulate among political conservatives and progressives. The assertions differ drastically, but function similarly to impute innocence. Let's start on the right. Conservatives will occasionally allow that colonization "may have" resulted in a certain degree of violence and dispossession, but such acknowledgments remain vague and general. Moreover, apologists are quick to invoke versions of the following four rationalizations:

iv. *Historical determinism.* Human and ecological harms were historically inevitable, this argument goes, as unavoidable "collateral damage" in the march of civilization. This is an appeal to "Progress," and assumes a Social Darwinist orientation: "stronger" cultures will always replace "weaker" ones. And if "we" didn't conquer, others would have. Such a determinist perspective implies it is ultimately futile to protest, impede, or lament these historical forces. It is sometimes flippantly stated as: "We won, get over it."[46]

---

43. Interview by Elaine Enns, Saskatoon, Saskatchewan, July 10, 2014.
44. Cited in DiAngelo, *White Fragility,* 64.
45. See Gilio-Whitaker, "Settler Fragility."
46. See e.g., Pearson, "Don't Tell Me to 'Get Over.'"

v. *Ideologies of superiority.* Closely related are implicit or explicit beliefs in northern European racial, cultural, and technological superiority, which function to justify conquest *and* to absolve us of transgression.[47] This approach portrays white settlers as protagonists in a self-congratulatory narrative, anchored either in theologies or secular ideologies of "chosenness": from Catholic Doctrines of Discovery to Protestant "errands in the wilderness," and from Manifest Destiny to American Exceptionalism.[48] An assumed agrarian supremacy legitimates taking land from subsistence hunter-gatherers and making it "productive" under a regime of yeoman colonial farmers. Because of these grandiose self-perceptions, it was impossible for settlers to see Indigenous peoples as fully and equally human: Native culture could only be either romanticized (the "Noble Savage") or demonized (the Indian as antithetical to civilization). This manic-depressive polarization lingers in our consciousness today.[49] All versions of our myth of superiority ignore how Indigenous hospitality facilitated European survival during initial settlement, and how this was followed by colonial state subsidies and racial prioritizing that advantaged white prosperity.

Some Mennonites I interviewed related comments they'd heard in our community that reflect superiority, using Indigenous "others" as a foil: "We've had enough of this Indigenous talk and the terrible things we did to them. Why can't they just pull themselves up by their bootstraps like we did? We've given them a good education, housing . . . We never got the privileges that Indigenous people got."[50] This attitude disingenuously takes credit for (vastly exaggerated) government-initiated programs to Native communities, while forgetting the many *Privilegia* and land subsidies from which Mennonites benefitted.[51] And the "bootstraps" trope recycles a chestnut of European pioneer hagiography.

47. In the U.S., "white superiority and racial power codes develop as early as preschool" (DiAngelo, *White Fragility,* 108).

48. For background, see e.g., Perry Miller's classic study of Puritan settler culture *Errand into the Wilderness,* and Roberts, *American Exceptionalism.*

49. This polarity was clearly expressed through nineteenth-century American settler art and culture (see Myers, *Who Will Roll Away the Stone?,* 120–22).

50. Interview by Elaine Enns, Saskatoon, Saskatchewan, July 10, 2014. See more in McLean, "'We Built a Life from Nothing.'"

51. As a *Russländer* descendent interviewee put it: "We went through a period of trauma, but then we came here and before long we were back in positions of privilege," pointing out that Indigenous peoples have "been second-class citizens in their own land since the arrival of Europeans. And it hasn't changed, and we don't get that." Interview by Elaine Enns, Rosthern, Saskatchewan, June 16, 2014.

Also problematic is how our community has carried certain strands of Germanic superiority brought from Europe.[52] Loyalties to German culture caused some Mennonites in both Europe and North America to tolerate or even support the Third Reich.[53] In my generation, these strands were more benign, but still lamentable: "Our institutions have fostered superiority for sure," said an interviewee, "including our schools."[54] Others express Mennonite exceptionalism in terms of durability and industry. One interviewee told me Mennonites endured the Russian Civil War because they were "tough."[55] In such comments are we reassuring ourselves that our people were *not* damaged by the trauma in Russia and Ukraine, or that the trauma was "resolved" by our hard work and faithfulness in Canada? Why, then, as we argued in chapter 3, do we exhibit symptoms of intergenerational trauma as individuals and as a community? Denial of untransacted pain not only diminishes our capacity to empathize with other traumatized people; it also feeds pejorative judgments of those who *are* "damaged" by oppression. Attitudes of paternalism and victim-blaming towards Indigenous peoples prevent us from understanding how poverty or addiction are deeply connected to the continuing legacy of colonial violence.

vi. *Intent vs. Impact.* If conservatives *do* harbor moral qualms about historical injustices, these are quickly eclipsed by assertions that European settlers were/are "humane" in our colonization, and that if damage occurred such was not the *intent*. The claim that intentions outweigh actual impacts is a classic move to innocence in contemporary racial politics; Robin DiAngelo calls it "the foundation of white fragility."[56]

52. Above 3D. One of my family history books contains contradictory testimonies. On one hand it notes pejorative attitudes among some Mennonite settlers in Russia toward (and lack of substantial social contact with) displaced Cossack, Bashkir, and Tartar neighbors: "They lived beside us in great backwardness, gladly offering their casual services . . . We must admit that we knew very little of these, the natives of the area, and little was taught of them in our schools" (Neufeld et al., *Ufa*, 112). On the other hand, the book states: "The Bashkirs are most hospitable people," alludes to being guests in their homes, and notes that some Mennonites learned to speak the Bashkir language (65).

53. Historian Ben Goossen has shown how "a substantial percentage of Europe's Mennonites benefited from and often sympathized with aspects of Nazism," and some even "developed robust fascist sensibilities" ("Mennonites and the Holocaust," paras. 3, 5).

54. Group interview by Elaine Enns, Carlton area, Saskatchewan, July 17, 2014.

55. *Russländer* Focus Group, interview by Elaine Enns, Saskatoon, Saskatchewan, June 25, 2014.

56. DiAngelo, *White Fragility*, 68–69. See Utt, "Intent vs. Impact," and Tannenbaum,

Nor is the claim true: the *publicly avowed* intentions of consequential historic policies such as the Indian Removal Act or Indian Residential Schools would be judged by any measure today as genocidal.[57] Taking refuge in the myth of our own essential "goodness" evades responsibility for past impacts of settler colonialism and undermines responseability regarding present ones.

vii. *Fictimization.* This is defined by the Urban Dictionary as "when a person or a group uses disingenuous and false arguments to claim they are the 'real' victims."[58] Of all conservative moves to innocence, this is the most odious—and in the U.S. today it is a common strategy of the Alt-Right (i.e., claims that white people and/or Christians are the *most* oppressed group). Another typical expression surfaces when marginalized communities protest injustice in the streets, or raise issues of discrimination in a workplace, only to have white people accuse them of using "violent" or "exaggerated" language. White reactivity thus endeavors (consciously or unconsciously) to trump the pain that people of color carry.[59]

A small example of fictimization was illustrated at the beginning of this chapter: in August 1976, Mennonites in the Stoney Knoll area complained that Young Chippewayans were being threatening, playing on settler stereotypes of "hostile Indian attacks" (which reverse the real direction of most historical violence). Another instance occurred at one of our Bartimaeus Institutes in a women's circle, where Indigenous participants were sharing experiences of trauma. After one mournful story of abuse by the church, a white woman responded: "I know what you mean, the church hurt me too." Such a move to render all pain equivalent—even if offered as a gesture of empathy—functions to replace Indigenous subjectivity with our own. There are appropriate

---

"'But I Didn't Mean It!'"

57. President Andrew Jackson told Congress on December 6, 1830 that clearing Alabama and Mississippi of their Indigenous populations would "enable those states to advance rapidly in population, wealth, and power" (https://www.ourdocuments.gov/doc.php?flash=false&doc=25#, para. 3). Carlisle School founder Captain Richard Pratt famously told a convention in 1892 that his goal was to "kill the Indian in him and save the man" (text of his speech at http://historymatters.gmu.edu/d/4929/, para. 1).

58. See https://www.urbandictionary.com/define.php?term=Fictimization.

59. DiAngelo writes that white people overstate our own sense of violation and can't articulate our feelings in racially stressful situations because our socialization doesn't give us the stamina or ability to respond differently (*White Fragility*, 109–10, 119–21). As we write, protests are breaking out around the U.S. in the wake of George Floyd's murder by police in Minneapolis; Fox News reports focus on property destruction while studiously avoiding mention of the cause of rage.

ways for settlers to speak about our trauma, but comparing it with that of Indigenous people is never one.

A related expression is what social-psychologist John Mack calls "egoism of victimization," in which groups that have experienced real trauma are not able to exhibit empathy for the losses of others, even if "palpably evident and comparable to or greater than one's own."[60] This becomes fictim-identity when descendants of traumatized people are now socially and materially advantaged, yet still center only *their* people's suffering. There is a lively conversation about this phenomenon in Jewish activist circles today, as there should be among North American Mennonites. As Mennonite poet Julia Spicher Kasdorf puts it, "Keeping bittersweet memories of past trespasses alive may blind writers to immediate injustice or prevent us from appreciating the privileged positions we now hold."[61]

On the liberal-Left of settler culture, responses focus not on denying agnosia about past or present injustice, but "fixing" it through critical consciousness. Social critics are eager to establish the culpability of structures and regimes in all manner of injustice—but too often we imagine our indictments somehow absolve us from culpability. The following three moves to innocence are particularly found among people who might read this book!

viii. *Exoneration by conscientization.* "Progressive" settler academics and activists combat mainstream unknowing with trenchant analysis, and political and moral censures of colonization. But our temptation is to assume a self-righteousness (or presumed moral superiority) of hindsight. Putative "wokeness" does not exonerate us; our entanglement in settler privilege won't end until the system itself does. And future generations will assuredly see *our* complicity in current technologies and structures of oppression. Analysis and critical literacy are indeed necessary—our project seeks to nurture both—but they are not sufficient for our work: knowledge alone doesn't empower change, healing, or response-ability. Tuck and Yang put it bluntly: a "focus on decolonizing the mind" cannot "stand in for the more uncomfortable task of relinquishing stolen land."[62]

ix. *Scapegoating Christianity.* A liberal humanist frame tends to lay the blame for *all* settler colonial pathologies and crimes over the last

60. Mack, *Cyprus, War and Adaptation*, ix–xxi.

61. Kasdorf, *Body and the Book*, 162. See also Stein, "'Chosen Trauma.'"

62. Tuck and Yang, "Decolonization Is Not a Metaphor," 19. See also Hiller, "Tracing the Spirals of Unsettlement."

half-millennium at the doorstep of Christendom. This move to innocence we see not only on the secular left, but also among socially
conscious settler colleagues who identify as post-Evangelical. Those
raised in conservative churches (which deny *any* responsibility for
the legacy of settler colonialism) tend to swing to the opposite pole,
and dissociate from a hopelessly culpable Christian tradition. There
are many reasons to be disenchanted with Christian history (some of
which we acknowledged in our Theological Interlude). But disowning
that tradition does not exonerate us, nor does it change how settler
colonialism shaped us, advantaged us, and inhabits our spirits still.
Moreover, Indigenous communities seeking justice and reparation are
not helped by settlers who simply "wash their hands" of their culture's
conflicted religious history. Solidarity for Christians requires facing
the abuses perpetrated by and in churches, and working to make our
tradition accountable to the demands of restorative justice. We believe
the Anabaptist history of dissidence and reconstruction—despite contradictions we've acknowledged throughout this book—can help in
forging a discipleship of decolonization.

x. *Appropriation.* If fictimization is the most aggravating move to innocence on the Right, attempts to appropriate the moral authority of
Native culture is its counterpart on the Left. Tuck and Yang name one
classic expression:

> Settlers locate or invent a long-lost ancestor who is rumored to
> have had "Indian blood," and use this claim to mark themselves
> as blameless in the attempted eradications of Indigenous peoples
> . . . It is an attempt to deflect a settler identity, while continuing
> to enjoy settler privilege and occupying stolen land.[63]

They point to nineteenth-century settlers who imagined that they
had been "adopted" by Native communities (to "alleviate the anxiety of
settler un-belonging"), or appointed as successor, "in which the Native
(understanding that he is becoming extinct) hands over his land, his
claim to the land, his very Indian-ness to the settler for safe-keeping."[64]
Today we see similarly devised fantasies in "spirituality" circles
where non-Indigenous ritualists (or worse, self-proclaimed "shamans") lead Native ceremonies, claiming to have been trained and

---

63. Tuck and Yang, "Decolonization Is Not a Metaphor," 10–11. Darryl Leroux explores this phenomenon in Francophone Canada in *Distorted Descent*.

64. Tuck and Yang, "Decolonization Is Not a Metaphor," 14–15.

commissioned to do so by Indigenous elders.[65] The problem of settler appropriation of Native spirituality in North America is widespread, and related, in our opinion, to settler religious homelessness—in part a result of renouncing our own traditions! Trickier still are recent settler efforts to trace (or imagine) one's deep European indigeneity through autoethnography. It may be instructive to speculate about our pre-civilizational ancestors' lifeways; indeed, we who are captive to a hyper-industrial society would do well to study and learn from hunter-gatherer cultures of all kinds.[66] But identifying *existentially* with a fabulated ancient progenitor is a way of simultaneously dis-identifying from whiteness *and* romanticizing indigeneity.[67] For most settlers it is difficult enough to trace back to our immigrant ancestors; we think the powerful tool of autoethnography is better deployed on our own settler socialization to innocence![68]

Each of the above moves to innocence are efforts by settlers, as DiAngelo puts it, to place ourselves on the "good side" of a moral binary set up by white culture.[69] Coming to terms with our conscious (and especially our unconscious) reliance upon such moves is hard work. But until and unless we recognize how they undermine response-ability, we will remain mired in a preoccupation with exoneration rather than liberation. This holds true especially for those of us who assume our solidarity activism or "knowledge of the issues" makes us virtuous, which only inhibits us from facing *our* disease and disabilities. Though it seems counterintuitive to an entitled people,

---

65. Roxanne Dunbar-Ortiz offers a useful overview of current and historical ways settlers profit from "playing Indian," which she points out is also a form of extractive exploitation ("White Americans Need to Stop").

66. For some of the relevant literature, see Myers, "Anarcho-Primitivism and the Bible." In their critique of the Occupy movement, Tuck and Yang also characterize contemporary settler urban homesteading and "back to the land" experiments as attempts at "playing Indian." While some "feral" lifestyles may indeed be a move to innocence, we do not think that pursuit of traditional arts such as native plant cultivation, herbalism, and small-scale horticulture are necessarily appropriative. Given the social and ecological ultimatums of climate catastrophe, recovery of sustainable lifeways can and should be pursued by settlers in a good way. Insofar as they draw upon Native traditions, practitioners should be accountable and apprentice to local Indigenous communities (Tuck and Yang, "Decolonization Is Not a metaphor," 8, 23, 24, 28).

67. On the other end of the spectrum, White Nationalists are weaponizing paganism in their versions of Nordic and Teutonic Ásatrú (see Samuel, "What To Do," and Southern Poverty Law Center, "New Brand of Racist Odinist Religion").

68. A good example is Dale, "Decolonizing the Empathic Settler Mind." For Indigenous autoethnographers seeking to reconstruct their identities, see St-Denis and Walsh, "Reclaiming My Indigenous Identity."

69. DiAngelo, *White Fragility,* 87.

the way to healing is through abandoning our innocence, so we can turn to face reality. This is the greatest challenge of de-assimilation.

6D. TURNING: REPENTANCE, RECOVERY, AND COMPLICITY

At this weighty juncture in our analysis, we bring in again the voice of the ancient gospel tradition, whose wisdom can break up the ice that traps us in settler colonial history. According to the earliest account of the life of Jesus of Nazareth, his core proclamation as recorded in his very first "sermon" was brief, concise, and razor-sharp:

> The time is fulfilled
> the kingdom of God has come near;
> repent
> and believe in the good news (Mark 1:15).

This summons comes in two parts.

The first two verbs state the matter unequivocally in terms of *here* and *now*. God's sovereignty (or "kingdom") is not to be relegated to some other place or time. This means justice cannot be put off until later, left to someone else, or turned into an abstraction. Jesus' very first line in this story means to get our attention: no more business as usual. Martin called it "the fierce urgency of now"; Malcom called it "chickens coming home to roost."[70]

The next two verbs (in the imperative mood) articulate what is required in light of this crisis. "Repent" (Greek *metanoeite*) commands us to reverse personal and political direction. The arc we are on is leading to inevitable destruction. This is a terminal diagnosis: our lifeways are killing us. But as we saw earlier, the prophet-healer understands that "only those who know they are dis-eased" will forsake their imagined "wellness" in order to "turn around" (Mark 2:17; above, 1B). "Believe (Greek *pisteuete*) the good news," in turn, connotes neither an irrational leap nor a cognitive assent to doctrine, but rather wholehearted *trust*. Those seeking to heal can rely on the powerful medicine of the gospel. At once individual altar-call and historical ultimatum, Jesus' proclamation articulates in the same breath hard words *and* hope, end *and* beginning.

This venerable discourse of repentance, though widely domesticated in our churches today, is grounded in the Hebrew prophetic tradition of

---

70. See Cone, *Martin & Malcolm & America*. For a contemporary discussion, see Bergen, "Whether, and How, a Church Ought to Repent," and Burn's extended reflection on repentance and Indigenous justice, *Liberating the Will of Australia*.

speaking inconvenient truth to hardened hearts. Early church father St. John Chrysostom put the matter this way: "Sin is the wound, repentance is the medicine."[71] (Sin was understood in antiquity as "missing the mark" or "incurring a moral debt.") Writing in 387 CE—the dawn of the Constantinian church, but dusk of the Roman Empire—Chrysostom understood that this diagnosis was counterintuitive to a self-absorbed and entitled culture, and that the work of turning around is a lifelong journey. Unfortunately, in today's imperial context, our ecclesial traditions tend to collapse this journey into singular cathartic experiences ("confession and absolution" for Catholics, "conversion" for Protestants). So do settler attempts at public apology and reconciliation! Dietrich Bonhoeffer rightly diagnosed this as "cheap grace," which coexists peaceably with fascism. He understood that de-assimilation would be "costly."[72]

We acknowledge, however, that for many people the religious semantics of sin and repentance carry too much problematic baggage, or simply don't resonate in a secular context. The demanding terrain of radical change requires a creative reassessment of language, old and new. So here we explore two contemporary analogues that say similar things differently.

i) *Recovery.* Today the Twelve-Step recovery movement more consistently embodies the ethos of repentance—namely, that captivity is lethal, that redemption is possible, and that healing is a community practice here and now—than do most churches.[73] As a diagnostic framework the Steps illuminate the task of decolonization. To paraphrase: Step One is a recognition that "life under settler colonialism is unmanageable." Denial is our arch-enemy; the moves to innocence surveyed above represent "stinking thinking." Steps Two and Three call for a necessary exodus from this captivity, accompanied by a divine power that originates outside the dominant system. Step Four requires a "searching and fearless moral inventory," or as we put it in chapter 1, "constructing the missing inventory of traces of colonization's historical processes in us." Step Five, in turn, requires honest admission of culpability and responsibility to God, self, and one other. Twelve-Steppers often use the rhetoric of

71. Chrysostom, *Fathers of the Church,* Homily 8.

72. Bonhoeffer, *Cost of Discipleship.*

73. On this, see Myers, "Beyond the 'Addict's Excuse,'" and Myers, *Who Will Roll Away the Stone?,* ch. 6. Indeed, Alcoholics Anonymous has roots in the revivalist Oxford Group Christian movement of the 1930s from which, Bill Wilson said, it "got its ideas of self-examination, acknowledgment of character defects, restitution for harm done, and working with others" (https://en.wikipedia.org/wiki/Oxford_Group#Relationship_to_Alcoholics_Anonymous). For a summary of the Twelve-Steps, see https://www.aa.org/assets/en_US/smf-121_en.pdf.

"house-cleaning," which resonates with Luke's Gospel parable about demons (above 1B).[74] Steps Six and Seven involve the "inner work" of *preparation*, and Steps Eight and Nine the "outer work" of *reparation*. Decolonization work must be specific about those we have damaged, beginning with Indigenous peoples. These disciplines of "doing our own work" are reiterated in Steps Ten and Eleven. Step Twelve recruits us to build the insurrection against settler colonialism.

While classic Twelve-Step practice addresses only the personal, it is profoundly relevant to the public addictions and historical injustices that shape our settler compulsions. One AA testimony speaks to the work of decolonization: "It takes a while for the 'fog' to begin to lift, so that we begin to see ourselves and the world around us more clearly."[75] Most importantly, the Twelve-Steps are understood as a widening and deepening *process*, not a single *event*.

> ii) *Complicity*. Another secular word for this kind of self-examination work is recognizing one's settler "complicity," an idea especially prevalent in contemporary decolonial political discourse. Alissa Macoun offers this definition: "Complicity establishes both a political responsibility and an intellectual imperative to understand and contest systems of domination in which we are enmeshed through deliberate respectful engagements with those who have experiences, knowledges and forms of authority that we do not."[76] Unfortunately, complicity language tends to provoke in settlers a spiral into shame, a response of white fragility. Because this functions to derail and paralyze—the opposite of response-ability—we need to address it here.[77]

We earlier made a distinction between toxic shame and a "healthy guilt" which animates change (above 1D). But in popular usage they are conflated, both understood to insinuate that we *are* wrong rather than that we've *done* wrong. Scholar Brené Brown agrees:

> There is a profound difference between shame and guilt. I believe that guilt is adaptive and helpful: holding something we've done or failed to do up against our values, and feeling psychological discomfort. I define shame as the intensely painful feeling or

74. See http://www.aachat.org/directions.htm, and https://12step.org/the-12-steps/step-5/.

75. "Buddy T.," at https://www.verywellmind.com/a-study-of-step-4-69406.

76. Macoun, "Colonising White Innocence," 85.

77. For a reflection on this dynamic in activist circles, see Stephens, "Left's Self-Destructive Obsession with Shame."

experience of believing that we are flawed and therefore unworthy of love and belonging. Something we've experienced, done,
or failed to do makes us unworthy of connection. I don't believe
shame is helpful or productive . . . [It] is much more likely to be
the source of destructive, hurtful behavior than the solution or
cure. I think the fear of disconnection can make us dangerous.[78]

The etymology of *complicit* is thus helpful. Like "complicate," it comes
from the Latin *complicare*, "to fold together," "intertwine," or "braid."
Throughout this book we advocate investigating how our settler lives are
braided into the vast web of colonization's traumatizing past and present.
Precisely because of our socialized presumptions of innocence, it is painful
to accept these "entanglements"—especially when others point them out! In
such moments, DiAngelo's suggestions for how to counter shame responses
when called to accountability for racist behavior apply to settler defensiveness as well. These include: conjuring gratitude and humility rather than reacting with anger or rationalizing; opening up emotionally by listening and
self-reflection rather than shutting down and withdrawing; and expressing
trust by soliciting feedback about our blind spots.[79]

As in the radical analysis of both gospel and Twelve-Step traditions,
naming our complicity with settler colonialism is about healing from
a system that is killing *us* as well as others. It is a process of restoration,
not self-abnegation. We must constantly navigate between (as the ancient
Greeks put it) the Scylla of self-justifying denial and the Charybdis of
self-righteous hindsight. Complicity as healthy guilt clearly and concretely
recognizes our entanglement, yielding neither to shaming nor blaming (of
self or others). It animates work toward our liberation through practices of
responsibility, restorative solidarity, and reparation. To invoke the second
part of John Chrysostom's dictum: "Sin is followed by shame; repentance is
followed by boldness."

~

If settler shame responses prevent us from embracing repentance/recovery/
complicity, so does our fear of consequences. This happens in two ways.

   i) *Anxiety about how kin or social groups will respond to how we re-vise
       and re-member our settler communal narratives.* We noted this at the
       outset (above introduction C). When an addict turns to sobriety, they

---

78. Brown, "Shame v. Guilt," paras. 1–3.
79. DiAngelo, *White Fragility*, 141–42.

often experience denial and resistance from friends and relatives who don't realize *their* complicity in the dysfunction. This same defensive reaction arises in the face of recovery from the public addiction of settler colonialism. Pushback from some of those close to us is inevitable, given that the family system is the primary socializing mechanism for both personal identity *and* political norms.

If stories of *victimization* are silenced in our most intimate narratives (above 3D), how much more are stories of *perpetration* suppressed? These will be seen as damaging to the public reputation (or private self-image) of one's family, church, or community. An anthropologist colleague in the southern U.S. doing family research discovered and documented that her ancestors were actively involved in the slave trade. She feels, however, that she cannot bring this story to public light as it would cause "serious trouble" for family members now holding upper-level political positions. She knows there is a psychic cost of *not* vetting these legacies, but worries about the ethics of distant kin paying the price of her truth-telling.

We find ourselves, then, not only working against the grain of the sanitized "received narratives" of our communal past, but also dealing with reactions of family and friends in the present who can't understand why we are exhuming "unsavory" matters. I have wrestled in this project with how much to share about my family and community story. The prospect of social ostracism from those we love and respect is real, especially in tight-knit ethnic or religious groups, or when relatives are prominent in the community's past or present. But "unsettling" our relational networks may be part of the cost of our discipleship. And though the truth inevitably disturbs, the gospel assures us that ultimately it sets us free (John 8:31–32).

If uncovering personal history is destabilizing, then critically revising *public* history is even more conflictive. Those who would dethrone settler "heroes" by exposing their complicity in genocidal policies can count on the wrath of apologists and "defenders of heritage." We see this in the U.S. in the fierce and polarizing struggles around removing Confederate statuary throughout the South.[80] In Canada, an example is the controversy around founding Prime Minister John MacDonald, particularly around his handling of the Northwest Resistance and his genocidal Indigenous policies.[81] The strategy of nam-

80. See e.g., Wallace-Wells, "Fight over Virginia's Confederate Monuments" and Southern Poverty Law Center,* "Whose Heritage?"

81. See e.g., Hopper, "Here Is What Sir John A. Macdonald Did to Indigenous People."

ing cities, universities, or landscapes after military and political icons who committed atrocities is perhaps the most "crazy-making" settler move to innocence, and also the most difficult to rectify. A handful of high school students from Evanston, Illinois learned this recently. They courageously questioned whether it was appropriate for their city to be named after the co-architect of the notorious 1864 Sand Creek massacre—and were studiously ignored.[82] But this is important work, and revising our own family histories provides good practice for the uphill battle regarding larger political narratives.

ii) *Fear of retribution.* A second and equally primal anxiety underneath denials of complicity arises from our socialization into a culture and cosmology of retributive justice: the dread of judgment without re-demption or mercy. While for some this fear may be theologically driven, for most it comes from a legal system that teaches us that the only solution to crime is punishment of the offender, quite apart from whether or not that brings relief or restitution to the victim(s).[83] Thus, when profound issues of Indigenous oppression and dispossession are raised, settlers worry "someone is going to lose" if justice is served. Admissions of culpability might bring retaliation in kind: somehow Indigenous descendants of colonial horrors will return upon us the violence we inflicted on their ancestors. Our personal and political imaginations remain mired in the same retributive logic that rational-ized many of those original injustices.

The adversarial legal system that both Canada and the U.S. inher-ited from Great Britain is steeped in concepts of justice in which a per-petrator is pitted against the state. This leaves actual victims out of the adjudicatory process, and punishes offenders instead of holding them

---

82. Colorado Governor John Evans and Methodist minister Col. John Chiving-ton were the authorities primarily responsible for the slaughter of over 150 unarmed Cheyenne and Arapaho people, mostly women and children (see Stratton, "Sand Creek Massacre"). Evanston, Illinois is one of four towns in the U.S. that bears Evans's name. Ched learned about the campaign during a 2019 visit to Garrett Evangelical Theological Seminary from eighteen-year-old Henry Eberhart, who coauthored an editorial in his school paper (Hughes and Eberhart, "Still Love These Lonely Places"). Ched is grateful to Henry for introducing him to a concept that became central to this book!

83. For a basic comparison of retributive vs. restorative justice paradigms, see Enns and Myers, *Ambassadors of Reconciliation*, 2:50–51; for elaboration of the "spiral of violence" model, see 5–10. Beliefs that violation can only be "satisfied" by retaliation or punishment long predate settler colonialism, of course. The primal human impulse to respond in kind is addressed in the ancient etiological narrative of Genesis 4, where Cain's "bloodguilt" is mitigated by the divine principle of sanctuary (see Myers and Enns, *Ambassadors of Reconciliation*, 1:64–65).

accountable for the relational, social, and economic impacts of their violations. This fails to bring real healing to victims. Moreover, sentencing of offenders is often based on negotiation, which disincentivizes honest admission of guilt.[84] Michelle Alexander argues that the U.S. education system increasingly reflects a similar mindset in zero-tolerance and expulsion policies that drive a "school to prison pipeline."[85] It is no wonder then that we, the progeny of this colonial system, equate complicity with retribution, assuming we are "innocent until proven otherwise," and thus avoid the work of facing our response-ability.

The good news is most Indigenous peoples are *not* captive to the settler retributive framework, having practiced relational forms of community justice that long predate colonization. In a worldview that perceives everything as connected in a web of life, misbehavior is understood as a sign of sickness of the soul (which requires healing) or ignorance (which requires instruction). Accountability focuses on reminding offenders who they are in their community, prescribing practices of self-reflection and restitution. Contemporary restorative justice work has much to learn from these Indigenous traditions.[86] In North America, many Indigenous communities who exercise sovereignty over criminal justice proceedings are returning to traditional practices of sweats, healing circles, and teachings of the medicine wheel to work towards justice, forgiveness, and reintegration.

In our experience, Indigenous colleagues bring this relational spirit into decolonization work, even regarding the fraught issue of repatriation. Young Chippewayans, for example, whose story is central to this book, have made it clear that reparation for historic dispossession from Opwashemoe Chakatinaw/Stoney Knoll does not necessarily require return of *that* land. Leaders are mindful that it is privately owned by settlers, and have indicated an openness to receiving comparable land elsewhere for a new reserve home. Settlers with a heart for justice and a spirit of humility born of culpability can expect to be surprised by grace.

84. In my years working in the restorative justice movement I met with countless teenagers who admitted to me that they had committed a different crime than that to which they had pled. Routinely public defenders advise juvenile offenders to plead guilty to a lesser crime in order receive a lesser sentence. While the aim of keeping offenders out of a punitive system that discriminates against people of color is understandable, it hardly fosters personal or social restoration.

85. See Alexander, *New Jim Crow.*

86. The relationship between traditional Indigenous practices and contemporary restorative justice is explored in Valandra and Hokšíla, *Colorizing Restorative Justice,* and McCaslin, *Justice as Healing.* See also Davis, *Little Book of Race and Restorative Justice.*

6E. "MY LOSS IS YOUR LOSS": PERPETRATOR TRAUMA OR MORAL INJURY?

Dutch psychiatrist Bessel van der Kolk talks about how trauma victims often adopt rote narratives "edited into a form least likely to provoke rejection."[87] Are settlers exhibiting symptoms of trauma by being stuck in our own compulsive repetition of "acceptable" narratives of innocence? Perpetration-Induced Traumatic Stress (PITS), developed by Rachel MacNair, explores posttraumatic stress disorder among those responsible for violence. She studied soldiers, executioners, and police officers whose "socially acceptable" but morally problematic roles involved killing.[88] PITS has been used in therapeutic diagnoses of active combatants, but might help explain the negative psychic feedback loop in settler family systems haunted by how their privileges are rooted in slavery or dispossession.

Turkish Cypriot psychiatrist Vamik Volkan describes a similar syndrome in victimizer groups who "cannot mourn the losses or overcome the shame associated with a past event":

> In Germany, for example, the shadow of the Nazi era and the German people's complicity in the Holocaust continue to influence how individuals and Germans as a group conceive themselves today . . . The inability of previous generations of Germans to mourn this period involves a shared defense against identification and association with the Third Reich and feelings of shame for its atrocities. These unresolved issues have passed on to the subsequent generations.[89]

Referring to complicity as "trauma," however, is tricky for several reasons, not least because it can imply an equivalence between the pain of victims and perpetrators of violation or oppression.[90]

We think the language of "moral injury" better characterizes the damage our complicity wreaks on us. Jeremy Jinkerson defines moral injury as "a particular type of trauma . . . that may develop following a perceived moral violation." He writes: "Guilt, shame, spiritual/existential conflict, and loss of trust are identified as core symptoms. Depression, anxiety, anger,

87. Van der Kolk, *Body Keeps the Score*, 246.

88. MacNair, *Perpetration-Induced Traumatic Stress.* See also http://www.rachel-macnair.com/pits.html, and https://en.wikipedia.org/wiki/Perpetrator_trauma.

89. Volkan, "Transgenerational Transmissions and Chosen Traumas," 88.

90. But see Resmaa Menakem's *My Grandmother's Hands,* a well-received study that deploys trauma language to understand the effects of white supremacy on both Black and white bodies and psyches. See https://www.resmaa.com.

re-experiencing, self-harm, and social problems are identified as secondary symptoms." Jinkerson, a U.S. Air Force psychologist, adds: "Moral injury does not develop through an experience of physiological distress. Instead, it develops through a moral conflict in which one's actions, or the actions of one's peers or leaders, are demonstrably inconsistent with one's moral code."[91]

Womanist theologian Chanequa Walker-Barnes, in her assessment of the long-term psychological effects of racism, insists on differentiating moral injury from trauma:

> To say that the souls and psyches of White Americans are afflict-
> ed with moral injury is not to cast them as victims of trauma.
> Indeed, I adamantly reject the racial reconciliation movement's
> increasing appropriation of trauma language to categorize
> the effects of racism upon White identity. Even scholars who
> conceptualize moral injury as a form of trauma are careful to
> distinguish it from PTSD.[92]

U.S. Iraq War veteran David Peters draws the same distinction starkly: "If PTSD results from being the *prey*—re-experiencing the feeling that something is hunting you, hurting you, trying to kill you—then moral injury results from being the *predator*—where you have done things to hurt people."[93] In decolonization work, settlers certainly encounter the ravages of moral injury.

But there are those for whom past and present violations of Indigenous peoples (and others) are *not* "inconsistent with their moral code." Some settlers live quite comfortably under canopies of rationalization, and others are defiantly defensive of white supremacist policies. We can refer to this in terms of addiction or illness, but moral injury pertains only to those upon whom the continuing legacy of dispossession and injustice weighs, and who are trying to "turn around."

All white settlers in North America have some sort of genealogy of complicity in the long colonial history of "killing and taking possession," as the ancient story of Naboth's vineyard so plainly put it (above Interlude B). This is true regardless of how minor or major our people's entanglements might have been; or how obscured by generations of denial, agnosia, and moves to innocence; or how directly or indirectly correlated it may be to our current race and class privileges. Discerning our moral injury and determining what repentance/recovery/complicity might mean is thus indeed

91. Jinkerson, "Defining and Assessing Moral Injury," 122, 125.

92. Walker-Barnes, *I Bring the Voices of My People*, 129.

93. Peters, "When War Lives on Inside You," para. 1. Peterson is the founder of the Episcopal Veterans Fellowship.*

settlers' "first task in producing ourselves as ethical subjects."[94] This we believe is the most compelling reason to probe our Landlines, Bloodlines, and Songlines. Only by peeling the onion of our conflicted settler identity "seven layers deep," as Jesus' parable suggests (above 1B), will we encounter how our entanglements have damaged *us*, and connect with our emotional body enough to actually experience the pain of moral injury. Again, only those who know in their bones they are sick/terminally addicted/morally culpable will seek healing, and be willing to embrace the lifelong disciplines demanded in the journey of repentance/recovery/complicity.

∿

A half century ago, sociologist Leo Driedger raised to our Mennonite community the poignant question cited at the top of this chapter: Did "serious compromise of our beliefs" arise from our participation in the "agricultural invasion" that dispossessed Indigenous peoples? This collective moral injury still hovers uneasily over us. And I feel personal loss as well.

What part of my community's struggles with mental health result from intergenerational trauma, and what part from moral injury by our entanglement with colonization in Canada? It may be impossible to know for sure. But surely an example of the latter is how many Mennonite families, including mine, participated in and were impacted by the "Sixties Scoop." Some 20,000 Indigenous children were placed in settler families between 1951 and 1991, now widely recognized as yet another government program of assimilation. Two of them were my cousins Larry and Glenn (above introduction B).

In August 2019, while in Saskatchewan interviewing elder relatives, we visited with my eighty-six-year-old paternal Aunt Elsie, Larry and Glenn's mother (above 3A). At an assisted living home in Carrot River, Elsie, her daughter Carolyn, and Carolyn's husband John Fell, sat together with Ched, my sister Janet, and me. We sipped coffee slowly while we carefully entered the painful conversation about those adoptions. It was indeed like doing surgery on living flesh (above 3E). We learned that before being adopted, Glenn and Larry were in foster homes (respectively in Regina and Saskatoon). Glenn likely also suffered from fetal alcohol syndrome, a condition resulting from alcohol exposure during the mother's pregnancy, causing irreversible brain damage and growth problems. Though he was in prison several times, he reconnected with two of his birth siblings, and found his way back to Indigenous culture and spirituality.

94. Kouri and Skott-Myhre, "Catastrophe," 14, cited above 2B.

My aunt admitted: "If I had this to do again, I would do it differently. At that time we had never even heard of fetal alcohol syndrome."[95] Elsie and Carolyn noted how Larry continues to be personable and outgoing. At the same time, they hadn't seen him in two years, though he lives only twenty-five miles away. It was agonizing to see Aunt Elsie wrestle, in frustrated confusion, with the fact that the way she raised her family has been characterized publically as cultural genocide.[96] Indeed, the July 1966 Conference of Mennonites in Canada had passed a "Welcoming Indian and Métis" resolution encouraging Mennonite families to adopt and foster Native children. Moreover, a prominent church member was the architect of Saskatchewan's Adopt Indian Métis program.[97] "We thought we were doing something good when we adopted them," Elsie lamented, "but as it turns out we were all out to lunch." She wondered if this conflict "is what bothers Larry. We used to get a long so good together. One time I asked him what I had done to bring this on, and he said 'You didn't do anything.' His distancing is hard to swallow." In that delicate moment we dared not presume the righteousness of hindsight.

At the same time, as we've argued above, the best intentions cannot cancel out the terrible impacts experienced by my Indigenous cousins (and thousands of others) as a result of having been wrested from their families and communities. Coming out of that conversation I *felt* what Justice Murray Sinclair, chair of the Canadian TRC, meant when he kept insisting that Indian Residential Schools and their legacies "are not an Indian problem, but a Canadian problem."[98] And I understood more deeply what Harry Lafond had told me a few years previously: "My loss," he said simply, "is your loss."

At our 2020 Bartimaeus Kinsler Institute, two of the Indigenous interlocutors asked me to share some of that pain with participants. "It can't always be us testifying to the damage of colonization," they said. I briefly told the story of my adopted cousins, but could barely get through it for my tears. I don't believe these emotions were "white women's tears of fragility," though I have cried those too.[99] I was not being "called out," but was "calling

95. This and the following quotes are from our conversation in Carrot River, August 9, 2019.

96. See Elliott, "Canada Grapples with a Charge of 'Genocide.'" On June 1, 2020, the Federal Court of Canada approved Sixties Scoop Class Action settlement payments to begin; over 12,500 persons are eligible to date (see www.sixtiesscoopsettlement.info).

97. Then-provincial Director of Child Welfare Otto Driedger (Leo's brother) started the AIM program. Today he "understands adoptees' criticisms," but has "mixed feelings." (Fowler, "Creator of Sixties Scoop Adoption Program.")

98. See Sinclair, "Reconciliation is Not an Aboriginal Problem."

99. On this, see DiAngelo, *White Fragility,* ch. 7, and Accapadi, "When White

up" familial hurt, connecting with a pool of grief much bigger than my own. At that moment I experienced what my Indigenous colleagues were referring to: the intense discomfort of having an audience spectating on one's ache. But this is part of the work of a settler "Remem-bearer" (above 3A, E): to carry the weight of complicity, grief, and moral injury that is lodged in us because of our entanglement in colonization.

6F. QUERIES FOR DE-ASSIMILATION

In contrast to colonial traditions of retributive justice and settler dodges of innocence, restorative justice seeks the personal and community healing of *both* victims and perpetrators of injustice. But for settlers, this requires an ongoing journey of repentance/recovery/complicity, the keystone practice of de-assimilation from settler colonialism.

As you consider the questions below, remember that if you cannot find the specifics of *your* ancestors' entanglements in settler colonialism (after persistent digging), then your Bloodlines work should focus on your own social story and landscape.

1. What are some of the privileges (or disadvantages) your ancestors/you accrued during settlement?

2. How was your family story lost, overwritten, or silenced by internal or external forces? How was it distorted by dominant cultural myth?

3. What is missing from your family/communal stories of settlement? What is intentionally passed over, and why? How does it feel to carry unknown pieces of your family history? How has this affected your identity?

4. When and how did you/your family "become white?" Do you retain any ethnic traditions (i.e., language, food, customs, music, trades)? What cultural losses do you feel existentially? If you don't really care, why not?

5. How might your immigrant ancestors have been complicit in events or systems that traumatized others?

6. What "moves to innocence" do you most employ? How can you interrupt these practices and work towards solidarity?

Women Cry." Their critiques are important; however, they may not sufficiently address how, in the division of emotional labor under settler patriarchy, women have been socialized to carry the sorrow, shame, and grief that men cannot or will not bear.

7. Which framework of "turning" most resonates with you: the theological rhetoric of repentance, the recovery language of Twelve-Steps or the juridical metaphor of complicity? Or do you draw from each, and if so, how?

8. How do you think you and/or your ancestors may suffer from moral injury as a result of entanglement with settler colonialism? Think not only of acts of "commission," but also losses due to "omission."

9. What are differences between the work of addressing the complicity of your ancestors, and that of your own where you now live? How can tackling one encourage work on the other?

10. What are concrete strategies of de-assimilation you've been pursuing? How might you deepen them?

Figure 27: Casa Anna Schulz Mural, panel 1 (*Täuferhöhle*, CH, with guardian angel). Artists: Dimitri Kadiev and Lisa Slavik (used with permission). Photo: Chris Wight (used with permission).

Figure 28: Casa Anna Schulz Mural, panel 5 (Painted Cave, CA, with guardian angel). Artist: Dimitri Kadiev (used with permission). Photo: Chris Wight (used with permission).

CHAPTER 7

Songlines II
Traditions of Restoration

> sitting under a black sky sprinkled with stars
> my eyes are called to the ones who have gone before—
> late at night they join hands—brilliant serpentine belt
> in the northern sky
>   purple splashes on green—shawl upon skirt
>
> great grandmothers—my ancestors love to dance
>
> I didn't know I could still hear them
> swishing in the wind—in the solitude of dark
>   great grandmothers who danced
>   to a drum only they could hear
> until I sit in silence . . .
>
>   —Mika Lafond, "my way back"[1]

7A. *TÄUFERHÖHLE* AND PAINTED CAVE, 2011

THE MURAL IN OUR front yard (depicted at several points in this book) serves as a daily reminder to us of the Landlines, Bloodlines, and Songlines to which we are accountable. Five feet tall and twenty-two feet long, its

---

1. Lafond, *nipê wânîn*, 15. Lafond is a contemporary Cree poet from Saskatchewan.

panels stretch across the adobe wall that encloses our patio. It is flanked by cactus, foregrounded by a riot of hot pink *Calandrinia spectabilis* in spring, and shaded by a three-story-tall Western sycamore that we transplanted as a seedling from the local mountains shortly after moving to the Ventura River Watershed.

In the first few months after the mural was painted, I was startled to see my ancestors each time I walked out our front door. I felt them watching me, interested in—perhaps wondering about—how I was engaging my discipleship. My Grandpa Franz was twenty-eight when he bent those rifles (above 4C). Great-grandmother Anna was forty-six when she offered hospitality to her enemies (above 2A). Their history transmitted intergenerational trauma, but also planted seeds of courage, strength, and love. I bear the effects of both. My "conversations" with these relatives holding vigil in my front yard have helped guide this project. As noted (above 4C), the mural project took place during our summer Bartimaeus Institute in 2012, a communal painting effort choreographed by Catholic Worker itinerant artist Dimitri Kadiev. It culminated the christening of our home as "Casa Anna Schulz," its design inspired by deeply impactful pilgrimages we'd just made.

In February 2011, four months after my visit to Ukraine, Ched and I went to Israel/Palestine for the first time. There we witnessed the disenfranchisement and displacement endured by Palestinians in the Occupied Territories, so painfully resonant with our North American history of settler colonialism.[2] This pilgrimage became a time of recommitment for us to a discipleship of decolonization. At the site of biblical Capernaum, just a few yards from the excavation of what is believed to have been the fisherman-apostle Peter's home, Ched reconfirmed his baptism in the Sea of Galilee. A few days later, on our return trip, we stopped over in Switzerland to visit Anabaptist sites in Zurich. We took a day's journey by train, bus, and foot to the *Täuferhöhle*, a large cave in the local mountains where early Radical Reformers had lived and worshipped in hiding from the authorities who hunted them.[3] The cave, 130 feet wide, 100 feet deep and thirteen feet high, punctuates a steep, forested slope. There I reconfirmed my baptism under a small waterfall flowing over the cave's mouth, feeling the spirits of Anabaptist ancestors. The shores of Capernaum and that Swiss cave are places that hold our origin stories of faith, our holiest Songlines.

---

2. See Veracini, "Israel-Palestine through a Settler-Colonial Studies Lens." We are profoundly grateful to Rev. Darrel Meyers who cajoled us to make this pilgrimage, then helped facilitate it; and to the Sabeel Ecumenical Liberation Theology Center* for faithfully curating opportunities for the world to "come and see" realities of the Occupation.

3. See Kaylor, "Global Baptists Worship in Anabaptist Cave."

Moved by our experience at the *Täuferhöhle*, soon after returning to California we went to pay respects to Painted Cave, a Chumash sacred place. Considered the most spectacular pictograph site in North America, it is tucked into a sandstone cliff about eleven miles northwest of Santa Barbara. Its smooth, undulating walls are adorned with many drawings created over the last millennium, complex designs painted in vivid red, black, and white by shamans and others depicting Chumash cosmology and life. Because settler graffiti (dating back to the nineteenth century) threatened to destroy this shrine—another expression of colonial "overwriting" of Indigenous culture—it is now protected by metal gates and State Historic Park status.[4]

To honor these two holy grottos, we asked Dimitri to frame the three main panels of our mural with depictions of each, adorned by appropriate symbols. Between the mural's two caves (representing Ched's Landlines and my Bloodlines respectively) are three Songlines from my family history we have related in this volume: Franz Enns subverting militarism (4C); Anna Schulz feeding those who invaded her home (2A); and Mennonite refugees departing Ukraine in boxcars (2D). The mural inspires me to learn other Songlines from my peoples' sojourn in Canada—especially stories of those who lived against the grain of colonization, often suppressed because of how they contradict mainstream communal narratives.

The following two modest vignettes, for example, illustrate how good relations between early Mennonite settlers and Indigenous women *did* exist on the prairies.

Katherina Hiebert emigrated from Russia in 1875, and became one of the first midwives to serve French, English, Métis, and Mennonite communities in southern Manitoba. A well-known herbalist, she gained "considerable herb healing information" from Indigenous women. When Katherina developed breast cancer she stayed with one of these Native healers for weeks, receiving treatments "that included poultices made from herbs and bark," and was "completely cured."[5] Intimate social interaction between Mennonite and Native communities was surely more common than the surviving record indicates.

Like other early European settlers, Mennonites relied upon the hospitality of Indigenous neighbors. One was Emilia Wieler, whose family arrived from Prussia to Rosthern, Saskatchewan, in 1894. Her husband died shortly after, leaving her to raise nine children. She moved to an abandoned homestead in Batoche that was made "available through the Indian Reservation

---

4. For images, see https://www.cyark.org/projects/chumash-painted-cave. There are numerous other Chumash rock art sites around our bioregion whose locations are kept from the public to prevent desecration.

5. Epp, *Mennonite Women in Canada*, 24, 41.

Superintendent."[6] Soon there was nothing to eat, so Emilia sent her two pre-teenaged sons to buy food at the Batoche trading post four miles away. After they left, a ferocious prairie blizzard blew up, and for three long days Emilia agonized with no word of her boys. Just as a brilliant sun finally appeared, to her tremendous joy and relief Emilia heard the boys singing through the crisp air. "An Indian picked us up and took us to the trading post," they reported, "gave us one of his blankets to sleep on beside the stove," and "brought us back on his sled . . . It was lots of fun!" Yet the supplies they brought back were meager, and before long the family faced hunger again. In desperation, Emilia sent them out once more for help to a nearby "Cree chief." The ice across the South Saskatchewan was breaking up, and it would shortly be impossible to cross the river to the store in Duck Lake. The Indigenous man risked his life by jumping across the ice floes to get to the store, then re-crossing it with arms laden with supplies for the widow and her children. It was an extraordinary and perilous feat of kindness.

A subsequent episode related by Emilia is equally poignant. A young Cree resister named *Kisse Manitou Wayo* (Almighty Voice) was fleeing the territorial police in what would become Canada's most notorious manhunt of that decade. He had been arrested for butchering a government steer—like the Young Chippewayans, people on his reserve were suffering from hunger—and broke out of jail for fear he would be lynched. Emilia's memoirs relate how Almighty Voice stopped at her cabin for food, and she shared what little she had (no mention of whether or not she knew she was aiding and abetting a fugitive). The eighteen-month chase ended in late May 1897, when dozens of militia members laid siege with heavy artillery to where Almighty Voice and two companions were trapped:

> The next morning, while Almighty Voice's mother sat on a near-by hill singing her son's war song and hundreds of local residents looked on, the Northwest Mounted Police bombarded the grove. After no sound was heard . . . the police rushed the bluff where they found the bodies of Almighty Voice, his brother-in-law Topean, and his cousin Little Saulteaux.[7]

That very hour Emilia was being baptized at Eigenheim Church (at the time a log building with an earthen floor) more than twenty miles away.

6. This and the following account was related by Emilia's granddaughter, Helen Regier, in 1980 (see Regier, "My Grandmother and Her Family").

7. Hanson, "KITCHI-MANITO-WAYA." His account adds this lament from the *Toronto Evening Telegram*: "Almighty Voice was the champion of a race that is 'up against it' in civilization. The wonder is, not that an occasional brave cuts loose, but that all the braves do not prefer sudden death to the slow extinction of their people" (para. 9).

During the service she "had a feeling that the end was near" as she heard sounds of distant cannon fire. "I will never forget this Sunday," she wrote; "it held much joy for me, but as I thought of young Almighty Voice, I also became sad. Surely there is another way for us to live together."[8]

The above two anecdotes of Mennonite women represent an important, if neglected, stratum of my communal history. Such stories are exceptions to the rule of rationalizing or racist settler narratives, and we typically have to scratch hard to disinter them from obscurity. Here in Ventura County, we are still searching for dissident tales from settler history, the kind that might fill out our mural between the two sacred caves. Were there European defectors from the local mission system, or defenders of Chumash rights during Mexican and early American periods? And who *else* is leaving gifts at the Asistencia memorial down the valley (above 1A)?

This chapter explores how Songlines nurture settler response-ability. We start with a short "detour" from our main focus, in order to illustrate how our own journey of recovery has been deepened through the discipline of pilgrimage, exploring landscapes and genealogies that hold liberative Storylines. This will take us for a moment into the haunted landscape of the Southern U.S..

7B. "A WAY THAT WITH TEARS HAS BEEN WATERED": PEDAGOGY OF PILGRIMAGE

Individual stories of courage and conscience both inspire and instruct us, as illustrated by family tales I've shared in this book, not to mention by the lives of recognized saints, heroes, and martyrs. Germane to our theme, for example, is the *Journal of John Woolman*, the poignant testimony of a Pennsylvania Quaker dissident against settler colonialism. He is perhaps the closest North American counterpart to the great voice of conscience in Latin America, Bartolomé de las Casas. Well before American independence, Woolman was lamenting English colonization of the eastern seaboard. "The seeds of great calamity and desolation are sown and growing fast on this continent," he wrote while on a 1763 pilgrimage to visit Delaware tribes considered enemies during the French and Indian War. Woolman hoped that settlers of conscience "might arise in God's strength, and like faithful

---

8. Regier, "My Grandmother and Her Family." The tragic story of Almighty Voice is memorialized on a beautiful public mural in Duck Lake, Saskatchewan. See https://ducklake.ca/visitors/murals.html, and artist's website at https://rkeighley.com/shop/almighty-voice/.

messengers work to check the growth of these seeds, that they many not ripen to the ruin of our posterity."[9]

But personal narratives are even more effective in animating change when they are contextualized as part of social movements; conversely, a good way to approach the history of movements is through the lens of key protagonists.[10] We explored this dialectic of personal and political in our 2009 *Ambassadors of Reconciliation II,* profiling nine current North American pioneers of restorative justice. We've mentioned several of them in the course of this volume, and below again highlight the work of Nelson Johnson, Lawrence Hart, Elizabeth McAlister, and Murphy Davis. Our profiles of these colleagues were offered not as hagiographies, but to illustrate how transformative social movements are populated by ordinary persons called to extraordinary work. Their impact is often invisible and rarely measurable in the short term, fully revealed only in hindsight, which is why preserving histories of popular movements of resistance to oppression and for democratic renewal is so important.[11]

How is learning such Storylines relevant to decolonization work? There are two basic reasons:

- Every social movement for justice—whether by and for women, racialized minorities, workers, low-income people, prisoners, LGBTQI, or disabled folks; or for environmental sustainability or human rights; or against war or economic apartheid—in some way *contests the settler colonial system.* Each is instructive for new generations engaging similar structural forces, if different particularities.

- An alternative history is *essential* to political imagination, precisely because settler colonialism legitimates and perpetuates itself through myths of innocence and nobility. Accounts of popular struggle not only expose, demystify, and discredit dominant fairytale thinking, they also offer us a more reliable and redemptive collective story and ethos. There was good reason that Ella Baker and Dr. King's Southern

---

9. Woolman, *Journal and Major Essays of John Woolman,* 129. See more in Myers, *Who Will Roll Away the Stone?,* 146–48, and Ellsberg, "Las Casas' Discovery."

10. A wonderful case in point is a recent documentary film, *Crip Camp* (https://www.netflix.com/title/81001496), which narrates the early disability rights movement in the U.S. through the perspectives of key individual leaders (see review in Rivers, "Crip Camp Reminds Us"). Two of those profiled are Denise Sherer and Neil Jacobson, dear friends with whom Ched got his start in activism in the mid-1970s.

11. Two exemplary efforts are Zinn's *A People's History of the United States* and Williams's *Empire as a Way of Life.*

Christian Leadership Conference* summarized its mission as "re-deeming the soul of America."[12]

For both reasons, mainstream education and media in North America ignore or marginalize social movement stories, or "adopt" them retrospectively in ways that sentimentalize and politically neuter them, Martin Luther King's legacy being an obvious case in point in the U.S..

It is up to regular citizens, therefore, to "re-school" ourselves (below 8B) by becoming students of justice movements, preferably learning directly from individuals and organizations who stand *in* living traditions of struggle. This is a challenge, since even activist culture neglects to devote time and energy to such a pedagogy. But as scholar activist Michelle Alexander says,

> If we are going to do the work that is required to build truly transformational movements in which there is any hope of us building a multiracial, multiethnic, multifaith, multi-gender democracy, in which every voice and every life truly matters, we are going to have to connect and tap into, embrace that revolutionary spirit and the spirits of the ancestors, the freedom fighters who came before us.[13]

Ched and I had the great privilege of being mentored by Dr. Vincent Harding, spiritual advisor to Dr. King and foremost historian of the Southern Freedom Struggle, the most consequential social movement in U.S. history. Harding believed "all moral imagination begins with memory," and repeatedly exhorted us to learn the story of "The Movement," as it was singularly called in the 1960s.[14] In his primer, *Hope and History*, Harding relates a conversation in 1990 with a young man in Boston who was caught up in street crime and trying to turn his life around. "What we need are signposts to help us find the way. I don't mean no regular signposts," said the teenager, "I mean like live human signposts. People we can look at, be with, listen to."[15]

At Harding's urging, we have apprenticed ourselves to civil rights history and to its elderly animators who are still with us (such as James Lawson, Ruby Sales, and the National Council of Elders*). No one in the

12. Fairclough, *To Redeem the Soul of America.*

13. Comments made during a panel in Chicago, July 3, 2017 (transcript at https://portside.org/2017–07–03/people-were-resisting-trump-michelle-alexander-naomi-klein-and-keeanga-yamahtta-taylor).

14. See Harding, *Hope and History*, though all of his books facilitate this learning.

15. Harding, *Hope and History*, 13. Dr. Harding emphasized and embodied the art of listening to young people.

U.S. can escape slavery's haunting of soil and soul, ghosts as omnipresent as those of Indigenous dispossession. Indeed, many Indigenous persons were also enslaved, a story rarely told.[16] Though neither of our Saskatchewan and Californian family histories were directly entangled in the system of chattel slavery, as white people our privileges are nevertheless rooted in the bitter legacy of American apartheid. So over the past twenty years we have continually sought to learn more about both the awful history of oppression and the vibrant traditions of overcoming. With the latest round of police violence against African American men in the U.S. in May 2020, and the surge of protest since that is contesting longstanding policies and practices, this commitment has only deepened.

The Movement was profoundly faith-rooted, fired by traditions of Black preaching and prayer.[17] By compelling people to move from the sanctuary out onto the streets, it reminded us the church is *meant* to be a social movement for liberation. Just as music was important to my forebears (above 4B), it played a strategic role in the Freedom Movement. Bernice Johnson Reagon, Sweet Honey in the Rock* leader and founding member of the Student Non-violent Coordinating Committee, believes group singing modulated sanity and balance amidst the pressures of organizing and actions.[18] Movement songs, many of which were reworked Negro spirituals that were easily taught and learned, allowed for expressions of rage, sadness, determination, and faith. As Dr. King put it:

> In a sense the freedom songs are the soul of the movement. They are more than just incantations of clever phrases designed to invigorate a campaign; they are as old as the history of the Negro in America. They are adaptations of the songs the slaves sang—the sorrow songs, the shouts for joy, the battle hymns and the anthems of our movement . . . We sing the freedom songs of today for the same reason the slaves sang them, because we too are in bondage and the songs add hope to our determination that "We shall overcome."[19]

Singing together served to unify, nurture, and strengthen protestors in the face of the guns, firehoses, and dogs of white supremacist police and Citizens Councils. It inspired courage and connection, especially in jail.

16. See Reséndez, *Other Slavery.*

17. See Marsh, *Beloved Community.*

18. See profile and interviews at https://folkways.si.edu/bernice-johnson-reagon-civil-rights-song-leader/african-american-struggle-protest-folk/music/article/smithsonian.

19. King, cited in Washington, *Testament of Hope,* 535.

And it illustrates how social movements draw on existing culture (hymns from the Black church) while creating their own unique expressions (assigning new words and meanings).

Our apprenticeship has received particular encouragement and challenge from long-time mentors Joyce and Nelson Johnson of the Beloved Community Center* in Greensboro, and Murphy Davis and Ed Loring of the Open Door Community* in Atlanta, whose work and witness remain formational for us.[20] At one point, Murphy and Ed solemnly gifted us all three volumes (over 2,500 pages of narrative!) of Taylor Branch's epic history *America in the King Years,* on the condition that we read the *whole* corpus (this took us several years to accomplish)! Learning from texts, interviews, or films is an enriching discipline; but *walking the hallowed ground* that holds this history brings it to life.

Mary Shawn Copeland writes that solidarity

> begins in *anamnesis*—the intentional remembering of the dead, exploited, despised victims of history. This memory cannot be a pietistic or romantic memorial, for always intentional recovery and engagement of the histories of suffering are fraught with ambiguity and paradox. The victims of history are lost, but we are alive. We owe all that we have to our exploitation and enslavement, removal and extermination of despised others . . .
> Our recognition and regard for the victims of history and our shouldering responsibility for that history form the moral basis of Christian solidarity.[21]

Pilgrimages to Movement sites, therefore, have become central to our "continuing education."

Our pedagogy of pilgrimage began in earnest in 2002 with the first of many week-long Word and World schools in cities with significant and diverse social movement histories (discussed below 8B). In 2003, we spent a longer stretch in Memphis, Tennessee, teaching the spring semester at Memphis Theological Seminary and Christian Brothers University. There we encountered in depth the story of Dr. King's commitment to the 1968 Sanitation Workers Strike, which ultimately cost him his life. We spent countless hours at the National Civil Rights Museum,* constructed at the site of the Lorraine Motel where King was gunned down. Our time in Memphis corresponded with the second Gulf War's terrible "Shock and Awe" campaign, so we deployed King's "Beyond Vietnam" speech as a catechism

---

20. See Nelson and Murphy's profiles in Enns and Myers, *Ambassadors II,* chapters 6B and 7B, and Myers, "Following Jesus in the Way of King"

21. Copeland, *Enfleshing Freedom,* 100.

during antiwar workshops and sermons in both Black and white churches.[22] And we experienced the discomforting realities of living in a profoundly segregated southern city.

In fall 2010, we traveled to Birmingham, Alabama, visiting Kelly Ingram Park, a central battleground in the 1963 Children's March. Here the notorious Bull Connor infamously turned dogs and high-powered water hoses on nonviolent demonstrators. Across the street we paid respects at the Sixteenth Street Baptist Church,* where in September 1963 a Klan bombing killed four little girls (and injured many others) during worship services. And we pored through the adjacent Birmingham Civil Rights Institute.* But our most recent and impactful pilgrimage took place in October 2019—in the middle of drafting this book. We strung together several work commitments into a month-long sojourn around the American southeast, highlights of which we relate here.

We began at the historic Haley Farm* for a retreat to plan the "Freedom Seminary" component of the next Proctor Institute.* This vibrant summer conference constitutes the largest gathering of progressive Black church leaders and activists in the U.S., curated over the last quarter century by the venerable and visionary Marion Wright Edelman of the Children's Defense Fund.* The Proctor Institute has become an annual destination for us since 2014, part of our continuing formation in a living civil rights movement history and theology. As we do each visit, we brought gifts of gratitude to the gravesites of mentors Rosemary and Vincent Harding and Gordon and Mary Cosby of Church of the Saviour,* tucked away at the edge of Haley's sacred grounds.

We next spent several days in New Orleans, our first visit. It began with a poignant personal moment, as we commemorated our twentieth wedding anniversary by renewing vows at the same Trinity Episcopal Church side chapel altar where Ched's parents were married seventy-five years earlier. That evening, at the wedding of two activist friends, we got to know Ronald Lewis, a revered labor and cultural activist from the Lower Ninth Ward; five months later he became one of the early victims of the COVID-19 pandemic.[23] We experienced the communal ecstasy of marching in a Second Line parade, a tradition Lewis did so much to preserve. Then we took the first

22. See Myers, "Time to Break the Silence—Again."
23. See Clapp, "Ronald Lewis."

of several deep dives during this sojourn into the history of the "Second Middle Passage," about which we knew too little.

Here is a concise summary of the era of domestic slave trafficking in the U.S.:

> When Congress outlawed the Transatlantic Slave Trade beginning in 1808, new demand for slaves had to be met by natural reproduction in the local slave population or by domestic trade. As a result of the increased demand for slave labor due to the booming cotton industry, an estimated one million slaves were forcibly transferred from the Upper South to the Lower South between 1810 and 1860 . . . Slave traders accumulated substantial wealth by purchasing slaves in the Upper South and transporting them to the Lower South. It is estimated that more than half of all slaves in the Upper South were separated from a parent or child, and a third of their marriages were destroyed by forced migration.[24]

This brutal trafficking, which surpassed in volume the transatlantic slave trade, enabled the rise of cotton and sugar economies in the deep South even as it further tore apart Black families. We could feel the hauntings as we traversed paths around New Orleans that had been walked by enslaved people and those who bought and sold them, from wharfs to markets to auction houses.[25]

On our way out of New Orleans we visited Whitney Plantation,* which focuses exclusively on the lives of enslaved people. It does an amazing job of rendering present the ghosts of former enslaved residents through art, narrative, and statuary. There we were reminded that "this inhuman traffic did not succeed in crushing its victims." Enslaved people resisted and survived:

> They clung to a sense of family and developed life-saving and heritage-preserving coping devices against a hostile white world. They learned to value themselves and their families in a society that looked upon them with loathing. And they learned to build a community that would grow into an extraordinarily dynamic and creative force in the nation through which they were moved in chains.[26]

24. At https://eji.org/news/history-racial-injustice-domestic-slave-trade/.

25. See the virtual walking tour and audio guide at https://www.neworleansslave-trade.org/.

26. From an essay providing context at "In Motion," an excellent resource (http://www.inmotionaame.org/print.cfm;jsessionid=f83010905315859888818298?migration=3&bhcp=1).

We next drove to Montgomery, Alabama, to spend a day each at Equal Justice Initiative's* two recently completed installations: the Legacy Museum ("From Enslavement to Mass Incarceration"); and the National Memorial for Peace and Justice* (commemorating the history of lynching). EJI's mission is to change the story about race in the U.S. by centering the voices of impacted individuals and groups, and by depicting the sheer scale of violence and trauma during American apartheid. These state-of-the-art exhibits accomplish this aim powerfully, tracing the history from kidnapping (slavery) to terrorism (lynching), and from segregation (Jim Crow) to incarceration (from convict-leasing in the nineteenth century to the racialized prison industrial complex of the twenty-first). We strongly commend the EJI complex as a pilgrimage destination for a catechism in this awful history, which also commissions visitors to organize in our own counties around America's violent past and continuing legacy of racism.

Our last day in Montgomery focused on the Rosa Parks Museum's* story of the revival of civil rights activism in the famous bus boycott, and Dexter Ave. Baptist Church,* where Dr. King was serving when he was pulled into a campaign being led by women. In Montgomery one sees a dramatic clash between memorials, monuments, and signage narrating two conflicting histories: the "glories" of the Confederacy on one hand, and the courage of the civil rights struggle on the other. As we navigated this public battle of legacies, we were confirmed in our conviction that white settlers can only discern the truth of our Landlines and Bloodlines through the lens of Songlines. And those Songlines *must* include the stories of those who forged "a way that with tears has been watered . . . through the blood of the slaughtered," in the famous words of James Weldon Johnson. That history can tutor us, too, to "sing a song full of the faith that the dark past has taught us."[27]

Our journey then turned to the hidden history of white folks who embodied repentance from supremacy and violence, as we visited places associated with some of our most important settler mentors in faith and justice. At the tail end of a tropical storm we arrived at Koinonia Farms* in Americus, Georgia, to honor the fiftieth anniversary of Baptist radical Clarence Jordan's passing. Florence and Clarence built a remarkable interracial community in the teeth of 1940s Jim Crow and 1950s Cold War America. This small but notorious "demonstration project" endured Klan terrorism and county-wide white hostility. A national network of supporters buying Koinonia's mail-order pecans helped them survive a strangling local white

27. For full lyrics and background to a song that became the Negro National Anthem, see Johnson, "Lift Every Voice and Sing."

boycott, thus helping their mission to "ship the nuts out of Georgia" (as Clarence's disarming wry wit put it). In 1966, Clarence called then-IBM executive Ladon Sheats onto the Way of discipleship, who in turn became a beloved mentor to many. In 1976, Ladon passed on that call to Ched, a genealogy of faith we were there to honor.[28] We strolled quietly through a small unmarked cemetery up in a pecan grove, and prayed at the desk where Clarence died suddenly in 1969. It was in this shack that he wrote influential books marked by both biblical eloquence and colloquial humor (such as his *Cottonpatch Gospel*), which continue to guide those seeking a more engaged gospel faith.[29] In the early 1970s, Koinonia incubated Habitat for Humanity,* now a global project promoting housing justice, and the Farm continues as the oldest ongoing experiment in Christian community, sustainable agricultural and racial justice in the U.S..

From the haunted red clay of Georgia fields we drove to coastal Brunswick to attend the trial of the Kings Bay Plowshares* defendants. Since 1980, Plowshares activists have nonviolently entered military bases and weapons manufacturing facilities to "disarm" symbolically nuclear components with hammers, their own blood, and subpoenas, actions seeking to expose weapons of mass destruction as crimes against humanity. On April 4, 2018—the fiftieth anniversary of Martin Luther King's assassination—our dearest living mentor Liz McAlister and six other Roman Catholic activists entered Kings Bay Naval Submarine base to enact the prophetic summons to "beat swords into plowshares." During their trial, supporters from around the world converged to sing and pray in a "Festival of Hope," and we saw many old friends from the peace movement. Yet we wrestled with the specter that we might never again see Liz, an amazing woman we honor as our singular "mother in the faith," now eighty years old and in faltering health.[30] The defendants were found guilty, and many face significant jail time.[31]

We headed north with a certain melancholy which deepened as we crossed the "Seminole Trail" at several points. The Trail of Tears network stretches over 5,000 miles across nine southeastern states. More than 60,000 Indigenous persons from multiple tribes (including Cherokee, Choctaw, Creek, Chickasaw, and Seminole) were forcibly dispossessed by President Andrew Jackson's notorious 1830 Indian Removal Act, widely considered

28. See Myers, "Caretaking the Gift."

29. For an overview of that legacy and a complete bibliography, see https://followingjesus.org/clarence-jordan/.

30. Enns and Myers, *Ambassadors of Reconciliation*, 2:95–104.

31. Find interviews and perspectives at https://www.ncronline.org/social-tags/plowshares-movement.

one of the worst crimes of U.S. settler colonialism.[32] Over 15,000 died on the journey west of the Mississippi.

Our heavy hearts were revived that evening through the hospitality of dear Methodist friends in Lumberton, North Carolina. Over a generous dinner we spoke with Sheryl and Steve Taylor about their work, which includes organizing with the local Lumbee tribe in their continuing struggle for recognition and respect. Steve, a former Air Force officer in command and control over nuclear weapons in Europe, underwent a remarkable conversion to the gospel and publicly apologized to those his weapons once targeted.[33]

In Richmond, Virginia, we stopped for a stretch break by the James River, and stumbled upon another artery of sorrow: the Richmond Slave Trail.* As we crept along its muddy banks we learned Richmond was the largest source for enslaved African Americans trafficked on the east coast from 1830 to 1860. We had unwittingly found the origin point of the domestic slave trade whose terminus in New Orleans had been the start of our pilgrimage. We then visited Sarah Nolan at St. Paul's Episcopal Church* (she had worked in the Ventura River watershed for many years founding the Abundant Table Farm Project* with whom we still partner). The parish Sarah now serves as a lay staff member is a virtual museum of Confederate symbols and memorials. She toured us around the parish buildings, and spoke about the congregation's sincere but halting efforts at a "History and Reconciliation Initiative."

We were grateful to settle in for a week's stay in Arlington, Virginia, where our hosts, Carter Echols and Bill Johnson, are white southerners who have done considerable work facing their respective family histories around slavery, even as they pursue peace and justice ministries today. Curating such stories was the focus of a writing retreat we then co-facilitated with veteran authors Rose Berger and Demetria Martinez and jazz musician Warren Cooper over the next several days. An intergenerational, multiracial group of participants practiced "writing from and for the Movement," probing their family and communal Landlines, Bloodlines, and Songlines. Our gathering was at Wellspring,* the retreat center of the Church of the Saviour,* an alternative Christian witness to justice since the 1940s whose witness has shaped us deeply.[34]

32. See Toensing, "Indian-Killer Andrew Jackson Deserves Top Spot," and Ehle, *Trail of Tears.*

33. See his moving testimony in Taylor, "I Believe in God," and at the conclusion to our "Introducing the Bartimaeus Institute" video (https://www.youtube.com/watch?v=TcvwqwzGgNY&feature=youtu.be).

34. See Abernethy, "Gordon Cosby and Washington's Church of the Savior." The

The northernmost edge of our sojourn was Baltimore, where we enjoyed an afternoon and evening with aforementioned mentors Murphy Davis and Ed Loring of Open Door Community.*[35] Their lives, faithfully walking with the poorest of the poor on the streets of Atlanta and on Georgia's Death Row for over thirty years, are Songlines for us. Not long after we returned to California we received a draft of Murphy's long-awaited memoir, which we read out loud to each other. Through a quarter-century-long battle with cancer, Murphy has faithfully wrestled with the principalities of death, both in her body and in the body politic.[36]

Our pilgrimage culminated in Greensboro, North Carolina, where we enjoyed the hospitality of Charlene Holler as we have for each of our almost annual visits over twenty-five years. Charlene and her late husband, Zee (a Presbyterian minister who often was a solitary voice for justice among local white clergy), have supported and collaborated with the Beloved Community Center* since its inception.[37] We had come to join the BCC in a fortieth-anniversary commemoration of a 1979 massacre, remem-bearing how Ku Klux Klan members, aided by police and Nazis, murdered five labor organizers and wounded ten others in an African American neighborhood in Greensboro. Joyce and Nelson Johnson, esteemed elders mentioned throughout this volume and survivors of that shooting, helped animate the Greensboro Truth and Community Reconciliation Project* from 2004 to 2006, the first TRC process to take place in the U.S..[38] The BCC's profound commitment to restorative justice has been a North Star to us, so it was a fitting conclusion to our trip to gather with colleagues from around the country to witness the exemplary care with which the Johnsons curate and honor their own story.

We will long be buoyed by Songlines forged and remembered by Black, white, and Indigenous people that we traced along this pilgrimage way. Learning Movement Storylines is a keystone spiritual and political discipline for us. The history of settler colonialism into which we are socialized may be devised and dismembered, but that doesn't mean we are without alternatives. Every corner of North America also holds memories of truthtelling, courage, and solidarity. Every community stewards biographies of

---

retreat was funded by a bequest from Kayla McClurg, a beloved member of the church (see https://chcov.org/1050524-2/), and facilitated by Mike Little of Faith and Money Network.*

35. Enns and Myers, *Ambassadors of Reconciliation*, 2:104–20.

36. Davis, *Surely Goodness and Mercy*.

37. See https://www.greensboro.com/obituaries/holler-jr-rev-zeb-north/article_4d91d550-9b11-58bc-8b64-04e8c98f529b.html.

38. See Magarrell and Wesley, *Learning from Greensboro*.

memorable figures who contributed healing, not just those who generated hauntings. Pilgrimage-as-pedagogy has introduced us to holy grounds, which though far from us geographically, are now woven into our consciousness.[39] We regularly commend this practice to younger settler colleagues, often mapping out places and people to visit; we have seen their pilgrimages similarly result in life changes.[40]

Songlines educate and inspire us to keep going, and to go deeper. And the ones most deeply held in the soil of North America are those of Indigenous communities. Settlers committed to decolonization need to pay particular attention to these Songlines, especially their most recent iterations.

7C. TRUTH AND RECONCILIATION

On June 11, 2008, in the middle of a theology conference in Truro, Nova Scotia, Rev. Russ Daye whispered to Ched: "Buddy, something historic is about to take place not far from here; let's go!" An hour later they were inside the Mi'kmaq tribal hall at *Sipekne'katik* (then Indian Brook) First Nation, where Russ had been invited. It was packed to the rafters and electric with anticipation: elders chanted and waved eagle feathers at a large screen where they were about to watch a live telecast of a special joint session of the Canadian House of Commons and the Senate. That afternoon, Prime Minister Stephen Harper issued a public apology to Indigenous leaders assembled before him for the government's role in the terrible history of Indian Residential Schools. The collective catharsis that swept through that room moved Ched to tears as he realized he would likely never see anything like this take place on the floor of the U.S. Congress.[41]

The neighboring Milbrook First Nation reserve also hosted a large gathering that day, because the Shubenacadie Indian Residential School

39. For examples of how the Southern Freedom Movement has shaped Ched's exposition of Scripture, see Myers and Enns, *Ambassadors I,* and most recently Myers, "Jesus' Risen, Mutilated Body."

40. We think of a suburban couple who changed course after visiting a dozen radical Christian communities across the U.S. one summer; activist friends we helped get to Standing Rock to stand with Water Protectors against the Keystone XL pipeline in 2016; and the many young mentees we've pointed to the places we've named above, as well as others such as Spiritus Christi Church,* Borderlinks,* Trinity UCC Chicago,* and Catholic Worker houses* around North America.

41. See https://www.cbc.ca/archives/government-apologizes-for-residential-schools-in-2008-1.4666041. Harper's apology was, from his side, a political calculus (see Barrera, "Harper's 2008 Residential School Apology"). Apologies are important, as the tidal wave of Indigenous response indicated, but ultimately require change of behavior (see below 8D).

had been located there. That reserve's most famous daughter, and survivor of that school, was Nora Bernard, though she was not there to see this moment; she had passed just six months earlier. Her remarkable story captures the essence of both courageous leadership and tragedy born of trauma. It also illustrates the powerful advocacy that has arisen from Indigenous communities over the last half century, as well as the ongoing impacts of oppression. Bernard was delivered by her grandmother in 1935 into the Milbrook community. At age nine she was forced to attend Shubenacadie, the only IRS in Atlantic Canada; she was there for five years. In 1955, she lost her tribal status for marrying a non-Indigenous man, which wasn't reinstated until 2007. But in 1995, Bernard began an organization for IRS survivors, and subsequently recruited legal help to file suit against that school, the first IRS class-action suit in Canada.

IRS abuses of children were not only sexual and physical, Bernard testified later to the House of Commons. They also included "being incarcerated through no fault of their own; the introduction of child labour; the withholding of food, clothing, and proper education; the loss of language and culture; and no proper medical attention."[42] Other survivor's associations were inspired to file similar suits, which were consolidated into the largest class-action suit in Canadian history, naming the government and churches as defendants, and representing some 79,000 survivors. A settlement was agreed to in 2005, and implemented in 2007 for more than 5 billion dollars. Tragically however, the life of this woman who initiated the historic turn toward accountability for past injustices in Canada was cut short by the very consequences of oppression she had worked so hard to expose. Bernard was murdered in 2008 by a grandson in the throes of addiction.

The IRS Settlement Agreement brought modest compensation for individual survivors (Nora used some of hers to help other band members pay bills). It also mandated the creation of a national Truth and Reconciliation process, which developed into an extraordinary experiment that became arguably the most significant movement of transformation in modern Canadian history. The Truth and Reconciliation Commission of Canada's* task was to document how survivors, their families, and communities were affected by the IRS experience, and to create an historical record that could render Canadians aware and accountable. Over seven generations, more than 150,000 Indigenous children between the ages of four and sixteen were taken—usually forcibly—from their homes and sent to residential schools, where they were forbidden to speak their Native language and forced to

42. Cited at https://en.wikipedia.org/wiki/Nora_Bernard, para 4. See also the testimonies of Bernard's lead attorney, John McKiggan, "Tribute to Nora Bernard," and Meili, "Nora Bernard Fought for Justice."

conform to European lifeways. Almost all were abused, and there was a staggering mortality rate.[43]

After a slow start, three formidable commissioners launched the TRC process in Winnipeg in June 2010, and over the next five years curated seven national, and many more regional, hearings around the country. Over 6,500 witnesses testified to the impacts of the IRS, and by association, many other aspects of settler colonization. This was the extraordinary fruit that came from seeds planted by a persistent Mi'kmaq woman, and grown through actions of survivors across the country. I had the privilege of attending two national TRC gatherings: in Halifax, Nova Scotia (October 2011) and in Saskatoon, Saskatchewan (June 2012). The latter began with an Inuk elder solemnly lighting a traditional *qulliq* whale oil lamp. After being brushed with cedar and smudged with sage, the three commissioners took their seats behind an elegantly carved bentwood box. A survivor began his testimony, haltingly narrating painful memories from sixty years ago. Soon tears began to flow, and a support person carefully collected the damp tissues into a basket, which at the end of the day were added to the sacred fire that burned around the clock outside the hall. In this space, so filled with sorrow and rage, every ritual communicated respect and empathy, transforming the sterile auditorium into a sanctuary for healing.[44]

We heard tale after tale of unthinkable violence and abuse. The pattern of brutality was captured by one woman's testimony that has stayed with me. Five years old when taken away from her family, she had been initially excited about receiving an education. But on her very first day she was stripped of her traditional clothing, her braids shaved off, raped by a nun, and then held under water until she nearly drowned "to teach her discipline." She related how one of her brothers died at that school and how two others have brain damage resulting from severe beatings they received. Though repeatedly told at the school that she was a "dumb Indian," she now pursues doctoral work, defiant and courageous. Like many survivors, she made it clear the IRS system was a reflection of the larger legacy of colonization and racism that continues in Canada.

Commission chair Justice Murray Sinclair opened the second day of the hearings with a poignant refrain he repeated all over Canada. This is what he told us:

> This IRS legacy is not an Indian problem; it is a *Canadian* prob-
> lem. At the same time that Native children were being taught

---

43. See Truth and Reconciliation Commission of Canada, *They Came for the Children*, and list of final Commission reports at http://nctr.ca/reports.php.

44. See Enns, "Shameful Legacy."

inferiority, non-Native children in the public schools were implicitly and sometimes explicitly taught superiority. This work
takes courage. Survivors: make sure that Canada and your
children know your story and understand what happened; put
aside your victimization, stand up and take charge of your life,
beginning today. Audience: you need to bear witness to what
you hear, and feel the strength of these tears. [45]

Grassroots restorative justice movements, from victim-offender dialogue to those working with torture survivors, have learned how important
it is for victims of violence to tell their stories, especially when their truth
has been publicly suppressed or distorted. Facilitators of such processes
must be vigilant about the potential for re-traumatization, and work closely
with victim participants to: acknowledge risks; establish conditions for
"brave space"; ensure that those testifying are in control of the process; and
curate rituals of solidarity and accompaniment. Truth-telling can be a key
step for violated persons to move from victim to survivor to healer.[46] Their
testimonies, in turn, have the moral authority to transform our ignorance,
denial, and complacency. The Canadian TRC hearings magnificently dem-
onstrated this caution, care, and courage.

There is a cost to those who speak their pain. As our Chumash/Ohlone
colleague Jonathan Cordero always reminds us, Indigenous leaders are "sick
and tired of having to share our pain in order for white people to get it."
Settlers, he says, need to share the emotional labor by getting in touch with
and sharing publicly the personal and familial pain *we* have experienced as
a result of colonization's dehumanization (above 6E). At the same time we
see repeatedly the contagious power of testimony to animate those "with
ears to hear" to make personal and political change. For example, several
of the settler Mennonite women who participated in my doctoral research
also attended the TRC hearings in Saskatoon, and shared their experiences
with me. One expressed how impressed she was by the TRC process: "I feel
like we've been mentored into such an amazing way of doing reconciliation work. We Mennonites come from a long history of peacebuilding, and
how do we not know about this kind of thing?" Another added: "As Native
women were telling their stories, strength was coming to them. That is when
healing occurs. And I thought: this could happen with Mennonites too!"[47]

45. Sinclair, June 22, 2012 TRC hearing, Prairieland Park, Saskatoon, Saskatchewan,
as recorded in my notes; emphasis Sinclair's.

46. See Enns and Myers, *Ambassadors of Reconciliation*, 2:157.

47. TRC Focus Group, interview by Elaine Enns, Saskatoon, Saskatchewan, June 26,
2014. Eileen Klassen Hamm, Executive Director of MCC Saskatchewan, believes the
influence of the TRC is "one of the key reasons that Mennonites in our area have been

In June 2015, the TRC released its Executive Summary, with ninety-four Calls to Action directed to all sectors of Canadian society, including fourteen addressed to churches.[48] These calls now function as both framework and measuring stick for concrete change. In 2018, the Indigenous Unit of the Canadian Broadcasting Corporation established the Beyond 94* website to track the status of each call, in order to "monitor the progress of one of Canada's most important tools for change." As of spring 2020, they mark ten as completed, twenty-one in progress and thirty-nine with projects proposed. Of twenty-four "not yet started," four are church-related, including an apology from the pope to IRS survivors.[49] Many churches are repudiating the Doctrine of Discovery.[50]

Sara Stratton serves as Reconciliation and Indigenous Justice Animator for the United Church of Canada.* She offered us this summary of how their churches are responding five years on:

> Canadian churches that ran residential schools welcomed the Calls to Action, and committed to help fulfill them. The Calls are clearly rooted in implementation of the United Nations Declaration on the Rights of Indigenous Peoples. So the United Church of Canada began by adopting the principles, norms, and standards of the Declaration as our framework for reconciliation; many other churches and religious organizations have done this as well. This has meant that we now approach everything from advocacy to investments with an Indigenous rights framework. It also resulted in a restructuring of the United Church so that its 64 Indigenous communities of faith and ministries are now part of a self-determining body within the United Church. We continue to advocate for Canada's implementation of the

able to engage in the Stoney Knoll story" (email correspondence with authors, May 15, 2020). See also McGuire and Denis, "Unsettling Pathways."

48. See Truth and Reconciliation Commission of Canada, *Calls to Action.*

49. In 2018, the pope refused "an invitation from the Canadian government to apologize for the Catholic Church's role in running residential schools" (Downey and Holscher, "What the U.S. Catholic Church Gets Wrong about Native Dispossession"). See also Cecco, "Pope Faces Indigenous Canadians' Anger," and Andraos, *Church and Indigenous Peoples in the Americas*, ch. 4.

50. Canadian denominations include Mennonites (see Woelk and Heinrichs, *Yours, Mine, Ours*); United Church (https://www.united-church.ca/sites/default/files/resources/doctrine-discovery-backgrounder.pdf); Presbyterians (https://presbyterian.ca/justice/doctrine-of-discovery/); and Anglicans (https://www.anglican.ca/wp-content/uploads/Doctrine-of-Discovery.pdf). In the U.S., see Gismondi, "American Churches Are Apologizing for a Centuries-Old Injustice"; Miller, "Denominations Repent for Native American Land Grabs"; and the Dismantling the Doctrine of Discovery Coalition (https://dofdmenno.org/).

Declaration, and for those Calls to Action regarding justice issues such as child welfare, education policy, and violence against
women. In terms of Calls directed to churches, we continue to
seek and provide information on missing children, and will
be collaborating in memorialization programs. The United
Church is also actively working, with the government, national
Indigenous organizations, and other churches, on a Covenant
of Reconciliation. All of this arises not just from the church's
commitment to confront and atone for its past actions, but also
to address the current ongoing impacts of colonial policies that
led to residential schools.[51]

We are grateful for how the Canadian TRC has shaped our own lives
and work, and support fledgling efforts to do similar education and advocacy in the U.S. around its parallel history.[52]

To be sure, the TRC didn't forge a consensus around (much less realize) the great dream of "reconciliation," which is still a contested notion
in Canada (below 8A). Nevertheless, Russ Daye, who served as a United
Church of Canada liaison to the TRC, asserts:

> One could legitimately say that despite the resistance, the TRC
> has been a game changer for Canada in terms of truth-telling
> about the genocide suffered by our first peoples. And it has fos-
> tered much greater change than any previous initiative, includ-
> ing the Royal Commission on Aboriginal Peoples (1991–96).[53]

Driven by IRS survivors, the TRC is, to date, the most notable example
of how, against all odds, Indigenous communities in North America have
not only survived colonial attempts at erasure, but are today strengthening
their nations and capacities to flourish through cultural renewal, economic
development, and political activism.

7D. INDIGENOUS RESURGENCE

In November 2019, our colleague, Dr. Jonathan Cordero (Chumash/
Ohlone), traveled up to San Francisco to welcome visitors to Ohlone

51. Stratton, email correspondence with authors, March 26, 2020. Hear her talk
about her settler family history in Newfoundland and its meaning for decolonizing
discipleship in Stratton, "Decolonizing Discipleship."

52. See Pember, "Death by Civilization," and the work of the National Native American Boarding School Healing Coalition* (https://boardingschoolhealing.org/healing/
for-churches/).

53. Daye, email correspondence with authors, May 15, 2020.

territory. He had done this many times before, but this was special: several thousand people were gathered for the fiftieth-anniversary commemoration of the Indigenous occupation of Alcatraz Island.[54] The energy around this convergence inspired him, he told us, a reminder of how a half century ago, Indigenous activist initiated a new chapter in the long history of resistance to colonization and genocide. Animated by the cultural and political turmoil of the late 1960s in the U.S., in the space of five years the American Indian Movement was founded to combat the Indian Termination Act (1968); Alcatraz was re-occupied for nineteen months (November 1969—June 1971); and a "second battle" erupted at Wounded Knee (1972).[55]

Gerald Vizenor (Chippewa) uses the term "survivance" (survival + endurance) to describe Native "renunciations of dominance, tragedy and victimry" through history.[56] Mohawk educator Gerald Taiaiake Alfred refers to contemporary streams of Native protest, advocacy, and revitalization as "Indigenous Resurgence":

> To decolonize we need to reclaim the sacred spaces of our traditional territories. Rename those spaces to sever the emotional and intellectual ties of colonially imposed names and restore the full histories and ancient significances embedded in Indigenous languages. Reoccupy to create a sense of community and purpose and to regenerate our traditional cultural practices. Find a way to give our younger generation access to the lands and waters that are their birthright. Restoring this connection is the crucial task of our survival.[57]

According to Michael Elliott, Indigenous Resurgence promotes three main premises: "(1) colonialism is an active structure of domination premised, at base, on Indigenous elimination; (2) the prevailing normative-discursive environment continues to reflect this imperative; and (3) Indigenous peoples must therefore turn away from this hostile environment and pursue independent programs of social and cultural rejuvenation."[58]

54. Cordero is active in both Ohlone (https://historysmc.org/ohlone-day-event) and Chumash revitalization efforts. See report by Frank and Carraher-King, "Commemorating the 50th Anniversary of the Occupation of Alcatraz."

55. See Wittstock and Salinas, "Brief History of the American Indian Movement." The Alcatraz occupation is summarized by McCallin, "Reclaiming the Rock." A recent documentary on Wounded Knee chronicles its conflicted and ambiguous aspects (see Martin, "Returning to Wounded Knee"). See also Weyler, *Blood of the Land.*

56. Vizenor, *Manifest Manner,* vii.

57. Alfred, "Don't Just Resist"; see also https://taiaiake.net/.

58. Elliott, "Indigenous Resurgence," 61. See also Simpson, "Indigenous Resurgence and Co-resistance."

Expressions of Resurgence activism have arisen all over Turtle Island (and beyond) in the last five decades. For example, in our bioregion a massive liquefied natural gas facility proposed for Point Conception sparked a major protest from Chumash organizers in 1978: "Three occupations of the site, one lasting eight months . . . stalled the momentum of the project, and gave impetus to the fledgling Native American movement in Santa Barbara County."[59] But that area continues to be impacted by Vandenberg Air Force Base to the north, which launches intercontinental ballistic missiles toward the Pacific Missile Test Range in the Marshall Islands more than 4,000 miles away. Indigenous Marshall Islanders were displaced by this testing from the 1950s to the present; their nonviolent reoccupation of their home islands in 1983 was another example of Resurgence.[60]

A watershed moment for Indigenous self-determination (and settler dis-illusionment) was the 1992 Columbus Quincentenary, during which Native peoples and their allies all over the world mobilized to push back on devised narratives of European "discovery" of the Americas.[61] The Quincentenary was a public spectacle that was never realized. Though many official bodies in the U.S. planned lavish commemorations, because of Indigenous counterorganizing, dozens of celebrations and reenactments were either downsized or canceled altogether.[62] This saga is chronicled in *Sinking Columbus*, coauthored by history professors Summerhill and Williams, the later having headed the Quincentenary Jubilee Commission before bailing

59. Burns, "Point of Contention," A1. Conception (Chumash *Humqaq*) is the northwest edge of the Southern California Bight, a dividing point for Pacific marine species north and south, and a marine navigation challenge (known to nineteenth-century sailors as the "Cape Horn of California"). Chumash may have traditionally considered the point to be a sacred place, the "Western Gate" where spirits of the dead jumped off to begin their journey to the next world (though this is still debated; see Rami, "Chumash as Keepers of the Western Gate," and Anderson, "Point Conception"). Though the port scheme was eventually defeated, various oil and real estate interests continue to threaten the relatively pristine area (see Robins, "Ecological and Historical Portrait"). Current initiatives seek to create a National Seashore and/or a Chumash Religious Sanctuary (see https://chumashsanctuary.com/).

60. See French, "Dark Side of Security Quest," and Johnson, "Collision Course at Kwajalein." This action was part of a pan-Pacific movement that in 1980 drew Ched into Indigenous solidarity work for the first time (see Myers, "Deadly Paradises"; "Wind that Diverts the Storm"; and Myers and Aldridge, *Resisting the Serpent*).

61. See Gonzalez, *Without Discovery,* and Myers, *Who Will Roll Away the Stone?,* 111–57.

62. An example was the Spanish government's replicas of the Niña, Pinta, and Santa María. Slated to tour around the Americas, the ships were welcomed by only a few ports, their failure to capture the popular imagination indicative of the groundswell of opposition. They were given to the City of Corpus Christi, and demolished in 2015. (Lessoff, "Ship Shape.")

out. As one review of the book put it, official tributes "could not escape being an anachronism . . . [because] the events, as planned, assiduously avoided examining the darker aspects and implications of the event"—the very issues Indigenous protestors *did* raise.[63] Since then, Columbus Day (established as a federal holiday in the U.S. in 1937) has become increasingly contested by countercelebrations of Indigenous People's Day, which has now been adopted by hundreds of cities and many states.[64] This subversion of a public U.S. holiday is not an insignificant skirmish in the war of myths swirling in and around our national historical unconscious.

Another milestone was the United Nations General Assembly's overwhelming adoption in 2007 of the landmark Declaration on the Rights of Indigenous Peoples (UNDRIP), after decades of Indigenous advocacy. Its affirmations include: rights to traditional lands, territories, and resources; rights to culture, identity, language, employment, health, and education; and the right to remain distinct and to pursue their own visions of economic and social development. Only four countries opposed the Declaration, objecting especially to its principle of free and informed prior consent. Each had significant histories of unresolved Native claims: Canada, the U.S., New Zealand, and Australia. As a consensus international human rights instrument, the UN Declaration affirms Indigenous rights of self-determination; prohibits discrimination and genocide; calls on states to honor and respect Treaties; protects Native languages and cultures; and upholds rights to lands, territories, and resources.[65] Though both Canada and the U.S. subsequently removed their objector status to UNDRIP, violations of its letter and spirit have led to a new era of Indigenous direct action around North America.

63. Kicza, "Getting It Right about Getting It Wrong," para. 20. As part of their response to the Quincentenary, the binational Mennonite General Conference and MCC Canada issued an apology that speaks to land reparations and set up a Jubilee Fund that continues today (https://www.mennonitechurch.ca/jubilee-fund).

64. The effort began in 1977 at the UN International Conference on Discrimination against Indigenous Populations in the Americas. South Dakota was the first to adopt "Native American Day" in 1989. For the growing list of cities and states who have changed over, see https://en.wikipedia.org/wiki/Indigenous_Peoples%27_Day. When the Los Angeles City Council voted to join the trend in 2017, Councilman Mitch O'Farrell (a member of the Wyandotte Nation in Oklahoma) supported it as an expression of restorative justice (Zahniser, "L.A. City Council Replaces Columbus Day"). For ongoing controversy, see Fadel, "Columbus Day or Indigenous Peoples' Day?"

65. Laguna Pueblo/Diné human rights lawyer June L. Lorenzo (see Foreword) has done several assessments of UNDRIP as a tool in Indigenous work for justice including: "*Kiskinohamatowin*"; "Spatial Justice and Indigenous Peoples' Protection of Sacred Places"; and "Report Submitted to the U.N. Human Rights Council" (a 2015 report, co-authored with Petuuche Gilbert, reviewing U.S. observance of UNDRIP). See also Heinrichs, *Wrongs to Rights*.

Idle No More* was founded in Saskatchewan in 2012 by three Indigenous women and a settler ally in response to the Canadian government weakening environmental laws.[66] Through Round Dance flash mobs and blockades, Idle No More continues to inspire political actions worldwide for Indigenous sovereignty and against ecological degradation.[67] The most visible of these to date was the witness of "Water Protectors" opposing the Dakota Access Pipeline at the Standing Rock Reservation in North Dakota, which captured international attention for much of 2016. Sioux tribal leadership had opposed the pipeline for years, and in April the first of four encampments was established on the pipeline's route. Over the following nine months, some 8,000 Indigenous and settler activists participated in an occupation of the contested site, including religious leaders, veterans, and, most importantly, representatives of more than 280 Native nations from around the world. The ceremonies and prayers of Indigenous elders centered the camps and grounded dramatic nonviolent confrontations with pipeline security. The Standing Rock resistance changed the face of ecojustice activism.[68]

Indigenous women were forerunners of Resurgence, both in California and Saskatchewan. The Saskatchewan Indian Women's Association (SIWA) predated Idle No More by four decades. Isabelle McNab, granddaughter of an important Treaty 4 negotiator in 1874, was SIWA president during the 1970s. She organized on reserves at a time, according to Allyson Stevenson,

> when government-designed third world conditions made survival precarious . . . The women of SIWA sought to present new images of First Nations women derived from a positive depiction of strong Indigenous mothers and women . . . waged a war on both alcohol and political apathy, calling on male First Nations leaders to step up and join them in the raising of the next

66. See Caven, "Being Idle No More."

67. See Hopper, "How the Idle No More Movement Started." INM priorities include implementing UNDRIP; monitoring Canada's Indigenous human rights record; resisting environmental devastation on First Nations land (especially by tar sands development and oil pipelines); Indigenous persons in the criminal justice system; and land repatriation.

68. For snapshots of the campaign, see https://www.ienearth.org/stand-with-standing-rock-no-dapl/. "Extractive industries have been part of the experience of every single tribe in the U.S.," said Kyle Powys Whyte, Michigan State professor and member of the Potawatomi Nation. "The activism, the acts of protection we engage in today are no different from what our ancestors were doing 200 years ago when they were facing the barrage of U.S. colonialism" (Bagley, "At Standing Rock," paras. 9, 21). See also Grossman, *Unlikely Alliances*, 188–92.

generations . . . [and] sought to decolonize Indian politics and fight for treaty rights.[69]

Mary Ellen Turpel-Lafond (Muskeg Lake Cree) worked with the Federation of Saskatchewan Indian Nations,* then became the first Indigenous provincial court judge in Saskatchewan in 1998. After doing cutting-edge work in aboriginal law she became British Columbia's first Representative for Children and Youth.[70]

Women continue to be prominent in Resurgence, from elder wisdom keepers to those reclaiming traditional midwifery to a new generation of politicians.[71] The growing Water Walking movement deserves special mention as a profound expression of Indigenous spirituality and ecological action. Around Turtle Island, women elders (and increasingly young girls) are leading pilgrimages on foot *with* water, *for* water health, sustainability and justice, organized by groups such as Mother Earth Water Walk,* Nibi Walks,* Great Lakes Water Walk,* and Nibi Emosaawdamajig.*[72] We had the honor of working with one of the movement's original animators, Ojibwe elder Sharon Day, at our Minneapolis Institute.[73] A few years later in northern California, we met another amazing Indigenous environmental prophet, Winnemem Wintu Chief Caleen Sisk, who is leading efforts to restore the salmon migration to the headwaters of the McCloud River on Mt. Shasta, her tribe's sacred origins site.[74]

69. Stevenson, "Hidden from History," paras. 2, 19, 26, 31. "In 1973, fewer than 4% of reserves had running water, and 2% had indoor toilets. Only half a per cent of the First Nations and Métis student population was in Grade 12 . . . 60% of Indigenous people were unemployed" (paras. 12, 13).

70. See Adam, "Mary Ellen Turpel-Lafond."

71. See Gilpin, "Indigenous Matriarchs Stand Together in Dark Times." For June L. Lorenzo (Laguna Pueblo/Diné), the turn back to native midwifery is significant: "It is so central to Indigenous women to have sovereignty over the birthing process" (correspondence with authors, May 30, 2020). Two examples of emerging national office holders are M.P. Leah Gazan (Wood Mountain Lakota First Nation, Saskatchewan) in Canada (https://www.leahgazan.ca/) and Rep. Deb Haaland (Laguna Pueblo) in the U.S. (https://haaland.house.gov/).

72. Thirteen-year-old Autumn Peltier (great-niece of Anishinaabe Water Walker Josephine Mandamin) gave moving testimony before the United Nations on World Water Day 2019; see it at https://www.waterdocs.ca/news/2019/3/8/the-women-who-walk-for-the-water-grandmother-josephines-legacy.

73. See Grillo, "Water Walk Along North Shore." We think Water Walking should resonate with Christians and others interested in "spiritual ecology" (see Zolli, "Toward a Contemplative Ecology").

74. See https://www.winnememwintu.us/caleen-sisk/ and Young, "Fight for Free and Wild Salmon Rivers." Their "Run 4 Salmon" is a 300-mile trek that follows the historical journey of the salmon from the Sacramento-San Joaquin Delta to the McCloud

At the same time, no group has been more exploited and dehumanized than Indigenous women, from the dawn of colonization to President Trump's racist tweets.[75] Nahanni Fontaine, an Ojibway politician in Manitoba, summarizes: "Canada's colonial history includes strategically, methodically and tragically racializing and sexually objectifying Indigenous women and girls' bodies, minds and spirits, as a means of purposefully oppressing Indigenous Peoples and territories."[76] This is seen acutely in the endemic crisis of missing and murdered Indigenous women and girls (MMIWG).[77] Though Indigenous women are 6 percent of Saskatchewan's population, they make up 60 percent of the province's missing women cases, and more than half of all reported homicides.[78] The U.S. National Institute of Justice recently released staggering statistics showing that 84 percent of Alaska Native and American Indian women have experienced some form of violence in their lifetimes, ranging from psychological to sexual and physical violence.[79]

MMIWG is a key issue in Resurgence organizing. Examples in Canada include: the Valentine's Day Women's Memorial March* started in Vancouver in 1992; Sisters in Spirit Vigils*; and Drag the Red* in Winnipeg (in which volunteers search the Red River for missing and murdered Indigenous women).[80] These have been joined by powerful artistic commemorations and mobilizations such as the REDress* and Faceless Dolls* projects. During one of my Saskatchewan research workshops in 2014, thirty of us went to Wanuskewin Heritage Park* to see the "Walking with our Sisters"* touring exhibit. It tells the grim story of MMIWG through more than 1,800 colorful, beaded moccasin vamps (tops), including 118 children's pairs,

River to raise awareness about the policies threatening Winnemem waters, fish, and lifeways" (http://www.run4salmon.org/); see the 2012 documentary *Dancing Salmon Home* (http://dancingsalmonhome.com/).

75. In February 2018, Trump referred to Sen. Elizabeth Warren as "Pocahontas." Perhaps because of this kind of disrespect, the 2018 U.S. midterm elections saw ten Native candidates (including three women) run for office—the highest number ever (Tolan, "Amid Trump's 'Pocahontas' taunts").

76. Fontaine, "Enduring Violence against Indigenous Women in Canada," para.5.

77. See Gray, "Forgotten Women"; Lucchesi and Echo-Hawk, "Missing and Murdered Indigenous Women and Girls Report."

78. See more at Radford, "Memorial Honours Murdered Women, Builds Dialogue," para. 12.

79. See Tauli-Corpuz, "Indigenous Women's Rights Are Human Rights," 6.

80. See Grabish, "Drag the Red Searchers Get Grim Lesson." See also the CBC podcast series "Who Killed Alberta Williams?" (https://www.cbc.ca/missingandmurdered/podcast) and documentary film *Quiet Killing* (trailer at https://womenandhollywood.com/under-the-radar-quiet-killing-delves-into-canadas-mistreatment-of-indigenous-women/).

each with a unique sewn pattern. Survivors of Indian Residential Schools, their descendants, and other artists created the vamps to honor victims of violence and their families. The moccasins are unfinished, symbolizing the lives of women and girls that were cut short. In Montana, teenaged Marita Growing Thunder (Assiniboine/Sioux) has launched similar commemorations through Save Our Sisters,* as the MMIWG movement continues to spread.[81]

∼

Native artists, writers, and academics have also carried forward Indigenous Resurgence. Musician Buffy Sainte-Marie (Cree) has been unmasking colonialism since the 1960s.[82] Indigenous artists Robbie Robertson (Mohawk), Rita Coolidge (Cherokee), and Jimi Hendrix (Cherokee) have also shaped mainstream musical culture.[83] Authors such as novelist Leslie Marmon Silko (Laguna Pueblo) and biologist Robin Wall Kimmerer (Potawatomi) have garnered wide settler audiences.[84] So have 2019 U.S. Poet Laureate Joy Harjo (Mvskoke) and professor/poet Emma LaRocque (Plains Cree Métis).[85] Artists and therapists are teaming up to work on healing Indigenous trauma, such as Donna Schindler's 2013 film "*Hozhonahaslíí*: Stories of Healing the Soul Wound," and Eduardo Duran, Allen Ivey, and Derald Wing Sue's *Healing the Soul Wound: Counseling with American Indians and Other Native People.*[86]

81. See profile by Manning, "Walking with Marita Growing Thunder."

82. This amazing woman (from Saskatchewan!) has for more than fifty years influenced music, politics, education, and culture. A ground-breaking folk singer-songwriter in the 1960s, her "Universal Soldier" is arguably the greatest anti-war song ever written (lyrics scrawled as graffiti on a Vietnam-bound troop ship found their way into the Smithsonian Institute; see story at http://buffysainte-marie.com/?p=809). Sainte-Marie is a fierce advocate for Indigenous rights as well as for children's literacy (from a long run on "Sesame Street" to her Cradleboard Teaching Project*), and an early adapter to digital media. See Warner, *Buffy Sainte-Marie,* and Joan Prowse's new documentary, *Buffy Sainte-Marie.*

83. See Robertson's *Music for the Native Americans,* and Grant, "Robbie Robertson Talks Native American Heritage." See https://ritacoolidge.net/, and https://www.jimi-hendrix.com/. We also give a shout-out to contemporary Canadian Native musicians, cultural workers, and friends Cheryl Bear (Nadleh Whut'en; https://cherylbear.com/) and Brander Raven (Peguis; https://branderraven.weebly.com/).

84. See Silko, *Ceremony;* Kimmerer, *Braiding Sweetgrass.*

85. See https://www.joyharjo.com/; LaRoque, *When the Other is Me,* and *Defeathering The Indian.*

86. See Schindler film at https://www.youtube.com/watch?v=FqaKN5iuNS8. In the same vein is the 2018 documentary "Dawnland" (see https://upstanderproject.org/

Vine Deloria's (Standing Rock Sioux) work helped launch a whole generation of activist scholars (it was reading his work in the mid-1970s that first turned Ched's attention and spirit to Indigenous justice).[87] Educator Marie Battiste (Mi'kmaq) heralded a Native approach to critical colonial studies, as did historians John Mohawk (Seneca) and Ranginui Walker (Māori).[88] The education system is a key arena for change.[89] Paradigm-changing work in theology has eclipsed the legacy of "Christianizing" Indigenous people with the project of Indigenizing Christianity. Early shapers include historian Tink Tinker (Osage), Māori public theologian Jenny Te Paa Daniel, Episcopal Bishop Steve Charleston (Choctaw; see above 4A), and the *First Peoples Theology Journal.*[*90] Harry Lafond (Muskeg Cree) addressed Pope John Paul II in 1997, urging the Catholic Church to recognize the spiritual role of elders in Indigenous communities.[91] More recently, Native Christian authors such as Adrian Jacobs (Cayuga), Randy Woodley (Keetoowah Cherokee), Richard Twiss (Lakota), Katilin Curtice (Potawatomi), and Mark Charles (Navajo) have developed strong followings in evangelical circles.[92]

A rising generation of Indigenous decolonial scholar activists such as Waziyatawin (Dakota), and journals like *Decolonization: Indigeneity, Education & Society,** have developed frameworks that have shaped our work.[93] In November 2019, we attended the historic Native Truth and Healing: California Genocide Conference* in San Diego, where we met Cutcha Risling Baldy. A member of the Hoopa Valley Tribe in Northern California and Department Chair of Native American Studies at Humboldt State

---

dawnland). Duran's earlier book is *Native American Postcolonial Psychology.*

87. See Deloria, *Custer Died for Your Sins; God is Red;* and *We Talk, You Listen.*

88. See Battiste, *Reclaiming Indigenous Voice and Vision;* Mohawk, *Utopian Legacies;* and Walker, *Ka Whawhai Tonu Matou.*

89. In a Carrot River, Saskatchewan secondary school, for example, a team of teachers are working with local elders and knowledge keepers to integrate Indigenous culture into their math curriculum (see Squires, "Carrot River Math Reconciliation Experience").

90. See Tinker, *American Indian Liberation;* Charleston and Robinson, *Coming Full Circle;* and https://anglicantaonga.org.nz/features/extra/jenny_te_paa_s_academic_profile. Charleston's recent *The Four Vision Quests of Jesus* is mandatory reading for our Institutes; see also Heinrichs, *Unsettling the Word,* and *Buffalo Shout Salmon Cry.*

91. See Lafond, "Church and the Indigenous Peoples of Canada," and Yard, "Cree, Christian, and Questioning the Catholic Church."

92. Jacobs ("History of Slaughter"), Woodley (*Shalom and the Community of Creation*), and Twiss (*Rescuing the Gospel from the Cowboys*) have been involved in the NAIITS* network. See also Curtice, *Native* (https://kaitlincurtice.com/), and Charles and Rah, *Unsettling Truths.*

93. See Waziyatawin, *What Does Justice Look Like?,* and *In the Footsteps of Our Ancestors.*

University, she has helped revitalize her people's Flower Dance, a women's coming-of-age ceremony that was suppressed after the Indian Island massacre of 1860.[94] "The Flower Dance supports an Indigenous decolonizing praxis by enacting Indigenous methodologies that center on ceremony to counteract the impact of settler colonial ideologies of gender, history, and spirituality," she writes.[95] Baldy seeks to break the monopoly of white, mostly male ethnography, and considers memories of elders and medicine women to be equally (or more) reliable as details found in museums and academic studies. Generations ago, she contends, her ancestors shared their cultural knowledge with anthropologists to preserve traditions they believed would one day be recovered and renewed by their posterity. "The ancestors planned for us," she asserts, "thinking, 'I am singing this song so my descendants will find it and sing it again.'"[96] Baldy celebrates the genius of those who shared language, customs, and songs in the nineteenth century in order to facilitate their recovery and renewal in the twenty-first.

This perspective illuminates two historic Chumash figures whose testimonies have been well-examined by white scholars, but which are now being deployed by Indigenous culture-rebuilders. Fernando Librado Kitsepawit (1839–1915) and Candelaria Valenzuela (1847–1915) were ethnographer John Harrington's most important cultural sources, and his interviews with them around the turn of the last century are now seeding Chumash revitalization.[97] In 1912, Kitsepawit directed the construction of a traditional *tomol*, the canoe that was central to Chumash maritime culture. In 1976, another *tomol* (*Helek*, or "Peregrine Falcon") was built based on Harrington's notes from the 1912 design, along with his ethnographic and archaeological data. The *Helek* was then paddled by a Chumash crew to the Channel Islands in an historic journey, a century and a half after the Brotherhood of the Canoe was disbanded under Mexican colonization. In 2001, a second *tomol* (*'Elye'wun*, "Swordfish") was built and paddled to *Limuw* (Santa Cruz Island), where a ceremony re-established a Chumash Maritime Association. These and subsequent voyages, writes Roberta Cordero, are "a

94. See Baldy, "Flower Dancers." On the massacre, see Rohde, "Genocide and Extortion." See below 8D for a story of repatriation at Indian Island.

95. Baldy, "no:'olchwin-ding, no:'olchwin-te," para 9. Her recent book is *We Are Dancing for You.*

96. Talk at California Genocide Conference, November 22, 2019, at San Diego State University.

97. See Librado, *Eye of the Flute,* and Johnson, "Trail To Fernando." Harrington was a quirky, intrepid, and dedicated linguist who traversed California in the early twentieth century recording Indigenous languages and customs. His voluminous notes have been employed to establish federal tribal recognition, settle territorial claims, protect sacred sites from development, and revive languages.

means of rediscovering our dignity and identity as a people sprung from this place. Against overwhelming odds, what we are seeing is a cultural spirit so compelling that the tree once considered dead has sent up strong, resilient shoots and branches."[98] Similarly, renowned Ventureño Chumash basket maker Valenzuela allowed her words and customs to be recorded by Harrington, testimony that has helped fuel contemporary revivals of traditional basketry.[99]

Our colleague Matthew Vestuto is scouring the Harrington notes to help revive the *mitsqanaqan* (Ventureño Chumash) language (one of six distinct languages within the Chumashan language family). He is part of a wider renaissance of Native linguistic revitalization efforts.[100] Matthew delights in the challenge of modernizing idioms so they can be learned and spoken today ("What," he asks, "might a Chumash word for 'refrigerator' be?") He teaches Chumash to tribal members, and offers tours of the region to settlers that focus on Chumash place names and customs (we were his "pilot" tour, and experienced it as a powerful way to see anew one's watershed). Like Baldy, Vestuto looks through the veil of anthropological studies; he too believes Kitsepawit was "singing it forward" to people like him. This mystical thread is central to Indigenous Resurgence, as beautifully expressed in Mika Lafond's poem at the start of this chapter celebrating reconnection with ancestors: "I didn't know I could still hear them."[101] Mika's father Harry is a key animator of Cree language learning in Saskatchewan, one of the strongest revitalization efforts in Canada.[102]

Another important front has been the fight to repatriate ancestral remains and cultural items that are sequestered in settler museums across North America. I was introduced to this crucial work twenty-five years ago by Northern Cheyenne Peace Chief and Mennonite pastor Lawrence Hart, whose Return to the Earth Project* insists that remains held as "artifacts"

---

98. Cordero, "Full Circle Chumash Cross Channel," para. 6. See a photo of the 1912 project in Holtzman, "Tomol Revival," and video of the crossing at https://northern-chumash.org/2011/12/02/tomol/.

99. For how Valenzuela and five other masters helped to preserve their craft across generations, see Brown et al., "'Song of Resilience.'"

100. Vestuto works with Advocates for Indigenous California Language Survival* (see an interview with him about his work at https://www.youtube.com/watch?v=ukga7igNi7c). For the wider language revitalization movement, see Lang and Begay, "Creating New Speakers"; Lutz, "Saving America's Endangered Languages"; and Administration of Native Americans.*

101. The many currents of cultural renewal among California's Indigenous communities are chronicled by the quarterly journal *News from Native California.* *

102. See Martell, "Learning Cree 'A Form of Medicine'"; Benjoe, "New Twists on an Old Language."

by museums and universities be repatriated to their tribal relatives so they can be reburied with dignity.[103] In our area, similar work is being led by Julie Tumamait-Stenslie, Tribal Chairperson for the Barbareño/Ventureño Band of Mission Indians* (formed in 2003 and still seeking federal recognition). Julie is a Cultural Resource Consultant serving on the state's Native American Heritage Commission,* laboring to preserve ceremonial artifacts and protect burial sites from vandalism and destruction by development. She struggles with local jurisdictions regarding building codes, and monitors excavations onsite. The most prominent Chumash cultural ambassador in our watershed, Julie each year graciously welcomes participants to Ventureño territory at our annual Bartimaeus Kinsler Institute (below 8B), part of her deep commitment to teaching settlers her people's culture and stories.[104]

There are, naturally, a plurality of perspectives within Indigenous communities, including critiques of some of the efforts related above. For example, Tamara Starblanket's concern (voiced at the 2019 California Genocide Conference) that neither the TRC nor UNDRIP have brought enough change or repatriation of land is echoed in many activist circles. Diversity of opinion is a sign of strength and maturity as resurgence grows throughout North America and abroad. "Indigenous struggles strike a very hopeful note," writes Ed Nakawatase, longtime National Representative for Native American Affairs for the American Friends Service Committee. "They operate in an almost stealth fashion, particularly for non-Native people, building something that incorporates a different relationship to the Earth, a different understanding of the people who live and work on it, and a fundamental challenge to the powers that think that they own it."[105]

This is why settlers should engage with currents of cultural and political resurgence. They are Songlines because they portend a different future, and offer pathways for us to practice restorative solidarity. Taiaiake Alfred summarizes what resurgence requires of settlers:

> Forgoing the need to be right, to be in charge, and to possess. Embracing the discomfort of the unsettled existence of an ally committed to the strength and well-being of Indigenous nations. Just as with the Indigenous people who are defining resurgence

---

103. See our profile in Enns and Myers, *Ambassadors of Reconciliation*, 2:121–32, and a book-length treatment by Hinz-Penner, *Searching for Sacred Ground*.

104. See Tumamait-Stenslie, "My Chumash Ancestral Legacy"; a video of Julie teaching about the *Sukinanik'oy* festival is at https://ravenredbone.com/tag/julie-tumamait-stenslie/.

105. Email correspondence with authors, May 14, 2020. Ed was one of Ched's mentors (see John-Hall, "Propelled into a Life of Fighting for Liberties").

through their unscripted creative contention and generative acts of love for the land, there is no template or menu for allyship.[106]

7E. QUERIES FOR RESTORATION

There are countless examples of renewal, restoration, and resurgence to be found today among both settler and Indigenous communities. Whether making headlines or quietly transforming lives in neglected corners of Turtle Island, Songlines are essential for our journey of decolonization. Take some time to map Songlines around you and within you, that are held by lands you love and embodied by those you know (or are learning about) who are working to heal the world.

1. What traditions of sacred story were passed on to you by your family or community, and how did these traditions contest the dominant narratives of your race and/or class upbringing?

2. Where have Songlines taken you across Landlines? Plot on a map where you were born and where you have moved (and why). How much of your mobility has been driven by external push-and-pull factors, and how much by your commitment to learn or embody a Songline?

3. What Songlines have helped you transcend the prejudices, wounds, and constraints of your own communal narratives? In what ways do Songlines animate your convictions and empower you to transcend the limits and dysfunctions of your Bloodlines?

4. How have Songlines helped you heal from inherited trauma or from moral injury?

5. Has your faith tradition inspired you to tackle decolonization work? Does it sustain you in this work? How has it been problematic?

6. Who are persons you look to—well-known or special just to you—for inspiration and guidance, and why ("biography as theology")? How have you learned stories of social movements, and how can you increase your literacy in this history?

7. How much do you know about Truth and Reconciliation experiments in South Africa; Canada; Greensboro, North Carolina; or elsewhere, and how has that work influenced you? What might such a process look like regarding places, people and/or issues of violation and healing you care about deeply today?

106. Alfred, "Don't Just Resist," paras. 14, 15.

8. What cultural or political expressions of Indigenous Resurgence have you encountered, either personally or through various media? Where are they happening in your area, and how might you get to know them better? How can you deepen and broaden the relationships you currently have with such movements?

9. What anxieties do you have about being in spaces where Indigenous people are exercising their power and leadership? What are steps you can take to learn more about reliable allyship?

10. How do local Indigenous people and their concerns help you decide priorities in your organizing, educational, or pastoral work? What are concrete opportunities for personal, ecclesial, and political practices of solidarity, reparations, and repatriation in your area (see chapter 8)?

Figure 29: Signing of "Declaration of Harmony and Justice" Memorandum at Opwashemoe Chakatinaw/Stoney Knoll, August 22, 2006 (l-r: Abram Funk, Mennonite; Chief Ben Weenie, Young Chippewayan First Nation; Robert Schultz, Lutheran). Photo: Les Klassen Hamm (used with permission).

CHAPTER 8

Healing Hauntings

A Discipleship of Decolonization

> There is no response, other than radical love, that is up to the
> task of healing transgenerational wounds . . . Questions that we
> lay on those inner altars and that receive no response in one
> generation are handed down to the next.
>
> —Barbara Holmes[1]

> We must become the wind and the current that diverts the on-
> coming storm. We must offer a new glimpse into the old and
> wounded hearts for a new hope . . . [to] build societies that are
> more genuine, more just, and which take root in sharing and
> love.
>
> —Bernard Narokobi[2]

AFRICAN AMERICAN THEOLOGIAN BARBARA Holmes warns us that unless
and until we respond to the history that haunts us and the wounds that
cripple us, they will keep cycling from generation to dysfunctional generation. The late Melanesian statesman Bernard Narokobi believed it was up to

---

1. Holmes, *Joy Unspeakable,* 58. Holmes is also a lawyer, mystic, and mentor.

2. Narokobi, "Pacific Identity and Solidarity," 29. Narokobi (1943–2010) was a
politician, jurist, and philosopher in Papua New Guinea and an early exemplar of Indigenous resurgence. He was a champion of human rights (including independence for
West Papua), an advocate for Melanesian identity (see his book *The Melanesian Way*),
and a devout and widely respected Catholic.

Indigenous leaders to take up the candle of hope and rekindle the possibility of societies characterized by justice, sharing, and love. These two elders—both followers of the decolonial gospel—summarize well what is at stake personally and politically in a discipleship of decolonization.

This book has outlined key constitutive aspects of Landlines, Blood-lines, and Songlines work for settlers, including:

- taking "inventory of the traces" of deformity and damage from settler colonialism within and around us;

- re-visioning and re-membering where our people came from; where, why, and how they settled in North America; and their impacts upon Indigenous land and life;

- reckoning with our inherited trauma, complicity, and moral injury, but also with traditions of resilience and response-ability;

- de-assimilating by turning from agnosia, white privileges, and myths of innocence in order to tend to covenants and build authentic relationships with Indigenous neighbors;

- learning from past, and engaging current, movements of justice, while exploring Songlines (our own and that of other communities of faith and conscience); and

- reinhabiting our bioregions as decolonizing treaty people committed to restorative solidarity and redistributive justice.

As we noted at the outset, the bottom line of this work is the "repatriation of Indigenous land and life."[3] "Decolonization may take various forms," says Canadian sociologist Katie Boudreau Morris, "but is at its core a process of actions and changes, not a position or an identification to claim."[4] LBS work finds its ultimate purpose in concretely contextual practices of re-schooling, restorative solidarity, reparation, and repatriation. We devote this final chapter to a discussion of these practices, which are for settlers the indispensable expressions of "radical love," *our* part in conjuring a wind to "divert the oncoming storm."

3. Above, introduction A; Tuck and Yang, "Decolonization Is Not a Metaphor," 21.
4. Morris, "Decolonizing Solidarity," 456.

8A. RECONCILIATION AS REDISTRIBUTIVE JUSTICE: AN ALLEGORY

Over the last thirty years, discourses of "reconciliation" have driven both public discussions and private initiatives trying to address longstanding issues of white-Black and settler-Indigenous tensions in North America, especially in religious circles. While this is due in part to the influence of the seminal Truth and Reconciliation experiment in South Africa, it is too often a product of settler sentimentality that presumes to resolve centuries of oppression with ritual apologies. But settler colonialism "is a structure and not an event," as Tuck and Yang put it, requiring systemic transformation, not rhetorical contrition.[5] Desires of a complicit group for reconciliation without cost or radical change are little more than another grand move to innocence (above 6C). It is hardly surprising that the semantics (and politics) of reconciliation are increasingly rejected as disingenuous by both Indigenous and Black activists.[6]

Christians are often responsible for injecting "cheapening" notions of grace into public conversations that seek to reckon with historical violations. But it is also the case that we have resources to correct this drift toward "instant" exoneration. We again find help at the scriptural roots of our tradition. The apostle Paul famously argues in 2 Corinthians 5:16—6:10 that reconciliation is indeed our core vocation(for full text see Appendix II):

> "God has given us the ministry of reconciliation . . . entrusting the message of reconciliation to us" (2 Cor 5:18–19). But his vocabulary was hardly sentimental: "The semantic field of the verb 'to reconcile' (Greek *katallassō*), used only by Paul in the New Testament is economic here, not expiatory. In Aristotle, it connotes an exchange of money to establish equivalence of value (we still speak of 'reconciling' a bank statement)."[7]

Reconciliation, in this view, is fundamentally the restoration of justice. But it is "the justice *of God*" (5:21), which Paul understands (in contradistinction to Roman *iustitia*) not as retribution but redistribution. In situations of disparity between groups this *specifically* means restoring equity:

---

5. Tuck and Yang, "Decolonization Is Not a Metaphor," 5. See more of their work at Tuck and Yang, *Toward What Justice?*

6. See e.g., https://unistoten.camp/reconciliationisdead/; Szeto, "'Is Reconciliation Dead?'"; Walters, *Price of Racial Reconciliation*; and Walker-Barnes "Until All of Us Are Free."

7. Myers and Enns, *Ambassadors of Reconciliation*, 1:11. See our detailed treatment of this passage there.

as the apostle puts it later in the same epistle, "your present surplus should help their need . . . in order that there may be equality" (2 Cor 8:14).[8]

Paul's exhortation to Christians to act as "ambassadors of reconciliation" (5:20) uses *political* rhetoric. "In the Greek-speaking Roman Empire, 'ambassador' (Greek *presbeutēs*; Latin *legatus*) had thoroughly political connotations. The *legatus* represented imperial interests, especially in foreign (and often occupied) lands."[9] Paul asserts the notion (radical for both the ancient world and our own) that regular people can act to restore an economic and political equity that cuts against the interests of the empire's system! This is the concrete meaning of grace. But *not* to embrace practices of restorative justice is to "receive" or "welcome" (Greek *dechomai*) grace "in vain" (2 Cor 6:1), argues Paul. This is precisely what white settlers are doing when we expect reconciliation without any discussion (much less practice) of equal justice.

The problem is that the culture of capitalism in North America has few ethical resources that consider seriously wealth redistribution of any kind, much less as reparation. Indeed, redistributive justice as a concept is roundly condemned as heretical.[10] In this social context, Songlines are crucial for reinvigorating political imagination, which is why we are turning here one last time to the biblical imaginary. To strengthen Paul's "course-correction" regarding reconciliation, we offer a reading of the infamous Gospel story of Jesus and the rich man as an evocative yet unequivocal allegory that clarifies the task facing us.[11]

We encounter this vignette at the crossroads of Mark's plot (Mark 10:17–31; see Appendix II for full text). Jesus is about to turn toward Jerusalem, a destination of confrontation with the powers that evoked dread and denial among Jesus' disciples (10:32). But Jesus' sharp exchange with an affluent Brahmin represents a theological junction as well. The man's question—"What must I do to inherit eternal life?"—seems a straightforward inquiry about salvation (10:17). Yet Jesus neither opens his arms in universal enfranchisement (as does modern liberal theology) nor does he

---

8. "The term 'equality' (Gk *isotēs*), so important to our modern notions of justice, is actually rare in the New Testament, appearing only here and in Colossians 4:1. Yet in the following verse Paul underlines this principle by invoking the central 'instruction' of the Exodus *manna* story: 'The one who had much did not have too much, and the one who had little did not have too little (2 Cor 8:15 = Exodus 16:8)'" (Myers and Enns, *Ambassadors of Reconciliation*, 1:8).

9. Myers and Enns, *Ambassadors of Reconciliation*, 1:12.

10. See e.g., Arnsperger, "Federation of Ways of Life."

11. The following exposition is an adaptation of Myers, *Biblical Vision of Sabbath Economics*, 30–37.

demand proper belief (as does conservative theology). Instead this man (a potential patron for the movement!) is challenged to redistribute his assets to those who have been dispossessed by the system that has enriched him (10:21). An encounter that begins with such theological promise thus concludes with the rich man's refusal of Jesus' call to discipleship—the only character in Mark's story to do so (10:22). Worse, Jesus appears to shrug off this rejection with a crude class explanation: "How difficult it is for the wealthy to enter the Kingdom of God!" (10:24).

This story has long held a place of ignominy in Christendom, yet never seems to be overly troubling, since preachers have exerted so much energy undermining its plain meaning. It has occasioned countless homilies (dating back to the medieval period) on how those "blessed" with wealth must take care not to let their affluence get in the way of their love for God and the church. This despite the fact that such an interpretation is precisely what this text rules out. To rescue it from centuries of domestication, we need to shift focus, as does the passage itself, from the rich man's concern about eternal life to Jesus' teaching about the "Kingdom of God." But how should we understand this notion, which most North America theologians have treated as little more than a nebulous metaphor or ignored altogether? To be sure, Mark's use of kingdom language is relatively sparing and somewhat imprecise. It can connote temporality (1:15; 9:1; 14:25), but also spatiality (9:47; 10:23–25). It is paradoxical: for disciples a "mystery," for others a "parable" (4:11). Nevertheless it can be concrete; when pressed for an analogy, Jesus chooses what is most familiar to peasants: the land (4:26, 30). We are never told definitively by Mark what the kingdom of God *is*. At one point, however, he makes it uncomfortably clear what it is *not*.

So the audience (which includes us) will not forget, and repetition being the key to pedagogy, Jesus offers a lyrical little verse whose point is sharpened with an edge of peasant humor:

> How difficult it will be for those with riches
> *to enter the Kingdom of God!*
> . . . Children, how difficult it is
> *to enter the Kingdom of God!*
> It is easier for a camel to go through a needle's eye than for a rich man
> *to enter the Kingdom of God!* (10:23–25)[12]

We have a seemingly unlimited supply of disingenuous reasons why this terrifying triplet cannot mean what it clearly says. Most are rooted in our anxiety (the product of capitalist cosmology and patronage culture) that Jesus might be saying something critical about the rich. Yet this ditty is not

12. See exegetical notes in Myers, *Binding the Strong Man*, 271–76.

about *them* at all. It concerns rather the nature of the kingdom, defined here as a social condition free of the killing disparities of wealth and poverty. By definition, then, the rich cannot "enter" it—at least not with their wealth intact. Let's take a closer look at this episode, which unfolds in three scenes.

i) *The encounter.* From his direct approach to Jesus we can tell that the man is socially powerful: he wants something and is willing to give deference in exchange, according to the protocols of honor culture (10:17). But his grandiose claim to innocence ("I have kept all the commandments," 10:20) flies in the face of Jesus' rejection of his original compliment ("No one is good but God alone," 10:18). Moreover, the man's putative religious concern is not as genuine as it appeared, because his question assumed he can *inherit* eternal life (Greek *klēronomeō*, from the root *klēros*, a parcel of land). This gentleman is exhibiting the false consciousness of class prerogative: eternal life is passed on like property. Indeed, beneficiaries of a socioeconomic system often envision religion as a reproduction of their own privilege (hence Marx's famous contention that material life determines consciousness). In first-century Palestine, land (not commodities) was the basis of wealth, so the gentry took great care to consolidate their holdings intergenerationally. Jesus' later parable about a struggle over deeded land, in which insurgent tenants kill the heir (*klēronomos*) in order to wrest the heritable estate (*klēronomis*) from its absentee landlord, illustrates how the politics of generational wealth transfer was often bloody business (Mark 12:1–10).

We are told our subject "possessed many properties" (10:22). In antiquity, estates of the rich grew in one (or more) of three ways:

- consolidation of households through marital or political alliances;
- distribution of expropriated or conquered land through political patronage; and/or
- land acquisition from those defaulting on debt.

The third of these targeted small agriculturalists groaning under burdens of rent, tithes, taxes, tariffs, and operating expenses (still a widespread phenomenon today). Forced to take out loans secured by their parcel, smallholders unable to service these loans lost their land to the lenders.[13] In most cases, this was large landowners, who in the absence of banking institutions made their surplus capital available at

13. See two monumental studies of this long, sordid history: Graeber, *Debt*, and Hudson, . . . *And Forgive Them Their Debts.*

exorbitant interest (despite its prohibition by Torah). This is how socioeconomic inequality had become so widespread at the time of Jesus, and almost certainly how this man ended up with "many properties."

An overlooked detail in this story provides a hermeneutic key: Jesus' "short list" of the Ten Commandments (10:21). Leaving out the first four "theological" commandments was not uncommon for rabbis; their meaning was not a matter of debate. Mark's twist lies in the last of the six "ethical" commands: "Do not covet what belongs to your neighbor" (Exod 20:17). In Jesus' recitation it has been replaced (we might say reframed) by an allusion to the Levitical censure: "Do not defraud" (Mark 10:19). Leviticus 19:13 appears in a longer passage addressing socioeconomic conduct in the Sabbath community: "You shall not defraud your neighbor; you shall not steal; you shall not keep for yourself the wages of a laborer." With this deft bit of *midrash*, Jesus snaps into focus the cycle of indebtedness just described: latifundialization is created and maintained through fraud.[14] Jesus unmasks ideologies of entitlement as rooted in the unjust expropriation of one's neighbor's land.

"Jesus looked at the man and loved him" (10:21). Nowhere else in Mark is such compassion portrayed! But "radical love" offers truth that refuses to equivocate—"tough love" in Twelve-Step parlance. "You *lack* one thing." The Greek *husterei* implies it is the rich man who is in debt to the dispossessed he has defrauded (like the widow later in the story who is rendered *hustereseōs* by predatory lawyers, 12:38–44). "Get up," pleads Jesus (the verb Mark uses most often in healing episodes), "sell what you have, give it to the poor, and come follow me."

Jesus here clearly commands the wealthy to repatriate land that has been stolen. This is a hard word to settlers: redistribution is our precondition for discipleship.

This man is not being invited to change his attitude toward his money, nor to treat his servants better, nor to reform his personal life. This is an intervention on behalf of a terminally addicted person (and system), an ultimatum of "recovery or death" (above 6D). The metaphor for healing is to "receive *treasure* in heaven" (10:21; the Greek *thēsauron* is distinct from the other words used to describe wealth in this episode). The economy has been radically revalued. Stung, the rich man whirls and stalks away (10:22), neither able nor willing to embrace liberation. But Mark's story does not end there. Two more scenes constitute an epilogue to this revelatory and disturbing exchange.

14. See definition above, Interlude, n. 36.

ii) *The teaching.* Jesus turns and looks at the disciples, eyebrows arched, perhaps bemused at their incredulity. He then offers a punchy "rhyme" about the kingdom of God, culminating in an absurdist image: his world's largest animal fitting through its smallest aperture (10:23–25). It is a summary dismissal of his disciples' worldview (and ours) that equates wealth accumulation with divine blessing and/or human meritocracy. His followers can only muster an anguished protest: "*Who, then, can be saved?*" (10:26). Why would someone need to be healed or liberated (the Greek verb *sōzō* connotes both), they wonder, if their condition is not understood as an illness or captivity (above 1B, 6D)? The same assumptions explain why this story circulates at such a low rate of exchange among us today.

Mark's Jesus is drawing on an old Songline here, knowing that only deeper, wiser traditions can shatter the monopoly on our consciousness held by the rich and their system. Specifically he is alluding to the Jubilee visions of Torah and the prophets, what Ched calls "Sabbath Economics."[15] In earlier episodes of Mark, sins are unilaterally forgiven (Mark 2:5–10); debt collectors share table fellowship with the indebted (2:13–17); disciples commandeer food from a grain field (asserting their gleaning rights, 2:23–28); Jesus spins visions of abundant harvests for poor peasants based on the natural fertility of the soil (4:8); and crowds are fed in a manna-like demonstration meal in the wilderness so that "everyone has enough" (6:42). These themes appear later in Mark's narrative as well, especially in Jesus' criticisms of how the Jerusalem Temple exploits the disenfranchised instead of being "a house for all peoples" (11:11–25; 12:38—13:2). And throughout this section's "discipleship catechism," the inverse economics of Jubilee redistribution is a refrain: the "last will be first" (9:35; 10:31, 44). Balancing the books is a constitutive expression of divine sovereignty for Mark as well as Paul.

iii) *The promise.* Though the rich man has repudiated this "Way," in part two of the epilogue the disciples muster some agency. They remind Jesus (and themselves!) that they indeed "left everything and followed" (10:28). The Greek verb *aphienai* (similarly used back in 1:18, 20 when the fishermen "left" their nets) also means "to release" from sin or debt (as in 2:5, 7, 9). This further knits together the theme of discipleship and economic justice in this narrative. "Enough for all" is generated if and when entitlements of *household* (the basic productive economic

15. As expressed in e.g., Exod 16, Lev 25, and Deut 15; for a summary, see Myers, *Biblical Vision of Sabbath Economics*; and above, n. 8.

unit), *family* (patrimony and inheritance), and *land* (the basic unit of wealth) are "released"—that is, restructured as community assets (10:29–30a). Jesus doesn't affirm whether or not his disciples have in fact realized this vision, but promises that "whosoever" (conditional subjunctive) practices this Way will *receive* (not inherit) community sufficiency. "Hundredfold" is an allusion to the Sower parable's punch line back in 4:8, and a metaphor for the divine economy of abundant grace. A sobering note of realism intrudes: persecution inevitably results from such subversive practices. The matter of eternal life, however, is left as a mystery of "the age to come" (10:30b).

࿇

This is the answer to the rich man's initial question. But he didn't stick around to hear it, unpersuaded by Jesus' alternative vision and thus unwilling to change his economic practice. This illustrates another point of Jesus' earlier Sower parable: some "hear the word, but the anxieties of this age, the love of riches, and the lust for everything else choke the word, so that it proves unfruitful" (4:19). In the sweep of Mark's narrative, the privileged cannot enter the kingdom of God through "intellectual assent" (as with the scribe in 12:34), nor through "sympathy" (as with Josephus in 15:43), and certainly cannot *inherit* it. Relinquishment and reparation are the only vaccine to the killing virus of entitlement.

In our opinion, Mark's archetypal tale speaks directly to the condition of North American settlers as a deeply unsettling allegory for those of us who are rich relative to the global distribution of wealth and power, and whose affluence has been built over centuries on the "murder and dispossession" of Indigenous peoples. Having done some exegetical work, let us re-narrate this story (with some poetic license) as an encounter between "Indigenous Jesus" and "powerful settler official." It begins with the latter's desire (command?) to be enlightened by a Native "shaman." Recognizing his religiously cloaked entitlement, Indigenous Jesus coolly rebuffs his attempt to ingratiate himself through idealizing Native spirituality (10:18). He sharply reminds him instead about the basic treaty obligations—in which this official is *supposed* to be well-versed—for emphasis underlining the abrogation of murder, theft, lying, and fraud (10:19). The settler, predictably, responds with a dramatic move to innocence (10:20).

Indigenous Jesus now practices decolonization as radical love, making it clear that liberation means repatriation (10:21). The official freezes, bound and blinded by his ideologies of ownership and control, which define his management of vast properties that were once Native homelands. Then he withdraws, no longer so interested in "reconciliation" (10:22). This surely should resonate with us. We too are practiced at stopping our inquiries and engagements well shy of reparation. But Indigenous Jesus is not done.

He now turns to his fellow Native insurgents to decode the encounter as an object lesson. *Settlers*, he says, *only ever negotiated treaties with our ancestors for that to which they already felt entitled. Through murder, theft, lying, and fraud they commandeered most of our territories. So,* he intones in a solemn refrain, *no reconciliation without repatriation* (10:23–25)!

It is now his companions' turn to retreat, convinced (from hard experience) that this is too much to ask of officials of the settler state. It is as dissonant to our ears as it was to theirs, and provokes the same kind of astonishment. Can we imagine a world in which stolen land has been returned, resources redistributed, and crimes atoned for? To their skepticism, and to ours, Indigenous Jesus replies simply: *I know it seems impossible to you, but for Creator all things are possible* (10:27). Decolonization is ultimately a matter of theological and political imagination.

Do you mean, asks one dispirited follower, *that we should return to our traditional ways, to which you called us at the beginning of our movement* (10:28)? The Teacher demurs about whether they have yet grasped his vision. But in the same breath he reiterates that the Good Way will restore original abundance for all—*if* the ancient laws of sufficiency, egalitarianism, and mutual aid are practiced (10:29–30). *And they will oppose us at every turn,* he adds. *But know this: though we who were first on this land are now last, this too will be reversed* (10:31).

Over two millennia this tale has rarely been received as good medicine by those of us who are inheritors of the rich man's system. Nevertheless, it speaks clearly to a settler Christian discipleship of decolonization. Its concluding promise that the world will be turned "right-side up" is distressing only to those of us who live near the top of a toxic hierarchy. Paul, one of Jesus' first interpreters, understood reconciliation as a metaphor for the deconstruction of all dehumanizing disparities: "It is a matter of equality" (2 Cor 8:13). This Second Testament vision of reconciliation as redistributive justice has eluded settler faith and practice for too long. It is time to "get up" onto this healing Way of shared abundance, to become ambassadors of *this* reconstituted social order. And for us that requires some determined re-schooling.

8B. EXPERIMENTS IN RE-SCHOOLING

Discipleship is a journey ever deeper into faith and practice. I pick up the story of my path toward restorative justice with my experience during college with a Cree "Little Sister," which impelled me to pursue work with juveniles caught in the criminal justice system (introduction B). In 1989, I left Saskatoon to work with Mennonite Voluntary Service in a Victim Offender Reconciliation Program in Fresno, California. There I learned to facilitate victim-offender dialogues, and witnessed the transformative power of personal testimony, accountability, and acts of restitution. I also observed the brokenness of a judicial and prison system that rarely brought healing or justice to victims or perpetrators, their families, or communities. Meeting with Black and Latino prisoners serving life sentences radicalized my understanding of both systemic injustice and courageous individual redemption.

In 1998, while I was teaching at the University of Winnipeg, Native Canadian leaders opened my eyes further to our predominately white restorative justice movement's blind spots regarding structural racism. A subsequent trip to Australia and Aotearoa/New Zealand offered two more opportunities to learn from Indigenous communities. Ched and I participated in a Uniting Church of Australia sponsored pilgrimage to rural Aboriginal communities in Victoria. Afterward I attended a national restorative justice *hui* (assembly) at a *marae* (a ceremonial space) in Auckland where Māori leaders shared about their use of traditional relational justice practices in the juvenile system. But it was my involvement with the Greensboro Truth and Community Reconciliation Project* in the early 2000s, under the tutelage of Joyce and Nelson Johnson, that turned my full attention to how restorative justice could be applied to historic injustices and violations. This interest deepened as I interviewed colleagues for our *Ambassadors of Reconciliation* project, and became very personal in 2010 during my pilgrimage to Ukraine (above 2A). Traveling along the Dnieper River, I had a pivotal conversation with my sister Janet, voicing aloud my heartfelt questions about how to make sense of the double legacy of trauma and peacemaking carried by our Mennonite community. She encouraged me to dig deeper, and has accompanied me faithfully since.

Attending public hearings of the Canadian TRC* was another personal and political stepping-stone (above 7C). All these experiences fueled doctoral studies, which allowed me to explore my ancestors' settlement on the Canadian prairies next to Native communities, and how their respective trauma interacted (or didn't). I interviewed many Mennonites about their relations with Indigenous people, and in public conversations (with Harry Lafond's accompaniment) I put my research before my community.

I continued to press my questions in lectures, publications, and hands-on workshops, slowly developing the bones of the LBS process articulated in this book. Through Capacitar,* an international network of solidarity and empowerment, I pursued training in practical, somatic ways to heal from trauma, which I have integrated into my pedagogy.[16] But the central commitment that has constellated for Ched and me over these years is to create spaces for "re-schooling": critically immersing ourselves in the Landlines, Bloodlines, and Songlines of our faith traditions, of exemplary social movements and of our own lives. These instruct, inspire, empower, and sustain our discipleship journeys.

Over the last twenty years, we have curated many opportunities for such immersion, employing pedagogies of popular education and drawing on the people and places important to past and current movements of faith and justice. After many years of dreaming, in 2001, we and a few trusted colleagues convened seventy-five faith-rooted social justice activists in Detroit to explore possibilities for grassroots, movement-based, theological education. This gathering birthed Word and World People's School,* which Ched described as an intersectional experiment "bridging the gulf between seminary, sanctuary and streets."[17] Between 2002 and 2007, a national collective organized annual weeklong schools of eighty to 150 participants in various locations around the U.S., each looking at different social issues:

- Greensboro, North Carolina: the 1960 Sit-In movement and subsequent local civil rights campaigns;

- Tucson, Arizona: immigrant rights, Indigenous justice and liberation theology;

- Philadelphia, Pennsylvania: disarmament, nonviolent direct action, and homelessness movements;

- Rochester, New York: feminist/womanist and LGBT struggles for inclusion;

16. For a fuller account, see Enns, "Journey into Restorative Justice." Capacitar* operates in over forty countries, training people in somatic practices (mostly based on traditional Chinese medicine) in and for communities affected by violence, poverty and trauma. On the importance of somatic therapies, see van der Kolk, *Body Keeps the Score*, and above 3B. As trauma therapies proliferate among white communities, practitioners draw from diverse religious and cultural traditions in ways that are sometimes appropriative (a reflexive habit of settler colonialism). When we borrow and adapt methods from traditions not our own it is important to practice respectful transparency, acknowledgment, permission, and, ideally, apprenticeship.

17. See Myers, "Reconnecting Seminary, Sanctuary, Streets and Soil."

- Minneapolis, Minnesota: a "biography as theology" focus on William Stringfellow;

- Memphis, Tennessee: faith and labor organizing and the 1968 sanitation worker's strike;

- Tar Heel, North Carolina: community unionism, economic justice, and the Smithfield meatpackers campaign.

Each place offered a unique "pedagogy of pilgrimage" for learning and teaching movement history alongside current pressing issues of justice. These rich gatherings were sustained on a shoestring: neither organizers nor faculty were paid, and we rarely garnered grant or institutional support (we were too political for religious entities and too religious for secular ones). After a creative run with limited capacity, our collaborative reluctantly had to scale back.[18]

Ched and I then began organizing a similar endeavor locally: the Bartimaeus Institute* in the Ventura River watershed. This has developed into our primary platform for re-schooling work, a space where predominantly white settler Christians (and others) can reckon with personal and political "blindness" in order to deepen our journeys from denial to discipleship. Our "patron saint" is Bartimaeus (Mark 10:46–52), a poor and marginalized man in Mark's Gospel who represents a contrasting archetype to the rich man just discussed. In a narrative sequence Ched calls the "discipleship triptych," the rich man (10:17), Jesus' disciples (10:32), and this blind beggar (10:46) are all positioned proximate to "the Way." Their responses to Jesus reveal respectively: refusal (10:22), self-delusion (10:35–40), and a desire to "see" above all else (10:51). This triptych culminates Mark's "catechism" in discipleship (8:22—10:52), the fulcrum on which his whole narrative balances.[19] And it deeply informs our re-schooling philosophy.

Since 2007, we have held twenty-four Institutes on a variety of topics.[20] Several times our theme has been decolonization, but our first attempt was disappointing. In the wake of our attendance at Canadian TRC hearings we

18. Word and World has subsequently convened several retreats, a mentoring program for young activists, and a school on intersections of Indigenous and Black ecojustice in Detroit in 2015.

19. See Myers et al., *Say to this Mountain*, 132–34.

20. For institute summaries, see https://www.bcm-net.org/study/bartimaeus-institute. In 2014, we expanded our name to the Bartimaeus Kinsler Institute to honor retired mentors Gloria and Ross Kinsler. The Kinslers were Presbyterian missionaries for three decades in Central America, involved in liberation education and solidarity during the region's wars (see Kinsler, *Biblical Jubilee and the Struggle for Life*). Ched has also helped develop another space where activists and church leaders can study: The Center and Library for the Bible and Social Justice* in New York.

decided to make this powerful experiment the focus of our 2012 Institute, only to have to cancel it for lack of sufficient registration. This impressed upon us that the U.S. is far behind Canada regarding these issues. We've had better responses since then. In fall 2015, we took the Institute on the road to the headwaters of the Mississippi River, in partnership with Minneapolis-based Church of All Nations,* where 100 participants looked at the relationship between watershed discipleship and Indigenous justice. A year later, we held another Institute in Saskatoon in collaboration with Canadian colleagues (including Harry Lafond and Idle No More cofounder Sylvia Mc-Adam) to explore the TRC's Calls to Action addressed to faith communities.

The following two years our Institutes focused on how best to understand and resist the new Trump era. But in 2019, we decided to re-center our attention on the roots of settler colonial pathology, of which Trumpian politics are symptom, not cause. A dozen Native leaders from North America and Australia helped us build literacy in core issues of Indigenous justice:

- Land: the long legacy of theft and ecological destruction, as well as contemporary efforts at land reparation and repair;

- Law: the devising of legal theories of white entitlement and the breaking of treaty covenants, as well as organizing to construct a more equitable human rights foundation for Indigenous survival and flourishing; and

- Language: the historic suppression of Native linguistic and cultural traditions, as well as the current struggle to rehabilitate them.

More than 175 participants learned from powerful Indigenous teaching and testimony, as well as from the inevitable episodes of settler fragility.

We continued this conversation in 2020, with the focus on how settlers can better imagine and strategize how to:

1. identify and work toward healing from the moral injury and haunting of colonization, through a

2. commitment to understanding, resisting, and transforming historical and current structures of settler colonialism within us and around us, in order to

3. embody deeper practices of restorative solidarity and relationship with Indigenous communities so as to become reliable allies, build trust, and forge a new path together.

We spent many hours discerning and designing a pedagogy of personal and communal exploration for this Institute, using parts of the process outlined in this book. Our aim was to involve each person as a subject of decolonization work, focusing not on *information* so much as *transformation*. Participants were asked to bring what they knew about their ancestors' immigration and settlement history. In cohorts each day, four to six persons spent intensive time sharing and reflecting on their family stories regarding immigrant roots; settlement and its impacts on Indigenous peoples; and current efforts at restorative solidarity. Individuals supported each other on deep dives into their own work. Cohorts then gathered in a Council to report salient points from their conversation to two Indigenous interlocutors, who listened, queried, and clarified. The final step was a plenary session in which interlocutors offered feedback, reflections, challenges, and encouragement to participants (see Figure 30). Each day explored a discrete set of questions (drawn from these chapters) designed to help participants peel back layers of our assimilation into settler colonialism, and to take steps deeper into decolonization.

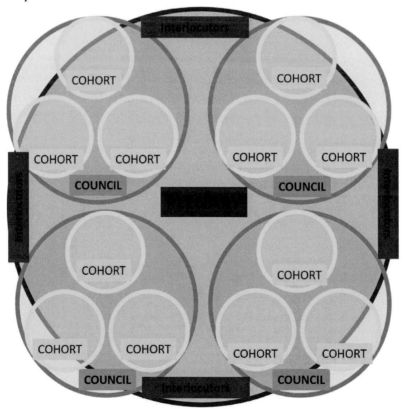

Figure 30: Cohort-Council-Plenary model used for LBS work at Bartimaeus Kinsler Institute, February 2020. Design by Chris Wight.

There are precious few spaces in settler society where we can lean into this kind of personal and political work, and it is up to those of us committed to liberation to create and maintain them. Since discipleship engages not only our heads but also our hearts, spirits, and hands, at each Institute we have artists-in-residence who help us go deeper through music and poetry, visual and participatory art, and body and liturgical movement.[21] And because re-schooling should lead to specific commitments, our closing liturgy always includes covenants of action. Each participant pens a "memo to self" on a postcard, which we mail to them at Easter as a reminder. In that spirit, we turn now to consider strategies of restorative solidarity, reparations, and repatriation.

8C. EXPERIMENTS IN RESTORATIVE SOLIDARITY

Our *Ambassadors of Reconciliation* project offered this working definition of restorative justice:
   A range of nonviolent responses with the aim of:

1. reducing or halting the presenting violence in order that

2. victims and offenders (as well as their communities and other stakeholders) can collectively identify harms, needs, and responsibilities so that

3. they can determine how to make things as right as possible, which can include covenants of accountability, restitution, reparations, and (possibly) reconciliation.[22]

This paradigm is predicated on two trajectories of truth-telling, which should encounter one another in the process: the narratives of those who have been injured; and complicit parties admitting responsibility. For both sides the vulnerability required is demanding, painful, and costly, described by an offender I worked with as "walking through a fire."[23]

In an appendix of that same volume we suggest how these principles might also inform situations of historical and group violation.[24] We subsequently developed this into what we call "restorative solidarity." This

---

21. Artists from our last two Institutes are listed in the Acknowledgments.

22. Enns and Myers, *Ambassadors of Reconciliation*, 2:xiii.

23. Enns and Myers, *Ambassadors of Reconciliation*, 2:57.

24. Enns and Myers, *Ambassadors of Reconciliation*, 2:153–62. The needs of victims, offenders, and their respective communities outlined there emerged out of our work with the aforementioned Greensboro Truth and Community Reconciliation* process.

involves both personal and political commitments and actions, but as Figure 31 portrays, it is an ongoing process of settler decolonization work, a continual circle of:

- "doing our own work";

- reckoning with harms and building capacity for "response-ability"; and

- making covenants and taking concrete steps of solidarity, reparation, and repatriation in relationship with communities injured by past and present injustices.

- Repeat (evaluating, digging deeper, showing up healthier and stronger).

Figure 31: Restorative Solidarity model. Design by Chris Wight.

For the rest of this chapter we focus on the third step in this process, without which the first two ring hollow. We will limit our discussion to just a few representative examples of the many on which we could report. We are clear that our settler efforts are "experiments in truth" (as Gandhi famously put it), which can always press deeper and reach more broadly.[25]

We begin with commitments of settler solidarity (which some Canadian colleagues prefer to call "common cause") in response to Indigenous-led initiatives.[26] This takes many forms, including accompaniment, direct action, service, and support. We'll start by looking at a few individual efforts.

A long-standing issue in British Columbia (as at Standing Rock) is the building of oil pipelines through Native territory. Two friends who are both faith leaders and activists were invited, after years of building relationships with local Indigenous communities, to stand with them during recent protests. Steve Heinrichs, director of Indigenous-Settler Relations for Mennonite Church Canada,* participated in a protest at Burnaby Mountain with Tsleil-Waututh* land defenders resisting pipeline expansion on April 20, 2018.[27] He and others were arrested for civil disobedience, and spent a week in jail. Laurel Dykstra is an Anglican priest who animates the Salal and Cedar Watershed Discipleship* community in Vancouver. On May 25, 2018, she and another parishioner were similarly arrested on Burnaby after chaining themselves to a tree outside the Trans Mountain terminal; they also served seven days in jail.[28] Laurel and Steve's pastoral ministries are equally as important as their direct actions: community-building with Indigenous leadership and educational outreach and accompaniment of settlers (and their respective denominations) who are moving into solidarity work. Laurel has developed beautiful liturgical resources, while Steve has produced a series of excellent publications on decolonizing discipleship distributed by CommonWord*; we highly recommend both. The veteran violence-reduction organization Christian Peacemaker Teams* has recently launched the Turtle Island Solidarity Network* that organizes similar sorts of direct action witness and accompaniment on both sides of the U.S.-Canadian border.

---

25. For respectively shorter and longer explications of this concept, see Dear, "Experiments of Gandhi," and Douglass, *Gandhi and the Unspeakable*.

26. Though our focus here is on settler work, solidarity is of course also expressed *between* Indigenous groups, notable recent examples being both the Standing Rock camps in 2016 and the blockades supporting *Wet'suwet'en* pipeline resistance (see https://unistoten.camp/timeline/timeline-of-the-campaign/). See Petronzio, "How Young Native Americans Built and Sustained the #NoDAPL Movement" and Ballingall, "With Blockades Coming Down, What Will the *Wet'suwet'en* Solidarity Movement Leave Behind?" See background of intertribal solidarity at https://www.wikiwand.com/en/Pan-Indianism; and also Grossman, *Unlikely Alliances*.

27. Waddell, "MC Canada Staffer Sentenced to Seven Days in Jail."

28. Fraser, "Pipeline Protestors Convicted of Civil Contempt of Court."

We asked two young, faith-rooted activists who have worked through the LBS process with us to share examples of how they've responded. Brenna Cussen is a founding member of St. Isidore Catholic Worker Farm,* an intentional community in southwest Wisconsin (Ho Chunk and Meskwaki territory) that cares for creation through prayer, farming, hospitality, and resistance. Brenna reported:

> I have been privileged to both participate in and support the logistical organizing of the annual Women and Water Coming Together Symposium* (WWCTS) held at Lac Courtes Oreilles Ojibwe reservation in Wisconsin. WWCTS is a five day gathering of Native and non-Native participants animated by Ojibwe elder Mary Ellen Baker. She gathers Native speakers to teach in a traditional way the importance of healing ourselves and the earth, particularly through the sacred relationship between women and water. With my local, majority white settler-descendant activist community I help lead workshops and immersive experiences that deepen awareness around colonization on this land, examining complicity and our collective need for healing. Our discussions try to center Indigenous voices through readings and speakers, and encourage concrete acts of reparation. And a group of us got Dubuque, IA to declare the second Monday of October Indigenous Peoples' Day.[29]

In 2019, Brenna bravely participated in a nonviolent action that shut down two Enbridge Energy tar sands oil pipelines, for which her group now faces felony charges. Their protest was offered in support of Anishinaabe resistance to these pipelines, which go through their traditional lands.[30]

Luke Winslow lives in Seattle, and works with Duwamish communities in "the storied and powerful place called the Salish Sea." He aspires to "skill up in tangible practices that can make concrete contributions to solidarity contexts, and do my own work to show up in healthy and productive ways."[31] Luke highlighted one of the efforts in which he is involved:

> Tribal Canoe Journeys* along the Northwest Coast is an annual tradition over the last thirty years of intertribal revitalization. "Canoe Families" work hard year round, practicing songs and dances, preparing regalia, making gifts to share, and getting in shape. They canoe to a different host nation each summer, for

29. Cussen, email correspondence with authors, April 7, 2020.

30. See Roewe, "Catholic Workers Charged."

31. This and the following excerpt are from Winslow's email correspondence with authors, April 7, 2020.

a week of feasting and cultural exchange called "Protocol." It is a powerful commitment to culture-based healing paths and sobriety, as well as a direct reoccupation of Indigenous land.

Canoe Journey Herbalists* was organized by Indigenous midwife and herbalist Rhonda Grantham (Cowlitz) to offer traditional medicine to support the Canoe Journeys. With experience in the medic/healing tent at the Standing Rock occupation, she turned her school bus (previously Standing Rock's kitchen) into a mobile apothecary. Rhonda works as "ground crew" at each stop along the way of the Canoe Journey, offering care to the "pullers" as they come ashore and gifting medicines and traditional healing.

My work to support her involves tending medicinal gardens, seasonal harvesting of native plants, and processing these into various medicines year round to be shared for common needs in the Journey communities. Many of these garden sites themselves represent small but significant acts of reparation, with access granted by private landowners to build relationships. This model of "many hands medicine" has grown for three years: offering Indigenous women and youth apprenticeship programs; providing traditional healing care unavailable to Native people in the colonial health system; and deepening alliances with other land projects led by people of color.

Luke has also participated in direct actions with Protectors of the Salish Sea.* In September 2019, they prayerfully walked forty-seven miles over five days, from a liquefied natural gas facility at the mouth of the Puyallup Tribe's river to the ancestral village site of *Sta,chas* (now buried under the state capitol building). They set up "tarp tipis" at the Capitol, sang, drummed, and demanded recognition of treaty rights. Elders described how 98 percent of their forests, salmon, and tribal lands have been lost. They remained there even after State riot troopers moved in and tore down the tents. This action continues as a public campaign of daily sunrise ceremonies on the capitol steps, educating about the intersection between climate emergency and Indigenous rights.

Solidarity work may take us to actions far from our homes, as it did, for example, for settler allies from around North America who traveled to support the 2016 Standing Rock Water Protectors. But the most important arena for our work is our home bioregions (see our earlier caution about "hypermetropia," above introduction C). Our primary responsibility is to overcome agnosia in order to learn the stories held by the land around us: where we dwell, at our place of work, where we shop and recreate, even the roads on which we bike or drive. Both Brenna and Luke pursued

relationships with nearby Indigenous communities, and found powerful expressions of Indigenous resurgence that welcome settler solidarity. Another
such local expression has been curated by Rev. Robert Two Bulls, a third-
generation Lakota Episcopal priest in Minneapolis and Canon Missioner
for the Department of Indian Work for the Diocese of Minnesota.*

Bob started First Nations Kitchen,* a ministry led by and for Indigenous people, but which welcomes local settlers to help serve home-cooked,
delicious "high-quality, fresh organic food in an environment of radical
hospitality and cultural empowerment. We understand that food is medicine and want to bring back the ancestral foods of the peoples indigenous
to this land to eradicate heart disease, Type Two diabetes, and obesity from
the Native community."[32] Located in the basement of All Saints Episcopal
Indian Mission, and supported by a large volunteer force from around the
city, the Kitchen has served meals every Sunday for the past nine years to an
average of over 100 guests, many from the streets. Menus feature traditional
food, including bison, wild rice, elk, fish, venison, turkey, and local vegeta-
bles. Like their ancestors, the cooks don't let anything go to waste. "We buy
an entire buffalo and use every bit of it," Two Bulls explains, "even tan the
hide as a raffle item at fundraisers." Guests are treated with dignity: greeted
at the door, shown to their seat, given the evening's menu and served their
order. When cooking and serving are done, volunteers come out to chat
with guests, contributing to everyone's sense of community. "We have some
regulars for whom this is like a night out; it's nice to see people enjoying the
food."[33] First Nations Kitchen, like our home, has been graced with a mural
by Dimitri Kadiev.[34]

Two Bulls facilitates another project for church volunteers on the
Pine Ridge Reservation in South Dakota, in which infrastructure in and
around his home village of Red Shirt is repaired or built (during the most
blistering weeks of summer).[35] His belief in the redemptive power of cross-
cultural relationships also resulted in a collaboration with the Taize Community* in France, which brought a large group of brothers and hundreds
of other pilgrims from around the world to Red Shirt in May 2013.[36] We

32. At https://firstnationskitchen.org/.

33. Quotes from Strickler, "First Nations Kitchen Serves Ancestral Foods," paras.
16 and 39. FNK collaborates with a local Indigenous-led farm that grows pre-colonial
foods and focuses on recovering knowledge of and access to healthy indigenous foods,
medicines, and lifeways (see www.dreamofwildhealth.org).

34. The mural was executed during the 2016 Carnival de Resistance* residency in
the Twin Cities.

35. See McCaughan, "At the Red Shirt Project."

36. See https://www.taize.fr/en_article14640.html.

are grateful that Bob serves at our annual Institutes as chaplain, liturgist, artist, and interlocutor. Other Indigenous colleagues with whom we've worked at our Institute similarly offer opportunities for settler education, service, and action.

Edith (Eastern Shoshone) and Randy Woodley (Keetoowah Cherokee) run Eloheh Indigenous Center for Earth Justice* as a space to learn about native seeds, peoples, and practices in an ecojustice context. Jim Bear Jacobs (Mohecan) curates Healing Minnesota Stories* to provide opportunities for people in the Twin Cities to learn stories held by the local landscape. Brooke Prentis (Waka Waka) directs Common Grace Australia,* which explores "lament and grief, apologies and forgiveness, friendship and solidarity" around issues of Aboriginal justice. June L. Lorenzo (Laguna Pueblo/Diné) has worked with settler allies to organize the Presbyterian Church USA to renounce the Doctrine of Discovery.[37] Germaine (Métis) and Harry Lafond (Muskeg Cree) are intentional about welcoming visitors to the Muskeg Lake Cree Nation* to learn, share culture, and build friendships, hosting circles of singing, story-telling, dance, and ecumenical worship.[38] They always remind us that settler solidarity must be predicated on genuine relationships with Indigenous people and communities. Neighborliness requires not heroic action, but consistent giving and receiving over many years of trust-building.

Deserving special mention here is the work of the national KAIROS: Canadian Ecumenical Justice Initiatives,* which has for two decades brought Indigenous and settler activists together in common cause.[39] The Kairos Blanket Exercise* is "a unique, participatory history lesson—developed in collaboration with Indigenous Elders, knowledge keepers and educators—that fosters truth, understanding, respect and reconciliation among Indigenous and non-indigenous peoples."[40] Used and adapted by groups all over North America in hundreds of venues, and now in its fifth edition, this hands-on exercise is a compelling and succinct catechism in and

37. Cole, "Native American Speaker."

38. See, for example, gatherings they curated with Mennonite settlers at Muskeg in 2017 and 2018 (Schulz, "We Sing the Same Songs," and "When Strangers Become Neighbours"). See also Gyapong, "Indigenous Couple Live a Life of Reconciliation."

39. KAIROS's predecessors, the Aboriginal Rights Coalition and Project North, brought churches together in solidarity work in the 1970s resisting the Mackenzie Valley Pipeline with Dene peoples.

40. Learn more at https://www.kairosblanketexercise.org/. We first experienced the exercise in an adapted U.S. version led by Erica Littlewolf (Northern Cheyenne) at Albuquerque Mennonite Church, in 2014 (see Miller, "MCC's Erica Littlewolf").

"performance" of the history of settler colonialism and its impacts. We strongly commend the Blanket Exercise as a learning tool.

A growing literature critically explores the prospects and pitfalls of settler solidarity. Liza Minno Bloom and Berkley Carnine's recent overview contains useful suggestions for linking other kinds of social justice commitments to correlated Indigenous issues, and reviews best practices.[41] Australian Clare Land's book, *Decolonizing Solidarity: Dilemmas and Directions for Supporters of Indigenous Struggles,* offers case studies and important discussions of mutuality, white privilege *within* movements, and the need to learn the "political genealogies" of previous solidarity activism.[42] Katie Morris reminds us settlers must learn to live with contingency and ambiguity: "Part of the challenge of working in solidarity with Indigenous peoples is reorienting our approach away from avoidance of settler uncertainty, or solidarity as a type of settler identity, and towards decolonization as a practice that includes nurturing a habit of discomfort."[43]

An ethic of restorative solidarity invites us to be expansive (and forgiving) in its experiments, and critical (but not ideological) in its self-assessments. Settler practices should include tasks of service (such as caretaking or cooking) as well as protests or public proclamations. Solidarity can also be expressed behind the scenes, whether in simple attentive listening, or in complicated research.[44] It is, as the SURJ Indigenous Solidarity Network* puts it, about "showing up." But it also needs to be accompanied by ongoing inner work, because we settlers will inevitably experience not only our own failures, but also disillusionment and disappointment. As white South African Dominican priest and liberation theologian Albert Nolan wrote thirty-five years ago, those we stand with also

> have faults . . . make mistakes . . . and sometimes spoil their own cause . . . Real solidarity begins when we recognize together the advantages and disadvantages of our different social backgrounds and present realities and the quite different roles that we shall therefore have to play while we commit ourselves together to the struggle against oppression.[45]

41. Bloom and Carnine, "Towards Decolonization and Settler Responsibility."

42. See also Gilbert, "Notes Towards a Theory of Solidarity," and Doreian and Fararo, *Problem of Solidarity Theories and Models.*

43. Morris, "Decolonizing Solidarity," 456. See further resources at Resource Generation* and Walia, "Decolonizing Together."

44. A recent example of the latter is an amazing piece of investigative journalism by Lee and Ahtone, "Land-Grab Universities."

45. Nolan, "Spiritual Growth and the Option for the Poor," paras. 27–29. Nolan was deeply immersed in the struggle against the apartheid regime, and has written wisely

The practice of restorative solidarity tests every layer of our settler fragility, and thus requires humility, patience (with others and ourselves), and above all, persistence. Because it is a lifelong journey "full of detours and wrong turnings."[46]

8D. EXPERIMENTS IN REPARATION AND REPATRIATION

We have arrived at the *sine qua non* of decolonization work: reparations and the repatriation of Indigenous land. This conversation spikes settler anxieties, and is usually dismissed as too complicated or "unrealistic." But we can and must think and organize together with Indigenous colleagues concerning how settler power, money, and land can be redistributed, personally and politically, here and now.

The Canadian Indian Residential Schools settlement has shown that monetary redress to individuals (or even communities) alone is insufficient and can even be problematic, providing a temporary boon without addressing structural change. Russ Daye, a United Church of Canada liaison to the TRC, notes that "redemptive transformation will require altering economies of opportunity, and shifting regulation to include community-based and cooperative enterprise compatible with Indigenous cultures. These will disrupt settler society to a much greater degree."[47] True reparation also necessarily involves the return of land. Our efforts inevitably start out more gestural than substantive; indeed, restitution is almost always symbolic when it comes to loss of life and land.[48] But reparative measures can propel further political imagination toward more strategic and systemic change.

---

about the many illusions that white middle-class persons bring to solidarity work. See also MacLaren, "Solidarity—Beyond the Clichés."

46. Jung, see above, introduction A. We commend some additional hard questions posed by African American Campus Minister Nii Addo Abrahams: "Does your solidarity: Last longer than a news cycle? Make you lose sleep at night? Cost you relationships? Take away time from other things you could be doing? Change the way you spend your money? Make you a disruptive presence in white spaces? Change how you read your Bible? Cause you to speak out when no one wants to listen? Cause you to shut up when you want to say something? Change the way you vote? Make you suspicious of predominantly white institutions? Cause you to believe in costly reparations? Have room for Black rage?" And above all: "Does your solidarity happen when no one is looking?" Found at http://www.liftinggenerations.com/anti_racism_resources_wylgpdd1t0hoqcizu6hgna

47. Daye, email correspondence with authors, May 15, 2020.

48. Restorative justice understands that in cases of interpersonal violation, restitution by offenders is symbolic because it cannot undo the trauma of violence or loss of

What follows is again a small but representative sampling of recent experiments by individuals, churches, and political entities. Given this book's focus on faith communities, we highlight efforts by persons and churches from different Christian traditions.

Individual initiatives. Before she travels, our friend Rose Marie Berger researches whose traditional territory she will be traversing, reaches out to ask permission to enter their land, and makes a small "entrance fee" donation. This practice has led to conversations with members of the Nansemond (Virginia), Muwekma Ohlone (California), Wannasaw (South Carolina), and the Yamasee (Florida) tribes. "This is part of what community economics leader Chuck Matthei called my 'social mortgage'; I do this because I'm a Christian," writes Rose, a Catholic who is a senior editor at *Sojourners* magazine. She got this note back from the Nansemond Nation: "Thank you so much for visiting Norfolk and for remembering us. Your support is greatly appreciated and a wonderful reminder that there are visitors who care about our ancestors and tradition."[49] This small but meaningful practice has helped Rose make connections with different tribes and the history and contemporary reality of the land on which she walks.

Florence Schloneger is a Mennonite pastor and descendent of immigrants who settled Kanza (or Kaw) land in the late 1870s. By 1846, twenty million acres of Kanza territory had been reduced to 256,000, and in 1873 the tribe was forcibly removed to Oklahoma. Learning that history, Florence gave $10,000—a portion of her share of the family homestead sale—to the Kanza Indigenous Heritage Society. This new organization works to maintain the legacy and memory of the people for whom Kansas is named, and to provide settlers with avenues to make things right.[50]

---

life. This is even more the case in historical and collective violence. Lukas Meyer suggests two conditions that can encourage citizens to "accept the duty" of symbolic reparation for past violence:

> First . . . if, as members of ongoing societies, they can identify with the public inheritance of their society in such a way that they will want to respond to what they consider inherited public evils by participating in public acts of symbolic reparation. Second, if transgenerational legal persons (usually states) in whose name previous members committed crimes against others can be understood to accept an obligation to provide indirect victims with compensation, currently living people who are members of such entities can accept a (civic) duty to support their legal person in carrying out its policies of reparation. ("Historical Injustice," para. 7)

49. Berger, "Nansemond Nation in Virginia" paras. 1, 3. Rose's most recent publication, *Bending the Arch*, is an amazing expression of "doing her own work" around settler colonialism through poetry.

50. See Huber, "Land of the Kanza," and Tanner, "Her Family Farm Once Belonged

In late July 2019, a collective of traditional Oneida women from New York, Wisconsin, and Ontario returned to their ancestral homeland to accept a gift of nearly thirty acres, two centuries after their ancestors' violent removal. Liseli Haines, a Quaker who had lived in the area for forty-three years, donated her land back to the newly formed nonprofit organization *Akwéku Ohshʌ'he Yukwayóte** (Oneida meaning "we work together"). For generations Oneida women have organized to get traditional territory back; *Akwéku* is now directed by a female from each of the three Oneida communities, including a six-year-old girl. "I feel honored to give back the land," Haines said, "I love this land and I could not imagine anyone being told to leave, leave your beautiful homelands! It rips your heart out." Oneida wolf clan member Michelle Schenandoah celebrated the return: "Our language was spoken and our songs were sung. We let the land know we were there."[51]

Denominational repatriation. It is even more powerful when institutions decide to make reparation, since these deliberations involve polity and structures, and can have wider impact on other organizations. As many denominations face dwindling congregations and underused church buildings, some parishes are closing their doors. Stony Point Presbyterian Church made this difficult decision in fall 2017, which led to a concrete gesture of repatriation. Fertile ground had been laid in 2016 when the Presbyterian Church USA General Assembly repudiated the Doctrine of Discovery, thanks to the work of our colleague June L. Lorenzo (Laguna Pueblo/Diné) and other Indigenous Presbyterians. Two years later, the General Assembly called on all levels of PCUSA to dialogue, strategize, and act with local Native communities as an expression of confession and repentance. Rick Ufford-Chase, former denominational moderator and current co-director of Stony Point Center,* proposed to Stony Point Presbyterian Church that they explore with local Indigenous leaders possibilities for repatriation. They began meeting with Chief Dwayne Perry of the Ramapough-Lenape Nation to discuss whether a transfer of property would be beneficial. This culminated in a November 2019 handover of "the former Stony Point Church and all its

---

to the Kaw Indians." In 2013, John Stoesz—after a 2,000-mile bike ride across the former Dakota homeland—similarly donated half the proceeds from the sale of family land to Oyate Nipi Kte (The People Shall Live), a Minnesota organization working to recover Dakota traditional knowledge and culture. "'It has been extraordinarily important for me to see a beneficiary of Dakota land loss take this step because it helps restore my sense of hope in the possibility of justice for our people,' said Oyate Nipi Kte founder Waziyatawin. "He has modeled a way to help make amends . . . [through] land recovery. We hope that others will be inspired to contribute to reparative justice projects" (Schrag and Espenshade, "Former MCC Director Trades Inheritance for Justice," para. 19). See also the work of the White Earth Land Recovery Project.*

51. Logan, "For Two Centuries," paras. 13, 11.

property to the newly created Sweetwater Cultural Center to promote the education, health and welfare of . . . Native peoples and to preserve their cultures and ceremonial practices locally, regionally, and around the western hemisphere."[52]

In 1819, John Stewart, a freed African American slave, became the first Methodist missionary to the Wyandotte Nation in Ohio. When the Wyandotte were forced to Oklahoma under the Indian Removal Act, they deeded three acres of their land to the church to secure it from desecration. The United Methodist denomination held this land in trust until September 2019—the bicentennial of Methodist missions in the U.S.—when the parcel (including the original mission building and a cemetery where tribal members and Stewart are buried) was returned to the Wyandotte nation. The ceremony brought together 100 tribal members, the most that had been back on the land since they were forced to leave. "People have been killed, and we have been complicit," acknowledged Thomas Kemper, general secretary of Global Ministries. He added that the repatriation did not diminish "responsibility that we have as Methodists," an allusion to Col. John Chivington's role in the 1864 Sand Creek Massacre.[53] Wyandotte Chief Billy Friend shared how he had taken "our elders and youth to the Mission, teaching them about our ancestors. It has been important in establishing our identity and helping us to reconnect with our ancestors who worshipped in that exact location."[54] Rev. Chebon Kernall, executive director of the denomination's Native American Comprehensive Plan and member of the Seminole Nation, added: "When we see a Christian denomination returning the land back to its original habitants it is significant . . . We are re-writing history and crafting our future in shared wellness for all of our peoples."[55]

In May 2017, the Jesuit-run St. Francis Mission returned to the Sioux 525 acres scattered throughout the Rosebud Indian Reservation in South Dakota. In 1880, when the reservation was established, a federal land grant was given to the Jesuits to support their missions work with the Lakota. "It's now time to give back to the tribe all of those pieces of land that were given to the church," said mission president Fr. John Hatcher (though it was a "cumbersome process" with the Bureau of Indian Affairs, according to his

52. Damico, "Presbytery of Hudson River Transfers Title," paras. 4, 1. See also Trawick, "Sweetwater Cultural Center."

53. Iati, "U.S. Once Forced This Native American Tribe to Move," para. 12. See above 6D, n. 82.

54. At http://www.umc-oimc.org/united-methodists-prepare-to-return-a-denomination-landmark-to-the-wyandotte-nation/, para. 7.

55. Underwood, "United Methodist Church Gives Historic Mission Site," para. 4. The celebration included descendants of Stewart.

chief operating officer). Russell Eagle Bear, Tribal Historic Preservation Officer of the Rosebud Sioux Tribe, was involved in the land transfer negotiations, and commended the Jesuits: "It's a big thing, just the idea of returning land. We'll see if some of the (other churches) will follow suit."[56]

None of the above six examples are heroic; indeed they are modest, and in most cases are redistributing "settler surplus." But they represent beginning steps in a longer journey, and can animate more substantial efforts among Christians and their denominations. Social change usually springs from small seeds of conscience, which by themselves seem relatively insignificant in the big picture. However, the power of vanguard thought and action is captured in an adage that is dear to radicals and widely confirmed by historical experience: "First truth is ridiculed; then violently opposed; and finally accepted as being self-evident."[57]

Political reparations. In the realm of public policy things quickly get more complicated (at least for the settler political imagination).[58] Recent grassroots experiments in "voluntary taxing as civil society reparations" are thus a good place to start. The Sogorea Te Land Trust* is an urban intertribal organization led by Indigenous women in Ohlone territory in the San Francisco Bay area. It is working to "rematriate" urban land to indigenous stewardship, and "to do the work that our ancestors and future generations are calling us to do," as their website says. A priority is to procure land where Ohlone ancestors can be properly reinterred, since every one of the 425 shell mounds (sacred burial grounds) around the Bay have been destroyed by development, while the remains of over 15,000 Ohlone are stored at local universities.[59] Some local settlers, in consultation with Sogorea Te, initiated the Shuumi Land Tax,* a voluntary payment that is both symbolic and substantive. The Shuumi website provides calculations based on one's rent or

---

56. Manning, "Jesuits Return 525 Acres to Rosebud Sioux Tribe," paras. 3, 15. The mission will continue to hold land on the reservation where it has active operation. For an important study of Lakota Catholicism by a settler Jesuit, see Costello, *Black Elk*. For other examples of denominational reparation, see e.g., Todd, "Metro Vancouver Anglicans to Direct Millions to Indigenous Efforts," and the repurposing of a Lutheran church and parsonage in Denver into the Four Winds American Indian Council Center* (see https://www.fourwindscenter.org/history).

57. Usually attributed to nineteenth-century philosopher Arthur Schopenhauer, its provenance (as is so often the case with proverbial wisdom) is murky (see https://quoteinvestigator.com/2016/11/18/truth-stages/).

58. See e.g., Alexander, "Complexities of Land Reparations"; Lee and Ahtone, "Land-Grab Universities."

59. The East Bay is ancestral homeland to Chochenyo-speaking Ohlone; no Ohlone tribe is federally recognized (see above 5B). As Lawrence Hart points out, settler warehousing of Native remains is a grotesque human rights violation (above 7D, n. 103).

mortgage (for both residential and commercial buildings) to help participants determine an annual residence tax. These funds "directly support Sogorea Te's work to acquire and preserve land; establish a cemetery to reinter
stolen Ohlone ancestral remains; and build urban gardens, community
centers, and sacred arbors so current and future generations of Indigenous
people can thrive in the Bay Area."[60] Similar symbolic tax initiatives have
sprung up among settler activists in the Pacific Northwest, New York City,
and in Wiyot territory, and we hope to start one here in Chumash territory.[61]

Land returns by public institutions are rare, and thus worth paying
attention to. The Wiyot Tribe on the North Coast of California has worked
for decades to repatriate the largest island in the Humboldt Bay, commonly
known as "Indian Island," site of a notorious massacre. In 1860, a small
group of settlers attacked sleeping Wiyots at night during their World Renewal Ceremony, murdering 250 (mostly women and children) and driving survivors into hiding. The ceremony was not held again until 2014.[62]
In 2000, after major fundraising efforts, the Wiyot got a foothold on the
island by purchasing a 1.5-acre former boatworks at the Duluwat village site
(though the land required years of toxic contamination remediation). Four
years later, the City of Eureka returned another forty acres. Then, in 2014,
Mayor Frank Jager (grandfather of two Wiyot girls) drafted an official letter
acknowledging the historic "massacre of unfathomable proportions." Fearing liability, the city attorney reissued Jager's letter with all mention of responsibility and apology removed. Two city council members subsequently
approached the tribe asking what they could do, and the answer was unequivocal: "Give us back the island." In October 2019, the city returned 200
additional acres to the Wiyot, transferring title without condition. This was
perhaps the first instance of a "local municipality repatriating hundreds of
acres of land to a local tribe in the absence of a sale or lawsuit settlement."[63]
The cultural and political healing that has resulted is deeply instructive.[64]

60. Wires, "Why We Charge the Shuumi Land Tax," para.2. See also Singh, "Native
American 'Land Taxes.'" A Bay Area permaculture project now includes the Shuumi
Tax in its costs (see Resource Generation,* a local foundation that encourages nonprofit
organizations to participate in the tax). Several synagogues also take part (see Mirsky,
"East Bay Jews Discuss").

61. Real Rent Duwamish* calculates amounts according to income; the Manna-
Hatta Fund* suggests a symbolic amount, and the Honor Tax Project* encourages
individuals to decide.

62. Mukherjee, "Wiyot Tribe Raising Funds for 2020 World Renewal Ceremony."

63. Above quotes at Greenson, "Duluwat Island Is Returned to the Wiyot Tribe,"
paras. 10, 12.

64. See the tribe's summary at https://www.wiyot.us/148/Cultural. Sabrina Imbler
narrates the long and poignant saga of tribal efforts to regain their "center of their

Government bodies of the settler state do not publicly accept responsibility for their complicity in historic violations until and unless it becomes
politically impossible *not* to do so, usually because of grassroots organizing
and advocacy. This was certainly the case with Canadian Indian Residential Schools, where it took a class action suit to provoke an official apology
and the subsequent TRC (above 7C). The same is true of corporations and
other institutions, including many churches. If and when such entities do
recognize past violations, they typically issue apologies that are as vague as
possible, accompanied by as little concrete restitution as possible. From the
perspective of restorative solidarity, such responses fall far short. Unless victims are truly heard and full responsibility taken, gestural remorse can even
re-victimize those originally harmed.[65] A personal or political apology that
functions primarily as a cathartic ritual for the complicit—in which offenders try to feel better about themselves without changing behavior, policies,
or structures—is merely another settler move to innocence (above 6C).

In 1993, Indigenous Hawaiians saw several sides of this phenomenon.
After years of grassroots advocacy the general synod of the United Church
of Christ instructed their president in 1991 "to offer a public apology to the
Native Hawaiian people and to initiate a process of reconciliation between
the UCC and Native Hawaiians . . . in recognition of our historic complici-
ties in the illegal overthrow of the Hawaiian monarchy in 1893."[66] Eighteen
months later, UCC President Paul Sherry delivered the apology, acknowledging the UCC's responsibility for the actions of "ancestors of ours in the
church." The date was poignantly January 17, 1993: the centenary of the
U.S.-backed coup against Queen Liliuo'kalani. And it was pointedly offered
to more than 10,000 people at the Royal Iolani Palace in Honolulu. For all
this symbolic power, it was only later and under pressure from Hawaiian
activists that the UCC *also* agreed to economic redress. Many were unhappy
that the eventual package (of over 4 million dollars and several parcels of
land) was earmarked mostly for Native Hawaiian church members. Still,
it was (to that date) the most substantive reparative step taken by a U.S.
denomination to Indigenous people.

Eleven months later, on November 23, 1993, Congressional Joint
Resolution 19 was adopted and signed by President Bill Clinton into Public
Law 103–150. Called the Apology Resolution, it

universe" ("How the Wiyot Tribe Won Back a Sacred California Island").

65. Regarding interpersonal crimes, see Bennett, "Taking the Sincerity Out of Saying Sorry"; on public apologies, see Cuypers et al., *Public Apology between Ritual and
Regret*; on political remorse, see Daye, *Political Forgiveness*.

66. See above, Interlude B, for background. McCollough, "Why Our Church Apologized to Hawai'i," para. 8. For a longer analysis, see Bissen, "Hawaiian Situation."

acknowledges that the overthrow of the Kingdom of Hawaii occurred with the active participation of agents and citizens of the
United States and further acknowledges that the Native Hawaiian people never directly relinquished to the United States their
claims to their inherent sovereignty as a people over their national lands, either through the Kingdom of Hawaii or through
a plebiscite or referendum.[67]

While this rhetoric was pregnant with possibility for the burgeoning
Hawaiian Sovereignty movement, it carried no actual political or economic
correlates. Any potential legal implications were later roundly eviscerated
by a March 2009 U.S. Supreme Court decision stating that "the 37 'whereas'
clauses . . . have no binding legal effect, nor does it convey any rights or
make any legal findings for Native Hawaiian claims."[68] That same year, however, well away from the spectacle of the White House apology-without-
reparation, a different initiative in Hawai'i was unfolding that would deliver
repatriation-without-apology.

Hawaiians came to Kaho'olawe, a small island off of Maui, at least a
millennium ago. More than 3,000 inventoried archaeological and historical sites show that it was a navigational center for voyaging, an agricultural
hub, and an important religious and cultural space. After U.S. occupation of
Hawai'i, Kaho'olawe was used as a penal colony, for sheep and cattle ranching, and then during World War II given to the Navy for a bombing range.
During the seventies and eighties, the island became a focal point for Hawaiian sovereignty activism, led by the Protect Kaho'olawe Ohana* (PKO).
Several nonviolent occupations of the island tried to halt bombings, and in
March 1977 two young Native activists—troubadour and PKO president
George Helm and local football star Kimo Mitchell—died during an action,
further galvanizing the movement.[69] Because of this persistent resistance
and advocacy, in 1980, a settlement was reached in a suit brought by the
PKO: "Under the Consent Decree and Order, the Navy agreed to survey
and protect historic and cultural sites on the island, clear surface ordnance
from 10,000 acres, continue soil conservation and revegetation programs,

67. See text of the Apology Resolution at http://hooponoponopeace.com/
APOLOGY%3AU.S.html.

68. See https://en.wikipedia.org/wiki/Apology_Resolution, para. 19. A remarkable
global database of hundreds of cases of apology and reparations has been curated by
Howard-Hassmann at the Political Apologies and Reparations website: http://political-
apologies.wlu.ca. See also the Fellowship of Reconciliation* grassroots reparations
initiative.

69. See Colleen Uechi's beautiful profile of Helm and Mitchell, "40 Years after Men's
Disappearance at Sea."

eradicate the goats from the island, limit ordnance impact training to the central third of the island, and allow monthly PKO accesses to the island."[70] The U.S. finally ended live-fire training exercises on Kahoʻolawe in 1990, and on May 9, 1994, "the Navy transferred Kahooʻlawe to the State of Hawaii for use as a cultural preserve—overseen by the Kahoʻolawe Island Reserve Commission* (KIRC)—for eventual transfer to a sovereign Hawaiian nation."[71] Ten years later, the Navy completed a $460 million cleanup and withdrew the last of its personnel. The KIRC now oversees ongoing cultural and restoration accesses to the island. "I see this whole island almost like a *hālau*, like a school," says Kui Gaspero, KIRC cultural resource project coordinator. "People want to come here and learn, practice their culture . . . There are so many elements of education that can be done on the island . . . how much there is out here with so little!"[72]

The possibilities for what our world could look like in the wake of concrete decolonization measures are, as Eve Tuck likes to say, *incommensurable* with settler colonial society as we know it. This means we will have to get used to working with questions that have no clear (much less easy) answers—something that is very difficult (even paralyzing) for us managerial-minded settlers. But the more we experiment with re-schooling, restorative solidarity, reparation, and repatriation, the more we'll be able to metabolize such questions. Taiaiake Alfred sums it up this way: "For all of us, Indigenous and settler alike, there is only self-questioning and embracing this commitment: listen to the voices of our Indigenous ancestors channeled through the young people of our nations, learn from Indigenous culture how to walk differently, and love the land as best you can."[73] A settler discipleship of decolonization can, we believe, contribute to the healing of our haunted history *and* to the liberation of our hostage future.

8E. KAHO'OLAWE, 1994 AND OPWASHEMOE CHAKATINAW, 2015

We close this chapter with two more personal experiences of Songlines that were key stepping stones for each of us. The extraordinary story of Kahoʻolawe just summarized is a compelling example of how Indigenous

70. Kahoʻolawe Island Conveyance Commission, "Kaho òlawe Island," 26. See history at http://www.kahoolawe.hawaii.gov/history.shtml.

71. Enomoto, "Kahoʻolawe Nine 30 Years Later," para. 25.

72. Reelitz, "Long Live Kahoʻolawe," para. 26 (the article has beautiful photographs of restoration work). See also http://www.kahoolawe.hawaii.gov/home.php.

73. Alfred, "Don't Just Resist," para. 15.

activism makes repatriation possible. It is also one that has shaped Ched, who began working in 1980 to support the PKO. In June 1994, he had the unparalleled privilege of participating in one of their first accesses to the island after its formal return. This profound experience of re-schooling on and by sacred land and its caretakers was bracketed by two mystical revelations.

A month before the access, Ched had a dream: "As I set foot on Kahoʻolawe there was music arising from the land, coming up from the ground and through my feet and into my mind. It felt like the whole universe was singing."[74] This portent was more than fulfilled as he joined five dozen folks from ages six to seventy-eight, in the initial swim from boat to beach (there is no natural harbor). "As one of the elders, or *kupuna*, puts it, 'We come to this island just as our ancestors arrived, by wading ashore.'" The PKO believes that just "by touching the *ʻaina* you will be converted to the cause . . . you can see the land bleeding to death, with acres and acres of hard packed dirt, because of the erosion from the bombing." During the day the group worked building basic infrastructure, and at night "talked story" and sang their own songs while camping out.

The last day was a pilgrimage to the sacred peak at the center of the island, where everyone was invited to remove their shoes over the final ascent "over very sharp rock. This is tradition, and also biblical, to remove one's shoes when on holy ground." The group offered gifts and made its way back down the mountain. What happened next was Ched's second numinous moment:

> In the saddle below the main peak was one *wiliwili* tree. We were told that these trees, gnarly and knobby, used to cover the whole island in a magnificent forest. But the island has been denuded, and here was this one last *wiliwili* tree left, kind of slunk over in the ground but still growing. A *kupuna* named Pualani Kanahele asked us and the conveyance commission, which included some military personnel, to gather in a circle around the tree. She began a chant in Hawaiʼian, which like so many Pacific Island languages rises and falls like the ocean in its intonation, mesmerizing you. One of my friends translated: She was thanking the tree for surviving the onslaught of the white man and of the military and of the holocaust inflicted upon Hawaiian land and culture. She was asking it to remember everything that it had seen, and never forget. Then she asked the tree to give its seed for renewal, so that the seeds of this one *wiliwili* tree would replant and reforest the whole island.

74. The following quotes are adapted from Wylie, "Singing for the *Wiliwili* Tree," 10–13.

Listening to that chant, Ched began weeping, realizing all that he, too, had lost from the colonial conquest of California, "and what could be found, if we dare to reconnect with the land, to understand who we are, and to go through the process of resistance, reclamation and reinhabitation."

Before leaving Kaho'olawe, Ched paid respects at an altar to Helm and Mitchell, martyrs of the PKO movement, which was located not far from the main camp along a little coastal trail.

> On the headstone, in Hawaiian, is a quote from the gospel of John: "Blessed is the one who comes in the name of the Lord." People lay wreaths and shell leis and flowers and coral. You just sit there and it all washes over you: If only we could come to the land in the name of the Creator, maybe healing could happen.

The image of a lone surviving tree amidst a devastated landscape, seeding renewal under the serenade of Indigenous elders, has been a guiding trope for Ched ever since.[75]

~

On a chilly, overcast May afternoon in 2015, we were at Janet and Rob's farm celebrating my graduation from St. Andrew's College, the program that allowed me to do much of the research for this book. As part of the gathering, Ched and I invited my siblings, their partners, and several friends to accompany us on a field trip to nearby Opwashemoe Chakatinaw (Stoney Knoll). Joining us there was Leonard Doell, who has helped animate and sustain Mennonite involvement in the land reparation efforts of the Young Chippewayans.[76] On the hill he told the story of the extraordinary assembly that had taken place at this spot a decade earlier. In August 2006, thirty years after the haunting related above (6A), Leonard worked with Young Chippewayan leaders, the Office of the Treaty Commissioner, representatives from Mennonite and Lutheran churches in the area, and Mennonite Central Committee Saskatchewan* (MCCS) to mark the 130th anniversary of the signing of Treaty Six. More than 100 people participated in a pipe ceremony.

75. In a similar vein, see cellist Audrey Nadeau's moving musical apology/lament to a lone fir tree on a clear-cut landscape at: https://www.youtube.com/watch?v=5lLTUC 9F_14&feature=youtu.be.

76. Leonard has been not only an exemplary advocate, but a student of Indigenous history. Raising his own family, he made a point of always telling paired Mennonite and Indigenous stories to his grandchildren—the kind of small but meaningful discipline that slowly changes culture.

Mennonite farmer Barb Froese, who lives at the bottom of the hill, reminisced about how markedly different the spirit of that day was from 1976:

> By eight am Lutherans were already dotting the hill. The sun was
> shining and people kept arriving, more than we ever expected.
> A large campfire was smoldering in the middle of the Lutheran
> churchyard, and a tent and teepee were set up, with a cluster of
> First Nations men in front. I introduced myself to them. The
> fire tender, who had camped there all night, joked that they
> should have come down to our farm at the bottom of the hill
> for breakfast, and I responded, "I wish you had." We laughed
> together. After speeches and signing, we ended the day with a
> presentation of gifts. I had the honor of presenting a patchwork
> quilt to Chief Ben Weenie and his wife Silvi.[77]

A Memorandum of Understanding was signed that read in part: "We
wish for ourselves and for future generations to live in conditions of peace,
justice, and self-sufficiency for all our communities. We will work together
to help bring about these conditions through a timely and respectful resolution of the issues which history has left to us."[78]

Elder Abe Funk, known for his electric blue cowboy hat, was another
Mennonite organizer behind that 2006 gathering, and a signatory to the
MOU. Funk was a persistent advocate for resolving the Opwashemoe
Chakatinaw land claim. In 2012, at age ninety-six, Abe passed away and,
like the biblical Moses, was unable to see the justice he longed for. "Until the
day he died," his son Ray told us, "my father was firm with me as his oldest
son, and with his oldest grandson, that our clan would commit ourselves
to working with the Young Chippewayans until this job of righting land
injustice is done."[79] Ray has been involved in the continuing conversations
between Mennonite Central Committee Saskatchewan leaders, local landowners, and tribal members, and helped inaugurate the Spruce River Folk
Festival.* This annual music and cultural event on his farm educates about
landless bands within Saskatchewan, proceeds of which go to support the
Young Chippewayan land claim and reconciliation efforts between Mennonites, Lutherans, and Young Chippewayans. In 2019, Ched and I attended

---

77. Tiefengrund Focus Group, interview by Elaine Enns, Carlton, Saskatchewan,
June 23, 2014.

78. The signing is captured in the photograph at beginning of this chapter. See Olfert, "Historic Meeting on Stoney Knoll," and Schulz, "Our Children Need to Know."

79. Interview by authors at Ray's farm outside of Prince Albert, Saskatchewan, July
4, 2014.

the tenth anniversary of this grassroots folkfest, witnessing its beautiful expressions of restorative solidarity.[80]

These are hopeful signs unfolding in my place and among my people,
exploring solidarity, reparation, and repatriation. But we have a long way to
go to heal the haunting of Reserve 107, and all the other wounds of colonization within and among us. Standing on Opwashemoe Chakatinaw that
afternoon, surrounded by family and friends, I thought about what was
here before Henry Kelsey and the Hudson's Bay Company; about how the
Indigenous stewards of this place could have taught us how to live more
sustainably had we listened; and about the solemn covenants about which
those Cree elders spoke (above 5E). I thought about the settler name of
this place: Stoney Knoll. "This stone heard all your words," Joshua of old
told the people at Shechem, "and shall be a witness against you if you break
faith" (Josh 24:27).

We, the children of the colonial settler project, have indeed broken faith towards lands, peoples, and Creator. There is so much history
to turn around.

Ched and I talked afterwards about another Scripture that employs a
similar metaphor:

> The stone that the builders rejected has become the cornerstone;
> this was the Creator's doing, and it is marvelous in our eyes.
>
> —Mark 12:10–11 (citing Ps 118:20)

The psalmist's counterintuitive wisdom was so important to our ancestors in faith that it is invoked half a dozen times in the Second Testament.[81]
This ancient Songline invites us to embrace Indigenous peoples—the very
ones whom the builders of the colonial project categorically rejected—as
the keystone of a decolonized future. This may be unthinkable to the keepers of empire, the spiritual descendants of the rich man who refused Jesus'
offer of liberation-as-reparation. But it is an article of faith among those
who follow Jesus of Nazareth, who himself was dismissed, criminalized, and

---

80. See https://donate.mcccanada.ca/registry/stoney-knoll-land-claim. In addition
to those named above, the circle working on this issue includes Indigenous leaders
Gary LaPlante and Harry Lafond and Lutheran leaders Jason Johnson and Charles
Schultz, as well as organizational resources of the Office of the Treaty Commissioner. A
recent award-winning documentary titled *Reserve 107* narrates this story well (available
online at www.reserve107thefilm.com/).

81. In each of the synoptic Gospels (also Matt 21:42, Luke 20:17), Acts 4:11, and
1 Pet 2:7 (where *kephalē gōnias* means "cornerstone" or "keystone"); alluded to in Eph
2:20 and 1 Pet 2:6 (where *akrogōniaios* means "cornerstone" or "capstone").

executed, only to rise to empower an insurrection of the dispossessed, with whom he forever mystically dwells.

At Opwashemoe Chakatinaw that day, I renewed my commitment to discipleship as an insurrection against settler colonialism. Healing and reconciliation will come to all of us only if and when Indigenous peoples, treated for 500 years as last and least, become again first (Mark 10:31). This will be "marvelous in our eyes."

Figure 32: Northern Lights, Waskesiu, SK, May 2017. Photo by Hamilton Fast (used with permission).

Epilogue
hukišunuškuy

"I WONDER WHETHER THERE might be an antonym for settler colonialism."

Matthew Vestuto was thinking aloud during a program committee meeting preparing for our 2020 Bartimaeus Kinsler Institute. Ever the teacher of Chumash language, Matthew proposed the Ventureño phrase *hukišunuškuy*.[1] "It connotes a different kind of settling," he explained. "It's what we would say to each other as an agreement to do something good together in the future, a promise or covenant." With his permission, we braided this phrase into our Institute theme (though it took us a while to learn how to pronounce it). The phrase summons us to become "treaty people," to partner with our Indigenous neighbors, to walk the way of decolonizing discipleship. We offer it here as a last word.

The spirit of this phrase was embodied in two Round Dances led by Harry Lafond to conclude two of our Bartimaeus Institutes. The first was in Saskatoon, place of my birth, during the closing ceremony of our "TRC Calls Churches to Action" gathering in October 2016. More than 100 of us—settler and Indigenous, Canadian and American—convened for a final ceremony at Station 20 West, a community center in a predominantly Native neighborhood. We ate, heard poetry (including Mika Lafond's), and testified to what we'd learned and how we would put it into practice going forward. As a benediction, Harry organized us into a Round Dance, a ritual of his people symbolizing friendship and solidarity. Around we went, arms linked, two-stepping sideways to drum and chant, smiling at each other across the circle. It was my first Round Dance.

According to Cree Elder John Cuthand, the origin of the dance lies in a story about a daughter who was grieving her departed mother. While

1. He notes: "Unlike English (a synthetic language) our language is polysynthetic. We don't have spaces between the word parts and *hukišunuškuy* is a phrase/sentence rather than a word." See above 7D.

walking alone on the prairie she saw her mom standing on a hill, feet not quite touching the ground:

> "I cannot find peace in the other world so long as you grieve," she said. "I bring something from the other world to help the people grieve in a good way." She taught her daughter ceremony and the songs that went with it. "Tell the people that when this circle is made, we the ancestors will be dancing with you and we will be as one." The daughter returned and taught the people the Round Dance.[2]

The tradition is linked to the northern lights, which the Cree believe are spirits of ancestors dancing in the "Green Grass world," their symbol of heaven.[3] As Harry's daughter Mika put it poetically: "Sitting under a black sky sprinkled with stars / my eyes are called to the ones who have gone before / late at night they join hands / brilliant serpentine belt in the northern sky."[4]

My second Round Dance came at the close of our 2020 Institute, in the Ventura River Watershed where I live now. Rev. Bob Two Bulls had just finished presiding at our closing eucharistic ceremony, using a beautiful indigenized liturgy he's created over the years. Harry again led the dance as benediction, and again it sealed a spirit of solidarity among our participants. This time the recorded song was longer, and at several points when the chanting paused, we settlers would move to break the circle, only to be pulled back into the dance as the song started up again. Harry was grinning, as if to say, "This is a lesson not to give up, to keep dancing in this work, even when you are getting tired."

If the Round Dance was originally for healing from grief, it is little wonder I experienced it as medicine, in and for both of my watershed homes. There is so much to lament, so many hauntings from which we must heal, so much restorative solidarity to realize. But as we danced round and round that circle of Landlines, Bloodlines, and Songlines, I felt the power of radical love, the warmth of a wind rising against the storm of settler colonialism.

hukišunuškuy: Let us agree to do something good together. Let us dance together into a decolonized future, that "by turning, turning we come round right."

---

2. Carlson, "Origin of the Round Dance Ceremony," para. 3. For a short video of a Northern Cree Round Dance and drumming circle, see https://www.youtube.com/watch?v=YKi7pVPVsJQ.

3. See Gowder, "What Is a Native American Round Dance?"

4. See above, beginning of ch. 7.

Afterword

by Harry Lafond

IT WAS ANOTHER ORDINARY Sunday meal, some years ago: the remains of a delicious roasted chicken on the table, surrounded by piles of little drumstick bones. My sister was home for a weekend visit from Edmonton. Lots of little stories were going around the table, with laughter and the odd teasing about her husband's fading hockey career. The stories often cycled back to the history of our Métis families.

"Maman, did you know your dad?" she asked my mother.

"pêkwaw nêstaw ki nakiskawaw, mitoni ki-apsîsin. Duck Lake miyâmâ ê-ki-ototat, *un magasin* ki paminam." ("I met him only once when I was a little girl; he ran a store in Duck Lake.")

Maman came from a Métis family, its origins somewhere south of Winnipeg with later connections to the Batoche people. She spoke very little English (never having felt the need to learn it). School was not an option for her; she learnt to maneuver her way comfortably using her Michief language and oral training. She raised a family of twelve children, to whom she told many stories about her grandfather Jonas, a restless buffalo hunter and veteran of the Batoche Resistance. She grew up under his loving care, and honed her skill to tell stories with detail and humor.

Maman's simple and honest statement about her slivered relationship to her dad caught my imagination, and eventually found its way into my heart. Who was this man, the grandfather we could only imagine? How had his absence impacted our identity as a family? Is it possible to connect to a grandfather long gone to the spirit world? Armed with these questions (and picking up more along the way), I set out to find answers, dragging my family with me. Some were interested, others just noted the little tidbits of information uncovered on the journey. This grandfather's only presence was his tombstone at Elmwood graveyard in Winnipeg, and a picture at Batoche museum, showing a marked resemblance to some of my siblings, including his blue eyes.

In my Cree world, the present is comfortably ensconced in the circle of life between past and future. In our Kihiw Waciston School we teach our children and grandchildren how to participate in a feast ceremony at least once for every season of the year. This is our way of teaching the importance of sustaining relationships with the ancestors (*anskochâpanak*). The ribbons of memory tying us to them are sustained through the food we share, the pipe we smoke, the cloth we bring to the sweat ceremony, and the offerings we gather for the ancestors. This is the keystone of our identity as Cree people. It is no wonder, then, that my heart feels the gaps of a lost grandfather, and a need to close them, to ensure my grandchildren can experience a balanced family tree. Experience has taught me that a leaning tree falls under the force of a strong wind.

I have been fortunate to be curious about people's histories, especially those of my community of Muskeg Lake, and to have had some resources to pursue the many paths of that curiosity. Others have not been so fortunate, haunted by the trauma brought into the lives of their grandparents when settlers arrived, by government attempts at genocide and/or assimilation, and by churches' collusion in the attempts to eradicate Cree institutions, which have left them with a broken understanding of their own identity and history. The overwhelming fog of unknowing, punctuated by brain-changing trauma, brings into a family an utter sadness, devoid of deep love. And so we reset . . . and reset . . . and reset inside ourselves, our families and our communities.

We work to instill the curiosity needed to seek family ties, and to understand Cree teachings of love, compassion, empathy and identity (*miskasowin*: finding your center). In our community we have established the *wahkotowin* (seeking to be related) Advisory Committee. The healing process has moved from a wish list to an action list. Everyone recognizes the committee by its powerful name, and *wahkotowin* has become everyday language.

Where does that leave my grandfather and me? The outline of the man my maman met only once is beginning to take on substance and color. We "met" when I visited his home in Duck Lake; an elderly woman formerly of Duck Lake pointed out the house to me. Then on three occasions I visited his grave at Elmwood and introduced myself. Later I brought my youngest son and two grandsons to meet their *anskochapan* (great-grandfather). With each visit, a sense of familiarity grows. In the spirit of the feast ceremony, my maternal grandfather is beginning to find his place with my paternal grandfathers, Andre and JB Lafond. Four of us (including my sister) made a trip to Germany to visit the small village that this grandfather's family left to come to Canada. Slowly the family tree is growing straighter. At every opportunity I bring his presence into family events, to help the children of my siblings get to know their *anskochapan*.

Canada has been on a rocky journey over the last ten years, trying to respond to the 94 Calls to Action issued by the national Truth and Reconciliation Commission. These are intended to guide us on our way across a map of reconciliation, from sea to sea to sea. It is rocky because, as usual, people want shortcuts. But there is no shortcut to a lasting, long-term relationship between Indigenous and settler communities. Each of us is called to remember the past, live the present, and set the framework for the next seven generations. And that will only happen under the spiritual nudging of *mâmawi-ohtâwîmâw* (God, the Father of all).[1]

July 2020
Muskeg Lake Cree Nation
Treaty 6 Territory
Saskatchewan, Canada

---

1. Harry Lafond is a former chief of Muskeg Lake Cree Nation and Executive Director of the Office of the Treaty Commissioner, Saskatchewan. He is board chair of the First Nations Trust, and Director of Education and Principal of Kihiw Waciston School. For more on his work for reconciliation and for indigenizing his Catholic faith, see Lafond, "Church and the Indigenous Peoples of Canada"; Yard, "Cree, Christian, and Questioning the Catholic Church"; and Gyapong, "Indigenous Couple Live a Life of Reconciliation." For background on the Batoche Resistance, see Prologue and 5C; on the Truth and Reconciliation Commission, see 7C.

APPENDIX I

Annotated Bibliography on Recent Intergenerational Trauma Studies

SHERRI NOZIK[2]

RESEARCH ON THE TRANSMISSION of intergenerational trauma has expanded significantly, both in the field of mental health and more widely among researchers and practitioners with a holistic vision of human flourishing. As the field of traumatology matures, our understanding of genetic, social, and environmental influences deepens. Summarized below are sixteen mostly recent peer-reviewed studies, selected with an eye to Enns and Myers's LBS rubric. For full references see the bibliography.

A. BLOODLINES

There is growing consensus that traumatic events affecting an individual's or group's health may also impact their grandchildren's well-being. Studies recognize that contexts, experiences, and responses to trauma are unique, such that present and future impacts vary.

---

2. Nozik is a doctoral student at Mississippi State University, focusing on counselor education and clinical mental health counseling.

Trauma's Impact upon Individuals

1. Van der Kolk, *The Body Keeps the Score: Brain, Mind and Body in the Healing of Trauma*, 2016.

   This influential book explores how trauma (from childhood neglect to war-time atrocities) lies beneath many of the diagnoses of contemporary Western medical models, and how our current treatment methods fall short. It contains an in-depth look at the neurobiology of trauma, utilizing case studies from the author's thirty years as a psychiatrist. Chronicling stories of pain and resilience, the study offers a holistic vision of trauma and recovery.

2. Conching and Thayer. "Biological Pathways for Historical Trauma to Affect Health: A Conceptual Model Focusing on Epigenetic Modifications," 2019.

   This article puts issues of social justice at the forefront, while reviewing current research in the field of epigenetics. It lays out two pathways through which historical trauma impacts the health of contemporary individuals: directly (via continued traumatization) and/or indirectly (through inherited, trauma-induced epigenetic modifiers). Both result in poor mental and physical health, and the toxicity resulting from historic traumatization of people groups is compounded by continuing subjugation.

Trauma's Impact upon Families

3. Moog, Entringer, Rasmussen, Styner, Gilmore, Kathmann, Heim, Wadhwa, and Buss, "Intergenerational Effect of Maternal Exposure to Childhood Maltreatment on Newborn Brain Anatomy," 2018.

   This study links a mother's history of childhood maltreatment to intrauterine influences upon her baby's brain development, specifically the cortical gray matter (the region of the brain implicated in several psychopathologies and neurodevelopmental disorders). Controls for other influencing factors, such as maternal stress during pregnancy, are considered. The findings illuminate the impacts of childhood maltreatment and their intergenerational consequences, and provide compelling evidence that those consequences begin in utero.

4. Costa, Yetter, and DeSomer, "Intergenerational Transmission of Paternal Trauma among US Civil War ex-POWs," 2018.

This study, which has received wide attention, compares the lon-
gevity of children of Civil War ex-POWs with those of non-POWs.
Results reveal that sons of ex-POWs born after their father's captivity were significantly more likely to die at younger ages than sons of
non-POWs born after the war. Sons of ex-POWs born *before* the war
were not impacted, however, indicating an epigenetic (as opposed to
environmental) cause. Interestingly, no impact on female children of
ex-POWs born after the war was found. More research is needed to
confirm and interpret upon these findings, but we can expect future
research to focus on sex-specific epigenetic transmission of trauma.

Trauma's Impact upon Groups

5. Volkan, "Transgenerational Transmissions and Chosen Traumas: An
   Aspect of Large-Group Identity," 2001.
      The originator of the psycho-political concept of "chosen trau-
   ma" gives several examples of historical traumas that manifest themselves in contemporary large-group identity. Volkan argues violent
   acts perpetrated against groups tend to influence how group members
   treat one another in subsequent generations. He also considers how
   perpetrator groups (such as Germans in the wake of the Nazi era) are
   impacted by an inability to grieve what past generations did. Failure to
   grieve negatively affects both victimized and perpetrator groups.

6. Stein, "'Chosen Trauma' and a Widely Shared Sense of Jewish Identity
   and History," 2014.
      This short study summarizes and applies Volkan's theory to Jew-
   ish tradition and history. It describes how ancient Jewish stories, and
   their representation in contemporary liturgy, display both "chosen
   trauma" and "chosen glories." Stein suggests those liturgies, along with
   contemporary struggles faced by Jewish peoples, have "collapsed time"
   and fostered a sense of never-ending terror. Recurrent terror, as well
   as an inability to grieve previous losses, leads to many problems. An
   example is violence within the modern Jewish family system (until
   recently a source of secret shame within the Jewish community). Stein
   also infers that deep communal feelings of loss surrounding Jewish
   holy sites, including the Temple Mount, have been exploited by some
   raising funds for Israel for the unlikely goal of rebuilding the Temple.
   By viewing a people group through several lenses—their traumatic
   histories; the stories they tell and language they use; and their religion,

geographic location, and family systems—this piece helps map how intergenerational trauma is transmitted.

B. LANDLINES

Just as Bloodlines carry the trauma and resilience of our ancestors, so does the land. Where intergenerational trauma focuses on experiences of individuals and groups, historical trauma looks at those experiences in the context of broader history, which is inextricably linked to specific *geographies* (e.g., lands from and to which settlers came). Historical trauma also includes how past violations—often erased by silenced stories, repressed memories, and whitewashed narratives—are reproduced in contemporary unjust policies, from discriminatory policy to disparities in public health to environmental degradation. Healing historical trauma thus requires attention to place as well as engaging social change in the present, including reparation for past injustices.

1. Harrison, "'We Need New Stories': Trauma, Storytelling, and the Mapping of Environmental Injustice in Linda Hogan's *Solar Storms* and Standing Rock," 2019.

     This article outlines the intimate connection between settler ecological destruction and the historical trauma and continued victimization of Indigenous bodies. The author utilizes trauma-informed theory, geographical mapping, and storytelling, analyzing Hogan's narrative of an Indigenous woman searching for the origin and healing of her personal trauma. She also looks at the link between ecological repair and the healing of soul and society, focusing on contemporary movements for ecological justice, grieving rituals for healing historical trauma, and the creation of a "more-than-human living community."

2. Mohatt, et al. "Historical Trauma as Public Narrative: A Conceptual Review of How History Impacts Present-Day Health," 2014.

     This article clarifies how historical trauma, mediated by modern-day narratives, impacts group health outcomes today. Traumatizing narratives filter through both personal reminders (e.g., microaggressions, loss, and discrimination) and public reminders (e.g., dominant cultural narratives, structural inequities, and public symbols such as monuments and holidays). This study illuminates how present-day social and political environments and discourses can either foster resilience in historically traumatized groups or trigger re-traumatization.

3. Women's Earth Alliance and Native Youth Sexual Health Network, *Violence on the Land, Violence on Our Bodies: Building an Indigenous Response to Environmental Violence*, 2016.

This e-book and interactive tool-kit offers an extensive collection of research, stories, and resistance strategies concerning violence at the intersection of the environment and bodies of Indigenous women and youth. Exploring the relationships between women and land, it shows how violence against one leads to violence against the other. The study surveys movements that resist this violence; possible legislative solutions and their limitations; educational resources to build coalitions; and self-care and healing strategies for activists. It includes a helpful glossary. At: http://landbodydefense.org/uploads/files/VLV-BReportToolkit2016.pdf.

4. Hartmann, et al. "American Indian Historical Trauma: Anti-Colonial Prescriptions for Healing Resilience and Survivance," 2019.

This article provides a timeline of how concepts of historical trauma developed, clarifies terms, and overviews current research directions and interventions. The authors look at historical trauma from its beginning, as a subset of posttraumatic stress disorder, to a less-pathologized concept today as critical discourse moves toward anti-colonial perspectives and organizing strategies. It overviews recent moves away from clinical and Western medical model treatments to those of collective healing and resilience-building, which avoid clinical diagnosis where appropriate (e.g., addressing historical trauma as a life-stressor rather than as PTSD).

C. SONGLINES

We carry the trauma of our ancestors, but also their resilience; pain but also strength and wisdom about how to overcome. However, the study of post-traumatic growth, adaptation, and resilience has lagged behind diagnostic research, and often fails to capture the amazing capacity of both humans and nature to heal, learn, and flourish.

Individual Resilience

1. Herman, *Trauma and Recovery: The Aftermath of Violence—From Domestic Abuse to Political Terror*, 2015.

One of the most significant works on trauma in the last half century, this book offers both laypersons and professionals an intermediate-level dive into the research on, and treatment of, trauma. It includes stories of both individual and collective trauma and resulting impacts, as well as a five-stage model of recovery: (1) A Healing Relationship; (2) Safety; (3) Remembrance and Mourning; (4) Reconnection; and (5) Commonality.

2. Levine et al. "Reintegrating Fragmentation of the Primitive Self: Discussion of 'Somatic Experiencing,'" 2018.

This model acknowledges that trauma is embodied, and focuses primarily on somatic methods of treatment. The authors discuss the Polyvagal Theory method, which is gaining credibility in trauma research and therapy. They also introduce the basic principles of somatic experiencing and the science upon which it is built. For more information, see https://traumahealing.org.

3. Riem et al. "Intranasal Oxytocin Enhances Stress-Protective Effects of Social Support in Women with Negative Childhood Experiences During a Virtual Trier Social Stress Test," 2020.

This study offers a neurobiological explanation of stress responses in women. Researchers administered intranasal oxytocin to a segment of participants; women who received it experienced higher levels of stress relief from friendship or support (tend-and-befriend). Interestingly, women who reported a history of adversity in childhood experienced even more significant levels of relief (a nod to resilience). Results indicate that when women are together with allies, oxytocin is an effective stress mediator and aids in recovery from stressful events.

Collective Resilience

1. Barlow, "Restoring Optimal Black Mental Health and Reversing Intergenerational Trauma in an Era of Black Lives Matter," 2018.

The Community Healing Network's patented model, Emotional Emancipation Circles, addresses historical, intergenerational, and personal trauma in African Americans. According to their website (https://www.communityhealingnet.org), their mission is "to mobilize Black people across the African Diaspora to heal from the trauma caused by centuries of anti-Black racism, to free ourselves of toxic stereotypes, and to reclaim our dignity and humanity as people of African ancestry." Barlow overviews various manifestations of trauma and how they impact physical and mental well-being. Personal and collective methods for overcoming trauma impacts are discussed, highlighting experiences of Black students and social justice movement leaders.

2. Salberg and Grand, *Wounds of History: Repair and Resilience in the Trans-Generational Transmission of Trauma*, 2016.

This collection of papers by a diverse group of contributors explores the resilience that follows wounding by collective traumas in contemporary history. Healing rituals and therapeutic interventions are discussed, as are various forms of resilience and self-in-community healing responses, including political activism, narrative truthtelling, embodied truth, song, dance, and drumming. This volume encourages readers to identify strength and resilience within individuals and groups who have faced trauma, and to listen to diverse professional voices.

3. Weaver, *Trauma and Resilience in the Lives of Contemporary Native Americans: Reclaiming Our Balance, Restoring Our Wellbeing*, 2019.

Weaver (Lakota) is Associate Dean for Diversity, Equity, and Inclusion at the University at Buffalo's School of Social Work. Grounded in an understanding of historical trauma and its systemic implications today, her book addresses contemporary issues concerning the health and social well-being of Native Americans. It acknowledges the reality of intergenerational trauma, while also focusing on the strength and resilience of Indigenous people (a growing body of research). The study looks at historical trauma, its contemporary manifestations, and aspects within Native American cultures that promote resilience. Weaver invites professionals to address the social and health-related concerns of Native American clients by drawing on their sources of resilience, and by participating in the deconstruction of racist systems that perpetuate and intensify historical trauma.

APPENDIX II

Longer Biblical Texts

Note: All texts are New Revised Standard Version with adjustments for inclusive language

1 KINGS 21 (INTERLUDE B)

Naboth the Jezreelite had a vineyard in Jezreel, beside the palace of King Ahab of Samaria. And Ahab said to Naboth, "Give me your vineyard, so that I may have it for a vegetable garden, because it is near my house; I will give you a better vineyard for it; or, if it seems good to you, I will give you its value in money." But Naboth said to Ahab, "The LORD forbid that I should give you my ancestral inheritance."

Ahab went home resentful and sullen because of what Naboth the Jezreelite had said to him; for he had said, "I will not give you my ancestral inheritance." He lay down on his bed, turned away his face, and would not eat. His wife Jezebel came to him and said, "Why are you so depressed that you will not eat?" He said to her, "Because I spoke to Naboth the Jezreelite and said to him, 'Give me your vineyard for money; or else, if you prefer, I will give you another vineyard for it'; but he answered, 'I will not give you my vineyard.'" His wife Jezebel said to him, "Do you now govern Israel? Get up, eat some food, and be cheerful; I will give you the vineyard of Naboth the Jezreelite."

So she wrote letters in Ahab's name and sealed them with his seal; she sent the letters to the elders and the nobles who lived with Naboth in his city. She wrote in the letters, "Proclaim a fast, and seat Naboth at the head of the assembly; seat two scoundrels opposite him, and have them bring a charge against him, saying, 'You have cursed God and the king.' Then take him out, and stone him to death."

The men of his city, the elders and the nobles who lived in his city, did as Jezebel had sent word to them. Just as it was written in the letters that she had sent to them, they proclaimed a fast and seated Naboth at the head of the assembly. The two scoundrels came in and sat opposite him; and the scoundrels brought a charge against Naboth, in the presence of the people, saying, "Naboth cursed God and the king." So they took him outside the city, and stoned him to death.

Then they sent to Jezebel, saying, "Naboth has been stoned; he is dead." As soon as Jezebel heard that Naboth had been stoned and was dead, Jezebel said to Ahab, "Go, take possession of the vineyard of Naboth the Jezreelite, which he refused to give you for money; for Naboth is not alive, but dead." As soon as Ahab heard that Naboth was dead, Ahab set out to go down to the vineyard of Naboth the Jezreelite, to take possession of it.

Then the word of the Lord came to Elijah the Tishbite, saying: Go down to meet King Ahab of Israel, who rules in Samaria; he is now in the vineyard of Naboth, where he has gone to take possession.

You shall say to him, "Thus says the Lord: Have you killed, and also taken possession?" You shall say to him, "Thus says the Lord: In the place where dogs licked up the blood of Naboth, dogs will also lick up your blood."

Ahab said to Elijah, "Have you found me, O my enemy?"

He answered, "I have found you. Because you have sold yourself to do what is evil in the sight of the Lord, I will bring disaster on you; I will consume you, and will cut off from Ahab every male, bond or free, in Israel; and I will make your house like the house of Jeroboam son of Nebat, and like the house of Baasha son of Ahijah, because you have provoked me to anger and have caused Israel to sin. Also concerning Jezebel the Lord said, 'The dogs shall eat Jezebel within the bounds of Jezreel.' Anyone belonging to Ahab who dies in the city the dogs shall eat; and anyone of his who dies in the open country the birds of the air shall eat."

2 CORINTHIANS 5:16—6:10 (8A)

From now on, therefore, we regard no one from a human point of view; even though we once knew Christ from a human point of view, we know him no longer in that way. So if anyone is in Christ, there is a new creation: everything old has passed away; see, everything has become new! All this is from God, who reconciled us to Godself through Christ, and has given us the ministry of reconciliation; that is, in Christ God was reconciling the world to Godself, not counting their trespasses against them, and entrusting the message of reconciliation to us.

So we are ambassadors for Christ, since God is making God's appeal through us; we entreat you on behalf of Christ, be reconciled to God. For our sake God made Jesus to be sin who knew no sin, so that in Jesus we might become the righteousness of God. As we work together with Jesus, we urge you also not to accept the grace of God in vain. For God says, "At an acceptable time I have listened to you, and on a day of salvation I have helped you." See, now is the acceptable time; see, now is the day of salvation!

We are putting no obstacle in anyone's way, so that no fault may be found with our ministry, but as servants of God we have commended ourselves in every way: through great endurance, in afflictions, hardships, calamities, beatings, imprisonments, riots, labors, sleepless nights, hunger; by purity, knowledge, patience, kindness, holiness of spirit, genuine love, truthful speech, and the power of God; with the weapons of righteousness for the right hand and for the left; in honor and dishonor, in ill repute and good repute. We are treated as impostors, and yet are true; as unknown, and yet are well known; as dying, and see—we are alive; as punished, and yet not killed; as sorrowful, yet always rejoicing; as poor, yet making many rich; as having nothing, and yet possessing everything.

MARK 10:17–31 (8A)

As Jesus was setting out on a journey, a man ran up and knelt before him, and asked him, "Good Teacher, what must I do to inherit eternal life?"

Jesus said to him, "Why do you call me good? No one is good but God alone. You know the commandments: 'You shall not murder; You shall not commit adultery; You shall not steal; You shall not bear false witness; You shall not defraud; Honor your father and mother.'"

He said to him, "Teacher, I have kept all these since my youth."

Jesus, looking at him, loved him and said, "You lack one thing; go, sell what you own, and give the money to the poor, and you will have treasure in heaven; then come, follow me."

When he heard this, he was shocked and went away grieving, for he had many possessions.

Then Jesus looked around and said to his disciples, "How hard it will be for those who have wealth to enter the kingdom of God!" And the disciples were perplexed at these words. But Jesus said to them again, "Children, how hard it is to enter the kingdom of God! It is easier for a camel to go through the eye of a needle than for someone who is rich to enter the kingdom of God."

They were greatly astounded and said to one another, "Then who can be saved?"

Jesus looked at them and said, "For mortals it is impossible, but not for God; for God all things are possible."

Peter began to say to him, "Look, we have left everything and followed you."

Jesus said, "Truly I tell you, there is no one who has left house or brothers or sisters or mother or father or children or fields, for my sake and for the sake of the good news, who will not receive a hundredfold now in this age—houses, brothers and sisters, mothers and children, and fields with persecutions—and in the age to come eternal life. But many who are first will be last, and the last will be first."

APPENDIX III

Organizations Cited

Abundant Table Farm Project, CA, https://theabundanttable.org/

Administration of Native Americans, About Native Languages, https://www.acf.hhs.gov/ana/programs/native-language-preservation-maintenance/about

Advocates for Indigenous California Language Survival, https://aicls.org/

Akwéku Ohshʌ'he Yukwayóte, NY, https://www.facebook.com/pages/Akw%C3%A9ku-Ohsh%CA%8Che-Yukway%C3%B3te%CC%B2/667901417012074

Allies for Change, https://www.alliesforchange.org/

Barbareño/Ventureño Band of Mission Indians, CA, https://www.bvbmi.com/

Bartimaeus Cooperative Ministries, CA, https://www.bcm-net.org/

Bartimaeus Kinsler Institute, CA, including past institute summaries: https://www.bcm-net.org/study/bartimaeus-institute

Beloved Community Center, NC, https://belovedcommunitycenter.org/

Beyond 94: Truth and Reconciliation in Canada, https://newsinteractives.cbc.ca/longform-single/beyond-94?&cta=1

Birmingham Civil Rights Institute, AL, https://www.bcri.org/

Borderlinks, Tucson, AZ, https://www.borderlinks.org/

Canoe Journey Herbalists, WA, https://www.facebook.com/canoejourneyherbalists/

Capacitar, https://capacitar.org/

Carnival de Resistance, NC, http://carnivalderesistance.com/

Catholic Worker Movement, https://www.catholicworker.org/

Center and Library for the Bible and Social Justice, NY, https://clbsj.org/

Central Coast Alliance United for a Sustainable Economy, CA, https://causenow.org/

Children's Defense Fund, DC, https://www.childrensdefense.org/

Christian Peacemaker Teams, https://www.cpt.org/

Church of All Nations, MN, https://www.cando.org/

Church of the Saviour, DC, http://inwardoutward.org/churches/

Common Grace Australia, https://www.commongrace.org.au/ aboriginal_and_torres_strait_islander_justice

Common Word Bookstore and Resource Center, MB, https://www.commonword.ca/Browse/868

Cradleboard Teaching Project, http://www.cradleboard.org/

Decolonization: Indigeneity, Education & Society, https://jps.library.utoronto.ca/index.php/des

Decolonizing the Heart, ON, https://www.decolonizingtheheart.org/

Department of Indian Work for the Diocese, Episcopal Church Minneapolis, MN, http://episcopalmn.org/department-of-indian-work

Dexter Avenue King Memorial Baptist Church, AL, https://www.dexterkingmemorial.org/

Dismantling the Doctrine of Discovery Coalition, https://dofdmenno.org/

Dr. Denis Mukwege Foundation, NL, https://www.mukwegefoundation.org/the-problem/ rape-as-a-weapon-of-war/

Drag the Red, MB, https://www.cbc.ca/news/canada/manitoba/ drag-the-red-bones-1.4166029

Eloheh Indigenous Center for Earth Justice, WA, https://www.elohehseeds.com/index.html

Episcopal Veterans Fellowship, https://episcopalveteransfellowship.org/

Equal Justice Initiative, AL, https://eji.org/; https://museumandmemorial.eji.org/

Faceless Dolls Project, https://www.nwac.ca/wp-content/up-loads/2015/05/2012_Building_on_the_Legacy_of_NWAC_Faceless_Doll_Project.pdf

Faith and Money Network, DC, https://faithandmoneynetwork.org/

Federation of Saskatchewan (Sovereign) Indian Nations, SK, https://www.first-nations.info/federation-sovereign-indigenous-nations.html

Fellowship of Reconciliation, NY, https://www.forreparations.org/

First Nations Kitchen, MN, https://firstnationskitchen.org

First Peoples Theology Journal, https://www.commonword.ca/ResourceView/11/9131

Four Winds American Indian Council Center, CO, https://www.fourwindscenter.org/

Great Lakes Water Walk, http://greatlakeswaterwalk.ca/

Greensboro Truth and Community Reconciliation Project, NC, https://belovedcommunitycenter.org/truth-reconciliation/

Habitat for Humanity, GA, https://www.habitat.org/about/history

Haley Farm, TN, https://www.childrensdefense.org/activism/haley-farm/explore-cdf-alex-haley-farm/.

Healing Minnesota Stories, MN, https://healingmnstories.wordpress.com/

Honor Tax Project, CA, http://www.honortax.org/

Idle No More, SK, www.idlenomore.ca

Indigenous Ministries Australia, https://www.gmp.org.au/what-we-do/projects/australia/ima

Indigenous Environmental Network, MN, https://www.ienearth.org/

Kahoʻolawe Island Reserve Commission, HI, http://www.kahoolawe.hawaii.gov/home.php

Kairos Blanket Exercise, ON, https://www.kairosblanketexercise.org/

KAIROS: Canadian Ecumenical Justice Initiatives, Indigenous Rights, ON, https://www.kairoscanada.org/what-we-do/indigenous-rights

Kings Bay Plowshares, https://kingsbayplowshares7.org/

Koinonia Farm, GA, https://www.koinoniafarm.org/brief-history/

Manna-Hatta Fund, NY, https://mannahattafund.org/

Mennonite Central Committee Canada, https://mcccanada.ca/

Mennonite Central Committee Saskatchewan, SK, https://mcccanada.ca/display-provinceregion/canada/saskatchewan

Mennonite Church Canada Indigenous-Settler Relations, MB, https://www.mennonitechurch.ca/indigenous

Mennonite Disaster Service, https://mds.mennonite.net/

Mennonite Voluntary Service, https://www.mennonitemission.net/Serve/Mennonite%20Voluntary%20Service

Mixteco/Indigena Community Organizing Project (MICOP), CA, http://mixteco.org/

Mother Earth Water Walk, http://motherearthwaterwalk.com

Muskeg Lake Cree Nation, SK, https://muskeglake.com/

NAIITS—An Indigenous Learning Community, https://naiits.com/

National Civil Rights Museum, TN, https://www.civilrightsmuseum.org/

National Council of Elders, http://nationalcouncilofelders.com/

National Native American Boarding School Healing Coalition, MN, https://boardingschoolhealing.org/

Native American Heritage Commission, http://nahc.ca.gov/about/

Native Truth and Healing: California Genocide Conference, CA, https://www.sdsu.edu/conferences/native-truth-and-healing

New Orleans Slave Trade, LA, https://www.neworleansslavetrade.org/

New Poor Peoples Campaign, https://www.poorpeoplescampaign.org/

News from Native California, CA, http://newsfromnativecalifornia.com/

Nibi Walks, http://www.nibiwalk.org/

Nibi Emosaawdamajig, https://trcbobcaygeon.org/nibi-emosaawdamajig/

Open Door Community, MD, https://opendoorcommunity.org/

Proctor Institute, TN, https://www.childrensdefense.org/programs/faith-based/samuel-dewitt-proctor-institute/proctor-event-page/

Protect Kahoʻolawe Ohana, HI, http://www.protectkahoolaweohana.org/

Protectors of the Salish Sea, WA, https://protectorsofthesalishsea.org/

RAW Tools: Forging Peace, Disarming Hearts, CO, https://rawtools.org/

Real Rent Duwamish, WA, https://www.realrentduwamish.org/

REDress Project, https://en.wikipedia.org/wiki/REDress_Project

Resource Generation, NY, https://resourcegeneration.org/land-reparations-indigenous-solidarity-action-guide/

Return to the Earth Project, OK, https://mcc.org/learn/more/return-earth

Richmond Slave Trade, VA, http://www.richmondgov.com/CommissionSlaveTrail/documents/brochureRichmondCityCouncilSlaveTrailCommission.pdf

Rosa Parks Museum, AL, https://www.troy.edu/student-life-resources/arts-culture/rosa-parks-museum/index.html

Sabeel Ecumenical Liberation Theology Center, Jerusalem, https://sabeel.org/

Salal and Cedar Watershed Discipleship, BC, http://salalandcedar.com/

Save Our Sisters, https://www.independent.co.uk/news/long_reads/native-american-women-missing-murder-mmiw-inquiry-canada-us-violence-indigenous-a8487976.html

Shuumi Land Tax, CA, https://sogoreate-landtrust.com/shuumi-land-tax/

Sisters in Spirit Vigils, https://www.nwac.ca/event/sisters-in-spirit-vigil-october-4th-2019/

Sixteenth Street Baptist Church, AL, https://16thstreetbaptist.org/

Sogorea Te' Land Trust, CA, https://sogoreate-landtrust.com/

Southern Christian Leadership Conference, GA, https://nationalsclc.org/

Southern Poverty Law Center, GA, https://www.splcenter.org/

Spirit House Project, GA, http://www.spirithouseproject.org/

Spiritus Christi Church, NY, https://www.spirituschristi.org/

Spruce River Folk Festival, SK, https://www.spruceriverfolkfest.com/

St. Isidore Catholic Worker Farm, WI, https://stisidorecatholicworkerfarm.org/

St. Paul's Episcopal Church, VA, https://www.stpaulsrva.org/HRI

Stony Point Center, https://stonypointcenter.org/

SURJ Indigenous Solidarity Network, https://www.showingupforracialjustice.org/indigenous-solidarity.html

Sweet Honey in the Rock, http://sweethoneyintherock.org/

Taize Community, France, https://www.taize.fr/en

The Takini Institute, NM, https://vivo.health.unm.edu/display/n12836

Tribal Canoe Journeys, WA, https://juustwa.org/program-areas/issues/first-american-indian-nations/our-work/tribal-canoe-journeys/

Trinity UCC Chicago, IL, https://www.trinitychicago.org/

Truth and Reconciliation Commission of Canada, http://www.trc.ca/

Tsleil-Waututh land defenders, BC, https://twnation.ca/about/

Turtle Island Solidarity Network, https://www.cpt.org/programs/tisn

Two Row Wampum Renewal Campaign, NY, https://honorthetworow.org/

United Church of Canada, Reconciliation and Indigenous Justice, ON, https://www.united-church.ca/social-action/justice-initiatives/reconciliation-and-indigenous-justice

Valentine's Day Women's Memorial March, https://en.wikipedia.org/wiki/Women%27s_Memorial_March

Victim and Offender Reconciliation Program (VORP), CA, https://servefresno.org/serve/ongoing/advocacy/victim-offender-reconciliation-program-vorp

Walking with Our Sisters, http://walkingwithoursisters.ca/

Wanuskewin Heritage Park, SK, https://wanuskewin.com/

Wellspring Conference Center, MD, http://wellspringconference.org/

White Earth Land Recovery Project, MN, https://www.welrp.org/

Whitney Plantation, LA, https://www.whitneyplantation.org/

Women and Water Coming Together Symposium, WI, https://www.spiri-tofthewater.org/

Word and World People's School, MI, http://www.wordandworld.org/

Bibliography

2bears, Jackson. "Mythologies of an [Un]dead Indian." PhD diss., University of Victoria, 2012. https://dspace.library.uvic.ca/bitstream/handle/1828/3855/Leween_Jackson_2bears_PhD_2012.pdf?sequence=1&isAllowed=y.

Abernethy, Bob. "Gordon Cosby and Washington's Church of the Savior." *PBS*, October 31, 1997. https://www.pbs.org/wnet/religionandethics/1997/10/31/october-31-1997-gordon-cosby-and-washingtons-church-of-the-savior/15297/.

Accapadi, Mamta Motwani. "When White Women Cry: How White Women's Tears Oppress Women of Color." *Accapadi* 26:2 (2007) 208–15.

Achebe, Chinua. *Things Fall Apart*. New York: Ballantine, 1959.

Adam, Betty Ann. "Mary Ellen Turpel-Lafond has Always Worked on the Law's Cutting Edge." *Saskatoon Star Phoenix*, March 7, 2017. https://thestarphoenix.com/news/saskatchewan/canada-150-mary-ellen-turpel-lafond/.

Ajrouch, Kristine, and Amaney Jamal. "Assimilating to a White Identity: The Case of Arab Americans." *The International Migration Review* 41:4 (2007) 860–79.

Albers, Gretchen. "Indigenous Land Claims." *The Canadian Encyclopedia*, April 20, 2015. https://www.thecanadianencyclopedia.ca/en/article/land-claims.

Alexander, Gregory. "The Complexities of Land Reparations." *Law & Social Inquiry* 39:4 (2014) 874–901.

Alexander, Michelle. *The New Jim Crow: Mass Incarceration in the Age of Colorblindness*. New York: New Press, 2010.

Alfred, Taiaiake. "Don't Just Resist. Return to Who You Are." *Yes Magazine*, April 9, 2018. https://www.yesmagazine.org/issue/decolonize/2018/04/09/dont-just-resist-return-to-who-you-are/.

Altschul, Jeffrey and Donn Grenda, eds. *Islanders & Mainlanders: Prehistoric Context for the Southern California Bight*. Tucson, AZ: Statistical Research, 2002.

Ambrose. *De Nabuthae: A Commentary*. Translated by Martin Rawson and Patrick McGuire. Washington, DC: The Catholic University of America Press, 1927.

Andersen, Chris. *Métis: Race, Recognition and the Struggle for Indigenous Peoplehood*. Vancouver: University of British Columbia Press, 2014.

Anderson, Alan B. *Settling Saskatchewan*. Regina, SK: University of Regina Press, 2013.

Anderson, John. "Point Conception: The Chumash Western Gate." http://www.angelfire.com/id/newpubs/conception.html.

Andraos, Michel. *The Church and Indigenous Peoples in the Americas: In Between Reconciliation and Decolonization.* Studies in World Catholicism 7. Eugene, OR: Cascade, 2019.

Andrews, Edward. *Native Apostles: Black and Indian Missionaries in the British Atlantic World.* Cambridge, MA: Harvard University Press, 2013.

Andrews, Evan. "What Was the Bear Flag Revolt?" *History,* October 19, 2018. https://www.history.com/news/what-was-the-bear-flag-revolt.

Angelou, Maya. "On the Pulse of Morning." In *Maya Angelou: The Complete Poetry,* 264–66. New York: Random House, 2015.

Arnold, Jeanne, ed. *Foundations of Chumash Complexity.* Perspectives in California Archaeology 7. Los Angeles: Cotsen Institute of Archaeology, 2004.

Arnsperger, Christian. "A Federation of Ways of Life: Towards a Globalized "Social Heresy." *Revue internationale de philosophie* 239:1 (2007) 81–104.

Azizeldin, Riham. "Do Human Bodies Act as Archives of Trauma?" *Mada Masr,* June 25, 2018. https://madamasr.com/en/2018/06/25/opinion/u/q53-do-human-bodies-act-as-archives-of-trauma/.

Bagley, Katherine. "At Standing Rock, a Battle over Fossil Fuels and Land." *Yale Environment 360,* November 10, 2016. https://e360.yale.edu/features/at_standing_rock_battle_over_fossil_fuels_and_land.

Baldwin, James. *The Fire Next Time.* New York: Knopf Doubleday, 2013.

———. "A Letter to My Nephew." *The Progressive,* December 1, 1962. https://progressive.org/magazine/letter-nephew/.

———. *The Price of the Ticket: Collected Nonfiction, 1948–1985.* New York: St. Martin's, 1985.

Baldy, Cutcha Risling. "The Flower Dancers: Reviving Hupa Coming-of-Age Ceremonies." *North Coast Journal,* August 2, 2018. https://www.northcoastjournal.com/humboldt/the-flower-dancers/Content?oid=10229320.

———. *"no:'olchwin-ding, no:'olchwin-te* (To Grow Old in a Good Way): The Hupa Flower Dance and the Revitalization of Women's Coming of Age Ceremonies in Native California." http://www.cutcharislingbaldy.com/blog/noolchwin-ding-noolchwin-te-to-growold-in-a-good-way-the-hupa-flower-dance-and-the-revitalization-of-womens-coming-of-age-ceremonies-in-native-california.

———. *We Are Dancing for You: Native Feminisms and the Revitalization of Women's Coming-of-Age Ceremonies.* Seattle: University of Washington Press, 2018.

Ballingall, Alex. "With Blockades Coming Down, What Will the Wet'suwet'en Solidarity Movement Leave Behind?" *The Toronto Star,* March 8, 2020. https://www.thestar.com/politics/federal/2020/03/06/the-wetsuweten-solidarity-movement-brought-indigenous-reconciliation-into-sharp-focus-for-canada.html.

Ballowe, James. "Review of *Trace,* by Lauret Savoy." *EcoLit Books,* September 22, 2016. https://www.ecolitbooks.com/2016/09/book-review-trace-by-lauret-savoy/.

Baptist, Edward. *The Half Has Never Been Told: Slavery and the Making of American Capitalism.* New York: Basic, 2016.

Barker, Adam, and Emma Lowman. "Settler Colonialism." *Global Social Theory* (undated). https://globalsocialtheory.org/concepts/settler-colonialism/.

Barlow, Jameta Nicole. "Restoring Optimal Black Mental Health and Reversing Intergenerational Trauma in an Era of Black Lives Matter." *Biography* 41:4 (2018) 895–908. doi:10.1353/bio.2018.0084.

Barrera, Jorge. "Harper's 2008 Residential School Apology Was 'Attempt to Kill the Story,' Says ex-PMO Speechwriter." *APTN National News,* September 10, 2015. https://aptnnews.ca/2015/09/10/harpers-2008-residential-school-apology-was-attempt-to-kill-the-story-says-ex-pmo-speechwriter/.

Bastian, Beverly. "Henry Wager Halleck, the *Californios,* and the Clash of Legal Cultures." *California History* 72 (1993) 310–23.

Battiste, Marie. *Reclaiming Indigenous Voice and Vision.* Vancouver: University of British Columbia Press, 2000.

Beaucage, Margorie, and Emma LaRoque. "Two Faces of the New Jerusalem: Indian-Metis Reaction to the Missionary." In *Visions of the New Jerusalem: Religious Settlement on the Prairies,* edited by Benjamin Smillie, 27–38. Edmonton, AB: NeWest, 1983.

Beck, Warren, and Ynez Haase. *Historical Atlas of California.* Norman: University of Oklahoma Press, 1974.

Beebe, Rose Marie, and Robert M. Senkewicz. "The End of the 1824 Chumash Revolt in Alta California: Father Vicente Sarría's Account." *The Americas* 53:2 (1996) 273–83. https://doi.org/10.2307/1007619.

Beeds, Tasha. "Movement and Ceremony." http://workingitouttogether.com/content/movement-and-ceremony/.

Bellegrade, Daniel, Carole Corcoran, and James Prentice. "Young Chippewayan Inquiry: Inquiry into the Claim of Stoney Knoll Indian Reserve 107." *Indian Claims Commission, Commissioners Report*, December 1994. https://www.academia.edu/32686538/THE_YOUNG_CHIPEEWAYAN_INQUIRY_into_the_Claim_Regarding_Stoney_Knou_Indian_Reserve_No._107_COUNSEL_For_the_Young_Chipeewayan_Claimants.

Beller, Erin, Robin M. Grossinger, Micha N. Salomon, Shawna J. Dark, Eric D. Stein, Bruce K. Orr, Pete W. Downs, Travis R. Longcore, Gretchen C. Coffman, Alison A. Whipple, Ruth A. Askevold, Bronwen Stanford, and Julie R. Beagle. "Historical Ecology of the Lower Santa Clara River, Ventura River, and Oxnard Plain: An Analysis of Terrestrial, Riverine, and Coastal Habitats." *San Francisco Estuary Institute,* August 2011. https://www.sfei.org/sites/default/files/biblio_files/VenturaCounty_HistoricalEcologyStudy_SFEI_2011_lowres.pdf.

Benjoe, Kerry. "New Twists on an Old Language: Efforts Flourish to Keep Cree Alive." *Regina Leader-Post,* April 21, 2017. https://leaderpost.com/news/local-news/new-twists-on-an-old-language-efforts-flourish-to-keep-cree-alive.

———. "Thomas Moore Keesick More Than Just a Face." *Regina Leader-Post,* December 22, 2015. https://leaderpost.com/news/local-news/thomas-moore-keesick-more-than-just-a-face.

Bennett, Christopher. "Taking the Sincerity Out of Saying Sorry: Restorative Justice as Ritual." *Journal of Applied Philosophy* 23:2 (2006) 127–43.

Bergen, Jeremy. "Whether, and How, a Church Ought to Repent for a Historical Wrong." *Theology Today* 73:2 (2016) 129–48.

Bergen, Rachel. "Saskatoon Gay Couple 1st to Be Married in Mennonite Church." *CBC News,* January 5, 2015. https://www.cbc.ca/news/canada/saskatoon/saskatoon-gay-couple-1st-to-be-married-in-mennonite-church-1.2888826.

Berger, Rose Maria. *Bending the Arch: Poems.* Eugene, OR: Resource, 2019.

———. "Nansemond Nation in Virginia." http://rosemarieberger.com/2019/05/10/nansemond-nation-in-virginia/.

Berry, Deborah Barfield. "I Was Writing about Colonial America's First Enslaved Africans; I Was Stunned to Find My Ancestors, Too." *USA Today,* October 17, 2019. https://www.usatoday.com/in-depth/news/nation/2019/10/16/black-history-slavery-reporter-uncovers-genealogy-1619-project/3847926002/.

Berry, Wendell. *What I Stand on: The Collected Essays of Wendell Berry 1969–2017.* New York: Library of America, 2019.

Bhangal, Naseeb, and Oiyan Poon. "Are Asian Americans White? Or People of Color?" *Yes Magazine,* January 15, 2020. https://www.yesmagazine.org/social-justice/2020/01/15/asian-americans-people-of-color/.

Binnema, Ted. *Common and Contested Ground: A Human and Environmental History of the Northwestern Plains.* Norman, OK: University of Oklahoma Press, 2001.

Birdsell, Sandra. *Return of the Day.* Toronto: Vintage Canada, 2006.

———. *The Russländer.* Toronto: McClelland & Stewart, 2001.

Bissen, Toni. "The Hawaiian Situation: An Overview of Hawaii's People, Politics, Religion, Spirituality and Culture, Yesterday and Today." In *Another World is Possible: Spiritualities and Religions of Global Darker Peoples,* edited by Dwight Hopkins and Marjorie Lewis, 77–96. Philadelphia: Routledge, 2014.

Bloom, Liza Minno, and Berkley Carnine. "Towards Decolonization and Settler Responsibility: Reflections on a Decade of Indigenous Solidarity Organizing." *CounterPunch,* October 3, 2016. https://www.counterpunch.org/2016/10/03/towards-decolonization-and-settler-responsibility-reflections-on-a-decade-of-indigenous-solidarity-organizing/.

Bonhoeffer, Dietrich. *The Cost of Discipleship.* New York: Macmillan, 1966.

Bornemann, Erin, and Lynn Gamble. "Resilience among Hunter-Gatherers in Southern California before and after European Colonization." In *Hunter-Gatherer Adaptation and Resilience: A Bioarchaeological Perspective*, edited by Daniel Temple and Christopher Stojanowski, 168–91. Cambridge: Cambridge University Press, 2019.

Borrows, John. "Wampum at Niagara: The Royal Proclamation, Canadian Legal History, and Self-Government." In *Aboriginal and Treaty Rights in Canada: Essays on Law, Equality, and Respect for Difference,* edited by Michael Asch, 155–72. Vancouver: University of British Columbia Press, 1997.

Bowen, Dawn. "Resistance, Acquiescence and Accommodation: The Establishment of Public Schools in an Old Colony Mennonite Community in Canada." *Mennonite Quarterly Review* 84:4 (2010) 551–80.

Bowling, Chris. "American Indian Storytelling Project Unearths Past to Educate, Heal." *Star Tribune*, August 3, 2018. https://www.startribune.com/untold-stories-of-minnesota-indian-history-offer-a-chance-for-healing/490041461/.

Boyd, Colleen E., and Coll Thrush, eds. *Phantom Past, Indigenous Presence: Native Ghosts in North American Culture and History.* Lincoln: University of Nebraska Press, 2011.

Boyd, Malia. "The Other Side of Paradise." *New York Times,* March 9, 2012. https://www.nytimes.com/2012/03/11/books/review/lost-kingdom-a-history-of-hawaii.html.

Brady, Miranda, and Emily Hiltz. "The Archaeology of an Image: The Persistent Persuasion of Thomas Moore Keesick's Residential School Photographs." *Canadian Journal of Cultural Studies* 37 (Spring 2017) 61–85.

Branch, Taylor. *At Canaan's Edge: America in the King Years,* 1965–1968. New York: Simon & Schuster, 2006.

————. *Parting the Waters: America in the King Years, 1954–63.* New York: Simon & Schuster, 1988.

————. *Pillar of Fire: America in the King Years, 1963–65.* New York: Simon & Schuster, 1998.

Brave Heart, Maria Yellow Horse. "The Historical Trauma Response among Natives and Its Relationship with Substance Abuse: A Lakota Illustration." *Journal of Psychoactive Drugs* 35:1 (2003) 7–13.

————. "*Oyate Ptayela*: Rebuilding the Lakota Nation through Addressing Historical Trauma among Lakota Parents." *Journal of Human Behavior and the Social Environment* 2 (1999) 109–26.

————. "The Return to the Sacred Path: Reflections on the Development of Historical Trauma Healing." https://www.ihs.gov/sites/telebehavioral/ themes/responsive2017/display_objects/documents/slides/historicaltrauma/ htreturnsacredpath0513.pdf.

Brave Heart, Maria Yellow Horse, J. Chase, J. Elkins, and D. B. Altschul. "Historical Trauma among Indigenous Peoples of the Americas: Concepts, Research, and Clinical Considerations." *Journal of Psychoactive Drugs* 43:4 (2011) 282–90.

Brave Heart, Maria Yellow Horse, J. Chase, J. Elkins, J. Nanez, J. Martin, and J. Mootz. "Women Finding the Way: American Indian Women Leading Intervention Research in Native Communities." *American Indian and Alaska Native Mental Health Research Journal* 23:3 (2016) 24–47.

Brennen, Christopher. "Yosemite's Haunted Canyon." http://www.dankat.com/mstory/ tenaya.htm.

Brett, Mark. *Political Trauma and Healing: Biblical Ethics for a Postcolonial World.* Grand Rapids: Eerdmans, 2016.

Brewer-Smyth, Kathleen, and Harold G. Koenig. "Could Spirituality and Religion Promote Stress Resilience in Survivors of Childhood Trauma?" *Issues in Mental Health Nursing* 35:4 (2014) 251–56.

Bridges, Alicia. "Saskatchewan's 'Landless Bands' Fight for Recognition, Reconciliation." *CBC News*, August 12, 2017. https://www.cbc.ca/news/canada/ saskatoon/landless-bands-saskatchewan-2017-reserve-107–1.4245184.

brown, adrienne maree. "Living through the Unveiling." http://adriennemareebrown. net/2017/02/03/living-through-the-unveiling/#:~:text=living%20through%20 the%20unveiling,to%20pull%20back%20the%20veil.

Brown, Brené. "Shame vs. Guilt." https://brenebrown.com/blog/2013/01/14/shame-v- guilt/.

Brown, Henry Box. *Narrative of the Life of Henry Box Brown.* New York: Oxford University Press, 2002.

Brown, Kaitlin, Jan Timbrook, and Dana Bardolph. "'A Song of Resilience': Exploring Communities of Practice in Chumash Basket Weaving in Southern California." *Journal of California and Great Basin Anthropology* 38:2 (2018) 143–62.

Budden, Chris. *Following Jesus in Invaded Space: Doing Theology on Aboriginal Land.* Princeton Theological Monograph Series. Eugene, OR: Pickwick, 2009.

Burn, Geoffrey. *Liberating the Will of Australia: Towards the Flourishing of the Land and All Its Peoples.* Eugene, OR: Wipf & Stock, 2021.

Burns, Melinda. "Point of Contention." *Santa Barbara News Press*, December 26, 1997. https://www.angelfire.com/sk/syukhtun/westgate.html.

Burrell, Kevin. "'How the West Was Won': Christian Expansion before and after the Protestant Reformation." *Andrews University Seminary Studies* 56:1 (Spring 2018) 115–40.

Cardinal, Harold, and Walter Hildebrandt. *Treaty Elders of Saskatchewan.* Calgary, AB: University of Calgary Press, 2000.

Carlson, Kay. "Origin of the Round Dance Ceremony." *WAVAW,* April 13, 2015. https://www.wavaw.ca/blogsround-dance-ceremony/.

Carr, David. *Holy Resilience: The Bible's Traumatic Origins.* New Haven, CT: Yale University Press, 2014.

Carson, Rachel. *Silent Spring.* Boston: Houghton Mifflin, 1962.

Carter, Sarah. *Aboriginal People and Colonizers of Western Canada to 1900.* Toronto: University of Toronto Press, 1999.

———. *Lost Harvests: Prairie Indian Reserve Farmers and Government Policy.* 2nd ed. McGill-Queen's Native and Northern Series. Montreal: McGill-Queen's University Press, 2019.

Cason, Colleen. "Chumash Beliefs Defy Easy Labels." *Ventura County Star,* October 10, 2015. http://archive.vcstar.com/news/columnists/colleen-cason-chumash-beliefs-defy-easy-labels-ep-1314946608–351049001.html/.

Castillo, Elias. *A Cross of Thorns: The Enslavement of California's Indians by the Spanish Mission.* Fresno, CA: Craven Street, 2015.

Cavanagh, Edward, and Lorenzo Veracini, eds. *The Routledge Handbook of the History of Settler Colonialism.* Philadelphia: Routledge, 2016.

Cave, Kate, and Shianne McKay. "Water Song: Indigenous Women and Water." *Resilience,* December 12, 2016. https://www.resilience.org/stories/2016–12–12/water-song-indigenous-women-and-water/.

Caven, Febna. "Being Idle No More: The Women behind the Movement." *Cultural Survival Quarterly,* March 2013. https://www.culturalsurvival.org/publications/cultural-survival-quarterly/being-idle-no-more-women-behind-movement.

Cecco, Leyland. "Pope Faces Indigenous Canadians' Anger over Refusal to Apologize for Past Abuse." *The Guardian,* March 30, 2018. https://www.theguardian.com/world/2018/mar/30/pope-francis-indigenous-canadians-residential-schools.

Chao, Melody Manchi, Ying-yi Hong, and Chi-yue Chiu. "Essentializing Race: Its Implications on Racial Categorization." *Journal of Personality and Social Psychology* 104:4 (2013) 619–34.

Charles, Mark, and Soong-Chan Rah. *Unsettling Truths: The Ongoing, Dehumanizing Legacy of the Doctrine of Discovery.* Downers Grove, IL: InterVarsity, 2019.

Charleston, Steve. *The Four Vision Quests of Jesus.* Atlanta: Morehouse, 2015.

Charleston, Steve, and Elaine Robinson, eds. *Coming Full Circle: Constructing Native Christian Theology.* Minneapolis: Fortress, 2015.

Chatwin, Bruce. *The Songlines.* London: Penguin, 1988.

Chavez, Yve. "Indigenous Artists, Ingenuity, and Resistance at the California Missions after 1769." PhD diss., UCLA, 2017. https://escholarship.org/content/qt355609rf/qt355609rf.pdf.

"Chief Rod Okemow Refuses Treaty Gifts." *Saskatchewan Indian* 6:8 (August 1976) 38.

Chrysostom, John. *The Fathers of the Church: St. John Chrysostom on Repentance and Almsgiving.* Translated by Gus George Christo. Washington, DC: The Catholic University of America Press, 2005.

Clapp, Jake. "Ronald Lewis, Culture Bearer and Director of House of Dance & Feathers, Has Died." *Gambit,* March 20, 2020. https://www.nola.com/gambit/music/article_32a067ee-6af8–11ea-af6e-b70b42dd9971.html?fbclid=IwAR266uziIuF_AYvUyiY4NuHi_HH9FpXjrFEEsvcE2v2qPoqmGIOxNiOLYTY.

Clark, Jerry L. "Thus Spoke Chief Seattle: The Story of an Undocumented Speech." *Prologue Magazine* 18:1 (1985). http://www.archives.gov/publications/prologue/1985/spring/chief-seattle.html#T21).

Clarke, Chris. "Untold History: The Survival of California's Indians." *KCET,* September 26, 2016. https://www.kcet.org/shows/tending-the-wild/untold-history-the-survival-of-californias-indians.

Cocker, Mark. *Rivers of Blood, Rivers of Gold: Europe's Conquest of Indigenous Peoples.* New York: Grove, 1998.

Cole, Pat. "Native American Speaker Says Repudiating 'Discovery' Doctrine Will Address Historic Harm: Lorenzo Says Generations Have Been Abused, Traumatized." *PCUSA General Assembly News,* June 20, 2018. https://www.pcusa.org/news/2018/6/20/native-american-speaker-says-repudiating-discovery/.

Committee of the Honorable the Privy Council, Canadian Superintendent General of Indian Affairs, Department of the Interior. "Report of the Committee of the Honorable the Privy Council, Approved by His Excellency on the 23rd January, 1895." Copies accessed in Leonard Doell private archives.

————. "Report of the Committee of the Honorable the Privy Council, Approved by His Excellency on the 11th May 1897." Copies accessed in Leonard Doell private archives.

Conching, Andie Kealohi Sato, and Zaneta Thayer. "Biological Pathways for Historical Trauma to Affect Health: A Conceptual Model Focusing on Epigenetic Modifications." *Social Science & Medicine* 230 (April 2019) 74–82.

Cone, James. *Martin & Malcolm & America: A Dream or a Nightmare.* 20th Anniversary ed. Maryknoll, NY: Orbis, 2012.

————. *The Spirituals and the Blues.* Maryknoll, NY: Orbis, 1992.

Copeland, M. Shawn. *Enfleshing Freedom: Body, Race, and Being.* Intersections in African American Theology. Minneapolis: Fortress, 2009.

Cordero, Jonathan. "Missionized California Indian Futures." *News from Native California* 28:2 (Winter 2014) 63.

Cordero, Roberta. "Full Circle Chumash Cross Channel in Tomol to Santa Cruz Island." https://channelislands.noaa.gov/maritime/chumash1.html.

Corrigan, Chris. "We Are All Treaty People." http://www.chriscorrigan.com/parkinglot/we-are-all-treaty-people/.

Costa, Dora, Noelle Yetter, and Heather DeSomer. "Intergenerational Transmission of Paternal Trauma among US Civil War ex-POWs." *Proceedings of the National Academy of Sciences of the United States of America* 115:44 (2018) 11215–20. https://www.pnas.org/content/115/44/11215.

Costello, Damien. *Black Elk: Colonialism and Lakota Catholicism.* Maryknoll, NY: Orbis, 2005.

Cox, Alicia. "Settler Colonialism." *Oxford Bibliographies,* July 26, 2017. https://www.oxfordbibliographies.com/view/document/obo-9780190221911/obo-9780190221911-0029.xml.

Crabtree, Vixen. "The Mystical Number Seven." *Human Religions*, May 3, 2015. http://www.humanreligions.info/seven.html.

Crespi, Juan. *A Description of Distant Roads, Original Journals of the First Expedition into California, 1769–1770.* Edited and Translated by Alan K. Brown. San Diego: San Diego State University Press, 2001.

Crook, Wilson, Jr., and R. King Harris, "A Pleistocene Campsite Near Lewisville, Texas." *American Antiquity* 23:3 (1958) 233–46.

Crous, Ernst, and Adolf Ens. "Privileges (Privilegia)." *Global Anabaptist Mennonite Encyclopedia Online* (1989). https://gameo.org/index.php?title=Privileges_(Privilegia)&oldid=161249.

Curtice, Kaitlin. *Native: Identity, Belonging, and Rediscovering God.* Grand Rapids: Brazos, 2020.

Cuypers, Daniël, Daniel Janssen, and Jacques Haers, eds. *Public Apology between Ritual and Regret: Symbolic Excuses on False Pretenses or True Reconciliation out of Sincere Regret?* Probing the Boundaries Series 86. Amsterdam: Rodopi, 2013.

Dahill, Lisa. "'Unworthy of the Earth': Fallibilism, Place, Terra Nullius, and Christian Mission." In *The Grace of Being Fallible in Philosophy, Theology, and Religion,* edited by Thomas John Hastings and Knut-Willy Saether, 67–88. New York: Palgrave Macmillan. Forthcoming.

Dale, Norman George. "Decolonizing the Empathic Settler Mind: An Autoethnographic Inquiry." PhD diss., Antioch University, 2014. https://aura.antioch.edu/cgi/viewcontent.cgi?article=1158&context=etds.

Damico, Noelle. "Presbytery of Hudson River Transfers Title of Former Church to Sweetwater Cultural Center." *The Presbyterian Outlook,* December 6, 2019. https://pres-outlook.org/2019/12/presbytery-of-hudson-river-transfers-title-of-former-church-to-sweetwater-cultural-center./.

Daschuk, James. *Clearing the Plains: Disease, Politics of Starvation, and the Loss of Aboriginal Life.* Regina, SK: University of Regina Press, 2013.

Davidson, Keay. "Did Ancient Polynesians Visit California? Maybe so." *SFGate News,* June 20, 2005. https://www.sfgate.com/news/article/Did-ancient-Polynesians-visit-California-Maybe-2661327.php.

Davis, Ellen. *Scripture, Culture and Agriculture: An Agrarian Reading of the Bible.* New York: Cambridge University Press, 2008.

Davis, Fania. *The Little Book of Race and Restorative Justice: Black Lives, Healing and U.S. Social Transformation.* New York: Good, 2019.

Davis, Murphy. *Surely Goodness and Mercy: A Journey into Illness and Solidarity.* Baltimore: Open Door, 2020.

Dawson, Anna-Lilja. "Buffalo Child Stone Rediscovered in Lake Diefenbaker." *The Sheaf,* September 11, 2014. https://thesheaf.com/2014/09/11/buffalo-child-stone-rediscovered-in-lake-diefenbaker/.

Day, Iyko. "Being or Nothingness: Indigeneity, Antiblackness, and Settler Colonial Critique." *Critical Ethnic Studies* 1:2 (2015) 102–21.

Daye, Russell. *Political Forgiveness: Lessons from South Africa.* Eugene, OR: Wipf & Stock, 2011.

Dear, John, S.J. "The Experiments of Gandhi: Nonviolence in the Nuclear Age." https://www.mkgandhi.org/articles/johndear.htm.

DeGruy, Joy. *Post Traumatic Slave Syndrome: America's Legacy of Enduring Injury and Healing.* Milwaukie, OR: Uptone, 2005.

De La Torre, Miguel. *Trails of Hope and Terror: Testimonies on Immigration.* Maryknoll, NY: Orbis, 2009.

Deloria, Vine. *Custer Died for Your Sins: An Indian Manifesto.* Norman: University of Oklahoma Press, 1969.

———. *Evolution, Creationism, and Other Modern Myths.* Golden, CO: Fulcrum, 2002.

———. *God Is Red: A Native View of Religion.* Ann Arbor, MI: Fulcrum, 2003.

———. *We Talk, You Listen: New Tribes, New Turf.* New York: MacMillan, 1970.

Dempsey, Hugh A. *Big Bear: The End of Freedom.* Regina, SK: University of Regina Press, 2006.

Desmarais, Annette, Darrin Qualman, André Magnan, and Nettie Wiebe. "Land Grabbing and Land Concentration: Mapping Changing Patterns of Farmland Ownership in Three Rural Municipalities in Saskatchewan, Canada." *Canadian Food Studies/La Revue canadienne des* études *sur l'alimentation* 2:1 (2015) 16–47.

DiAngelo, Robin. *White Fragility: Why It's so Hard for White People to Talk about Racism.* Boston: Beacon, 2018.

Dickason, Olive Patricia. *Canada's First Nations: A History of Founding Peoples from Earliest Times.* Toronto: McClelland and Stuart, 1992.

Dickman, Cassie. "Protesters of Christopher Columbus 'Genocide' Climb Statue, Get Arrested at California Capitol." *The Sacramento Bee,* June 05, 2018. https://www.sacbee.com/news/politics-government/article212594239.html.

Dodd, Elizabeth S., and Carl Findley, eds. *Innocence Uncovered: Literary and Theological Perspectives.* Philadelphia: Routledge, 2017.

Doell, Leonard. "History of Mennonites and Natives in the Last One Hundred Years." Report to MC Canada. Unpublished manuscript, August 31, 1977.

———. "The 1976 Treaty Six Commemoration: Mennonites Learning the Story." Unpublished manuscript, August 2012.

———. "Report to Mennonite Central Committee Saskatchewan." Unpublished manuscript, February 2011. https://mcccanada.ca/sites/mcccanada.ca/files/media/saskatchewan/documents/young_chippewayan_indian_reserve.pdf.

———. "Young Chippewayan Indian Reserve No.107 and Mennonite Farmers in Saskatchewan." *Journal of Mennonite Studies* 19 (2001) 165–67.

Doreian, Patrick, and Thomas Fararo, eds. *The Problem of Solidarity Theories and Models.* Philadelphia: Routledge, 1998.

Dougherty, Michael. *To Steal a Kingdom: Probing Hawaiian History.* Honolulu: Island Style, 2000.

Douglas, Kelly Brown. *The Black Christ.* Maryknoll, NY: Orbis, 1993.

Douglass, James. *Gandhi and the Unspeakable: His Final Experiment with Truth.* Maryknoll, NY: Orbis, 2012.

Downey, Jack, and Kathleen Holscher. "What the U.S. Catholic Church Gets Wrong about Native Dispossession." *Religion & Politics,* January 29, 2019. https://religionandpolitics.org/2019/01/29/covington-what-the-u-s-catholic-church-gets-wrong-about-native-dispossession/.

Driedger, Leo. "Changing Mennonite Family Roles: From Rural Boundaries to Urban Networks." *International Journal of Sociology of the Family* 13:2 (1983) 63–81.

———. "Louis Riel and the Mennonite Invasion." *The Canadian Mennonite* 18 (August 28, 1970) 6ff.

————. "Native Rebellion and Mennonite Invasion: An Examination of Two Canadian River Valleys." *Mennonite Quarterly Review* 46 (1972) 290–300.

Driedger, Leo, Roy Vogt, and Mavis Reimer. "Mennonite Intermarriage: National, Regional and Intergenerational Trends." *Mennonite Quarterly Review* 41 (1983) 132–44.

Dugdale, John. "Roots of the Problem: The Controversial History of Alex Haley's Book." *The Guardian*, February 9, 2017. https://www.theguardian.com/books/booksblog/2017/feb/09/alex-haley-roots-reputation-authenticity.

Dunbar-Ortiz, Roxanne. *An Indigenous Peoples' History of the United States*. Boston: Beacon, 2015.

————. "White Americans Need to Stop Assuming Native American Culture Belongs to Them, too." *Quartz*, October 10, 2016. https://qz.com/805704/columbus-day-cultural-appropriation-white-americans-need-to-stop-assuming-native-american-culture-belongs-to-them-too/.

Duran, Eduardo, Allen Ivey, and Derald Wing Sue, eds. *Healing the Soul Wound: Counseling with American Indians and Other Native People*. New York: Teachers College Press, 2006.

Duran, Eduardo, and Bonnie Duran. *Native American Postcolonial Psychology*. Reprint ed. New York: State University of New York Press, 1995.

Dyck, Harvey, John Staple, and John B. Toews. *Nestor Makhno and the Eichenfeld Massacre: A Civil War Tragedy in a Ukrainian Mennonite Village*. Kitchener, ON: Pandora, 2004.

Dykstra, Laurel, and Ched Myers, eds. *Liberating Biblical Study: Scholarship, Art, and Action in Honor of the Center and Library for the Bible and Social Justice*. The Center and Library for the Bible and Justice Series 1. Eugene, OR: Cascade, 2011.

Ehle, John. *Trail of Tears: The Rise and Fall of the Cherokee Nation*. New York: Anchor, 1988.

Eidt, Jack. "Chumash Story: Seeds of Creation and the Rainbow Bridge." *Wilder Utopia*, March 20, 2016. https://www.wilderutopia.com/traditions/myth/chumash-story-seeds-of-creation-and-the-rainbow-bridge/.

Elliott, Alicia. "Canada Grapples with a Charge of 'Genocide.' For Indigenous People, There's No Debate." *The Washington Post*, June 11, 2019. https://www.washingtonpost.com/opinions/2019/06/11/canada-grapples-with-charge-genocide-indigenous-people-theres-no-debate/.

Elliott, Michael. "Indigenous Resurgence: The Drive for Renewed Engagement and Reciprocity in the Turn Away from the State." *Canadian Journal of Political Science* 51:1 (2018) 61–81.

Ellsberg, Robert. *All Saints: Daily Reflections on Saints, Prophets, and Witnesses for Our Time*. Chestnut Ridge, NY: Crossroads, 1997.

————. *Blessed among All Women: Women Saints, Prophets, and Witnesses for Our Time*. Chestnut Ridge, NY: Crossroads, 2005.

————. "Las Casas' Discovery: What the 'Protector of the Indians' Found in America." *America*, November 5, 2012. https://www.americamagazine.org/issue/las-casas-discovery.

Enns, Beno, and Ernest Baergen, eds. *Family of Franz and Katharina Enns*. Saskatoon, SK: Self-published, 2000.

Enns, Elaine. "Facing History with Courage: Toward Restorative Solidarity with Our Indigenous Neighbors." *Canadian Mennonite* 10:5 (2015) 4–9.

———. "Journey into Restorative Justice." *Rock! Paper! Scissors!* 1:3 (March 2019). https://www.jesusradicals.com/vol-1-no-3/journey-into-restorative-justice.

———. "A Shameful Legacy." *Sojourners* 41.11(December 2012) 8–9.

———. "Trauma and Memory: Challenges to Settler Solidarity." *Consensus* 37:1 (2016) 1–12.

Enns, Elaine, and Ched Myers. *Ambassadors of Reconciliation, Vol II: Diverse Christian Practices of Restorative Justice and Peacemaking.* 2 vols. Marynoll, NY: Orbis, 2009.

Enns, S. Touser. *Sooner or Later: Where the Enns Meet.* Saskatoon: Riel Crescent, 1977.

Enomoto, Kekoa Catherine. "The Kahoʻolawe Nine 30 Years Later." *The Maui News,* April 4, 2006. https://www.moolelo.com/kahoolawe-nine.html.

Ens, Adolf. "Mennonite Relations with Governments: Western Canada, 1870–1925." PhD diss., University of Ottawa, 1978.

———. *Subjects or Citizens? The Mennonite Experience of Canada, 1870–1925.* Ottawa: University of Ottawa Press, 1994.

Epp, Frank H. *Mennonite Exodus: The Rescue and Resettlement of the Russian Mennonites Since the Communist Revolution.* Altona, MB: Canadian Mennonite Relief and Immigration Council, 1962.

———. *Mennonites in Canada, 1786–1920: The History of a Separate People,* Vol. 1. 2 vols. Toronto: Macmillan, 1974.

———. *Mennonites in Canada, 1920–1940: A People's Struggle for Survival,* Vol. 2. 2 vols. Toronto: Macmillan, 1982.

Epp Frank H. and Leo Driedger. "Mennonites." *The Canadian Encyclopedia,* April 15, 2015. https://www.thecanadianencyclopedia.ca/en/article/mennonites.

Epp, George, ed. *Roots & Wings: 100 Years of Rosthern Junior College.* Rosthern, SK: Rosthern Junior College Press, 2005.

Epp, Henry, and Tim E. H. Jones. "Prehistory, Southern Saskatchewan." https://teaching.usask.ca/indigenoussk/import/prehistory_southern_saskatchewan.php.

Epp, Marlene. "The Memory of Violence: Soviet and East European Mennonite Refugees and Rape in the Second World War." *Journal of Women's History* 9:1 (1997) 58–87.

———. *Mennonite Women in Canada: A History.* Winnipeg: University of Manitoba Press, 2008.

———. *Women without Men: Mennonite Refugees of the Second World War.* Toronto: University of Toronto Press, 2000.

Epp, Roger. "'There Was No One Here When We Came': Overcoming the Settler Problem." *The Conrad Grebel Review* 30:2 (2012) 115–26. https://uwaterloo.ca/grebel/sites/ca.grebel/files/uploads/files/cgr-30-2-s2012-2.pdf.

———. *We Are All Treaty People: Prairie Essays.* Edmonton: University of Alberta Press, 2008.

Erlandson, Jon, and Terry Jones, eds. *Catalysts to Complexity: Late Holocene Societies of the California Coast.* Perspectives in California Archaeology 6. Los Angeles: Cotsen Institute of Archaeology, 2002.

Estep, William. *The Anabaptist Story.* Grand Rapids: Eerdmans, 1963.

Fadel, Leila. "Columbus Day or Indigenous Peoples' Day?" *NPR,* October 14, 2019. https://www.npr.org/2019/10/14/769083847/columbus-day-or-indigenous-peoples-day.

Fairclough, Adam. *To Redeem the Soul of America: The Southern Christian Leadership Conference and Martin Luther King, Jr.* Rev. ed. Athens: University of Georgia Press, 2001.

Fast, Henry. *A Grandson Remembers: Family of Jakob K. Fast (1871–1947) and Helena Wiebe (1871–1941).* S.l.: Self-published, 2018.

Fellows, Mary Louise, and Sherene H. Razack. "The Race to Innocence: Confronting Hierarchical Relations among Women." *The Journal of Gender, Race and Justice* 1:2 (1998) 335–52.

Field, Nigel P., Sophear Muong, and Vannavuth Sochanvimean. "Parental Styles in the Intergenerational Transmission of Trauma Stemming from the Khmer Rouge Regime in Cambodia." *The American Journal of Orthopsychiatry* 83:4 (2013) 483–94.

Fontaine, Nahanni. "The Enduring Violence against Indigenous Women in Canada." *Dateline,* November 1, 2018. https://www.sbs.com.au/news/dateline/the-enduring-violence-against-indigenous-women-in-canada.

Foster, Wayne. "The Makhnovists and the Mennonites: War and Peace in the Ukrainian Revolution." *Libcom.org,* May 25, 2011. https://libcom.org/history/makhnovists-mennonites-war-peace-ukrainian-civil-war#footnote2_35xei88.

Fowler, Jennifer. "Creator of Sixties Scoop Adoption Program Says It Wasn't Meant to Place Kids with White Families." *CBC News,* October 20, 2018. https://www.cbc.ca/news/indigenous/creator-of-sixties-scoop-adoption-program-says-it-wasn-t-meant-to-place-kids-with-white-families-1.4584342.

Francis, Douglas, and Howard Palmer. *The Prairie West: Historical Readings.* Edmonton: University of Alberta Press, 1992.

Frank, Miriam Anne, and Alexandra Carraher-King. "Commemorating the 50th Anniversary of the Occupation of Alcatraz." *Cultural Survival,* November 20, 2019. https://www.culturalsurvival.org/news/commemorating-50th-anniversary-occupation-alcatraz.

Fraser, Keith. "Pipeline Protestors Convicted of Civil Contempt of Court Get 7 Days in Jail." *The Province,* November 23, 2018. https://theprovince.com/news/local-news/pipeline-protesters-convicted-of-civil-contempt-of-court-get-7-days-jail/wcm/f2112e27-ca3f-46db-b496-b8664f3a2955.

Freeman, Victoria. "Indigenous Hauntings in Settler-Colonial Spaces." In *Phantom Past, Indigenous Presence,* edited by Colleen Boyd and Coll Thrush, 209–54. Lincoln: University of Nebraska Press, 2011.

French, Howard. "Dark Side of Security Quest: Squalor at an Atoll." *The New York Times,* June 11, 2001. https://www.nytimes.com/2001/06/11/world/dark-side-of-security-quest-squalor-on-an-atoll.html.

Friesen, Gerald. *The Canadian Prairies: A History.* Toronto: University of Toronto Press, 1987.

Friesen, Jeff, and Steve Heinrichs, eds. *Quest for Respect: The Church and Indigenous Spirituality.* Special issue of *Intotemak.* Winnipeg: Mennonite Church Canada, 2017.

Friesen, Katarina. "The Great Commission: Watershed Conquest or Watershed Discipleship?" In *Watershed Discipleship: Reinhabiting Bioregional Faith and Practice,* edited by Ched Myers, 26–41. Eugene, OR: Cascade, 2016.

Galloway, Jim. "Raphael Warnock and a Sunday Sermon for a Shell-Shocked City of Atlanta." *The Atlanta Journal Constitution*, May 31, 2020. https://www.ajc.com/blog/politics/raphael-warnock-and-sunday-sermon-for-shell-shocked-city-atlanta/EcFL2Tz9TuxvgB3fIgxosN/.

Gamble, Lynn H. *The Chumash World at European Contact: Power, Trade and Feasting among Complex Hunter-Gatherers.* Berkeley: University of California Press, 2008.

Gerbrandt, Irma Toews, ed. *Remembering the Schulzes: From Pomerania to Russia to Canada.* Saskatoon, SK: Self-published, 1999.

Gibson, Robert. *The Chumash.* New York: Chelsea House, 1990.

Giesbrecht, Donovan. "Métis, Mennonites and the 'Unsettled Prairie,' 1874–1896." *Journal of Mennonite Studies* 19 (2001) 103–11.

Giladi, Lotem, and Terece Bell. "Protective Factors for Intergenerational Transmission of Trauma among Second- and Third-Generation Holocaust Survivors." *Psychological Trauma* 5:4 (2013) 384–91.

Gilbert, Jeremy. "Notes Towards a Theory of Solidarity." https://jeremygilbertwriting.wordpress.com/notes-towards-a-theory-of-solidarity/.

Gilio-Whitaker, Dina. "Settler Fragility: Why Settler Privilege Is so Hard to Talk About." *Beacon Broadside,* November 14, 2018. https://www.beaconbroadside.com/broadside/2018/11/settler-fragility-why-settler-privilege-is-so-hard-to-talk-about.tml?fbclid=IwAR2HxGPbcx5D1f4bBD1lVwlF82WOns9W5oXVaY79jQoPriOeULuGIlGabk4.

Gilley, Christopher. "Makhno, Nestor Ivanovich." *International Encyclopedia of the First World War,* October 8, 2018. https://encyclopedia.1914–1918-online.net/article/makhno_nestor_ivanovich.

Gilpin, Emilee. "Indigenous Matriarchs Stand Together in Dark Times." *Canada's National Observer*, May 7, 2019. https://www.nationalobserver.com/2019/05/07/features/indigenous-matriarchs-stand-together-dark-times?fbclid=IwAR3YgOI7WxMcWyxkfzz_drhu6IGr95v1tiYkecV2JruOzWogfbUbpDboU38.

Giroux, Henry. "The Terror of the Unforeseen: Rethinking the Normalization of Fascism in the Post-Truth Era." www.semcoop.com/terror-unforeseen-rethinking-normalization-fascism-post-truth-era-henry-giroux.

Gismondi, Melissa. "American Churches Are Apologizing for a Centuries-Old Injustice That Still Reverberates Today." *Washington Post*, September 14, 2018. https://www.washingtonpost.com/outlook/2018/09/14/american-churches-are-apologizing-centuries-old-mistake-that-still-reverberates-today/.

Goatley, David Emmanuel. *Were You There? Godforsakenness in Slave Religion.* Maryknoll, NY: Orbis, 1996.

Gonzalez, Ray, ed. *Without Discovery: A Native Response to Columbus.* Seattle: Broken Moon, 1992.

Goodwin, Rob. *Eclipse in Mission: Dispelling the Shadow of Our Idols.* Eugene, OR: Resource, 2012.

Goossen, Ben. *Chosen Nation: Mennonites and Germany in a Global Era.* Princeton: Princeton University Press, 2017.

———. "Mennonites and the Holocaust: An Introduction." *Anabaptist Historians,* February 7, 2018. https://anabaptisthistorians.org/2018/02/07/mennonites-and-the-holocaust-an-introduction/#fnref-4707–5.

Gordon, Avery. *Ghostly Matters: Haunting and the Sociological Imagination.* Minneapolis: University of Minnesota Press, 1997.

———. "Some Thoughts on Haunting and Futurity." *borderlands* 10:2 (2011) 2–3. http://averygordon.net/files/GordonHauntingFuturity.pdf.

Gowder, Paul. "What Is a Native American Round Dance? History, Music, & Meaning." *PowWows.com*, February 26, 2020. https://www.powwows.com/what-is-a-native-american-round-dance-history-music-meaning/.

Grabish, Austin. "Drag the Red Searchers Get Grim Lesson on Finding, Identifying Bones." *CBC News*, June 17, 2017. https://www.cbc.ca/news/canada/manitoba/drag-the-red-bones-1.4166029#:~:text=Drag%20the%20Red%20started%20in,to%20pull%20up%20possible%20remains.

Graeber, David. *Debt: The First 5,000 Years*. Brooklyn, NY: Melville House, 2011.

Gramsci, Antonio. *Selections from the Prison Notebooks of Antonio Gramsci*. Edited by Quentin Hoare and Geoffrey Nowell Smith. New York: International, 1971.

Grant, Sarah. "Robbie Robertson Talks Native American Heritage, New Children's Book." *Rolling Stone*, December 4, 2015. https://www.rollingstone.com/music/music-news/robbie-robertson-talks-native-american-heritage-new-childrens-book-43669/.

Gray, Lucy Anna. "Forgotten Women: The Conversation of Murdered and Missing Native Women Is Not One North America Wants to Have—But It Must." *Independent,* August 14, 2018. https://www.independent.co.uk/news/long_reads/native-american-women-missing-murder-mmiw-inquiry-canada-us-violence-indigenous-a8487976.html.

Greenson, Thadeus. "Duluwat Island Is Returned to the Wiyot Tribe in Historic Ceremony." *North Coast Journal*, October 21, 2019. https://www.northcoastjournal.com/NewsBlog/archives/2019/10/21/duluwat-island-is-returned-to-the-wiyot-tribe-in-historic-ceremony?fbclid=IwAR0fvMrf5tO5SMhhChGQS1bfFI5UiyvOPEgglEvZ3VC7Z9dGSLwfZIFUvlk.

Greenwood, David. "A Critical Theory of Place-Conscious Education." In *International Handbook of Research on Environmental Education*, edited by Robert B. Stevenson, Michael Brody, Justin Dillon, and Arjen E. J. Wals, 93–100. Philadelphia: Routledge, 2013.

Greenwood, Roberta S., and R. O. Browne. "The Chapel of Santa Gertrudis." *Pacific Coasts Archaelogical Society Quarterly* 4:4 (1968) 1–60.

Griffith, Andrew. "Building a Mosaic: The Evolution of Canada's Approach to Immigrant Integration." *Migration Policy Institute*, November 1, 2017. https://www.migrationpolicy.org/article/building-mosaic-evolution-canada-approach-immigrant-integration.

Grillo, Gina. "Water Walk Along North Shore Shines Light on Conservation and Stewardship." *Chicago Tribune*, March 25, 2019. https://www.chicagotribune.com/suburbs/wilmette/ct-wml-nibi-water-walk-tl-0328-story.html.

Gringauz, Lev. "Young Jews Created an Online Community for Kvetching—Jewbook." *New Voices,* April 17, 2018. https://newvoices.org/2018/04/17/young-jews-created-an-online-community-for-kvetching-its-called-jewbook/.

Grossman, Zoltán. *Unlikely Alliances: Native Nations and White Communities Join to Defend Rural Lands*. Seattle: University of Washington Press, 2017.

Guenter, Doreen, ed. *Hague-Osler Mennonite Reserve, 1895–1995*. Saskatoon, SK: Hague-Osler Reserve Book Committee, 1995.

Gura, Philip. *The Life of William Apess, Pequot*. Chapel Hill: University of North Carolina Press, 2015.

Gyapong, Deborah. "Indigenous Couple Live a Life of Reconciliation." *Canadian Catholic News*, November 25, 2016. https://www.catholicregister.org/item/23682-indigenous-couple-live-a-life-of-reconciliation.

Haley, Alex. *Roots: The Saga of an American Family*. Philadelphia: Da Capo, 1976.

Hamm, Peter. *Continuity and Change among Canadian Mennonite Brethren*. Waterloo, ON: Wilfrid Laurier University Press, 1987.

Hampton, Carol, and Malcolm Naea Chun, eds. *Creation and Other Stories*. Themed issue of *First Peoples Theology Journal* 2:1 (September 2001).

Hanson, Erin. "The Indian Act." https://indigenousfoundations.arts.ubc.ca/the_indian_act/.

Hanson, Stanley D. "KITCHI-MANITO-WAYA." *Dictionary of Canadian Biography*. http://www.biographi.ca/en/bio/kitchi_manito_waya_12E.html.

Haraway, Donna. *Staying with the Trouble: Making Kin in the Chthulucene*. Durham, NC: Duke University Press, 2016.

Harder, Helmut. *David Toews Was Here, 1870–1947*. Winnipeg: Canada Mennonite Bible College Press, 2002.

Harding, Vincent, Jr. *Hope and History: Why We Must Share the Story of the Movement*. Rev ed. Maryknoll, NY: Orbis, 2010.

———. *There Is a River: The Black Struggle for Freedom in America*. New York: Houghton Mifflin Harcourt, 1981.

Harrison, Summer. "'We Need New Stories:' Trauma, Storytelling, and the Mapping of Environmental Injustice in Linda Hogan's *Solar Storms* and Standing Rock." *The American Indian Quarterly* 43:1 (2019) 1–35. https://www.muse.jhu.edu/article/720012.

Hartmann, W. E., Dennis C. Wendt, Rachel L. Burrage, Andrew Pomerville, and Joseph P. Gone. "American Indian Historical Trauma: Anti-Colonial Prescriptions for Healing Resilience and Survivance." *American Psychologist* 74:1 (2019) 6–19.

Heath, Jessica. "The Bison: From 30 million to 325 (1884) to 500,000 (today)." https://www.flatcreekinn.com/bison-americas-mammal/.

Heinrichs, Steve. "Confessing the Past: Mennonites and the Indians School System." https://www.commonword.ca/ResourceView/43/16436.

Heinrichs, Steve, ed. *Buffalo Shout, Salmon Cry: Conversations on Creation, Land Justice and Life Together*. Harrisburg, PA: Herald, 2013.

———. *Unsettling the Word: Biblical Experiments in Decolonization*. Altona, MB: Mennonite Church Canada, 2018.

———. *Wrongs to Rights: How Churches Can Engage the United Nations Declaration on the Rights of Indigenous Peoples*. Special issue of *Intotemak*. Winnipeg: Mennonite Church Canada, 2016.

Heizer, Robert. *The Destruction of California Indians*. Lincoln: University of Nebraska Press, 1974.

———. "The Eighteen Unratified Treaties of 1851–1852 between the California Indians and the United States Government." Berkeley, CA: Archaeological Research Facility, Department of Anthropology, University of California Berkeley, 1972. https://digitalassets.lib.berkeley.edu/anthpubs/ucb/text/arfs003-001.pdf.

———. "Treaties." In *Handbook of North American Indians, Vol 8: California*, edited by William Sturtevant, 701–4. 20 vols. New York: HarperCollins, 1978.

Henderson, Phil. "Imagoed Communities: The Psychosocial Space of Settler Colonialism." *Settler Colonial Studies* 7:1 (2017) 40–56. www.tandfonline.com/doi/abs/10.1080/2201473X.2015.1092194.

Hendricks, Obrey. *The Universe Bends toward Justice: Radical Reflections on the Bible, the Church, and the Body Politic*. Maryknoll, NY: Orbis, 2011.

Herman, Judith. *Trauma and Recovery: The Aftermath of Violence—From Domestic Abuse to Political Terror*. Rev. ed. New York: Basic, 2015.

Heschel, Abraham. *The Prophets II*. 2 vols. New York: Harper & Row, 1962.

Hiller, Chris. "'No, Do You Know What Your Treaty Rights Are?' Treaty Consciousness in a Decolonizing Frame." *Review of Education, Pedagogy, and Cultural Studies* 38:4 (2016) 381–408.

———. "Tracing the Spirals of Unsettlement: Euro-Canadian Narratives of Coming to Grips with Indigenous Sovereignty, Title, and Rights." *Settler Colonial Studies* 7:4 (2016) 415–40. https://www.tandfonline.com/doi/full/10.1080/220147 3X.2016.1241209.

Hinz-Penner, Raylene. *Searching for Sacred Ground: The Journey of Chief Lawrence Hart, Mennonite*. Telford, PA: Cascadia, 2007.

Hiskey, Michelle. "Pilgrims Bear Witness to Racial Reconciliation at Georgia Lynching Site." *Episcopal News Service*, October 25, 2016. https://www.episcopalnewsservice.org/2016/10/25/pilgrims-bear-witness-to-racial-reconciliation-at-georgia-lynching-site/.

Hoare, Quentin, and Geoffrey Nowell Smith. "Introduction to Gramsci." In *Selections from the Prison Notebooks*, edited and translated by Quentin Hoare and Geoffrey Nowell Smith. New York: International, 1971.

Hollyday, Joyce. *Clothed with the Sun: Biblical Women, Social Justice, and Us*. Louisville: Westminister John Knox, 1994.

Holmes, Barbara. *Joy Unspeakable: Contemplative Practices of the Black Church*. Minneapolis: Fortress, 2004.

Holtzman, Bob. "The Tomol Revival." *Indigenous Boats (Blog)*, February 9, 2013. http://indigenousboats.blogspot.com/2013/02/the-preservation-and-revival-of-tomol.html.

Hopkins, Dwight, and George Cummings, eds. *Cut Loose Your Stammering Tongue*. Louisville: Westminster John Knox, 2003.

Hopper, Tristin. "Here Is What Sir John A. Macdonald Did to Indigenous People." *The National Post*, August 28, 2018. https://nationalpost.com/news/canada/here-is-what-sir-john-a-macdonald-did-to-indigenous-people.

———. "How the Idle No More Movement Started and Where It Might Go from Here." *The National Post*, December 26, 2012. https://nationalpost.com/news/canada/idle-no-more-first-nations-protest-movement-theresa-spence.

Horne, Gerald. *The Apocalypse of Settler Colonialism: The Roots of Slavery, White Supremacy, and Capitalism in Seventeenth-Century North America and the Caribbean*. New York: Monthly Review, 2018.

Horsley, Richard, ed. *Paul and Empire: Religion and Power in Roman Imperial Society*. Harrisburg, PA: Trinity, 1997.

Howard-Brook, Wes, and Anthony Gwyther. *Unveiling Empire: Reading Revelation Then and Now*. Maryknoll, NY: Orbis, 1999.

Hsu, Hsuan. "Introduction." In *The Life and Adventures of Joaquín Murieta: The Celebrated California Bandit,* edited by Hsuan Hsu, xv–xxx. New York: Penguin, 2018.

Huber, Tim. "Land of the Kanza: Descendant of Immigrants Gives Portion from Sale of Family Land to Indigenous Heritage Society." *Mennonite World Review,* March 4, 2019. http://mennoworld.org/2019/03/04/news/land-of-the-kanza/.

Hudson, Michael. . . .*And Forgive Them Their Debts: Lending, Foreclosure and Redemption from Bronze Age Finance to the Jubilee Year.* Dresden: Institute for the Study of Long-Term Economic Trends, 2018.

Hughes, Quin, and Henry Eberhart. "Still Love These Lonely Places: A Hauntological Analysis of Evanston." *Evanstonian,* April 26, 2019. https://www.evanstonian.net/feature/2019/04/26/still-love-these-lonely-places-a-hauntological-analysis-of-evanston/.

Hurtado, Albert. *Indian Survival on the California Frontier.* New ed. New Haven: Yale University Press, 1990.

Iati, Marisa. "The U.S. Once Forced This Native American Tribe to Move. Now They're Getting Their Land Back." *The Washington Post,* September 20, 2019. https://www.washingtonpost.com/religion/2019/09/19/us-once-forced-this-native-american-tribe-move-now-theyre-getting-their-land-back/.

Ignatiev, Noel. *How the Irish Became White.* New York: Routledge, 1995.

Imbler, Sabrina. "How the Wiyot Tribe Won Back a Sacred California Island, and Finally Completed a Ceremony Interrupted by a Massacre in 1860." *Atlas Obscura,* November 15, 2019. https://www.atlasobscura.com/articles/wiyot-won-back-sacred-island.

Irland, Basia, "What the River Knows: Saskatchewan Delta at Cumberland House, Canada." *National Geographic,* July 1, 2017. https://blog.nationalgeographic.org/2017/07/01/what-the-river-knows-saskatchewan-delta-at-cumberland-house-canada/.

Jacobs, Adrian. "A History of Slaughter: Embracing Our Martyrdom on the Margins of Encounter." *Journal of North America Institute for Indigenous Theological Studies* 6 (2008) 159–72.

Jenkin, Paul. "The Manure Problem." *Ventura River Ecosystem,* November 23, 2009. https://www.venturariver.org/2009/11/manure-problem.html.

———. "Recovering Ventura River Steelhead." *The Osprey* 72 (2012) 10–12. http://friendsofventurariver.org/wp-content/themes/client-sites/venturariver/docs/ventura-river-steelhead-osprey-72.pdf.

Jinkerson, Jeremy. "Defining and Assessing Moral Injury: A Syndrome Perspective." *Traumatology* 22:2 (2016) 122–30.

John, Maria. "Toypurina: A Legend Etched in the Landscape of Los Angeles." *KCET,* May 15, 2014. https://www.kcet.org/history-society/toypurina-a-legend-etched-in-the-landscape-of-los-angeles.

John-Hall, Annette. "Propelled into a Life of Fighting for Liberties." *Philadelphia Inquirer,* April 23, 2010. https://www.inquirer.com/philly/news/local/20100423_Annette_John-Hall__Propelled_into_a_life_of_fighting_for_liberties.html.

Johnson, Giff. "Collision Course at Kwajalein." *Bulletin of Concerned Asian Scholars* 18:2 (1986) 28–41.

———. *Don't Ever Whisper: Darlene Keju, Pacific Health Pioneer, Champion for Nuclear Survivors.* Self-published: CreateSpace, 2013.

Johnson, James Weldon. "Lift Every Voice and Sing." https://www.poetryfoundation.org/poems/46549/lift-every-voice-and-sing.

Johnson, John. "Arlington Man." *National Park Service*, June 7, 2016. https://www.nps.gov/chis/learn/historyculture/arlington.htm.

———. "The Chumash Indians after Secularization." In *The Spanish Missionary Heritage of the United States: Selected Papers and Commentaries from the November 1990 Quincentenary Symposium*, edited by Howard Benoist and Sr. Maria Carolina Flores, 143–64. N.p.: United States National Park Service, 1993.

———. "The Trail to Fernando." *Journal of California and Great Basin Anthropology* 4:1 (1982) 132–38.

Jones, Serene. *Trauma and Grace: Theology in a Ruptured World*. 2nd ed. Louisville: Westminister John Knox, 2009.

Jordan, Clarence. *Cottonpatch Gospel: The Complete Collection*. Macon, GA: Smyth & Helwys, 2014.

Joseph, Bob. "21 Things You May Not Have Known about the Indian Act." *Indigenous Corporate Training*, June 2, 2015. https://www.ictinc.ca/blog/21-things-you-may-not-have-known-about-the-indian-act-.

Jung, Carl. *Psychology and Alchemy*. The Collected Works of C. G. Jung 12. Princeton: Princeton University Press, 1968.

Jungkunz, Vincent, and Julie White. "Ignorance, Innocence, and Democratic Responsibility: Seeing Race, Hearing Racism." *The Journal of Politics* 75:2 (2013) 436–50.

Kahoʻolawe Island Conveyance Commission. "Kaho òlawe Island: Restoring a Cultural Treasure: Final Report of the Kaho òlawe Island Conveyance Commission to the Congress of the United State." Washington, DC, March 31, 1993.

Kasdorf, Julia Spicher. *The Body and the Book: Writing from a Mennonite Life: Essays and Poems*. University Park, PA: Penn State University Press, 2009.

Kaufman, Roy. *The Drama of a Rural Community's Life Cycle: The Prehistory, Birth, Growth, Maturity, Decline, and Rebirth*. Eugene, OR: Wipf & Stock, 2020.

Kaylor, Brian. "Global Baptists Worship in Anabaptist Cave." *Word & Way*, July 1, 2018. https://wordandway.org/2018/07/01/bwa-anabaptist-cave/.

Kellermann, Natan. "Epigenetic Transmission of Holocaust Trauma: Can Nightmares Be Inherited?" *The Israel Journal of Psychiatry and Related Science* 50:1 (2013) 33–39.

Kenez, Peter. *A History of the Soviet Union from the Beginning to the End*. New York: Cambridge University Press, 1999.

Keningsber, Ben. "'Crip Camp' Review: After Those Summers, Nothing Was the Same." (March 25, 2020). https://www.nytimes.com/2020/03/24/movies/crip-camp-review.html.

Khazan, Olga. "Inherited Trauma Shapes Your Health." *The Atlantic*, October 16, 2018. https://www.theatlantic.com/health/archive/2018/10/trauma-inherited-generations/573055/.

Kicza, John. "Getting It Right about Getting It Wrong." Review of *Sinking Columbus: Contested History, Cultural Politics, and Mythmaking During the Quincentenary*, by Stephen Summerhill and John Alexander Williams. April 2002. https://www.h-net.org/reviews/showrev.php?id=6197.

Kidwell, Clara Sue, Homer Noley, and George E. Tinker. *A Native American Theology.* Maryknoll, NY: Orbis, 2001.

Kimmerer, Robin Wall. *Braiding Sweetgrass: Indigenous Wisdom, Scientific Knowledge and the Teachings of Plants.* Minneapolis: Milkweed, 2015.

King, Chester. "The Names and Locations of Historic Chumash Villages." *The Journal of California Anthropology* 2:2 (1975) 171–79. https://escholarship.org/content/qt8833ss5k5/qt8833ss5k5.pdf.

King, Martin Luther, Jr. *Why We Can't Wait.* Signet Classic ed. New York: Harper & Row, 2000.

King, Thomas. *The Inconvenient Indian: A Curious Account of Native People in North America.* Toronto: Doubleday Canada, 2012.

King, Tiffany Lethabo. *The Black Shoals: Offshore Formations of Black and Native Studies.* Durham, NC: Duke University Press, 2019.

———. "Settler Colonialism and African Americans." *Oxford Bibliographies,* May 29, 2019. https://www.oxfordbibliographies.com/view/document/obo-9780190280024/obo-9780190280024-0071.xml.

Kinsler, Ross, and Gloria Kinsler. *The Biblical Jubilee and the Struggle for Life.* Maryknoll, NY: Orbis, 1999.

Koithan, Mary, and Cynthia Farrell. "Indigenous Native American Healing Traditions." *Journal of Nurse Practitioners* 6:6 (2011) 477–78. https://www.ncbi.nlm.nih.gov/pmc/articles/PMC2913884/.

Kouri, Scott, and Hans Skott-Myhre. "Catastrophe: A Transversal Mapping of Colonialism and Settler Subjectivity." *Settler Colonial Studies* 6:3 (2016) 279–94. www.academia.edu/20441952/Catastrophe_a_transversal_mapping_of_colonialism_and_settler_subjectivity.

Krahn, Elizabeth. "Lifespan and Intergenerational Legacies of Soviet Oppression: An Autoethnography of Mennonite Women and Their Adult Children." *Journal of Mennonite Studies* 29 (2011) 21–43.

Kraus, Dan. "Why Canada's Prairies Are the World's Most Endangered Ecosystem." *Nature Conservancy Canada,* November 27, 2018. http://www.natureconservancy.ca/en/blog/archive/grasslands-the-most.html.

Kropotkin, Pëtr. *Mutual Aid: A Factor in Evolution.* New ed. Manchester, NH: Extending Horizons, 1976.

Kulish, Nicholas. "What It Costs to Be Smuggled across the U.S. Border." *New York Times,* June 30, 2018. https://www.nytimes.com/interactive/2018/06/30/world/smuggling-illegal-immigration-costs.html.

Kuykendall, Ralph. *The Hawaiian Kingdom, 1778–1854, Foundation and Transformation.* Honolulu: University of Hawaii Press, 1965.

Kylie, Aaron. "Connecting to 6,000 Years of History at Wanuskewin Heritage Park." *Canadian Geographic,* December 20, 2017. https://www.canadiangeographic.ca/article/connecting-6000-years-history-wanuskewin-heritage-park.

LaDuke, Winona. *All Our Relations: Native Struggles for Land and Life.* Boston: SouthEnd, 1999.

Lafond, Harry. "The Church and the Indigenous Peoples of Canada: A Cree Vision of the Church and My Experience as a Cree Catholic." In *Concilium 4 (Christianity and Indigenous Peoples),* edited by Michael Andraos, Bernardeth Caero Bustillos, and Geraldo De Mori, 50–58. London: SCM, 2019.

Lafond, Mika. *nipê wânîn (my way back): poems.* Saskatoon, SK: Thistledown, 2017.

Land, Clare. *Decolonizing Solidarity: Dilemmas and Directions for Supporters of Indigenous Struggles.* London: Zed, 2015.

Landy, David, Hilary Darcy, and José Gutiérrez. "Exploring the Problems of Solidarity." *Interface* 6:2 (2014) 26–34.

Lang, Julian, and Kayla Begay. "Creating New Speakers for a New Decade." *News from Native California* 33:3 (2020) 10–13.

LaRoque, Emma. *Defeathering the Indian.* Ottawa, ON: Book Society of Canada, 1975.

———. *When the Other is Me: Native Resistance Discourse 1850–1990.* Winnipeg: University of Manitoba Press, 2010.

Lee, Jo-Anne. "Non-White Settler and Indigenous Relations: Decolonizing Possibilities for Social Justice." *Lectora* 22 (2016) 13–26.

Lee, Robert, and Tristan Ahtone. "Land-Grab Universities: Expropriated Indigenous Land Is the Foundation of the Land-Grant University System." *High Country News,* April 1, 2020. https://www.hcn.org/issues/52.4/indigenous-affairs-education-land-grab-universities.

Leidos, Stephen Bryne. "The Wind Sycamore: A Chumash Sacred Site Near Ventura." *Society for California Archaeology Proceedings* 28 (2014) 50–60. https://scahome. org/wp-content/uploads/2014/10/Proceedings.28Bryne3.pdf.

Leroux, Darryl. *Distorted Descent: White Claims to Indigenous Identity.* Winnipeg: University of Manitoba Press, 2019.

Lessoff, Alan. "Ship Shape." *Texas Observer,* January 26, 2015. https://www. texasobserver.org/corpus-christi-columbus-ships/.

Levine, Ellen. *Henry's Freedom Box: A True Story from the Underground Railroad.* New York: Scholastic, 2007.

Levine, Peter, Abi Blakeslee, and Joshua Sylvae. "Reintegrating Fragmentation of the Primitive Self: Discussion of 'Somatic Experiencing.'" *Psychoanalytic Dialogues* 28:5 (2018) 620–28.

Levitz, Eric. "America Will Only Remain 'Majority White' if Blacks Remain an Underclass." *New York Intelligencer,* May 3, 2018. https://nymag.com/intelligencer/2018/05/for-america-to-be-white-blacks-must-be-an-underclass.html.

Lev-Wiesel, Rachel. "Intergenerational Transmission of Trauma across Three Generations." *Qualitative Social Work* 6:1 (2007) 75–94.

Lewis, Ted. "Take into Account All That Menno Wrote." *The Mennonite,* July 7, 2009. https://themennonite.org/feature/true-evangelical-faith/.

Librado, Fernando. *The Eye of the Flute: Chumash Traditional History and Ritual as Told by Fernando Librado Kitsepawit to John P. Harrington.* Santa Barbara: Santa Barbara Museum of Natural History, 1977.

Lightfoot, Kent. *Indians, Missionaries, and Merchants: The Legacy of Colonial Encounters on the California Frontier.* Berkeley: University of California Press, 2006.

Liliuokalani. *Hawaii's Story by Hawaii's Queen.* Boston: Lee and Shepard, 1898. https://digital.library.upenn.edu/women/liliuokalani/hawaii/hawaii.html.

Little, Becky. "How Boarding Schools Tried to 'Kill the Indian' through Assimilation: Native American Tribes Are Still Seeking the Return of Their Children." *History,* November 1, 2018. https://www.history.com/news/how-boarding-schools-tried-to-kill-the-indian-through-assimilation.

Logan, Leslie. "For Two Centuries These Lands Have Not Heard the Songs or Felt the Oneida's Feet on the Ground." *Indian Country Today,* July 22, 2019. https://indiancountrytoday.com/news/for-two-centuries-these-lands-have-not-heard-the-songs-or-felt-the-oneida-s-feet-on-the-ground-mdeEFNplZES5raKBEBzpA.

Lorde, Audre. *Sister Outsider: Essays and Speeches by Audre Lorde.* Berkeley, CA: Crossing, 1984.

Lorenzo, June L. "*Kiskinohamatowin*: An International Academic Forum on the Human Rights of Indigenous Peoples." Conference Report for Centre for International Governance Innovation, Winnipeg, MB, January 2019.

———. "Spatial Justice and Indigenous Peoples' Protection of Sacred Places: Adding Indigenous Dimensions to the Conversation." *justice spatiale | spatial justice* 11 (2017) 1–17. https://www.jssj.org/wp-content/uploads/2017/03/JSSJ11_5_VA.pdf.

Lorenzo, June, and Petuuche Gilbert. "Report Submitted to the United Nations Human Rights Council in Regard to the Universal Periodic Review Concerning the United States of America." Second Cycle-22nd Session, Geneva, Switzerland, April-May 2015. https://uprdoc.ohchr.org/uprweb/downloadfile.aspx?filename=1786&file=EnglishTranslation.

Lucchesi, Annita, and Abigail Echo-Hawk. "Missing and Murdered Indigenous Women and Girls Report." https://www.uihi.org/wp-content/uploads/2018/11/Missing-and-Murdered-Indigenous-Women-and-Girls-Report.pdf.

Lutz, Ellen. "Saving America's Endangered Languages." *Cultural Survival Quarterly,* June 2007. https://www.culturalsurvival.org/publications/cultural-survival-quarterly/saving-americas-endangered-languages.

Mack, John. *Cyprus, War and Adaptation: A Psychoanalytic History of Two Ethnic Groups in Conflict.* Charlottesville: University of Virginia Press, 1979.

MacLaren, Duncan. "Solidarity—Beyond the Clichés: A Theological Perspective." *New Blackfriars* 72:854 (1991) 489–96.

MacNair, Rachel. *Perpetration-Induced Traumatic Stress: The Psychological Consequences of Killing.* Westport, CT: Praeger, 2002.

Macoun, Alissa. "Colonising White Innocence: Complicity and Critical Encounters." In *The Limits of Settler Colonial Reconciliation: Non-Indigenous People and the Responsibility to Engage,* edited by Sarah Maddison, Tom Clark, and Ravi de Costa, 85–102. Singapore: Springer, 2016.

Madley, Benjamin. *An American Genocide: The United States and the California Indian Catastrophe, 1846–1873.* New Haven: Yale University Press, 2016.

Magarrell, Lisa, and Joya Wesley. *Learning from Greensboro: Truth and Reconciliation in the United States.* Philadelphia: University of Pennsylvania Press, 2010.

Manning, Sarah. "Jesuits Return 525 Acres to Rosebud Sioux Tribe." *Indian Country Today,* May 19, 2017. https://indiancountrytoday.com/archive/jesuits-return-525-acres-to-rosebud-sioux-tribe-KjrSAhb-XkSvJUmFkul7bw.

———. "Walking with Marita Growing Thunder and the Young Revolutionaries among Us." *Truthdig,* March 30, 2018. https://www.truthdig.com/articles/walking-with-marita-growing-thunder-and-the-young-revolutionaries-among-us/.

Manuel, Arthur. *Unsettling Canada: A National Wake-Up Call.* Toronto: Between the Lines, 2015.

Marsh, Charles. *The Beloved Community: How Faith Shapes Social Justice, from the Civil Rights Movement to Today.* New York: Basic, 2005.

Martell, Creeden. "Learning Cree 'A Form of Medicine' at Sask. Language Revitalization Camp." *CBC News,* August 5, 2017. https://www.cbc.ca/news/canada/saskatchewan/sask-cree-immersion-camp-1.4235884.

Martens, Raina, and Brittney Robertson. "How the Soil Remembers Plantation Slavery." *Edge Effects,* March 28, 2019. http://edgeeffects.net/soil-memory-plantationocene/.

Martin, Joel. *The Land Looks after Us: A History of Native American Religion.* New York: Oxford University Press, 1999.

Martin, Nick. "Returning to Wounded Knee." *The New Republic,* November 20, 2019. https://newrepublic.com/article/155743/returning-wounded-knee.

Martin, Thomas. "Devolutionism: The New Nationalist Movements Transform the World." *Utne Reader* 30 (1988) 78–83.

Mawhinney, Janet. "'Giving up the Ghost': Disrupting the (Re) Production of White Privilege in Anti-Racist Pedagogy and Organizational Change." Masters Thesis, University of Toronto, 1998.

McCallin, Rylee. "Reclaiming the Rock." *Lakota People's Law Project,* November 19, 2019. https://www.lakotalaw.org/news/2019-11-19/alcatraz.

McCaslin, Wanda. *Justice as Healing: Indigenous Ways.* University of Saskatchewan Native Law Centre. St. Paul, MN: Living Justice, 2005.

McCaughan, Pat. "At the Red Shirt Project: 'Talk Is Cheap; You Come Here to Work.'" *Episcopal News,* August 23, 2017. https://episcopalnews.ladiocese.org/dfc/newsdetail_2/3187506.

McClendon, James. *Biography as Theology: How Life Stories Can Remake Today's Theology.* Eugene, OR: Wipf & Stock, 2002.

McCollough, Charles. "Why Our Church Apologized to Hawai'i." In *UCC@50–Our History, Our Future,* edited by J. Martin Bailey and W. Evan Golder. http://d3n8a8pro7vhmx.cloudfront.net/unitedchurchofchrist/legacy_url/11261/mccollough.pdf?1418437063.

McGuire, Mollie, and Jeffrey S. Denis. "Unsettling Pathways: How Some Settlers Come to Seek Reconciliation with Indigenous Peoples." *Settler Colonial Studies* 9:4 (2019) 505–24. https://www.tandfonline.com/doi/abs/10.1080/2201473X.2019.1598701?journalCode=rset20&.

McIntosh, Peggy. "White Privilege: Unpacking the Invisible Knapsack." *Peace and Freedom Magazine* (July/August 1989) 10–12.

———. "White Privilege and Male Privilege: A Personal Account of Coming to See Correspondences through Work in Women's Studies." Wellesley, MA: Center for Research on Women, 1988.

McKenna, Ryan. "Saskatchewan Premier Scott Moe Apologizes to '60s Scoop Survivors." *The Toronto Star,* January 7, 2019. https://www.thestar.com/news/canada/2019/01/07/saskatchewan-premier-scott-moe-to-apologize-to-60s-scoop-survivors.html.

McKenzie-Jones, Paul. "What Does 'We Are All Treaty People' Mean, and Who Speaks for Indigenous Students on Campus?" *The Conversation,* August 29, 2019. https://theconversation.com/what-does-we-are-all-treaty-people-mean-and-who-speaks-for-indigenous-students-on-campus-119060.

McKiggan, John. "A Tribute to Nora Bernard." https://www.apmlawyers.com/a-tribute-to-nora-bernard/.

McLean, Sheelah. "'We Built a Life from Nothing.' White Settler Colonialism and the Myth of Meritocracy." OS|OS (2018) 32–33. https://www.policyalternatives.ca/sites/default/files/uploads/publications/National%20Office/2017/12/McLean.pdf.

McLendon, Sally, and John R. Johnson. *Cultural Affiliation and Lineal Descent of Chumash Peoples in the Channel Islands and the Santa Monica Mountains: Final Report*. Washington, DC: National Park Service, 1999.

Mehl-Madrona, Lewis. *Narrative Medicine: The Use of History and Story in the Healing Process*. Rochester, VT: Bear, 2007.

Meili, Dianne. "Nora Bernard Fought for Justice in the Lives of Family and Friends." *Windspeaker* 25:12 (2008). https://ammsa.com/node/7019.

Menakem, Resmaa. *My Grandmother's Hands: Racialized Trauma and the Pathway to Mending Our Hearts and Bodies*. Las Vegas: Central Recovery, 2017.

Messersmith-Glavin, Paul. "Between Social Ecology and Deep Ecology: Gary Snyder's Ecological Philosophy." *The Anarchist Library,* January 9, 2011. https://theanarchistlibrary.org/library/paul-messersmith-glavin-between-social-ecology-and-deep-ecology-gary-snyder-s-ecological-philos.

Meyer, David, and Dale Russell. "'Through the Woods Whare Thare Ware Now Track Ways': Kelsey, Henday and Trails in East Central Saskatchewan." *Canadian Journal of Archaeology* 32 (2007) 163–97. https://www.researchgate.net/figure/Map-of-central-Saskatchewan-and-adjacent-west-central-Manitoba_fig2_291344958.

Meyer, Lukas. "Historical Injustice." *Encyclopedia Britannica*. https://www.britannica.com/topic/historical-injustice#ref1225857.

Mierau, Peter, and Ellie Reimer, eds. *Sojourners: The Story of the Enns Family.* Winnipeg: Self-published, undated.

Milgrom, Genie. *My 15 Grandmothers*. Scotts Valley, CA: CreateSpace, 2012.

Miller, Bruce. *Chumash: A Picture of Their World*. Los Osos, CA: Sand River, 1988.

Miller, Emily. "Denominations Repent for Native American Land Grabs." *Religion News Service*, August 22, 2018. https://religionnews.com/2018/08/22/denominations-repent-for-native-american-land-grabs/.

Miller, J. R. "Residential Schools in Canada." *The Canadian Encyclopedia*, October 10, 2012. https://www.thecanadianencyclopedia.ca/en/article/residential-schools.

Miller, Larisa K. "The Secret Treaties with California's Indians." *Prologue* (2013) 38–45. https://www.archives.gov/files/publications/prologue/2013/fall-winter/treaties.pdf.

Miller, Mackenzie. "MCC's Erica Littlewolf: 'We Are Still Alive. We Really Do Exist.'" *Mennonite World Review*, October 23, 2017. http://mennoworld.org/2017/10/23/feature/mccs-erica-littlewolf-we-are-still-alive-we-really-do-exist/.

Miller, Perry. *Errand into the Wilderness*. Cambridge, MA: Belknap, 1956.

Miller, Robert J. *Discovering Indigenous Lands: The Doctrine of Discovery in the English Colonies*. New York: Oxford University Press, 2010.

Mirsky, Maya. "East Bay Jews Discuss What It Means to Live as Jews on Ohlone Land." *J*, November 22, 2019. https://www.jweekly.com/2019/11/22/east-bay-jews-discuss-what-it-means-to-live-as-jews-in-the-ohlone-homeland/.

Mohatt, Nathaniel, Azure Thompson, Nghi Thai, and Jacob Kraemer Tebes. "Historical Trauma as Public Narrative: A Conceptual Review of How History Impacts Present-Day Health." *Social Science & Medicine* 106 (2014) 128–36.

Mohawk, John. *Utopian Legacies: A History of Conquest and Oppression in the Western World.* Santa Fe, NM: Clear Light, 2000.

Moog, Nora, Sonja Entringer, Jerod Rasmussen, Martin Styner, John H. Gilmore, Norbert Kathmann, Christine M. Heim, Pathik D. Wadhwa, and Claudia Buss. "Intergenerational Effect of Maternal Exposure to Childhood Maltreatment on Newborn Brain Anatomy." *Biological Psychiatry* 83:2 (2018) 120–27. https://www.biologicalpsychiatryjournal.com/article/S0006-3223(17)31809-7/fulltext.

Mooney, James. *The Ghost-Dance Religion and the Sioux Outbreak of 1890.* Lincoln: University of Nebraska Press, 1991.

Morris, Katie Boudreau. "Decolonizing Solidarity: Cultivating Relationships of Discomfort." *Settler Colonial Studies* 7:4 (2017) 456–73.

Mukherjee, Shomik. "Wiyot Tribe Raising Funds for 2020 World Renewal Ceremony." *Times Standard*, April 8, 2019. https://www.times-standard.com/2019/04/08/wiyot-tribe-raising-funds-for-2020-world-renewal-ceremony/.

Munger, Sean. "Civilizers or Conquerors? The First Missionaries to Hawaii." https://seanmunger.com/2013/12/03/civilizers-or-conquerors-the-first-missionaries-to-hawaii/.

Murray, Stephen. *American Gay.* Worlds of Desire: The Chicago Series on Sexuality, Gender, and Culture. Chicago: University of Chicago Press, 1996.

Myers, Ched. "Anarcho-Primitivism and the Bible." In *The Encyclopedia of Religion and Nature*, edited by Bron Taylor, 56–59. New York: Continuum, 2004.

———. "Beyond the 'Addict's Excuse': Public Addiction and Ecclesial Recovery." In *The Other Side of Sin: Woundedness from the Perspective of the Sinned-Against*, edited by Susan Nelson and Andrew Sung Park, 77–108. Albany: State University of New York Press, 2001.

———. *The Biblical Vision of Sabbath Economics.* Washington, DC: Tell the Word, 2001.

———. *Binding the Strong Man: A Political Reading of Mark's Story of Jesus.* Maryknoll, NY: Orbis, 1988.

———. "Caretaking the Gift: A Journey in Hospice." In *Bury the Dead: Death and Dying in the Radical Christian Left*, edited by Laurel Dykstra, 49–58. Eugene, OR: Cascade, 2013.

———. "Deadly Paradises: Encounters with War and Love in the Pacific." *National Outlook*, Sydney, Australia. (January 1986) 36–38.

———. "Following Jesus in the Way of King: An MLK Birthday Special." https://www.youtube.com/watch?v=Pd_AXkkzQtI.

———. "If an Ancient Cathedral Had Burned: A Lament for Grandmother Oak." https://chedmyers.org/2017/12/30/blog-2017-12-30-if-ancient-cathedral-had-burned-lament-grandmother-oak-ched-myers/.

———. "Jesus' Risen, Mutilated Body: Reckoning with the Traumatic Somatic." *The Christian Century*, September 3, 2019. https://www.christiancentury.org/article/critical-essay/jesus-risen-mutilated-body.

———. "Nature against Empire: Exodus Plagues, Climate Crisis and Hardheartedness." *Direction* 49:1 (Fall 2020) 5–17.

———. "Reconnecting Seminary, Sanctuary, Streets and Soil: Curating Alternative Spaces for Theological Education." In *Let Your Light Shine: Mobilizing for Justice with Children and Youth*, edited by Reginald Blount and Virginia A. Lee, 59–74. Chester Heights, PA: Friendship, 2019.

———. "A Shaman Appeared in Ventura." In *Unsettling the Word: Biblical Experiments in Decolonization*, edited by Steve Heinrichs, 190–94. Altona, MB: Mennonite Church Canada, 2018.

———. "A Time to Break the Silence—Again: A Reflection on the 40th Anniversary of M. L. King's Riverside Speech." https://chedmyers.org/2007/03/01/articles-peacemaking-time-break-silence-again-reflection-40th-anniversary-kings-riverside-speech/.

———. *Who Will Roll Away the Stone? Discipleship Queries for First World Christians.* Maryknoll, NY: Orbis, 1994.

———. "The Wind That Diverts the Storm: The Nuclear Free and Independent Pacific Movement." *Sojourners* (August 1983) 10–13.

Myers, Ched, ed. *Watershed Discipleship: Reinhabiting Bioregional Faith and Practice.* Eugene, OR: Cascade, 2015.

Myers, Ched, and Bob Aldridge. *Resisting the Serpent: Palau's Struggle for Self-Determination.* Baltimore: Fortkamp, 1990.

Myers, Ched, and Matthew Colwell. *Our God Is Undocumented.* Maryknoll, NY: Orbis, 2012.

Myers, Ched, and Elaine Enns. *Ambassadors of Reconciliation, Vol. I: New Testament Reflections on Restorative Justice and Peacemaking.* 2 vols. Maryknoll, NY: Orbis, 2009.

———. "Healing from the 'Lies That Make Us Crazy': Practices of Restorative Solidarity." *Intotemak* 49 (2016) 138–42.

Myers, Ched, Marie Dennis, Joseph Nangle, Cynthia Moe-Lobeda, and Stuart Taylor. *Say to This Mountain: Mark's Story of Discipleship.* Maryknoll, NY: Orbis, 1996.

Myerson, Jesse A. "White Anti-Racism Must Be Based in Solidarity, Not Altruism." *The Nation,* February 5, 2018. https://www.thenation.com/article/white-anti-racism-must-be-based-in-solidarity-not-altruism/.

Nabokov, Peter, ed. *Native American Testimony: A Chronicle of Indian-White Relations from Prophecy to the Present, 1492–1992.* New York: Penguin, 1991.

Nadeau, Denise. *Unsettling Spirit: A Journey into Decolonization.* Montreal: McGill-Queens University Press, 2020.

Najdowski, Cynthia J. and Sarah E. Ullman. "PTSD and Self-Rated Recovery among Adult Sexual Assault Survivors: The Effects of Traumatic Life Events and Psychosocial Variables." *Psychology of Women Quarterly* 33 (2009) 43–53.

Narokobi, Bernard. *The Melanesian Way.* Rev. ed. Suva, Fiji: Institute of Pacific Studies, 1983.

———. "Pacific Identity and Solidarity." *Asian Bureau Australia Newsletter,* September 1981, no. 59. Reprinted in Helen O' Brien, ed., "Your Kingdom Come," *Youth and Development,* Point, Forum for Melanesian Affairs no. 1 (1980) 23–29.

Neff, Christian, and J. Howard Kauffman. "Intermarriage." *Global Anabaptist Mennonite Encyclopedia Online.* https://gameo.org/index.php?title=Intermarriage&oldid=145818.

Neufeld, Elsie. "Madness in One Family's Journey: From Ukraine to Germany to Canada." *Journal of Mennonite Studies* 29 (2011) 11–19.

Neufeld, J. "Mennonites Have Yet to Reckon with Their Role in 'Sixties Scoop.'" *Canadian Mennonite* 19:18 (September 2015) 20–21. https://canadianmennonite. org/stories/mennonites-have-yet-reckon-their-role-%E2%80%98sixties-scoop%E2%80%99.

Neufeld, Nikolai J., H. F. Klassen, and Peter Mierau. *Ufa: The Mennonite Settlements (Colonies) 1894–1938*. Steinbach, MB: Derksen, 1977.

Newcomb, Steve. "Five Hundred Years of Injustice: The Legacy of Fifteenth Century Religious Prejudice." *Shaman's Drum* (Fall 1992) 8–20.

———. *Pagans in the Promised Land: Decoding the Doctrine of Christian Discovery*. Golden, CO: Fulcrum, 2008.

Neylan, Susan. "Canada's Dark Side: Indigenous Peoples and Canada's 150th Celebration." *Origins* 11:9 (2018) . https://origins.osu.edu/article/canada-s-dark-side-indigenous-peoples-and-canada-s-150th-celebration.

Nicholls, Christine. "A Wild Roguery: Bruce Chatwin's The Songlines Reconsidered." *Text Matters* 9:9 (2019) 22–49. https://search.proquest.com/openview/47fa420d3 07820d71fb59cf0ee717f17/1?pq-origsite=gscholar&cbl=2026642.

Niessen, Shuana. *Shattering the Silence: The Hidden History of Indian Residential Schools in Saskatchewan*. Regina, SK: Faculty of Education, University of Regina Press, 2017. http://www2.uregina.ca/education/saskindianresidentialschools/ regina-indian-industrial-school/.

Nolan, Albert, OP. "Spiritual Growth and the Option for the Poor." Talk given to the Catholic Institute for International Relations, London, June 29, 1984. http:// www.maryknollmissiontraining.org/Shroeder-English/nolanpdf.pdf.

Nolt, Steven M. "Formal Mutual Aid Structures among American Mennonites and Brethren: Assimilation and Reconstructed Ethnicity." *Journal of American Ethnic History* 17:3 (1998) 71–86.

O'Connor, Elizabeth. *Journey Inward, Journey Outward*. New York: HarperCollins, 1975.

Odahl, Charles. *Constantine and the Christian Empire*. Philadelphia: Routledge, 2005.

Ogg, Arden. "An Infamous Anniversary: 130 Years Since Canada's Largest Mass Hanging 27 November 1885." *Cree Literacy Network,* November 26, 2015. https:// creeliteracy.org/2015/11/26/130th-anniversary-of-infamy-canadas-largest-mass-hanging-27-november-1885/.

Olfert, Eric. "An Historic Meeting on Stoney Knoll." *Intotemak* 35 (2006) 1–4.

O'Loughlin, Margie. "Sacred Sites Tours Seek Healing through Storytelling." *Longfellow Nokomis Messenger*, December 1, 2019. http://www. longfellownokomismessenger.com/sacred-sites-tours-seek-healing-through-storytelling/.

Oudshoorn, Dan. "A Crash Course on Settler Colonialism in Canadian-Occupied Territories." https://www.danoudshoorn.com/2019/a-crash-course-on-settler-colonialism-in-canadian-occupied-territories/?fbclid=IwAR2ypIJJ9lQJ6hXlejKC sZ_2kTUxOEsDWMDaDD0KR1TXAYXO4idw6dGKMAI.

Pacosz, Christina. *Some Winded, Wild Beast*. Detroit: Black & Red, 1985.

Parker, Pat. *Movement in Black: An Expanded Edition*. Ithaca, NY: Firebrand, 1999.

Patowary, Kaushik. "The Stunning Beauty of Braided Rivers." *Amusing Planet,* February 26, 2016. https://www.amusingplanet.com/2016/02/the-stunning-beauty-of-braided-rivers.html.

Patterson, Sean. "The Eichenfeld Massacre: Recontextualizing Mennonite and Makhnovist Narratives." *Journal of Mennonite Studies* 32 (2014) 151–74.

Pearson, Luke. "Don't Tell Me to 'Get Over' a Colonialism That Is Still Being Implemented Today." *The Guardian*, April 1, 2016. https://www.theguardian.com/australia-news/commentisfree/2016/apr/02/dont-tell-me-to-get-over-a-colonialism-that-is-still-being-implemented-today.

Pember, Mary Annette. "Death by Civilization: Thousands of Native American Children Were Forced to Attend Boarding Schools Created to Strip Them of Their Culture." *The Atlantic*, March 8, 2019. https://www.theatlantic.com/education/archive/2019/03/traumatic-legacy-indian-boarding-schools/584293/.

Peters, David. "When War Lives on Inside You." *Sojourners* (March 2020). https://sojo.net/magazine/march-2020/when-war-lives-inside-you.

Peters, Victor. *Nestor Makhno: The Life of an Anarchist.* Winnipeg: Echo, 1970.

Petronzio, Matt. "How Young Native Americans Built and Sustained the #NoDAPL Movement." *Mashable*, December 7, 2016. https://mashable.com/2016/12/07/standing-rock-nodapl-youth/.

Peyer, Bernd. *The Tutor'd Mind: Indian Missionary-Writers in Antebellum America.* Native Americans of the Northeast: Culture, History, and the Contemporary. Amherst, MA: University of Massachusetts Press, 1997.

Phung, Malissa. "Are People of Colour Settlers Too?" In *Cultivating Canada: Reconciliation through the Lens of Cultural Diversity*, edited by Ashok Mathur, Jonathan Dewar, and Mike DeGagné, 289–98. Ottawa: Aboriginal Healing Foundation Research Series, 2011.

Pitawanakwat, Brock. "Indigenous Treaty Rights." *Indigenous Saskatchewan Encyclopedia*, University of Saskatchewan. https://teaching.usask.ca/indigenoussk/import/indigenous_treaty_rights.php.

Polian, Pavel. *Against Their Will: The History and Geography of Forced Migrations in the USSR.* Budapest: Central European University Press, 2004.

Polk, Dora Beale. *The Island of California: A History of the Myth.* Lincoln: University of Nebraska Press, 1991.

Premnath, Devadasan N. "Latifundialization and Isaiah 5.8–10." *Journal for the Study of the Old Testament* 40 (1988) 49–60.

Prowse, Joan, dir. *Buffy Sainte-Marie: A Multimedia Life.* Phoenix: True North Studio, 2014.

Radford, Evan. "Memorial Honours Murdered Women, Builds Dialogue." *The Star Phoenix*, October 30, 2014, http://www.pressreader.com/canada/saskatoon-starphoenix/20141031/281724087824487.

Radford, Jynnah. "Key Findings about U.S. Immigrants." *Fact Tank—Pew Research Center*, June 17, 2019. https://www.pewresearch.org/fact-tank/2019/06/17/key-findings-about-u-s-immigrants/.

Rami, Theo. "The Chumash as Keepers of the Western Gate." http://www.angelfire.com/sk/syukhtun/westgate.html.

Redekop, Calvin. *Mennonite Displacement of Indigenous Peoples: An Historical and Sociological Analysis*. Calgary: University of Calgary for the Canadian Ethnic Studies Association, 1982.

Reelitz, KeʻŌpūlaulani. "Long Live Kahoʻolawe: Restoring the Former Military Bombing Site off the Coast of Maui." *Mana Magazine*, February 4, 2020. http://www.honolulumagazine.com/Honolulu-Magazine/June-2019/Long-Live-Kahoolawe-Restoring-the-Former-Military-Bombing-Site-Off-the-Coast-of-Maui/.

Regan, Paulette. *Unsettling the Settler within: Indian Residential Schools, Truth Telling, and Reconciliation in Canada*. Vancouver: University of British Columbia Press, 2010.

Regehr, T. D. "Mennonites and the New Jerusalem in Western Canada." In *Visions of the New Jerusalem: Religious Settlement on the Prairies*, edited by Benjamin Smillie, 109–11. Edmonton: NeWest, 1983.

Regier, Helen (Buhr). "My Grandmother and Her Family." Unpublished manuscript sent to the seventieth anniversary of Tiefengrund Rosenort Mennonite Church, Laird, Saskatchewan, October, 1980. Accessed in Leonard Doell's unpublished *Collected Archives and Articles*, Saskatoon, Saskatchewan.

Reimer, Al. *My Harp Is Turned to Mourning*. Winnipeg: Hyperion, 1985.

Rentería, Tamis Hoover. "The Elijah/Elisha Stories: A Socio-Cultural Analysis of Prophets and People in Ninth-Century B.C.E. Israel." In *Elijah and Elisha in Socioliterary Perspective,* edited by Robert Coote, 75–126. Atlanta: Scholars, 1992.

Reséndez, Andrés. *The Other Slavery: The Uncovered Story of Indian Enslavement in America*. New York: Mariner, 2016.

Reynolds, Henry. *Why Weren't We Told? A Personal Search for the Truth about Our History*. Melbourne: Penguin, 1999.

Reynolds, Lynda Klassen. "The Aftermath of Trauma and Immigration Detections of Multigenerational Effects on Mennonites Who Emigrated from Russia to Canada in the 1920s." PhD diss., Fresno University, 1997.

Ridge, John Rollin. *The Life and Adventures of Joaquín Murieta: The Celebrated California Bandit*. New York: Penguin, 2018.

Riem, Madelon, Laura Kunst, Marrie Bekker, Monica Fallon and Nina Kupper. "Intranasal Oxytocin Enhances Stress-Protective Effects of Social Support in Women with Negative Childhood Experiences during a Virtual Trier Social Stress Test." *Psychoneuroendocrinology* 111 (January 2020) . https://www.sciencedirect.com/science/article/pii/S0306453019306432.

Rindfleisch, Bryan. "Native American History and the Explanatory Potential of Settler Colonialism." *Early Americanist*, February 10, 2016. https://earlyamericanists.com/2016/02/10/native-american-history-the-explanatory-potential-of-settler-colonialism/.

Risher, Dee Dee. *The Soulmaking Room*. Nashville: Upper Room, 2016.

Rivers, Joshua. "Crip Camp Reminds Us That, in America, Nothing Improves without Massive Sacrifice." *The Verge*, March 27, 2020. https://www.theverge.com/2020/3/27/21197088/crip-camp-review-netflix-documentary.

Roberts, Laura Schmidt, Paul Martens, and Myron Penner, eds. *Recovering from the Anabaptist Vision: New Essays in Anabaptist Identity and Theological Method*. New York: Bloomsbury, 2020.

Roberts, Timothy, ed. *American Exceptionalism Volume I: Land and Prosperity.* 4 vols. Philadelphia: Routledge, 2016.

Robertson, Robbie. *Music for the Native Americans with The Red Road Ensemble.* Cema/Capitol 28295, 1994. http://theband.hiof.no/albums/music_for_the_native_americans.html.

Robins, Spencer. "An Ecological and Historical Portrait of the Coast at Hollister Ranch." *KCET,* October 25, 2018. https://www.kcet.org/shows/earth-focus/an-ecological-and-historical-portrait-of-the-coast-at-hollister-ranch.

Robinson, Amanda. "Turtle Island." *The Canadian Encyclopedia,* November 6, 2018. https://www.thecanadianencyclopedia.ca/en/article/turtle-island.

Robinson, William W. *Land in California: The Story of Mission Lands, Ranchos, Squatters, Mining Claims, Railraod Grants, Land Scrip, Homestead.* Berkeley: University of California Press, 1948.

Roediger, David R. *Working toward Whiteness: How America's Immigrants Became White: The Strange Journey from Ellis Island to the Suburbs.* New York: Basic, 2006.

Roewe, Brian. "Catholic Workers Charged with Damaging Minnesota Pipeline in Climate Protest." *National Catholic Reporter,* February 6, 2019. https://www.ncronline.org/news/earthbeat/catholic-workers-charged-damaging-minnesota-pipeline-climate-protest.

Rogalsky, Dave. "Mutual Aid or Financial Institution?" *Canadian Mennonite* 18:9 (April 23, 2014) . https://canadianmennonite.org/articles/mutual-aid-or-financial-institution.

Rohde, Jerry. "Genocide and Extortion: 150 Years Later, the Hidden Motive behind the Indian Island Massacre." *North Coast Journal,* February 25, 2010. https://www.northcoastjournal.com/humboldt/genocide-and-extortion/Content?oid=2130748.

Romero, Robert Chao. *Brown Church: Five Centuries of Latina/o Social Justice, Theology, and Identity.* Downers Grove, IL: Intervarsity, 2020.

Rose, Wendy. "For Some, It's a Time of Mourning." In *Without Discovery: A Native Response to Columbus,* edited by Ray Gonzalez, 3–7. Seattle: Broken Moon, 1992.

Ross, Heather. "We Are All Treaty People." *Educatus,* May 1, 2013. https://words.usask.ca/gmcte/2013/05/01/we-are-all-treaty-people/.

Roth, John. "The Complex Legacy of the Martyrs Mirror among Mennonites in North America." *Mennonite Quarterly Review* 87 (July 2013) 277–316.

Sagi-Schwartz, Abraham, Marinus H. van Ijzendoorn and Marian J. Bakermans-Kranenburg. "Does Intergenerational Transmission of Trauma Skip a Generation? No Metaanalytic Evidence for Tertiary Traumatization with Third Generation of Holocaust Survivors." *Attachment & Human Development* 10:2 (2008) 105–21.

Saint-Onge, Rex, John Johnson, and Joseph Talaugon. "Archaeoastronomical Implications of a Northern Chumash Arborglyph." *Journal of California and Great Basin Anthropology* 29:1 (2009) 29–57. https://escholarship.org/uc/item/94n052j7.

Salberg, Jill, and Sue Grand, eds. *Wounds of History: Repair and Resilience in the Trans-Generational Transmission of Trauma.* Philadelphia: Routledge, 2016.

Sales, Ruby. "The Guardians of Whiteness." *Radical Discipleship*, July 7, 2019. https://radicaldiscipleship.net/2019/07/07/the-guardians-of-whiteness/?utm_source=dlvr.it&utm_medium=facebook&fbclid=IwAR2mjULWockE-vmDxvit2J tkwnLW2WUu4Qkr8GAavCtgwwGcseZ-b6RaKeE.

———. "Pull Out the Root." *Radical Discipleship*, December 12, 2019. https://radicaldiscipleship.net/2019/12/02/pull-out-the-root/.

———. "Where Does It Hurt?" Interview with Krista Tippet. *On Being*, NPR, September 15, 2016. https://onbeing.org/programs/ruby-sales-where-does-it-hurt-aug2017/.

Salverson, Julie. "Loopings of Love and Rage: Sitting in the Trouble." *Canadian Theatre Review* 181 (2020) 34–40.

Samuel, Sigal. "What to Do When Racists Try to Hijack Your Religion." *The Atlantic*, November 2, 2017. https://www.theatlantic.com/international/archive/2017/11/asatru-heathenry-racism/543864/.

Sanchez, Nikki. "Decolonization Is for Everyone." https://unsettlingamerica.wordpress.com/2019/10/23/decolonization-is-for-everyone.

Sanders, Ronald. *Lost Tribes and Promised Lands: The Origins of American Racism*. Westland, MI: Perennial, 1992.

Santayana, George. *The Life of Reason: The Phases of Human Progress*. New York: Scribner, 1905.

Savage, Candace. *A Geography of Blood: Unearthing Memory from a Prairie Landscape*. Vancouver: D&M, 2012.

Savoy, Lauret. *Trace: Memory, History, Race, and the American Landscape*. Berkeley, CA: Counterpoint, 2016.

Sawatsky, Walter. "Dying for What Faith: Martyrologies to Inspire and Heal or to Foster Christian Division?" *The Conrad Grebel Review* 18:2 (2000) 31–53.

Schick, Matthies, Naser Morina, Richard Klaghofer, Ulrich Schnyder, and Julia Müller. "Trauma, Mental Health, and Intergenerational Associations in Kosovar Families 11 Years after the War." *European Journal of Pyschotraumatology* 4 (2013) . https://www.ncbi.nlm.nih.gov/pmc/articles/PMC3744842/.

Schrag, Tina, and Linda Espenshade. "Former MCC Director Trades Inheritance for Justice: Cyclist Uses 2,000-Mile Bike Trip for Land Advocacy." *Mennonite World Review*, October 14, 2013. http://www.mennoworld.org/archived/2013/10/14/former-mcc-director-trades-inheritance-justice/?print=1.

Schroeder, William, and Helmut Huebert. *Mennonite Historical Atlas*. 2d ed. Winnipeg: Springfield, 1996.

Schulz, Donna. "Our Children Need to Know: Young Chippewayan People Host Mennonites and Lutherans at Treaty Anniversary Gathering." *Canadian Mennonite* 20:18 (September 7, 2016) . https://canadianmennonite.org/treaty-6-anniversary.

———. "Students Learn about Indigenous Land Issues." *Canadian Mennonite* 19:11 (May 20, 2015) . https://canadianmennonite.org/stories/students-learn-about-indigenous-land-issues.

———. "We Sing the Same Songs: Mennonites Join Cree Community for Music, Dancing and Food." *Canadian Mennonite* 21:17 (September 6, 2017) . https://canadianmennonite.org/stories/%E2%80%98we-sing-same-songs%E2%80%99.

———. "When Strangers Become Neighbours: Saskatchewan Mennonite Worship with Indigenous Community." *Canadian Mennonite* 22:10 (May 2, 2018) . https://canadianmennonite.org/stories/when-strangers-become-neighbours.

Schwinghamer, Steven. "'The Problem Is a Vexing One': Mennonites and Canadian Accommodation." https://pier21.ca/research/immigration-history/mennonites-and-canadian-accommodation.

Scott, James C. *Weapons of the Weak: Everyday Forms of Peasant Resistance.* New Haven: Yale University Press, 1987.

Seaton, Erin E. "Common Knowledge: Reflections on Narratives in Community." *Qualitative Research* 8:3 (2008) 293–305.

Siler, Julia Flynn. *Lost Kingdom: Hawaii's Last Queen, the Sugar Kings, and America's First Imperial Adventure.* New York: Atlantic Monthly, 2012.

———. "The Queen and the Clevelands (Grover and George . . .)." https://juliaflynnsiler.com/2012/09/the-queen-and-the-clevelands-grover-and-george/.

Silko, Leslie Marmon. *Ceremony.* Anniversary ed. New York: Penguin, 2006.

Simpson, Leanne Betasamosake. "Indigenous Resurgence and Co-resistance." *Critical Ethnic Studies* 2:2 (2016) 19–34. http://blogs.ubc.ca/564b/files/2017/11/Resurgace-LBS.pdf.

———, ed., *Lighting the Eighth Fire: The Liberation, Resurgence, and Protection of Indigenous Nations.* Winnipeg: Arbeiter Ring, 2008.

Sinclair, Murray. "Reconciliation Is Not an Aboriginal Problem, It Is a Canadian Problem. It Involves All of Us." *CBC Radio*, June 2, 2015. https://www.cbc.ca/radio/asithappens/as-it-happens-tuesday-edition-1.3096950/reconciliation-is-not-an-aboriginal-problem-it-is-a-canadian-problem-it-involves-all-of-us-1.3097253.

Singh, Maanvi. "Native American 'Land Taxes': A Step on the Roadmap for Reparations." *The Guardian*, December 31, 2019. https://www.theguardian.com/us-news/2019/dec/31/native-american-land-taxes-reparations.

Slagel, Allogan. "Unfinished Justice: Completing the Restoration and Acknowledgment of California Indian Tribes." *American Indian Quarterly* 13:4 (1989) 325–45.

Smillie, Benjamin, ed. *Visions of the New Jerusalem: Religious Settlement on the Prairies.* Edmonton, AB: NeWest, 1983.

Smith, C. Henry. *Smith's Story of the Mennonites.* Newton, KS: Faith and Life, 1981.

Smith, Linda Tuhiwai, Eve Tuck, and K. Wayne Yang, eds., *Indigenous and Decolonizing Studies in Education.* Philadelphia: Routledge, 2019.

Smoak, Gregory. *Ghost Dances and Identity: Prophetic Religion and American Indian Ethnogenesis in the Nineteenth Century.* Berkeley: University of California Press, 2006.

Smucker, Barbara Claassen. *Days of Terror.* Toronto: Penguin Global, 2008.

Smucker, Donovan, ed. *The Sociology of Canadian Mennonites, Hutterites and Amish: A Bibliography with Annotations.* Waterloo, ON: Wilfrid Laurier University Press, 1977.

Snell, Cathy Carter. "Psychological Effects of Trauma." Webinar for Center for Rural Community Leadership and Ministry, Saskatoon Theological Union, May 22, 2014.

Snell, Kelsey, "Suicide Is Rising among American Farmers as They Struggle to Keep
    Afloat." *NPR,* May 16, 2018. https://www.npr.org/2018/05/16/611727777/
    suicide-is-rising-among-american-farmers-as-they-struggle-to-keep-afloat.
Snyder, Gary. "Reinhabitation." *Manoa* 25:1 (2013) 44–48. https://sites.tufts.edu/
    mythritualsymbol2017/files/2017/08/snyder-reinhabitation.pdf.
Southern Poverty Law Center. "New Brand of Racist Odinist Religion on the March."
    The Intelligence Report, March 15, 1998. https://www.splcenter.org/fighting-hate/
    intelligence-report/1998/new-brand-racist-odinist-religion-march.
———. "Whose Heritage? Public Symbols of the Confederacy." https://www.
    splcenter.org/20190201/whose-heritage-public-symbols-confederacy.
Squires, Lisa. "The Carrot River Math Reconciliation Experience Described as
    Awesome." *The Saskatchewan Teachers Federation Bulletin,* March 18, 2020.
    https://www.stf.sk.ca/about-stf/news/carrot-river-math-reconciliation-
    experience-described-awesome.
Stan, Adele. "America the Traumatized: How 13 Events of the Decade Made Us the
    PTSD Nation." *Truthout,* December 2009. https://truthout.org/articles/america-
    the-traumatized-how-13-events-of-the-decade-made-us-the-ptsd-nation/#.
Stanek, Dörte. "Bridging Past and Present: Embodied Intergenerational Trauma and
    the Implications for Dance/Movement Therapy." *Body, Movement and Dance in
    Psychotherapy* 10:2 (2015) 94–105. https://www.tandfonline.com/doi/full/10.108
    0/17432979.2014.971872.
Stannard, David. *American Holocaust: The Conquest of the New World.* New York:
    Oxford University Press, 1993.
Starblanket, Tamara. *Suffer the Little Children: Genocide, Indigenous Nations and the
    Canadian State.* Atlanta: Clarity, 2018.
Starr, David. "Robert Wilcox and the Revolution of 1895: Hawaiian Revolutionary
    Honored." *Solidarity* (July-August 1995) . https://solidarity-us.org/atc/57/p2642/.
St-Denis, Natalie, and Christine Walsh. "Reclaiming My Indigenous Identity and
    the Emerging Warrior: An Autoethnography." *Journal of Indigenous Social
    Development* 5:1 (2016) 1–17. https://umanitoba.ca/faculties/social_work/media/
    V5i1–01st-denis_walsh.pdf.
Stein, Howard. "'Chosen Trauma' and a Widely Shared Sense of Jewish Identity and
    History." *The Journal of Psychohistory* 41:4 (2014) 236–57.
Stephens, R. L. "The Left's Self-Destructive Obsession with Shame." *Orchestratedpulse,*
    August 1, 2014. http://www.orchestratedpulse.com/2014/08/shame-left/.
Stevenson, Allyson. "Hidden from History: Indigenous Women's Activism in
    Saskatchewan." *National Post,* January 14, 2019. https://nationalpost.com/pmn/
    news-pmn/hidden-from-history-indigenous-womens-activism-in-saskatchewan.
Stratton, Billy. "The Sand Creek Massacre Took Place More Than 150 Years Ago: It
    Still Matters." *Time,* November 29, 2016. https://time.com/4584022/sand-creek-
    massacre-anniversary/.
Stratton, Sara. "Decolonizing Discipleship." United Church of Canada Webinar filmed
    March 31, 2020. YouTube video. 29:29. https://www.youtube.com/watch?v=26
    wzjJCFx4w&fbclid=IwAR1tpjCKlm9jqy2JqPJvMolQaho1IcPGH9iWUCofjZ_
    IxcEiJgKEXlT_qQg.

Strickler, Jeff. "First Nations Kitchen Serves Ancestral Foods to the Native American Community." *Faith & Leadership,* November 28, 2017. https://faithandleadership. com/first-nations-kitchen-serves-ancestral-foods-native-american-community? fbclid=IwAR1KRrjQicM2OVN9DlNlKH37cEqW7uo7IyGXC2w7BRvrKYf290T RLCeKxxY.

Sugiman, Pamela. "Passing Time, Moving Memories: Interpreting Wartime Narratives of Japanese Canadian Women." *Histoire Sociale/Social History* 37:73 (2004) 51–79.

Suleimenov, Arman. "Weeping in the Steppe: The Tragedy of the Nogai People." Translated by Raushan Makhmetzhanova. https://e-history.kz/en/publications/ view/3000.

Summerhill, Stephen, and John Alexander Williams. *Sinking Columbus: Contested History, Cultural Politics, and Mythmaking during the Quincentenary.* Gainesville: University Press of Florida, 2000.

Swyripa, Frances. *Storied Landscapes: Ethno-Religious Identity and the Canadian Prairies.* Winnipeg: University of Manitoba Press, 2010.

Szeto, Winston. "'Is Reconciliation Dead?' Debate Continues among Indigenous Advocates." *CBC News,* February 29, 2020. https://www.cbc.ca/news/canada/ british-columbia/victoria-dialogue-reconciliation-dead-1.5480927.

Talaugon, Sabine. "Four Things You Should Know about the Chumash Revolt of 1824." *Chumash Science Through Time,* September 11, 2018. https:// chumashscience.com/2018/09/11/the-chumash-revolt-of-1824/.

Tannenbaum, Melanie. "'But I Didn't Mean It!' Why It's so Hard to Prioritize Impacts over Intents." *PsySociety (blog). Scientific American,* October 14, 2013. https:// blogs.scientificamerican.com/psysociety/e2809cbut-i-didne28099t-mean-ite2809d-why-ite28099s-so-hard-to-prioritize-impacts-over-intents/.

Tanner, Beccy. "Her Family Farm Once Belonged to the Kaw Indians. She Decided to Pay Them Back." *The Witchita Eagle,* February 9, 2019. https://www.kansas.com/ news/local/article225981195.html.

Tauli-Corpuz, Victoria. "Indigenous Women's Rights Are Human Rights." *Cultural Survival* (February 2018). https://www.culturalsurvival.org/publications/ cultural-survival-quarterly/indigenous-womens-rights-are-human-rights.

Taylor, Shelley E., Laura Cousino Klein, Brian P. Lewis, Tara L. Gruenewald, Regan A. R. Gurung, and John A. Updegraff. "Biobehavioral Responses to Stress in Females: Tend-and-Befriend, Not Fight-or-Flight." *Psychological Review* 107:3 (2000) 411–29.

Taylor, Steve. "I Believe in God—Demetri Lee." *North Carolina Conference—The United Methodist Church,* May 12, 2016. https://nccumc.org/conflict/ko/believe-god-demetri-lee-guest-blogger-steve-taylor/.

Thomas, Adele. "Stolen People on Stolen Land: Decolonizing While Black." *Racebaitr,* May 24, 2016. https://racebaitr.com/2016/05/24/stolen-people-stolen-land/.

Thomas, Ashleigh-Rae. "Who Is a Settler, According to Indigenous and Black Scholars." *Vice,* February 15 2019. https://www.vice.com/en_us/article/gyajj4/ who-is-a-settler-according-to-indigenous-and-black-scholars.

Thomas, David Hurst. *Skull Wars: Kennewick Man, Archaeology and the Battle for Native American Identity.* New York: Basic, 2000.

Timbrook, Jan. *Chumash Ethnobotany: Plant Knowledge among the Chumash People of Southern California.* Santa Barbara: Santa Barbara Museum of Natural History, 2007.

Tinker, George. *American Indian Liberation: A Theology of Sovereignty.* Maryknoll, NY: Orbis, 2008.

———. *Missionary Conquest: The Gospel and Native American Cultural Genocide.* Philadelphia: Fortress, 1993.

Tobani, Sunera. *Exalted Subjects: Studies in the Making of Race and Nation in Canada.* Toronto: University of Toronto Press, 2007.

Todd, Douglas. "Metro Vancouver Anglicans to Direct Millions to Indigenous Efforts." *Vancouver Sun,* May 30, 2019. https://vancouversun.com/news/local-news/metro-vancouver-anglicans-to-direct-millions-to-indigenous-efforts.

Todd, Judith. "The Pre-Deuteronomistic Elijah Cycle." In *Elijah and Elisha in Socioliterary Perspective,* edited by Robert Coote, 1–36. Atlanta: Scholars, 1992.

Toensing, Gale Courey. "Indian-Killer Andrew Jackson Deserves Top Spot on List of Worst US Presidents." *Indian Country Today,* September 10, 2017. https://indiancountrytoday.com/archive/indian-killer-andrew-jackson-deserves-top-spot-on-list-of-worst-us-presidents-q-Qg-O3lJUCE1bdhzyeS-A.

Toews, John B. "The Origins and Activities of the Mennonite *Selbstschutz* in the Ukraine (1918–1919)." *Mennonite Quarterly Review* 46 (1972) 5–40.

Tolan, Casey. "Amid Trump's 'Pocahontas' Taunts, Native Americans Run for Office in Record Numbers." *The Mercury News,* October 22, 2018. https://www.mercurynews.com/2018/10/22/native-american-candidates-deb-haaland-elizabeth-warren-dna-test/.

Trawick, Robert. "Sweetwater Cultural Center: The First Steps to Repentance and Reconciliation." *Unbound* (December 3, 2019) . https://justiceunbound.org/sweetwater-cultural-center-the-first-steps-to-repentance-and-reconciliation/.

Truettner, William. *The West as America: Reinterpreting Images of the Frontier, 1820–1920.* Washington, DC: Smithsonian, 1991.

Truth and Reconciliation Commission of Canada. *Calls to Action.* Winnipeg: Truth and Reconciliation Commission of Canada, 2015. http://nctr.ca/assets/reports/Calls_to_Action_English2.pdf.

———. *They Came for the Children: Canada, Aboriginal Peoples, and Residential Schools.* Winnipeg: Public Works & Government Services Canada, 2012. https://en.wikipedia.org/wiki/File:TRC_Canada_They_Came_for_the_Children.pdf.

Tuck, Eve, and C. Ree. "A Glossary of Haunting." In *Handbook of Autoethnography,* edited by Stacy Holman Jones, Tony E. Adams, and Carolyn Ellis, 639–58. Philadelphia: Routledge, 2016.

Tuck, Eve, and K. Wayne Yang. "Decolonization Is Not a Metaphor." *Decolonization* 1:1 (2012) 1–40.

———. *Toward What Justice? Describing Diverse Dreams of Justice in Education.* Philadelphia: Routledge, 2018.

Tumamait-Stenslie, Julie. "My Chumash Ancestral Legacy." *Ojai History,* August 11, 2011. http://ojaihistory.com/my-chumash-ancestral-legacy/.

Turcotte, Yanick. "James Bay and Northern Quebec Agreement." *The Canadian Encyclopedia,* July 3, 2019. https://www.thecanadianencyclopedia.ca/en/article/james-bay-and-northern-quebec-agreement#.

Turner, Christina. "What Does It Mean to Be a Toronto Treaty Person?" *rabble.ca,* July 3, 2015. https://rabble.ca/news/2015/07/what-does-it-mean-to-be-toronto-treaty-person.

Twiss, Richard. *Rescuing the Gospel from the Cowboys: A Native American Expression of the Jesus Way.* Downers Grove, IL: Intervarsity, 2015.

Uechi, Colleen. "40 Years after Men's Disappearance at Sea, Their Vision for Kahoolawe Has Become a Reality." *The Maui News,* March 5, 2017. https://www.mauinews.com/news/local-news/2017/03/40-years-after-mens-disappearance-at-sea-their-vision-for-kahoolawe-has-become-a-reality/.

Underwood, Ginny. "United Methodist Church Gives Historic Mission Site and Land Back to Wyandotte Nation." *Indian Country Today,* September 23, 2019. https://indiancountrytoday.com/news/united-methodist-church-gives-historic-mission-site-and-land-back-to-wyandotte-nation-Hfo6x3-aGoy-LXNhKZXjPg.

Urry, James. *None but the Saints: The Transformation of Mennonite Life in Russia 1789–1889.* Kitchener, ON: Pandora, 1989.

Utt, Jamie. "Intent vs. Impact: Why Your Intentions Don't Really Matter." *Everyday Feminism,* July 30, 2013. https://everydayfeminism.com/2013/07/intentions-dont-really-matter/.

Valandra, Edward C., and Waŋbli Wapȟáha Hokšíla. *Colorizing Restorative Justice: Voicing Our Realities.* St. Paul, MN: Living Justice, 2020.

Van Bragt, Thieleman. *Martyrs Mirror: The Story of Seventeen Centuries of Christian Martyrdom from the Time of Christ to A.D. 1660.* Harrisonburg, VA: Herald, 1938.

Van der Kolk, Bessel. *The Body Keeps the Score: Brain, Mind and Body in the Healing of Trauma.* New York: Penguin, 2016.

Vellon, Peter. *A Great Conspiracy against Our Race: Italian Immigrant Newspapers and the Construction of Whiteness in the Early 20th Century.* New York: New York University Press, 2017.

Veracini, Lorenzo. "Decolonizing Settler Colonialism: Kill the Settler in Him and Save the Man." *American Indian Culture and Research Journal* 41:1 (2017) 1–18.

———. "Israel-Palestine through a Settler-Colonial Studies Lens." *Interventions* 21:4 (2019) 568–81.

Vimalassery, Manu, Juliana Hu Pegues, and Alyosha Goldstein. "Introduction: On Colonial Unknowing." *Theory & Event* 19:4 (October 2016) . https://muse.jhu.edu/article/633283.

Vizenor, Gerald. *Manifest Manner: Narratives of Postindian Survivance.* Lincoln: University of Nebraska Press, 1999.

Volkan, Vamik. "Transgenerational Transmissions and Chosen Traumas: An Aspect of Large-Group Identity." *Group Analysis* 34:1 (2001) 79–97. doi:10.1177/05333160122077730.

Vowel, Chelsea. "Undermined at Every Turn: The Lie of the Failed Native Farm on the Prairies." *Apihtawikosisan,* May 23, 2012. https://apihtawikosisan.com/2012/05/undermined-at-every-turn-the-lie-of-the-failed-native-farms-on-the-prairies/.

Waddell, Amy Rinner. "MC Canada Staffer Sentenced to Seven Days in Jail." *Canadian Mennonite,* August 10, 2018. https://canadianmennonite.org/stories/mc-canada-staffer-sentenced-seven-days-jail.

Waiser, Bill. "Saskatchewan's Oldest Graveyard Is Ancient." https://billwaiser.com/saskatchewans-oldest-graveyard-is-ancient/.

Walia, Harsha. "Decolonizing Together: Moving Beyond a Politics of Solidarity Toward a Practice of Decolonization." *Briarpatch,* January 1, 2012. https://briarpatchmagazine.com/articles/view/decolonizing-together.

Walker, John Frederick. *A Certain Curve of Horn: The Hundred-Year Quest for the Giant Sable Antelope of Angola.* New York: Grove, 2004.

Walker, Phillip, and Trevor Hudson. *Chumash Healing: Changing Health and Medical Practices in an American Indian Society.* Banning, CA: Malki Museum, 1993.

Walker, Ranginui. *Ka Whawhai Tonu Matou (Struggle without End).* Auckland: Penguin, 1990.

Walker-Barnes, Chanequa. *I Bring the Voices of My People: A Womanist Vision for Racial Reconciliation.* Grand Rapids: Eerdmans, 2019.

————. "Until All of Us Are Free: How Racial Reconciliation Fails Black Women." Lecture given at Pittsburgh Theological Seminary, July 31, 2018. Youtube Video, 46:22. https://www.youtube.com/watch?v=FxNB3W9I6n4.

Wallace-Wells, Benjamin. "The Fight over Virginia's Confederate Monuments: How the State's Past Spurred a Racial Reckoning." *The New Yorker,* November 27, 2017. https://www.newyorker.com/magazine/2017/12/04/the-fight-over-virginias-confederate-monuments.

Walters, Ronald W. *The Price of Racial Reconciliation.* Ann Arbor: University of Michigan Press, 2009.

Walzer, Michael. *Exodus and Revolution.* New York: Basic, 1986.

Warner, Andrea. *Buffy Sainte-Marie: The Authorized Biography.* Vancouver: Greystone, 2018.

Washington, James, ed. *A Testament of Hope: The Essential Writings and Speeches of Martin Luther King, Jr.* New York: HarperCollins, 1986.

Waziyatawin, ed. *In the Footsteps of Our Ancestors: The Dakota Commemorative Marches of the 21st Century.* St. Paul, MN: Living Justice, 2008.

Waziyatawin, Angela Wilson. *What Does Justice Look Like? The Struggle for Liberation in Dakota Homelands.* St. Paul, MN: Living Justice, 2008.

Weaver, Hillary N. *Trauma and Resilience in the Lives of Contemporary Native Americans: Reclaiming Our Balance, Restoring Our Wellbeing.* Philadelphia: Routledge, 2019.

Weaver, J. Denny. *Becoming Anabaptist: The Origin and Significance of Sixteenth Century Anabaptism.* Scottdale, PA: Herald, 1987.

Weil, Simone. *The Need for Roots: Prelude to a Declaration of Duties towards Mankind.* Philadelphia: Routledge, 2001.

Weisman, Ze'ev. *Political Satire in the Bible.* Society of Biblical Literature, Atlanta: Scholars, 1998.

Wenger, John. "Covenant Theology." *Global Anabaptist Mennonite Encyclopedia Online.* https://gameo.org/index.php?title=Covenant_Theology&oldid=162869.

West, Cornel. *Prophesy Deliverance! An Afro-American Revolutionary Christianity.* Philadelphia: Westminster, 1982.

Weyler, Rex. *Blood of the Land: The Government and Corporate War against First Nations.* Philadelphia: New Society, 1992.

Wiebe, Rudy. "Living on the Iceberg: 'The Artist as Critic and Witness' 36 Years Later." *The Conrad Grebel Review* 18:2 (2000) 85–92.

————. *Peace Shall Destroy Many.* Toronto: Vintage Canada, 1962.

————. *The Temptations of Big Bear.* Athens: Ohio University Press/Swallow, 2000.

Williams, Robert A. *The American Indian in Western Legal Thought: The Discourses of Conquest.* Reprint ed. New York: Oxford University Press, 1992.

Williams, William Appleman. *Empire as a Way of Life: An Essay on the Causes and Character of America's Present Predicament along with a Few Thoughts about an Alternative.* Brooklyn, NY: IG, 2006.

Wilson-Hartgrove, Jonathan. *Reconstructing the Gospel: Finding Freedom from Slaveholder Religion.* Downers Grove, IL: InterVarsity, 2018.

Winter, Miriam Therese. *WomanWisdom: A Feminist Lectionary and Psalter. Women of the Hebrew Scriptures: Part One.* New York: Crossroad, 1991.

———. *WomanWitness: A Feminist Lectionary and Psalter. Women of the Hebrew Scriptures: Part Two.* New York: Crossroad, 1992.

———. *WomanWord: A Feminist Lectionary and Psalter. Women of the New Testament.* New York: Crossroad, 1992.

Wires, Nicole. "Why We Charge the Shuumi Land Tax." *Planting Justice,* November 27, 2019. https://plantingjustice.org/blog/why-we-charge-the-shuumi-land-tax.

Wittstock, Laura, and Elaine J. Salinas. "A Brief History of the American Indian Movement." https://www.aimovement.org/ggc/history.html.

Woelk, Cheryl, and Steve Heinrichs, eds. *Yours, Mine, Ours: Unraveling the Doctrine of Discovery.* Special issue of *Intotemak.* Winnipeg: Mennonite Church Canada, 2016.

Wolfchild, Sheldon, dir. *The Doctrine of Discovery: Unmasking the Domination Code.* 2015. Morton, MN: 38 Plus 2 Productions. https://doctrineofdiscovery.org/the-doctrine-of-discovery-unmasking-the-domination-code/.

Wolfe, Patrick. "Settler Colonialism and the Elimination of the Native." *Journal of Genocide Research* 8:4 (2006) 387–409.

Women's Earth Alliance and Native Youth Sexual Health Network. *Violence on the Land, Violence on Our Bodies: Building an Indigenous Response to Environmental Violence.* 2016. http://landbodydefense.org/uploads/files/VLVBReportToolkit2016.pdf

Woodley, Randy. *Shalom and the Community of Creation: An Indigenous Vision.* Grand Rapids: Eerdmans, 2012.

Woolman, John. *The Journal and Major Essays of John Woolman.* Edited by Phillips Moulton. Richmond, IN: Friends United, 1971.

Worden, Leon. "Treaty between the United States and the Indians of 'Castaic, Tejon, Etc.' 1851." https://scvhistory.com/scvhistory/heizer1972.htm.

Worral, Simon. "When, How Did the First Americans Arrive? It's Complicated." *National Geographic,* June 9, 2018. www.nationalgeographic.com/news/2018/06/when-and-how-did-the-first-americans-arrive—its-complicated-/.

Wylie, Jeanie. "Exchanging Birthrights: A Nation of Esaus." *The Witness* (October 1992) 5–6.

———. "Singing for the *Wiliwili* Tree: An Interview with Ched Myers." *The Witness* (April, 1995) 10–13. https://chedmyers.org/1995/04/01/articlesecology-faith-singing-wiliwili-tree-reflections-hawaiian-sovereignty-and-earthregeneration/.

Wysote, Travis, and Erin Morton. "'The Depth of the Plough': White Settler Tautologies and Pioneer Lie." *Settler Colonial Studies* 9:4 (2019) 479–504. https://www.tandfonline.com/doi/abs/10.1080/2201473X.2018.1541221?journalCode=rset20.

Yard, Bridget. "Cree, Christian, and Questioning the Catholic Church: One Man's Journey in Faith." *CBC News*, March 19, 2018. https://www.cbc.ca/news/canada/ saskatchewan/cree-christian-and-questioning-the-catholic-church-one-man-s-journey-in-faith-1.4477750.

Yehuda, Rachel. "Biological Factors Associated with Susceptibility to Posttraumatic Stress Disorder." *Canadian Journal of Psychiatry* 44:1 (1999) 34–39.

———. "Biology of Posttraumatic Stress Disorder." *Journal of Clinical Psychiatry* 62:17 (2001) 41–46.

———. "Clinical Relevance of Biologic Findings in PTSD." *Psychiatric Quarterly* 73:2 (2002) 123–33.

Yehuda, Rachel, and Linda Bierer. "The Relevance of Epigenetics to PTSD: Implications for the *DSM-V*." *Journal of Traumatic Stress,* Special Issue: Highlights of the ISTSS 2008 Annual Meeting, 22:5 (2009) 427–34.

Yehuda, Rachel, Stephanie M. Engel, Sarah R. Brand, Jonathan Seckl, Sue M. Marcus, and Gertrud S. Berkowitz. "Transgenerational Effects of Posttraumatic Stress Disorder in Babies of Mothers Exposed to the World Trade Center Attacks during Pregnancy." *Journal of Clinical Endocrinology & Metabolism* 90:7 (2005) 4115–18.

Yehuda, Rachel, Jim Schmeidler, Abbie Elkin, Elizabeth Houshmand, Larry Siever, Karen Binder-Brynes, Milton Wainberg, Dan Aferiot, Alan Lehman, Ling Song Guo, and Ren Kwei Yang. "Phenomenology & Psychobiology of the Intergenerational Response to Trauma." In *Intergenerational Handbook of Multigenerational Legacies of Trauma,* edited by Yael Danieli, 639–56. New York: Plenum, 1997.

Yehuda, Rachel, James Schmeidler, Earl Giller, Larry Siever, and Karen Binder-Brynes. "Relationship between Posttraumatic Stress Disorder Characteristics of Holocaust Survivors and Their Adult Offspring." *American Journal Psychiatry* 155:6 (1998) 841–43.

Yoder, Carolyn. "European Anabaptist History and Current Reconciliation Efforts: Reflections through a Collective Trauma Theory Lens." *Mennonite Family History* 26:2 (2007) 95–100.

———. *The Little Book of Trauma Healing: When Violence Strikes and Community Security Is Threatened.* Intercourse, PA: Good, 2005.

Young, Ayana. "Fight for Free and Wild Salmon Rivers: Interview with Chief Caleen Sisk." *Minding Nature* 11:3 (Fall 2018) 34–43. https://www.humansandnature. org/fight-for-free-and-wild-salmon-rivers-interview-with-chief-caleen-sisk.

Zacharias, George. *Wilhelm Zacharias and Descendants: Early 1700 to 1996.* Saskatoon, SK: Self-published, 1996.

Zacharias, Isaak. *Meine Lebensgeschichte: Isaak Isaak Zacharias 1868–1945 (Autobiography of Isaak Isaak Zacharias).* Edited by George Zacharias. Translated by Agnes and Nick Peters. Saskatoon, SK: Self-published (undated).

Zacharias, Robert. *Rewriting the Break Event: Mennonites and Migration in Canadian Literature.* Winnipeg: University of Manitoba Press, 2013.

Zahniser, David. "L.A. City Council Replaces Columbus Day with Indigenous Peoples Day on City Calendar." *Los Angeles Times,* August 30, 2017. https://www.latimes. com/local/lanow/la-me-ln-indigenous-peoples-day-20170829-story.html.

Zinn, Howard. *A People's History of the United States.* New York: Harper Perennial Modern Classics, 2005.

Zlomislic, Diana. "Field of Dreams." *The Toronto Star*, June 20, 2019. https://projects.
     thestar.com/climate-change-canada/saskatchewan/.
Zolli, Andrew. "Toward a Contemplative Ecology: A Conversation with Douglas
     Christie and Andrew Zolli." *Garrison Institute*, April 21, 2017. https://www.
     garrisoninstitute.org/blog/toward-contemplative-ecology/.

Index of Subjects and Places

Note: Bolded numbers indicate places in text where entry is explained or defined.

159, 221, 228–29, 234, 242,
251, 255, 260n64, 276,
283–84, 288, 296n48
Restorative solidarity, 10, **12**, 14,
19, 23–24, 36, 44, 48, 51, 88,
109, 133, 150, 154, 192, 226,
268, 274, 286–89, 295–96,
302, 304, 308, 312
Retribution, 99, 228–29, 234, 275
Re-vising (devised histories), 14, **45**,
54, 153, 162, **167**, 226, 274
Richmond Slave Trail (VA), 250
Roman Empire, 53, 122, 133–34,
150–51, 161–62, 224, 275–76
Romanticizing, 52, 70, 87, 121,
164, 217, 222, 245
Rosthern (SK), 5–6, 73n34, 83, 112,
167, 172–73, 204, 239
Rosthern Junior College (RJC; German English Academy, SK), 6,
86, 198–99, 208–9
Round Dance, 261, **311–12**
Rupert's Land, 165
Russian Revolution (Civil War), 5,
15, 44, 59–60, 62, 68, 71–72, 82,
115, 118, 124, 218

Sabbath Economics/Jubilee, 40, 146,
203, 276n11, 279–80
Sand Creek massacre, 228, 299
Sanitizing (history, communal narra-
tives), 36, 98, 105, 227
Santa Barbara (CA), 34, 130–31, 164,
180, 182–83, 239, 259
Santa Cruz Island (*Lim-
uw*, CA), 164, 266
Santa Rosa Island (*Wima'l*, CA), 163
Saskatchewan Indian
newspaper, 5, 200
Saskatchewan Indian Women's
Association, 261
Saskatchewan Rivers: watershed,
3, 6, 24, 26, 185; South Sask.
River, 21, **157–59**, 164, 167, 240;
Sask. River Valley, 158–59, 163,
166–67, 172, 176, 184, 192
Schulz Fabrik (Ukraine), 58, 62

Second Corinthians (Sec-
ond Testament epistle),
140n15, 275–76, 282
Secularization Act (of CA missions),
34n5, 135, 181–83
Selbstschutz (Mennonite self-defense
force, Ukraine), 60–61
Settler colonialism (definition), xxvi, **10–13**
Severality (agricultural policy, Canada), 171
Shaman, 151n39,
181n79, 221, 239, 281
Shame, 39, **46**, 52, 99–100, 106,
108, 127, 213, 225, 226,
230, 234n99, 319
Showing Up for Racial Justice (SURJ), 295
Siberia (Russia), 73, 83–85, 102
Silences (historical, group), xxvii, 15,
17–18, 20, 42, 44, 47, 52, 66, 78,
88, **96–106**, 108, 111, 122, 195,
213, 215, 227, 234, 246n22, 320
Sin, xxvi, 100, 140, 148, 224, 226, 280
Sixteenth St. Baptist Church (AL), 246
Sixties Scoop (Canada), 17, 232–33
Slavery: xxivn4, 11, 13, 33, 37, 38n15,
45, 49–50, 53, 63, 66–68, 88,
91–92, 108, 122, 133, 135, 149,
162, 164, 181, 206, 215n42, 227,
230, 244–45, 299; domestic slave
trafficking, 247–50
Social Darwinism, 216
Socialization, 12, 18, 41, 43, 46–48,
51, 64, 87, 94, 114, 128, 145, 154,
181, 189, 213, 215, 219n59, 222,
226–28, 234n99, 251
Sogorea Te Land Trust/Shuumi
Land Tax, 300–301
Somatic, 87, 92, 120, 284, 322
Songlines (defined), xxv, xx-
vin6, **22**, 11, **113–14**
Southern Freedom Strug-
gle, 243, 252n39
Soviet Union/USSR, 5, 60, 65, 71–72,
74–75, 83–84, 95, 99–100,
102, 105–6, 125

Index of Persons and Groups

Note: Bolded numbers indicate places in text where entry is explained or defined. Surnames of my female family relatives/ancestors are alphabetized by either maiden or married names according to how they are most recognizable by my family/community.

Elaine Enns has worked across the restorative justice field since 1989, from facilitating victim-offender dialogue in the Criminal Justice System to addressing historical violations and intergenerational trauma. With a DMin from St. Andrew's College Saskatoon, she trains and teaches throughout North America, and with her partner Ched published the two-volume *Ambassadors of Reconciliation: A New Testament Theology and Diverse Christian Practices of Restorative Justice and Peacemaking* (Orbis Books, 2009). They codirect Bartimaeus Cooperative Ministries (www.bcm-net.org).

Ched Myers is an activist theologian and New Testament expositor working with peace and justice issues. He is a popular educator, animating scripture and literacy in historic and current social change movements. Myers has published over a hundred articles and eight books, including *Binding the Strong Man: A Political Reading of Mark's Story of Jesus* (Orbis, 1988). He and Elaine are ecumenical Mennonites based in the Ventura River Watershed of southern California in traditional Chumash territory.

Made in the USA
Columbia, SC
21 April 2021